THE COMPLETE GUIDE TO FINDING THE BIRDS OF AUSTRALIA

RICHARD THOMAS
and
SARAH THOMAS

Published by Frogmouth Publications, 59 Coolidge Gardens, Cottenham

THE COMPLETE GUIDE TO FINDING THE BIRDS OF AUSTRALIA
by Richard and Sarah Thomas

Copyright © Frogmouth Publications 1996

Reprinted 1997

ISBN 0 9528065 0 9

No part of this publication may be reproduced or transmitted in any form or by any means without the prior written permission of the publisher

Line Drawings © M J Carr, except Inland Dotterel, © P A J Morris

Cover photograph, Australian Pelican © P A J Morris

Back cover photograph, Blue-winged Kookaburra © P A J Morris

Printed by **Athenaeum Press Ltd**, Gateshead, England

CONTENTS

CHAPTER 1: INTRODUCTION 1
    Air Travel 1
    Car Hire 2
    Buying a Car 3
    Accommodation 4
    Climate 5
    Timing Your Trip 5
    Field Guides 5
    Tapes 6
    Using this Guide 6

CHAPTER 2: VICTORIA 8
    A Melbourne Area 9
        2.1 Melbourne Airport 10
        2.2 Ferntree Gully National Park 10
        2.3 Phillip Island 11
        2.4 Laverton Saltworks 11
        2.5 Werribee Sewage Farm 11
        2.6 You Yangs Forest Park 12
        2.7 Brisbane Ranges National Park 12
        2.8 Swan Island 13
        2.9 The Great Ocean Road 14
    B Inland Victoria 15
        2.10 Clunes State Forest 16
        2.11 The Western Highway 16
        2.12 Big Desert Wilderness Park 16
        2.13 Wyperfield National Park 17
        2.14 Hattah-Kulkyne National Park 19
    C Chiltern State Forest 21

CHAPTER 3: TASMANIA 23
        3.1 Bruny Island 25
        3.2 Mount Wellington 27
        3.3 Pittwater Road 28
        3.4 Maria Island National Park 29
        3.5 Freycinet National Park 30
        3.6 Forest Glen Tea Gardens 30
        3.7 Cradle Mountain 30
        3.8 Strahan 30
        3.9 Lake St Clair 31
        3.10 Melaleuca 31

CHAPTER 4: NEW SOUTH WALES 32
    A South of Sydney 33
        4.1 Barren Grounds Bird Observatory 34
        4.2 Morton National Park 36
        4.3 Lake George 38
        4.4 Jervis Bay 39
        4.5 Kioloa Rest Area 40

- 4.6 Nadgee Nature Reserve 41
- B Sydney Area 42
  - 4.7 Royal National Park 43
  - 4.8 Cronulla Swamp 45
  - 4.9 North Epping 46
  - 4.10 Dharug National Park 47
  - 4.11 Pierces Pass 48
  - 4.12 Glen Davis 48
- C North of Sydney 49
  - 4.13 Barrington Tops 50
  - 4.14 Coffs Harbour 50
  - 4.15 Red Rock Caravan Park 50
- D South-west New South Wales 50
  - 4.16 Yass 51
  - 4.17 Leeton Swamp 52
  - 4.18 Deniliquin Area 52
  - 4.19 Back Yamma State Forest 54
  - 4.20 Round Hill Nature Reserve 54
- E North-west New South Wales 56
  - 4.21 Nyngan to Bourke 57
  - 4.22 Bourke to Tibooburra 57
  - 4.23 Pyampa Station 57
  - 4.24 Tibooburra to Cameron Corner 58

CHAPTER 5: AUSTRALIAN CAPITAL TERRITORY 59

- 5.1 Australian National Botanic Gardens 61
- 5.2 Jerrabomberra Wetlands 61
- 5.3 Campbell Park 61
- 5.4 Tidbinbilla Nature Reserve 63
- 5.5 Corin Dam 64
- 5.6 Namadgi National Park 64
- 5.7 The Brindabellas 65

CHAPTER 6: QUEENSLAND 66

- A Brisbane Area 68
  - 6.1 Manly Yacht Club 68
  - 6.2 J C Slaughter Falls 70
  - 6.3 Redcliffe 70
  - 6.4 Lake Samsonvale 70
  - 6.5 Mount Glorious 70
  - 6.6 North Stradbroke Island 71
  - 6.7 Lamington National Park 71
  - 6.8 Girraween National Park 74
  - 6.9 Neumgna State Forest 75
  - 6.10 Bunya Mountains National Park 76
- B South-west Queensland and the Channel Country 77
  - 6.11 Sixty-three km West of Charleville 77
  - 6.12 Eighty-four km East of Windorah 77
  - 6.13 Lake Bindegolly 78
  - 6.14 Eulo Bore 79
- C The Central Queensland Coast 79
  - 6.15 Cooloola National Park 79

- 6.16 Bundaberg and the Reef ... 80
- 6.17 Eungella National Park ... 82
- 6.18 Cape Hillsborough National Park ... 82
- 6.19 Horseshoe Lagoon ... 83
- 6.20 Townsville Town Common Environmental Park ... 83
- 6.21 Mount Spec National Park ... 83
- 6.22 Ingham ... 84
- 6.23 Mission Beach ... 84
- D Cairns Area ... 84
  - 6.24 Cairns Esplanade ... 86
  - 6.25 The Great Barrier Reef ... 86
  - 6.26 Cairns Botanic Gardens ... 86
  - 6.27 Mount Whitfield Environmental Park ... 87
  - 6.28 Thomsons Road ... 88
  - 6.29 Edmonton and Yarrabah Turf Farms ... 88
  - 6.30 Yule Point ... 89
  - 6.31 Daintree River Cruises ... 89
- E The Atherton Tablelands ... 89
  - 6.32 The Crater National Park ... 91
  - 6.33 Hasties Swamp ... 92
  - 6.34 Lake Eacham and Lake Barrine ... 92
  - 6.35 The Cathedral Fig Tree ... 92
  - 6.36 Nardellos Lagoon ... 92
  - 6.37 Tinaroo Creek Road ... 92
  - 6.38 Pickford Road ... 93
  - 6.39 Big Mitchell Creek ... 93
  - 6.40 Mount Lewis ... 94
  - 6.41 Abattoir Swamp ... 95
  - 6.42 Mount Carbine Road ... 95
  - 6.43 Mount Molloy ... 96
- F Cape York Peninsula ... 96
  - 6.44 Musgrave ... 97
  - 6.45 Iron Range National Park ... 99
- G North-west Queensland and the Gulf Country ... 102
  - 6.46 Georgetown ... 102
  - 6.47 Karumba ... 103
  - 6.48 Cloncurry ... 104
  - 6.49 Mount Isa ... 105
  - 6.50 Lady Loretta Project ... 105

CHAPTER 7: NORTHERN TERRITORY ... 107

- A The Gulf Region ... 110
  - 7.1 Barkly Homestead ... 110
  - 7.2 Cape Crawford ... 110
  - 7.3 Boroloola ... 111
- B Darwin ... 113
  - 7.4 Daly River ... 113
  - 7.5 Middle Arm ... 114
  - 7.6 Howard Springs Nature Park ... 114
  - 7.7 Holmes Jungle Swamp ... 115
  - 7.8 Knuckey's Lagoon ... 116
  - 7.9 Lee Point and Buffalo Creek ... 117
  - 7.10 East Point Recreation Reserve ... 117

  7.11 Fogg Dam...118
  7.12 Adelaide River 119
 C Kakadu National Park 119
  7.13 Arnhem Highway 119
  7.14 Mamukala..120
  7.15 Nourlangie Rock 121
  7.16 Yellow Waters Boat Cruises...121
  7.17 Old Darwin Road 122
  7.18 Waterfall Creek 122
  7.19 Stag Creek 124
 D Katherine 124
  7.20 Fergusson River 125
  7.21 Edith River 125
  7.22 Katherine Gorge National Park..127
  7.23 Chinaman Creek 127
  7.24 Victoria River Roadhouse 128
  7.25 Dingo Creek..129
 E Tennant Creek Area..129
  7.26 Tennant Creek...129
  7.27 Tennant Creek to Alice Springs..130
 F Alice Springs...130
  7.28 Kunoth Well 131
  7.29 Simpson's Gap...132
  7.30 Ellery Creek Big Hole Nature Park 133
  7.31 Ormiston Gorge and Pound National Park 133
 G South of Alice 135
  7.32 Twenty-one km North of Erldunda 135
  7.33 Ayers Rock 136
  7.34 Six km North of South Australia State Border..137

CHAPTER 8: WESTERN AUSTRALIA 138

 A Northern Western Australia 140
  8.1 Lake Argyle..141
  8.2 Kununurra 141
  8.3 Dunham River...142
  8.4 Wyndham 142
  8.5 The Gibb River Road 143
  8.6 Halls Creek 146
  8.7 The Canning Stock Route 146
  8.8 Derby...147
  8.9 Broome Bird Observatory...147
  8.10 Port Hedland to Broome...148
 B Mid Western Australia 148
  8.11 Point Samson...148
  8.12 Maitland River...148
  8.13 Cape Range National Park...149
  8.14 Carnarvon...150
  8.15 New Beach 150
  8.16 Denham and Monkey Mia 150
  8.17 Mount Magnet 152
 C Southern Western Australia 152
  8.18 Monger Lake 154
  8.19 Dryandra State Forest 154

```
8.20 Two Peoples Bay ............................................................................... 155
8.21 Porongurup National Park ................................................................ 156
8.22 Stirling Ranges National Park .......................................................... 157
8.23 Forests East of Manjimup.................................................................. 158
8.24 Sugarloaf Island ................................................................................ 158
```

CHAPTER 9: SOUTH AUSTRALIA 159

    A Adelaide Area 160
```
9.1 Adelaide ICI Saltworks...................................................................... 161
9.2 Port Gawler and Port Prime............................................................... 162
9.3 Mount Remarkable National Park .................................................... 162
9.4 Innes National Park ........................................................................... 162
9.5 Bool Lagoon...................................................................................... 163
```
    B The Eyre Peninsula 163
```
9.6 Salt Lake 52 km South of Elliston..................................................... 164
9.7 Big Swamp........................................................................................ 165
9.8 Lincoln National Park ....................................................................... 165
9.9 Coffin Bay National Park .................................................................. 166
9.10 Lake Gilles Conservation Park........................................................ 167
9.11 Port Augusta.................................................................................... 167
```
    C North-east South Australia 167
```
9.12 Cameron Corner.............................................................................. 167
9.13 The Strzelecki Track ....................................................................... 168
9.14 The Chestnut-breasted Whiteface Site ........................................... 169
9.15 The Birdsville Track ....................................................................... 170
```
    D Great Victoria Desert Region 172
```
9.16 Great Victoria Desert ...................................................................... 174
9.17 Cook Airfield .................................................................................. 175
9.18 Nullarbor Roadhouse ...................................................................... 175
```

CHAPTER 10: PELAGIC TRIPS 177

```
10.1 Wollongong .................................................................................... 178
10.2 Portland .......................................................................................... 179
10.3 Tasmania ......................................................................................... 180
10.4 Eden................................................................................................ 180
10.5 Brisbane.......................................................................................... 180
```

CHAPTER 11: BIRD FINDING GUIDE... 181

```
Non-Passerines ........................................................................................ 182
Passerines ................................................................................................ 218
```

Appendix 1: Taxonomy of Australian Birds..256
Appendix 2: Vagrants Recorded in Australia 257
Appendix 3: Introduced Birds 259
Appendix 4: Useful Addresses and Contacts 260
Appendix 5: Glossary..261

Scientific Name Index..263
Bird Index 269
Locality Index 276

Acknowledgments

Many people have helped and given us encouragement as we have put this guide together. We would particularly like to thank the following: Dave Andrew, Keith Betton, Louis Boon, Canberra Ornithologists Group members, Scott Chandry, John Crowhurst, Richard Donaghey, Rod Dowling, Dave Fisher, Ian Fraser, Chris Gladwin, Dion Hobcroft, Richard Jordan, Alan McBride, Margaret McJannett, Chris Padley, Tony Palliser, Ian Puckrin, Trevor Quested, John Rogers, Paul Walbridge, Bill, Alexander and James Watson, and Brenda Wheeler. Particular thanks to Connor Jameson and Stella Green for help with writing the back cover, Brian Fletcher for proof reading, Mike Carr for his excellent line drawings, Peter Morris for permission to use his photographs on the front cover and for the Inland Dotterel line drawing, and especially Dave and Alistair Stewart for those brilliant birding trips through the remote outback. Finally many thanks to Peter Milburn and Phil Hansbro for the many birding and pelagic trips. Lastly a big thank you to all bird watchers in Australia for being so helpful and forthcoming with accurate information.

We have made every effort to ensure that the information included in this guide is as accurate as possible, however a number of the sites are under threat of development so some details are bound to change over time. We hope to revise and update the *Complete Guide to Finding The Birds of Australia* at some future date and would very much appreciate any comments, criticisms or difficulties in using it so that they can be rectified in any future editions. Please write to Richard Thomas, 59 Coolidge Gardens, Cottenham, Cambrigde CB4 4RQ, UK. Any contributions will be gratefully acknowledged. Good Birding!

INTRODUCTION

Australia has one of the most diverse and unique avifaunas of any single country. Approximately 750 species have been recorded, of which about 320 are endemic. Several families are endemic as well as a few shared only with New Guinea. The majority of species are landbirds, with about 100 seabird species, many of which are only rare vagrants. Since many of the landbirds are either resident or regular visitors, it is possible for the travelling birder with enough time to see a very high proportion of Australia's birds - a full circular tour of Australia including a trip through the centre should comfortably record 600 species. If some time is spent on pelagics, to observe some of the seabird species, 650 is a realistic possibility. Many of the sites described in this book have a bias towards the south-east; this is inevitable but reflects the fact that the east coast of Australia is by far the richest area for birds. This guide is based upon the three years my wife and I spent living in Australia and is intended to give precise information on exactly how to find every species of bird in the continent. Knowing the correct habitat is the key to finding the majority of the birds in Australia so that if you fail to see what you are after at the suggested site, make a note of what the habitat looks like and if you see a similar area within the range of the bird, there is a good chance the species you are searching for will be present. One feature of Australia is the very unpredictable rainfall patterns, particularly in the arid interior. Some bird species have adapted to this by becoming nomadic. For this reason it is very hard to give definite sites for a few birds - if the conditions are not right at the time of your visit, the birds will have moved on. Pied Honeyeaters for example roam from the west coast of Western Australia right across central Australia to western New South Wales and Queensland. They are always somewhere within this region, usually where it has rained heavily two months or so previously and the *Eremophola* bushes, on which they feed, are flowering. In such a suitable place, there may be hundreds of Pied Honeyeaters which will display, mate, breed and move on all within a few weeks. Clearly it is impossible to write in a guide exactly where to find them at a particular point in time; fortunately for nearly all species there are certain areas that are favoured haunts. It is inevitable in travelling the truly vast distances around Australia that at some point you will pass through an area which is optimal for some of these nomadic species. One thing that is certain, however, is that the Australian avifauna is truly amazing and includes the most beautiful parrots in the world as well as a host of other exciting birds. You just cannot fail to enjoy birding there.

A good travel guide to Australia is definitely worth investing in and whilst it is not the purpose of this guide to repeat all the information that you will find in one, some useful tips of particular interest to birdwatchers for exploring this fascinating country are given below.

Air Travel
Australia is well connected by air to the rest of the world. All the major cities have international airports with Perth, Sydney and Melbourne being the most favoured arrival points for international travellers. Make sure you have the

necessary visas and, if applicable, a work permit. Many special offers for reduced cost internal flights are often available for travellers arriving by air and it would be a good idea to find out about these if you intend to fly between major cities. The two main internal airlines are Ansett and Qantas. Having arrived in the country you will need some form of transport to cover any area adequately since public transport rarely goes to any of the birding sites and hitch hiking is notoriously difficult given the small volume of traffic on many roads.

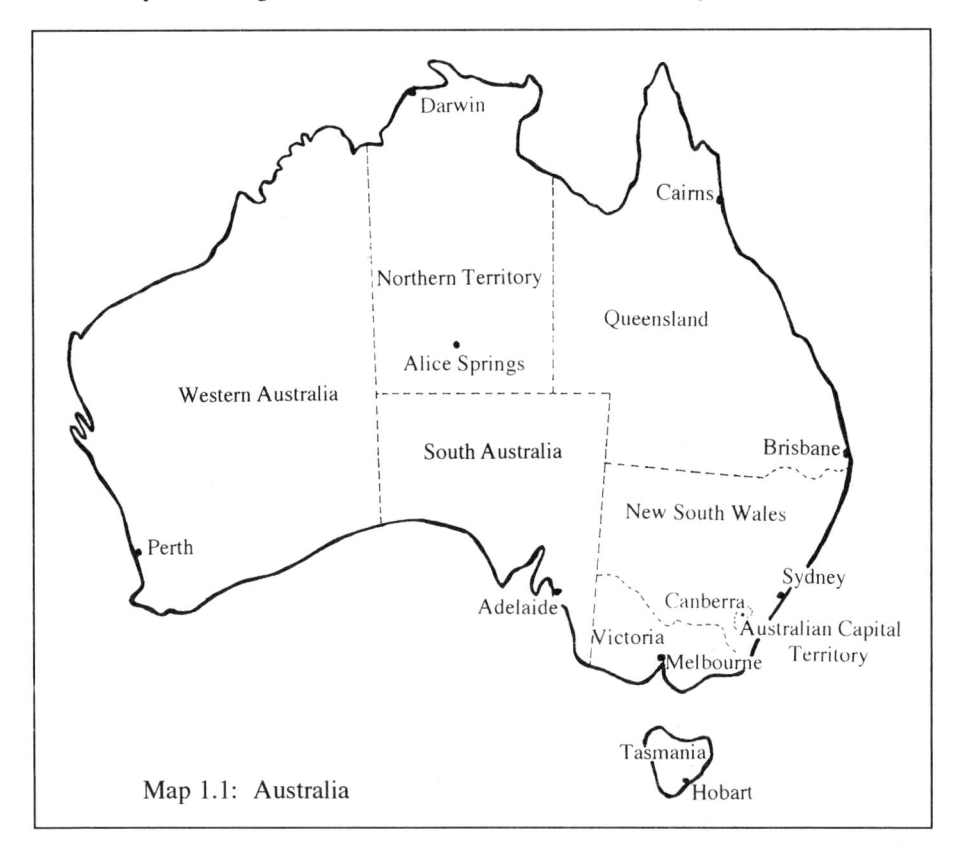

Map 1.1: Australia

Car Hire

If you are just on a short visit it may be worthwhile to hire a car. Make sure you hire a car that allows unlimited mileage. This is especially important but difficult in the Northern Territory where distances are vast. Unfortunately, many hire companies either do not allow their cars to be driven on unsealed roads, or if they do, you are not covered for underbody damage to the vehicle. Windscreen damage is also normally the responsibility of the hirer. Four wheel drive vehicles can be taken on any track but they are expensive to hire.

Buying a Car

Anyone who is planning to spend more than a few weeks birding in Australia should consider buying a vehicle. The choice of vehicle will depend very much on how much money you have to spend. For those with unlimited funds and planning on covering all sites, a Toyota Land Cruiser is probably the ultimate vehicle, but try to get a basic diesel model without all the unnecessary, complicated fuel injection extras. You can pick a good one of these up for around $20,000. For those on a more realistic budget a car is the only answer. The important thing to bear in mind when buying one is that it must be strong, reliable and have a good ground clearance. Whilst many of the familiar European makes of car are found in Australia, they tend to be expensive, particularly on spare parts and not designed for the rigours of Australian dirt roads. Fortunately cheap, reliable and sturdy cars do exist, and these are the old Ford Falcon and Holden (e.g. Kingswood) models. Kingswoods were made from the late 1960s until 1979. Of several models made, probably the best were the HQ and HZ. Do not be put off by the age or miles covered by these cars, the only thing that kills them is rust. The quality of engineering is superb and they are very reliable. There is of course a down side and that is that they are extremely big and heavy with enormous engines so consequently they are very thirsty on fuel. Fortunately petrol is about half the price that it is in the UK. A Kingswood in good condition will cost around $2,000, depending on the engine size. Usually they come with a 202 cubic inch motor (3.3 litres) which is renowned as a real work horse engine, rarely letting anyone down. It is better to buy a manual rather than an automatic car since they can be push started if you have battery problems in the bush. The older models have column gear changes. Parts are available, cheaply, from any scrap-yard in Australia and every mechanic in the country can fix a Holden in his sleep. We bought a 1973 HQ Kingswood stationwagon in Canberra for $1350 and sold it two years later for $1400; they keep their value well! It never let us down and had only the most minor of faults that were easy to fix with simple tools. The Ford Falcons are equally large and thirsty; the XA, XB and XC models are best, although they do not have such a good reputation as Holdens and can develop suspension problems. Other more modern cars to consider are the early Holden Commodores, or for a more economical car, try a Toyota Corolla. Many people opt for buying a camper van and of these, the old Volkswagon buses are very popular since they have a good ground clearance. Try to buy the model with the 1800 cc engine as the smaller engines tend to overheat in the tropical north.

Advertisements for old cars can be found on the noticeboard of any backpacker hostel or in any local paper. All cars must have a current 'rego'. This is roughly the equivalent of an MOT and road tax in the UK. The price varies regionally, up to about $400 in Queensland. Bear in mind when buying a vehicle that some states (WA, NT) do not inspect the car for this certificate. In NSW and Qld there is an annual inspection which includes a brief vehicle check. The rego fee includes road tax, and a compulsory third party insurance. Note that this only covers you for damage to someone else and not to his property, however for travellers this is probably quite adequate. It is highly advisable to join a motoring organisation, either the RACQ in Queensland or the NRMA elsewhere. These are excellent value for money and can arrange additional insurance if you require it. You can enter the office of either motoring organisation and obtain detailed road maps for any area in Australia just by showing your membership card. The NRMA also runs a road worthiness inspection service, where for around $100 you can have your potential car purchase given a thorough inspection by a qualified mechanic. Rules on driving licences vary between states; an international driving permit together with a UK licence was valid for up to one year in most states but beyond that you need to take an Australian driving test. It is a good idea to try to carry a few basic tools with you in case of breakdown in the outback. The NRMA will come out to fix your car but they won't be able to tow it for more than a few kilometres for free. Also it is a good idea to carry at least two spare tyres, particularly if travelling on dirt roads. The most dangerous areas to drive through are in the remote outback. It is essential to check with a motoring organisation or police station about the current state of the roads and in some remote areas about the availability of fuel. Always carry lots of water with you and allow for plenty of extra fuel; a jerrycan or two is essential. If you are travelling to a really remote area e.g. the Canning Stock Route, always let someone know where you are going and when you expect to be back.

Accommodation
Many of the birding sites are located well away from any towns so that the only way in which they can be reasonably covered is by camping. Nearly every national park has designated campsites but it is a good idea to carry your own jerrycan of water in case water is not available at the park or in short supply. You should also carry all your own food which you can either cook on a camp fire, (although they are banned in some parks) or take a small stove with you. Alternatively, many national parks and picnic areas provide barbecues places where you can build a fire. Every village has a store where you can buy supplies and in many remote areas, particularly in the interior, it is possible to get a shower at the local petrol station where you should also be able to fill up with drinking water. The showers are sometimes even free! If after a few nights camping in the bush you fancy a bit of luxury, there are many roadside motels (often in the petrol stations) which are often quite inexpensive, about $40 for a double room. For a cheaper alternative, look out for the many caravan parks where a van for the night will cost as little as $20. In the tropical north it is quite easy to sleep outside on the ground although the mosquitoes can be a problem and I would strongly recommend carrying a tent with you throughout your trip. Some indication of the level of campsites at each site is given in the text. A 'Bush Campsite' means that you should bring all your own food and water, and toilets are not provided. A 'Basic Campsite' means that toilets are provided, a 'Good Campsite' indicates drinking water will be available as well and finally an 'Excellent Campsite' means there are full facilities including showers. In all arid regions I would recommend carrying your own water to all sites as supplies can be unreliable. Often the water provided is 'bore water' which although drinkable has a lot of dissolved minerals in it and can taste very unpleasant.

Climate
Australia is a land of great extremes of climate. In Tasmania it can snow even at the height of summer so you should take plenty of warm clothing with you whatever time of year you visit. The southern mainland is very cold during the winter months and it can be bitterly cold on winter pelagics. The interior, although pleasantly warm during the day, can be bitterly cold at night during the winter months. In the summer months it becomes dangerously hot and, coupled with the annoyance from bush flies, means that you are well advised to avoid the outback between December and March. One English birder visited the Birdsville Track and the Channel Country at Christmas time. The heat and dehydration killed him so do not take these warnings lightly. The best time to visit these areas is during the spring. Rainfall is very unpredictable in the outback and it is possible for huge downpours to make roads impassable for weeks. Take careful note of any weather warnings. The north of the continent has a regular wet season from about November to March when roads are frequently impassable and can be cut off for months. It is therefore recommended that you visit the Top End (the northern part of the Northern Territory) during the dry season when, in any case, the birds are confined to drinking pools and are therefore easier to locate. There are a number of birds that are only found in the north during the wet season, however it is possible to see most of them in north-east Queensland which, although it is hot and wet, is worth the effort of visiting during the summer months. At all times you are well advised to wear a broad-brimmed hat, cover yourself up as far as possible and to put high factor sun block on any exposed areas of skin. This is because the hole in the ozone layer above the earth falls directly over Australia, particularly during March and the sunlight then becomes particularly intense and dangerous.

Timing Your Trip
Whether you are able to visit Australia for a long time or just a few days will affect your choice of sites to visit. There are several species that are only found in Australia at certain times of the year and others that it is only really practical or wise to look for during the cooler months of the year. As a rough guide, you should visit the tropical north between May and September and the southern half of the country during the rest of the year. Obviously exactly how you plan your trip will depend very much on how much time and money you have available. By visiting the sites given in this guide over a full year, you will not fail to see at least 600 species in Australia. Obviously you should try to slot in as many pelagic trips as you possibly can to increase the number of species you will record. If you are going for less than six weeks then I would recommend spending the majority of your time in the eastern and northern states where you will see the greatest variety of birds.

Field Guides
Australia has at least four excellent field guides and it is largely a matter of personal preference which one(s) you buy. My particular favourite is 'The Birds of Australia' by Simpson and Day which has very good plates but rather brief text. This guide is also now available on CD-ROM which also gives the songs and calls

for many of the birds. Undoubtedly the best background information on habitats and calls is found in 'A Field Guide to the Birds of Australia' by Pizzey and this makes this book invaluable. The plates by Doyle are rather outdated, however a new edition is planned for release in 1997. Perhaps the most accurate plates are found in the 'Slater Field Guide' by Slater and Slater. One or two birds appear rather mis-shapen but the feather detail in the pictures is accurate although the text is fairly minimal. Recently a photographic Guide to Australia's birds has appeared and will be useful although the first edition is full of errors (mis-labelled photographs *etc.*).

Tapes
You will be able to locate all the birds more easily if you have a good knowledge of their calls. The best way to learn these is to buy 'The field Guide to Australian Birdsong' which is available from the Royal Australian Ornithologists Union (RAOU) or through Wildsounds or the Natural History Book Service in Britain. By thorough home study of these you will be amazed just how much easier it is to locate scarce species, particularly in forest environments. If you plan to visit Iron Range National Park it is definitely worth buying a copy of 'Birds of the Iron Range' by R. J. Swaby from the RAOU. Highly recommended is 'Voices of the Sub-tropical Rainforest', the first CD in a series being produced by David Stewart. This covers the birds found around the Lamington area near Brisbane and includes recordings of some of the best species in that area such as Rufous Scrub-bird, Albert's Lyrebird and White-eared Monarch. Finally, a word of caution; the playing of tapes to attract elusive and shy species is not to be encouraged, especially during the breeding season when the persistent playing of tapes can cause distress to the birds concerned and even lead to nest desertion.

Using this Guide
This guide is intended to give the travelling birder as much help as possible in finding as wide a range of species as possible in Australia.

Each state (or territory) is treated in a separate chapter which begins with a brief introduction and lists all the endemic and speciality species of the state. The speciality species are those which can most easily be found at one of the places mentioned in the text for that particular state although they do not exclusively occur there. Many speciality species in Queensland are only shared with New Guinea so that the only chance of finding them in Australia is to search for them in Queensland. By summarising the important birds in each state in this way it quickly becomes obvious which are the areas in which you should spend the majority of your time, i.e. Queensland is by far and away the richest bird area in Australia. In order to see a really good selection of birds it will obviously be necessary to see all those species listed as endemics for each state and you should then concentrate your efforts on finding as many of the speciality species as you possibly can. For the larger states a map is also included with the introduction showing how the area has been sub-divided into smaller regions for separate treatment in the text.

Each sub-region is given a very brief introduction with a map showing the relative position of each of the sites covered within it. These maps help greatly when planning you route through a particular area. Each site is then treated separately beginning with a list of the key species found there in bold type. These are the species that you should concentrate on searching for during your visit. Sometimes the site described is easily the best known or possibly the only place where you can hope to see a particular bird. In this case the species is listed not only in bold but also italicised. Where relevant or useful, brief sketch maps of the actual site are included with the text. A selection of the better birds found at each site is also included. These are given in bold type to make them easier to locate in the text and since we visited the vast majority of sites covered in this guide, they are often those species recorded by ourselves. Full species lists for each location are not given as this would soon become impracticable in terms of space. In a country the size of Australia it is clearly not possible to cover all the good bird watching locations so rather than trying to give brief details on a large number of different places I have restricted myself to only the best localities. By visiting each of them you will give yourself an excellent chance to find all of the Australian landbirds, except perhaps Paradise Parrot! During our three years in Australia we only failed to find Red Goshawk, Night Parrot and Paradise Parrot.

Clearly any national park or nature reserve in Australia is worth visiting and I would strongly urge you to explore as many of them as you have time for and not restrict yourself to only those sites covered in this guide. In particular you should make the effort to contact local birdwatchers and bird societies as there is no substitute for really up to date information.

The states are treated in an anti-clockwise order beginning with Victoria. This is because the majority of birders arriving in Australia will do so at either Melbourne or Sydney. They will then wish to travel north to Queensland so an anti-clockwise tour of the country seems logical. Furthermore, those birders unable to cover the whole of the continent will wish to spend most of their time in the eastern states. Following this order these states are treated in consecutive chapters.

Following the chapters on the bird sites in each state there is a 'Bird Finding Guide'. This gives information about finding every landbird species in Australia, even the commonest ones. For each species there is a brief indication of its' world status and distribution in Australia together with some notes on the preferred habitat and an indication of the places where you are most likely to find it. For many species there is also an indication of their particular habits or behaviour which will enable you to track them down more easily. I hope that you will find this section useful as it is very frustrating when you are especially keen to see a particular bird to have no real indication of where to find it. Inevitably by birding at the sites given in this guide and searching for the key species at each locality you will encounter all the commoner species in Australia.

CHAPTER 2

VICTORIA

Malleefowl, widespread in the mallee of north-west Victoria, although very much under threat.

Introduction (Map 2.1)

Although Victoria is a relatively small state and none of the Australian endemics are found solely within its boundaries, it nevertheless has many important birding sites and a diverse range of interesting habitats.

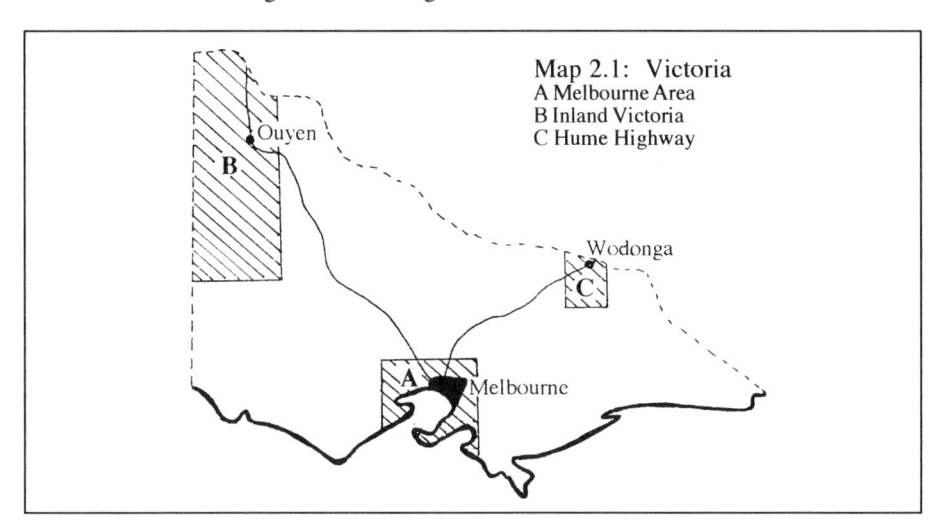

Map 2.1: Victoria
A Melbourne Area
B Inland Victoria
C Hume Highway

Specialities: Malleefowl, Swift Parrot (winter), Regent Parrot, Blue-winged Parrot, Orange-bellied Parrot (winter), Mallee Emuwren, Rufous Bristlebird.

A Melbourne Area (Map 2.2)

Despite being one of the largest urban areas in Australia, the immediate vicinity of Melbourne offers some of the most exciting bird watching in the whole continent. Melbourne would make an ideal point to start a birding tour of Australia as well as making an excellent base for exploring the following sites. The main attraction during the Austral summer (November to March) is the huge flocks of over wintering northern hemisphere waders which are found in particular on the western shores of Port Phillip Bay. During the winter months (May-September), the most exciting bird to be regularly found near Melbourne is the endangered Orange-bellied Parrot. The world population of this delightful species numbers only a few hundred birds and the entire population breeds in the remote south-western corner of Tasmania. They winter on the mainland near Port Phillip Bay, where a few birds are always seen on Swan Island. Other highlights include the world famous 'Penguin Parade' of Little Blue Penguins which takes place nightly on Phillip Island and the Great Ocean Road.

CHAPTER 2: VICTORIA

Map 2.2: Melbourne Area
1 Melboune Airport
2 Ferntree Gully NP
3 Phillip Island
4 Laverton Saltworks
5 Werribee Sewage Farm
6 You Yangs Forest Park
7 Brisbane Ranges NP
8 Swan Island
9 The Great Ocean Road

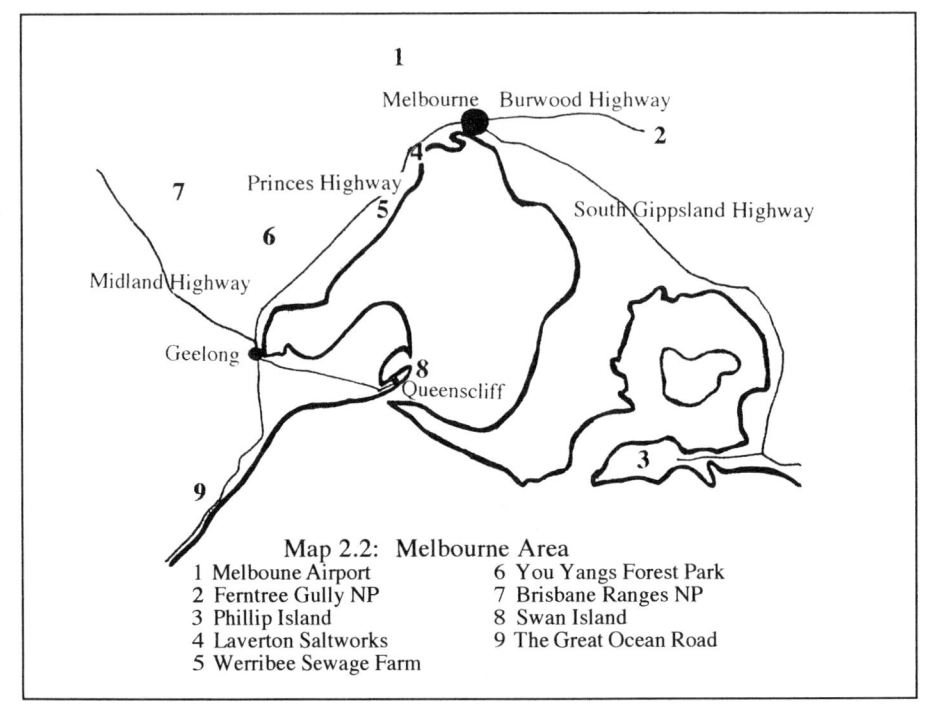

2.1 Melbourne Airport

Key Species: **Purple-crowned Lorikeet**
The main international airport in Melbourne, known as Tullamarine, is well signposted and situated just west of the suburb of Tullamarine. Check the flowering eucalypts around the car-park for **Purple-crowned Lorikeets** which are nearly always present and can be easily located by their constant chattering.

2.2 Ferntree Gully National Park (Map 2.3)

Key Species: **Powerful Owl**
Take the Burwood Highway east out of Melbourne and after 36 km you will reach Upper Ferntree Gully. Shortly past this, and before Highway 22 branches to the north towards Sassafras, there is a road leading to the ranger station in the national park with a car-park on the right. If you are going spotlighting, leave your car outside the park since it closes at 5.00 pm. Walk in to the north, passing the ranger station on the left and keep going beyond the pillars on either side of the track. About 250 m past the pillars the track splits into three; the **Powerful Owls** are normally found along the centre track and the track off to the right. Listen for them calling, especially at dusk. **Satin Flycatchers** also occur here in the summer.

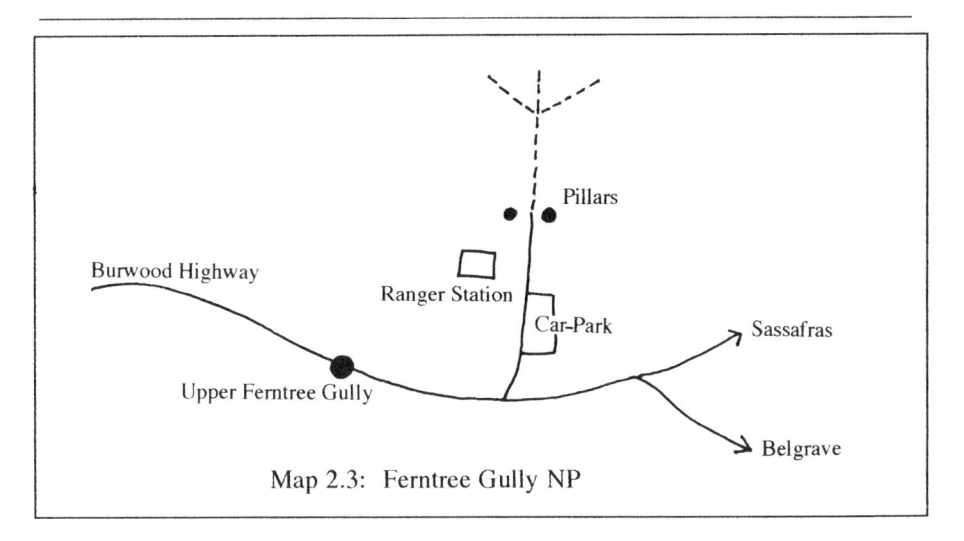

```
                    Map 2.3:  Ferntree Gully NP
```
(Map showing Burwood Highway, Upper Ferntree Gully, Ranger Station, Car-Park, Pillars, with routes to Sassafras and Belgrave)

2.3 Phillip Island

Key Species: **Little Blue Penguin**
Phillip Island is situated on the east side of Port Phillip Bay. You can drive onto the island from San Remo, which is to the east. It is chiefly famous for the nightly 'Penguin Parade', which is a big tourist attraction, at the western edge of the island. A viewing stand has been erected and every evening just at dark you can watch the **Little Blue Penguins** return to their burrows. There is a small entrance fee and it is well worth visiting. There is a good chance of seeing koalas and fur seals here as well.

2.4 Laverton Saltworks

Key Species: **Banded Stilt**
Laverton Saltworks is a large private saltworks and permission to enter must be obtained from the main office; there was no problem when we asked. Leave Melbourne south-west on the Princes Highway. Just past Laverton turn off south towards Point Cook along Aviation Road. After about 3 km you will pass the entrance to the salt works on your left. Go into the office and ask permission. You can drive out along the tracks between the salt pans. We saw **Banded Stilt** (1500).

2.5 Werribee Sewage Farm

Key Species: **Pacific Gull, Fairy Tern, Orange-bellied Parrot, Blue-winged Parrot, Lewin's Rail, Australian Crake,** waders (Austral summer)
The sewage farm covers a large area adjacent to the coast, south-west of Werribee and centred around the mouth of the Little River. It is a private area and to gain

access you really need to go in with someone who has a permit. Alternatively you can make your own arrangements well in advance, for more information contact the RAOU in Melbourne. Bear in mind that it is not usually open at weekends. It can be reached from the road running east from the Princes Highway opposite the Little River turning. It is noted as a regular wintering area for **Orange-bellied Parrots** although **Blue-winged Parrots** are actually commoner there. Also during the winter **Double-banded Plovers** are numerous. At any time of year **Fairy Terns** and **Australian Crakes** can usually be found on the lagoons whilst **Lewin's Rail** is sometimes seen here. A good number of rarities has been seen here and it is advisable to check with local birders for any current information.

2.6 You Yangs Forest Park

Key Species: **Purple-crowned Lorikeet, Swift Parrot** (winter), **White-browed Woodswallow**
To get to You Yangs Forest Park leave the Princes Highway about 30 km south-west of Melbourne at the Little River exit. Drive through Little River and then head west for 4 km to a T-junction. Turn left then right after 2 km, after a further 5 km a road off to the right leads to the picnic area. Note that it is not possible to camp overnight here. Once in the park, explore the dirt roads and walking tracks and especially any flowering eucalyptus trees. The area is renowned for **Purple-crowned Lorikeet** (year round), and **Swift Parrot** (only in the winter months), also **White-browed Woodswallow** and **Diamond Firetail** are resident. Camping is not allowed in this park.

2.7 Brisbane Ranges National Park (Map 2.4)

Key Species: **Powerful Owl**
This site is well worth visiting if you wish to see koalas which are common in the park and it is also known as a good place to find **Powerful Owl**. To get to Brisbane Ranges, leave Geelong north-west on the Midland Highway and after about 8 km turn right and continue for 23 km until you reach Anakie Junction. Bear left towards Ballan and after about 2 km, turn right along a dirt track which descends quite steeply to the Stony Creek picnic area. Park here and walk along the trail towards Anakie Gorge, look alongside the creek for koalas, they were extremely noisy and active even during the day when we were there (December 1992). The best area to search for **Powerful Owl** is to walk along the track to Lower Stony Creek Reservoir but turn left off it on to the Outlook walk. The owls are seen about 500 m along here. Alternatively they can be found around the picnic area; try and locate them by listening for their calls. We heard none in December, but they are winter breeders; May to July would be better. Note that camping is not allowed in this park.

Map 2.4: Brisbane Ranges NP

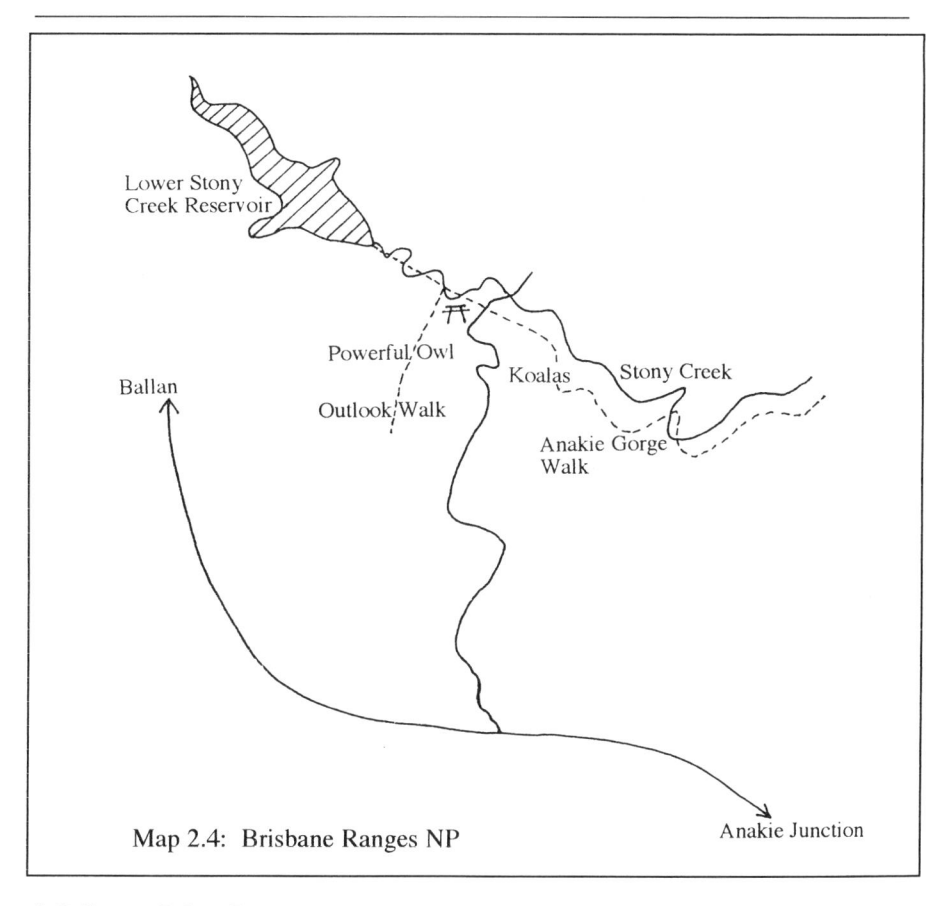

2.8 Swan Island

Key Species: **Orange-bellied Parrot** (May - July)
Situated on the west side of Phillip Bay, this island is reached from Queenscliff *via* a short causeway. In Queenscliff turn left off the main road through the town into Bridge Street and the causeway entrance is at the end of this road. Swan Island is a regular feeding area for **Orange-bellied Parrots**, but only from about late June to September when their particular food plant is available. Earlier than this, from about late April to June, they are often found at Lake Connewarre between Geelong and Queenscliff. It is highly advisable to check with the RAOU about the current whereabouts of the parrots, ask for John Stark. You may also be able to participate in census work in the winter months, again ask the RAOU for details. From October to April the birds are breeding in Tasmania (see that section for details of how to see them at Melaleuca). To visit Swan Island you will need permission from the military since there is a short causeway and army checkpoint to go through to reach the island. Telephone (052) 520011 and ask for Bill Clifton

who may want some reassurance you are a *bona fide* birder. After crossing the causeway, turn left to the golf club and park in their car-park. You will have to go into the club house and ask permission to walk around the edge of the course. They were friendly and used to birders visiting when we went there. The best area to search for **Orange-bellied Parrot** is the salt marsh on the far side of the golf course from the car-park. One of the golfers put us onto them and we saw at least 25 in July 1991. Around the muddy edges of the saltbush, **Buff-banded** and **Lewin's Rails** are regularly seen. There is also a wader roost on Swan Island. This is reached by turning right to the Yacht Club after you have crossed over the causeway. Park at the end of this track and walk around the edge of the island to the spit at the far side. **Asiatic Dowitcher** was recorded here in December 1992.

2.9 The Great Ocean Road

Key Species: **Blue-winged Parrot, Rufous Bristlebird**
The Great Ocean Road is a scenic route along the south coast from Geelong to Warrnambool. It is very popular with tourists, particularly the offshore rock formations such as the Twelve Apostles and there are many excellent campsites and places to stay along the route. **Rufous Bristlebirds** are to be found in the coastal heath and scrub all the way from Point Addis in the east (a short way off the Great Ocean Road, 7 km east of Anglesea) to at least Peterborough in the west. We heard at least seven whilst driving this section with the car windows down in December 1992. They have become quite tame at a number of the tourist spots along the way. The best of these is The Arch, which is 5 km to the west of Port Campbell. We saw the birds hopping around the car-park and also across the track that leads down to the viewpoint. We also saw birds at the London Bridge car-park about 3 km further west and they were heard (but not looked for) at Loch Ard Gorge car-park, just to the east of Port Campbell. Airlies Inlet is another good site with birds around the edge of the car-park and along the tracks down to the beach. The other specialty of this area is **Blue-winged Parrot**. We bush camped in the Sherbrook picnic area in April 1991 which is just to the west of The Twelve Apostles beside a bridge over the road (it is signposted). In the morning about 100 **Blue-winged Parrots** flew over in small parties and we even saw 12 on the short grass at the picnic site. Around the heath here we also saw **Rufous Bristlebird** (2) and **Olive Whistler**. Other good places for **Blue-winged Parrot** are the car-park at Loch Ard Gorge and the heath at Point Addis, but in general, just keep your eyes open as you drive through the heathy areas along the road.

B Inland Victoria (Map 2.5)

The chief attraction of the north-west of Victoria is the superb areas of mallee and their associated avifauna, with such specialities as Malleefowl, Chestnut Quail-Thrush, Southern Scrub-Robin, Shy Hylacola, Striated Grasswren and Mallee Emuwren. In the spring/early summer months Painted Honeyeaters are found in inland Victoria. *En route* from Melbourne the area around Horsham should be visited since Long-billed Corellas are locally very common here. This species is very numerous within its restricted range, which just extends as far as Deniliquin in New South Wales. Although the mallee areas are delightful places to visit in winter and spring, daytime temperatures and flies can get unbearable in the summer months.

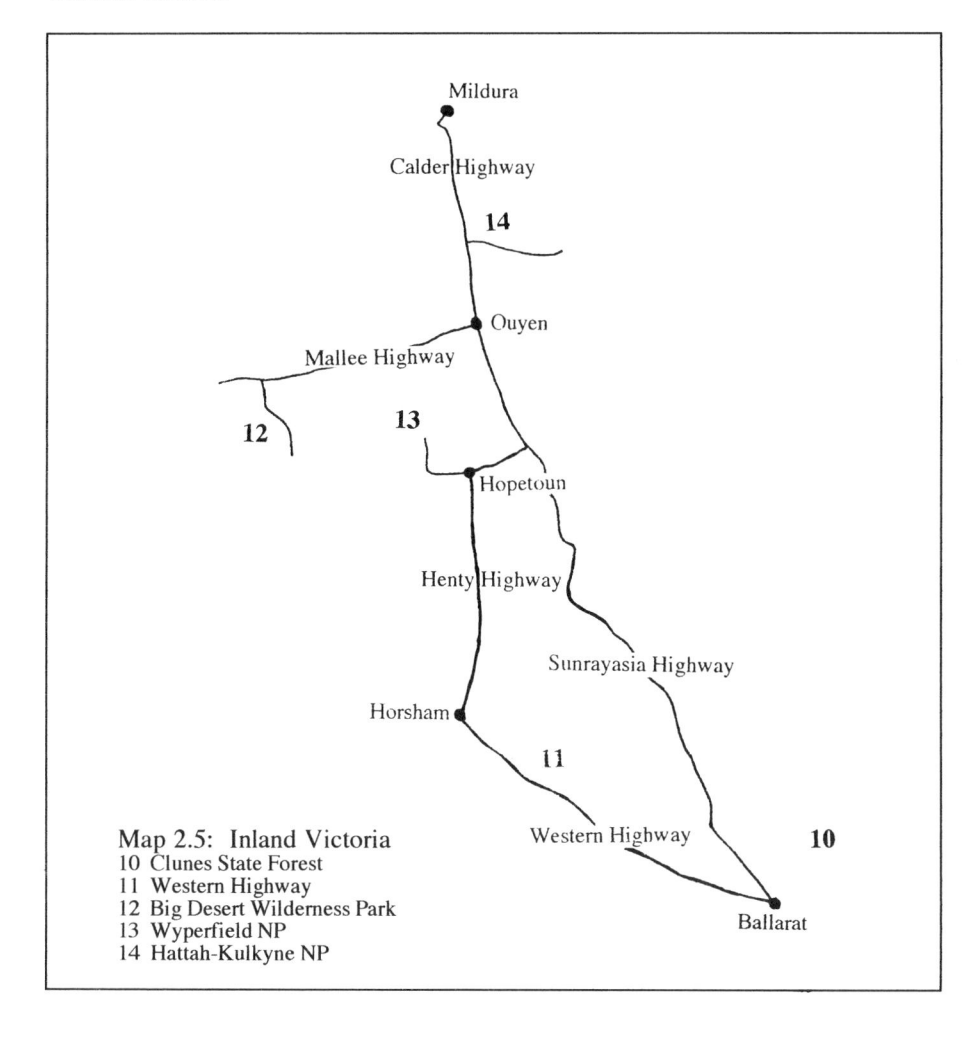

Map 2.5: Inland Victoria
10 Clunes State Forest
11 Western Highway
12 Big Desert Wilderness Park
13 Wyperfield NP
14 Hattah-Kulkyne NP

2.10 Clunes State Forest

Key Species: **Painted Honeyeater**
Situated north of Ballarat, this is the most reliable site in Victoria for **Painted Honeyeater** during the late spring (October to November). Leave Clunes north-westwards towards Campbelltown, then turn left towards Clunes State Forest. After 1.5 km you get to a T-junction. Turn left but stop after 200 m by a gate. About 50 m beyond the gate is a huge eucalyptus tree infested with mistletoe. The honeyeaters are found in this tree when the mistletoe is flowering in spring. Another site, worth checking for this species in spring, is Kingower near Inglewood on the Calder Highway north-west of Bendigo. Check the scrub and eucalyptus trees behind the cricket pitch at the east end of town.

2.11 The Western Highway

Key Species: **Long-billed Corella**
The Western Highway between Ballarat and Horsham goes right through the heart of **Long-billed Corella** territory and is particularly good between Ararat and Horsham. Just drive along the road until you find a corella flock, check carefully though them as they are sometimes mixed in with **Little Corellas** and **Sulphur-crested Cockatoos**. If you are having trouble locating them on the highway, detour into Hall's Gap in The Grampians where **Long-billed Corellas** are even more numerous.

2.12 Big Desert Wilderness Park

Key Species: **Purple-gaped Honeyeater, Shy Hylacola, Southern Scrub-Robin**
This park contains a large mallee area and is a good place to see **Purple-gaped Honeyeaters** which do not seem to occur very much in other mallee areas in Victoria. To reach Big Desert Wilderness Park, drive west from Ouyen on the Ouyen Highway. After 110 km turn south in Murrayville onto the road signposted to Nhill. This is a rather muddy and sandy track and it was officially closed when we were there in October 1991 so we only went 10 km down it. We saw **Purple-gaped Honeyeater** (fairly common in flowering mallee trees), **Shy Hylacola** (at least six, they seem particularly common here), **White-fronted Honeyeater** and **Southern Scrub-Robin**. Thirty-four km down the track from Murrayville is a windmill and dam, known as Big Billy Bore, a further 15.5 km south is a pull-in; both areas are known as **Red-lored Whistler** sites. These are not nearly as good as Round Hill Nature Reserve in New South Wales for the whistler, but you might have a remote chance of finding them if they were singing in spring. All the usual mallee species occur down this road but be very careful driving it, particularly if it has been raining. Bush camping only is available.

2.13 Wyperfield National Park (Map 2.6)

Key Species: **Malleefowl, Chestnut Quail-Thrush, White-browed Treecreeper**

Wyperfield National Park is a very pleasant mallee area which is notable as a stake-out for **Malleefowl**. The main entrance is reached by driving west from Hopetoun for 31 km until you reach a T-junction. Turn right and head north until you enter the park. **Bluebonnets** and **White-browed Woodswallows** are regularly seen along this section of road. Follow the entrance road to the information centre and good campsite. The main birding area is along the 15 km Eastern Lookout Nature Drive which is a one-way dirt track loop starting at the campsite. The route is a nature trail marked with wooden posts. The key area to concentrate on is the mallee between the Dattuck and Lowan Tracks (posts 11 to 16). **Malleefowl** can be seen from a screen built in front of an active mound. This is found by following the obvious track into the mallee on the left just beyond post 12 for about 200 m. This ends at the screen and just beyond this is the mound. Early morning is the best time to see the birds, but note that the mounds are not tended much between about March to May although we saw one bird close to the screen in April 1991.

Along the start of the Lowan Track is another good area; in the mallee just off this track we saw **Chestnut Quail-Thrush** (a male in song, October 1992, and 3-4 birds on the track, April 1991), **Southern Scrub-Robin, Malleefowl, Regent Parrot** and **Pink Cockatoo**. Look very carefully at any **Yellow-throated Miners**; we saw a party of ten **Yellow-throated Miner** x **Black-eared Miner** hybrids in April 1991 which included at least two 'pure bred' individuals. There are officially only two birds of this (doubtful) species still in existence, one of them in this area although others probably still exist in South Australia. It is possible that they are only a race of Yellow-throated Miner, but you don't have a lot of time to make up your own mind before they are hybridised out of existence by the more aggressive species.

Around the campground **Emus** are exceptionally common. The 3 km walk to Lake Brambruk is worth a look, we saw **Southern Scrub-Robin** and **Shy Hylacola** along it. Between the main entrance and the campground we saw a party of over 50 **Regent Parrots** feeding on grass seeds in October 1992.

The other important area to visit is the northern entrance which is a stake-out for **White-browed Treecreeper**. To get here, return to Hopetoun and drive north for 47 km, turn west at the cross-roads and drive through Patchwollock. When you reach a dirt cross-roads, turn left, take the first right and follow the road which has a sharp left bend to the national park gate. It is 8.2 km from the dirt cross-roads to the gate. Park here and check the trees along the edge of the sandy track between the entrance gate and the campsite, but be warned that **Brown Treecreepers** are also numerous in this area.

18   CHAPTER 2: VICTORIA

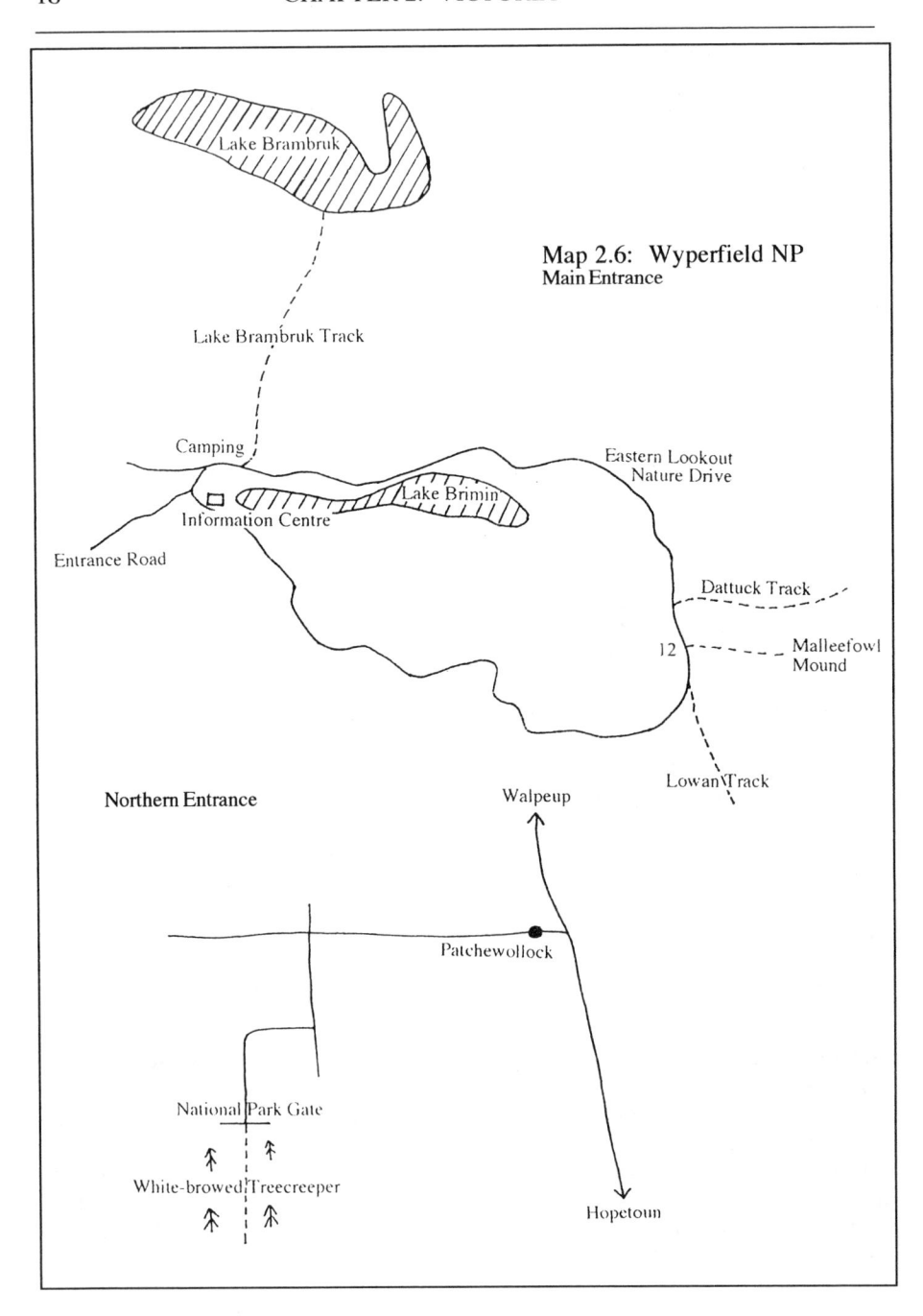

Map 2.6: Wyperfield NP
Main Entrance

2.14 Hattah-Kulkyne National Park (Map 2.7)

Key Species: **Regent Parrot, Pink Cockatoo, Striated Grasswren,** *Mallee Emuwren*
This is probably the best mallee area in Victoria and most of the mallee speciality species can be found here. The park is located at the intersection of the Murray Valley and Calder Highways, 36 km north of Ouyen. The entrance to the park is a left turn off the Murray Valley Highway about 3 km from the intersection. It is well signposted. Follow the entrance road past the visitors centre to the car-park and around to the left is the campsite. You can camp here in a good campsite for a small fee. Lake Hattah, in front of you, is a drinking spot for parrots, mostly at dawn and dusk. We saw **Regent Parrot, Pink Cockatoo, Mallee Ringneck, Purple-crowned Lorikeet, Yellow (Blue-cheeked) Rosella, Mulga Parrot, Sulphur-crested Cockatoo** and **Red-rumped Parrot**. The lake itself has a reasonable selection of waterbirds, the best we saw were **Great Crested Grebe** and **Black-tailed Native-Hen** on each of our three visits in April 1991, October 1992 and May 1993.

Within the National Park there are several good places for birds. Along the Old Calder Highway there are two sites to visit. Turn north onto this track off the park entrance road and after about 8 km, look out for a small wooden sign on the left which says 'Beesite 8' (it had fallen down on the ground in May 1993), it is about 10 m past a particularly tall eucalyptus tree. This was formerly a site for Black-eared Miner although, sadly, none are left now at Hattah. There is some reasonable spinifex here; we saw **Mallee Emuwren** and **White-fronted Honeyeater**. Try tapping any trees with suitable hollows in them for **Australian Owlet-Nightjars**. Further north along the Old Calder Highway, a track goes off to the right signposted the 'Nowingi Track' (it is the first road on the left coming from the north) drive down here for about 300 m to where there are two small pull-ins on the left. Park here and check the spinifex on either side of the track; we saw **Striated Grasswrens** on both sides. In each case they were about 100 m into the spinifex from the track and were easy to see in October 1991 when they were singing and calling a lot. They were harder to find in May 1993, listen for the high pitched call. Around this area we also recorded **Gilbert's Whistler, Chestnut Quail-Thrush, Shy Hylacola** and **Southern Scrub-Robin**. Further north along the Nowingi Track there are **Malleefowl** and an active mound is close to the track a further 1 km along the track. Another good site for **Striated Grasswren** is found when you drive out of the park along the entrance road, stop at the junction with the Murray Valley Highway. Walk over the rise opposite and you will find a fire-break. The grasswrens regularly cross over this fire-break, particularly in the evening. The track north from the Lake Hattah campsite to Lake Mournpall is good for **Chestnut-crowned** and **White-browed Babblers**. Another spinifex area which is excellent for **Mallee Emuwren** is west of the Calder Highway. Drive north from Hattah store, but almost immediately turn left across the railway, then turn right. Follow the track through a gate and stop after 1.5 km where you can see good spinifex on the right. Check the largest clumps between the track and the railway line; **Mallee Emuwren** is reasonably common here and we saw three; listen for their high pitched call, although they can be very skulking. **Striated Grasswrens** also occur in the larger clumps, but they are easier to find along the Nowingi Track. A good mallee area for **Southern Scrub-Robin, Chestnut Quail-Thrush** and **Shy Hylacola** is the area to the west of the Calder Highway, south of the Hattah store opposite the national park sign. Keep an ear open for **Black-eared Cuckoos** which occur throughout the park and for **Tawny Frogmouths** around the campsite at night.

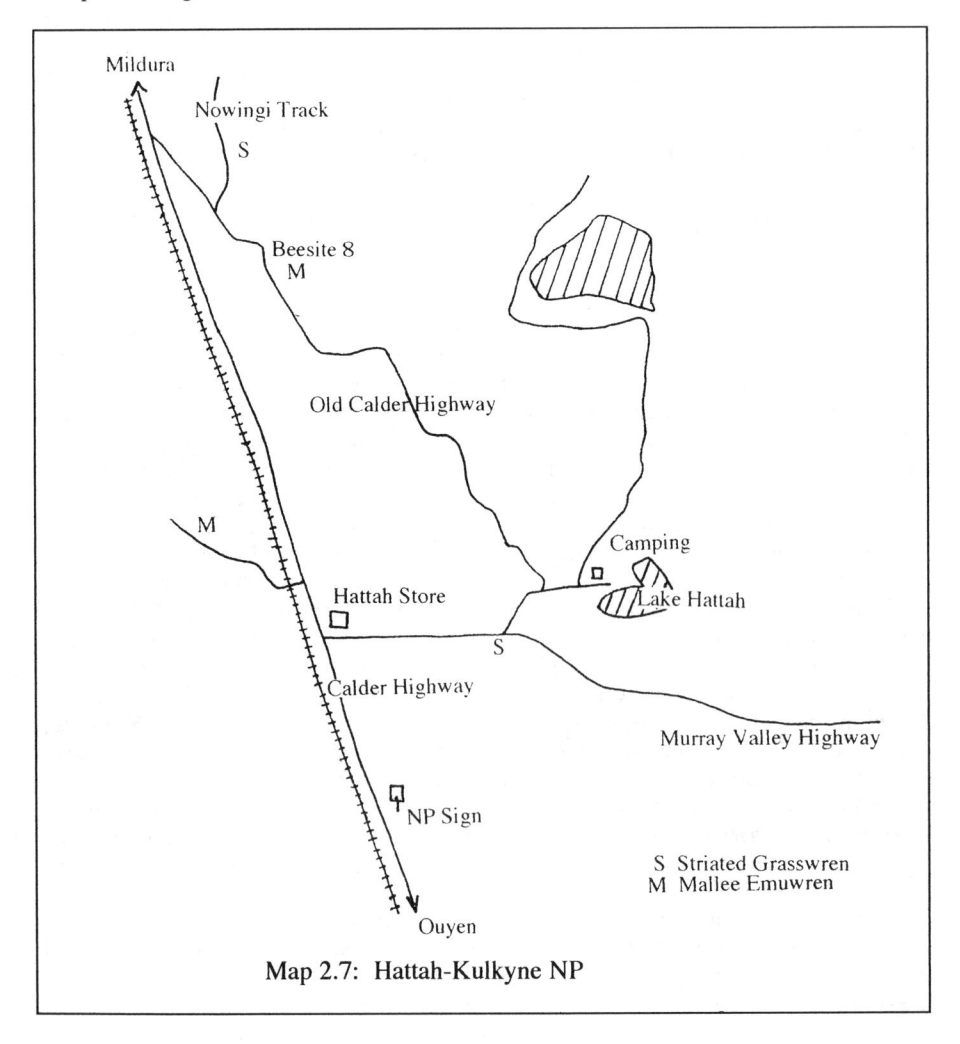

Map 2.7: Hattah-Kulkyne NP

S Striated Grasswren
M Mallee Emuwren

C Chiltern State Forest (Map 2.8)

Key Species: **Painted Button-Quail, Turquoise Parrot, Regent Honeyeater, Black-chinned Honeyeater**

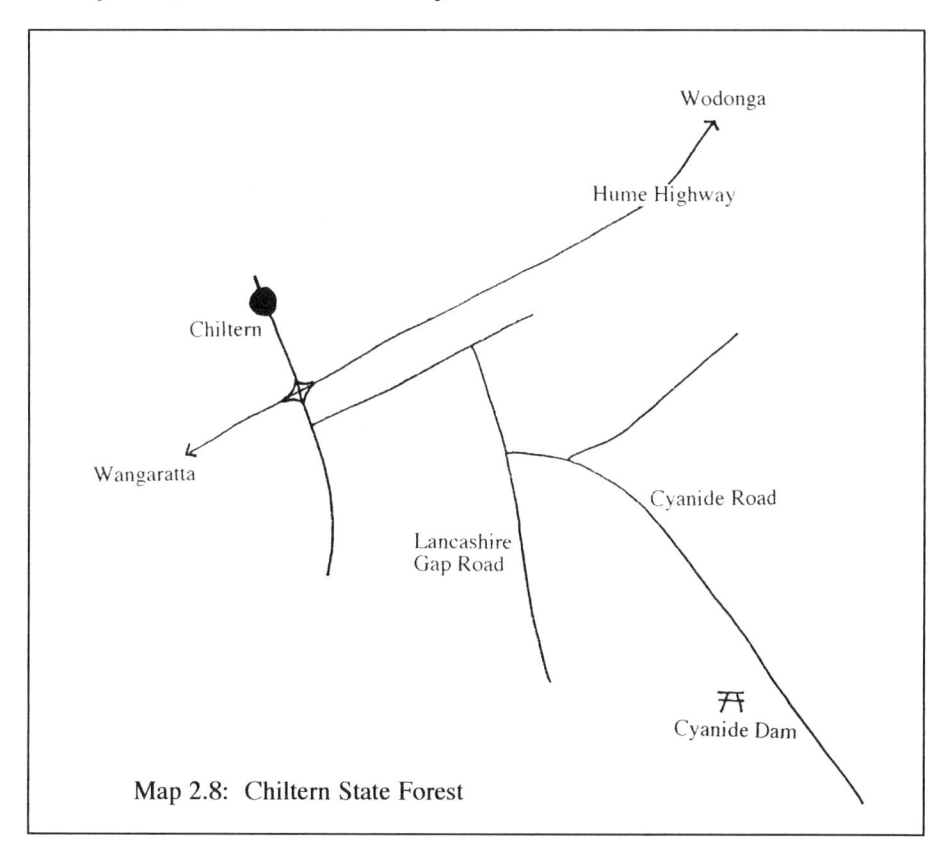

Map 2.8: Chiltern State Forest

Chiltern State Forest is just in Victoria, close to the New South Wales border on the Hume Highway, just south of Albury. It is well worth a visit, particularly during the late winter or spring months when honeyeaters and parrots may be present in good numbers. The main species to concentrate on at other times is Painted Button-Quail which seems to be particularly numerous here. Take the Chiltern exit off the Hume Highway going south. At the end of the slip road, turn left and left again so you are going back parallel to the Hume Highway. Take the first right turn, Lancashire Gap Road, then turn left along Cyanide Road. This eventually leads to a picnic table near Cyanide Dam.

Camping is not strictly allowed and water is not available. The best areas to concentrate on are around the dam, and the tracks off to the east of it which lead up the slope. When the ironbarks are flowering, the forest is alive with honeyeaters and parrots. The following birds are usually around: **Black-chinned**, **Fuscous** and **Yellow-tufted Honeyeaters** (all common), **Regent Honeyeater** (a reliable site, but tends to be much more regular in spring although it has been recorded in May. They favour feeding in the ironbark trees with red flowers on them, particularly along Lancashire Gap Road), **Little** and **Musk Lorikeets** (dependant on flowering, we saw plenty in March 1991), **Turquoise Parrot** (resident, a good site for this species; try the tracks east of Cyanide Road), **Swift Parrot** (regular in winter), **Chestnut-rumped Hylacola** (fairly common in the heathy under storey; we saw them on the first road leading east off Cyanide Road after Lancashire Gap Road), **White-throated Nightjar** (they hawk insects over Cyanide Dam on summer evenings), **Rufous Songlark**, **Little Friarbird**, **Crested Shrike-Tit**, **White-browed Babbler**, **Restless Flycatcher**, **Brown Treecreeper**, **Diamond Firetail**, **Painted Button-Quail** (this is one of the most regular sites for this species; you will find them by searching for fresh platelets, particularly along any dry ridges east of Cyanide Road. The birds are shy and tend to flush rather easily), **White-browed Woodswallow** and **Rainbow Bee-eater**. Sadly the area is under threat from mining.

CHAPTER 3

TASMANIA

Black-headed Honeyeater, one of four endemic honeyeaters found in Tasmania

Introduction (Map 3.1)

Tasmania is a really beautiful island, reminiscent of western Scotland, and like Scotland the weather can be very unpredictable, wet and windy. It can snow at any time of the year so take plenty of warm clothing with you. The absence of foxes means native animals abound on Tasmania, which makes for some excellent spotlighting.

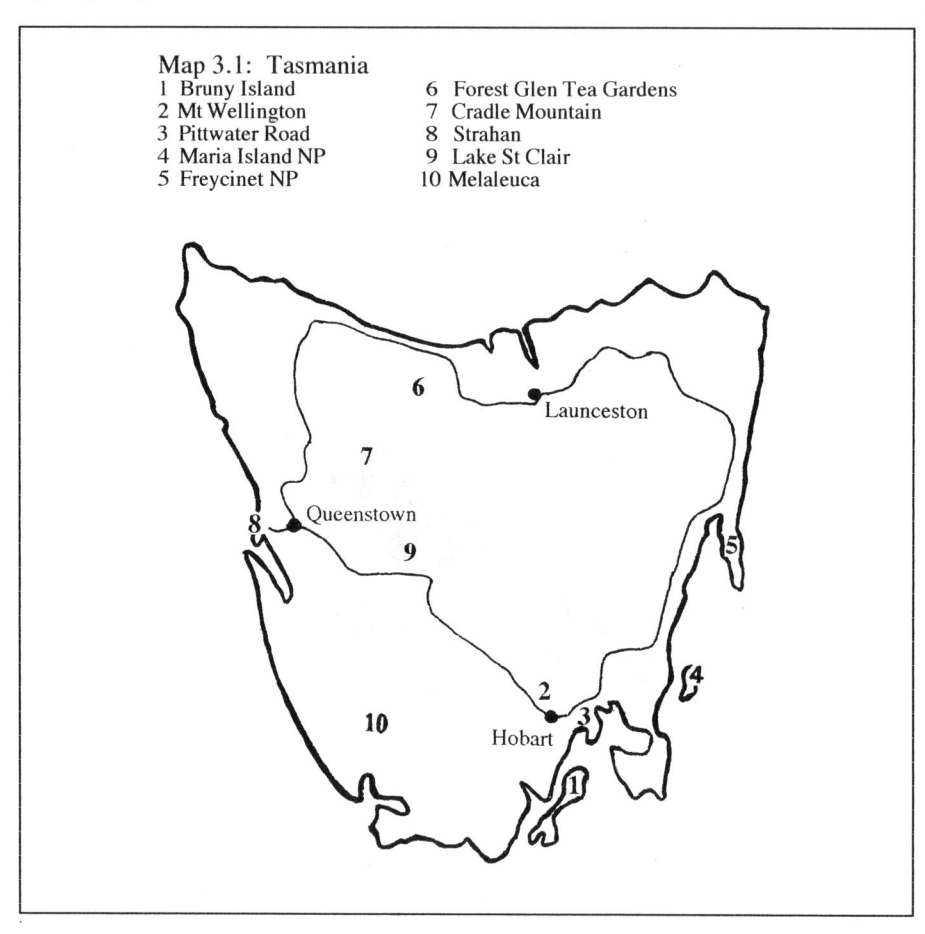

Map 3.1: Tasmania
1 Bruny Island
2 Mt Wellington
3 Pittwater Road
4 Maria Island NP
5 Freycinet NP
6 Forest Glen Tea Gardens
7 Cradle Mountain
8 Strahan
9 Lake St Clair
10 Melaleuca

Obviously you must either fly or get the boat to Tasmania. Both these options can be rather expensive however, particularly during school holiday periods when all forms of transport to Tasmania are booked up weeks in advance. The advantage of going on the boat from Melbourne is that you can take a vehicle across, although this is costly and you may find that it is cheaper to fly over and hire a car since they are relatively inexpensive on Tasmania. We spent eight days in Tasmania in March 1991 and paid just $26.00 a day for an old Ford Falcon stationwagon which was ideal for sleeping in as well. We flew there with Ansett on a 'rock bottom special' fare booked three weeks in advance. The cost was $165 return from Melbourne to Hobart, booked through the Tasmanian Travel Centre in Canberra. These travel centres are found in the capital cities of each state and are well worth visiting. They publish a monthly free newspaper *Travelways* which is definitely worth getting, it gives up to date information on car hire, flight prices and any special offers available.

It is possible to see all the endemics birds in a couple of days by visiting Bruny Island but unless you are really pushed for time it is well worth spending a few extra days in Tasmania to catch up with many additional species. Also note that the rarer penguins are sometimes recorded moulting on Tasmania's beaches, particularly Fjordland Crested Penguin. They are usually seen in March so keep an eye open for them, particularly on the west coast beaches if you visit the island in autumn.

Endemics: Tasmanian Native-Hen, Green Rosella, Forty-spotted Pardalote, Brown Scrubwren, Scrubtit, Tasmanian Thornbill, Yellow-throated Honeyeater, Black-headed Honeyeater, Strong-billed Honeyeater, Yellow Wattlebird, Dusky Robin, Black Currawong
Specialities: Black-faced Cormorant, Masked Owl, Hooded Plover, Pacific Gull, Kelp Gull, Musk Lorikeet, Crescent Honeyeater, Tawny-crowned Honeyeater, Pink Robin, Satin Flycatcher (summer), Forest Raven, Beautiful Firetail
Both Orange-bellied Parrot and Swift Parrot breed exclusively in Tasmania, but winter on the mainland.

3.1 Bruny Island (Map 3.2)

Key Species: **Swift Parrot, Forty-spotted Pardalote, Dusky Robin, Beautiful Firetail**
This island is reached by vehicle ferry from Kettering 35 km south of Hobart. There is a regular service beginning at 7.15 am from Kettering (see the *Travelways* paper). The cost for a car was $12.00 return when we did the trip. The island is really picturesque especially in the southern half and the birding is easy. The roads are mostly unsealed and can be rough in places. Whilst waiting for the ferry at Kettering jetty we easily found **Yellow Wattlebird, Yellow-throated** and **Black-headed Honeyeaters** and **Tasmanian Thornbill** in the surrounding gardens. All twelve Tasmanian endemics can be seen on Bruny Island - in one and a half days we saw eleven and heard the twelfth (**Black Currawong**). Most are common in the correct habitat. The following areas we found to be very good.
3.1a Dusky Robin Pool
Along the road leading from the ferry landing point (after about 5 km) there is a small pool on the left hand side of the road. **Dusky Robins** were plentiful around the edge, either perched up on dead trunks or on the barbed wire fences.

Map 3.2: Bruny Island
1a Dusky Robin Pool
1b Waterview Hill
1c Cape Queen Elizabeth Track
1d Seabird Colony
1e Wader area
1f Adventure Bay to Lunawanna Road
1g Cape Bruny

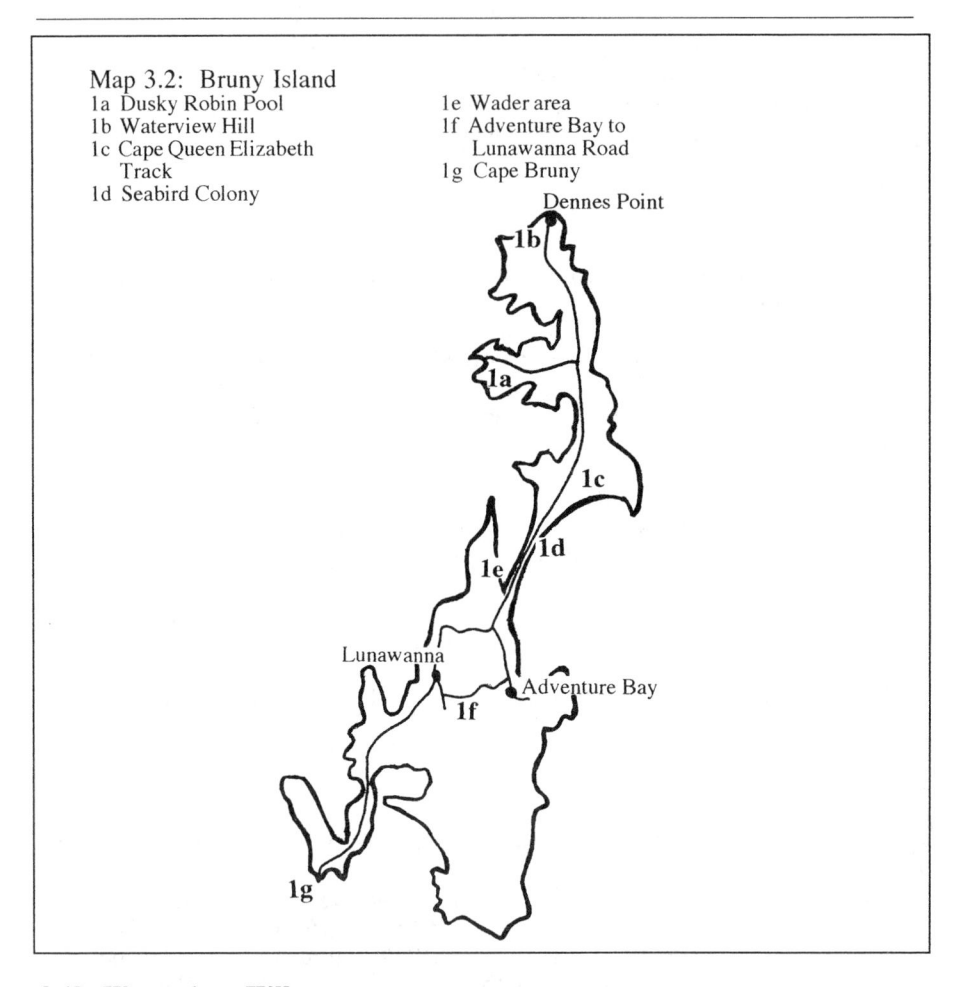

3.1b Waterview Hill

There is a fair sized colony of **Forty-spotted Pardalotes** on the northern slopes of Waterview Hill. Drive south from the shop at Dennes Point on the main east coast road. After about 3 km you begin to enter eucalypt woodland and after 3.5 km pull off on the right hand side of the road. On the left is a high fence (above waist height) and some tall trees (30 m), whilst on the right above you there is a steep slope with rather smaller trees (15 m). We climbed the steep slope on the right where viewing the tree tops is easy since they are at eye level with the steep slope. We saw **Forty-spotted Pardalote** here easily. We got much better views here than on Maria Island where the pardalotes inhabit much higher trees. **Striated** and **Spotted Pardalotes** were also in this area, and also **Dusky Robin**. Another good site for the pardalote on the other side of Waterview Hill is reached by driving south from Dennes Point along the west coast road. After 2-3 km stop at McCrackens Gully and search the eucalypts there. **Swift Parrot** is also sometimes seen at this site.

3.1c Cape Queen Elizabeth Track
About 2 km north of the isthmus there is a well signposted walking track leading east to Cape Queen Elizabeth. In the grassy field alongside the road by this track we saw several **Dusky Robins** and also several in the first 2 km along the track. In the coastal scrub we found a large mixed flock of honeyeaters, robins and pardalotes which surprisingly included one **Forty-spotted Pardalote**.

3.1d Seabird Colony
On the east side of the isthmus road there is a well signposted **Short-tailed Shearwater** and **Little Blue Penguin** colony; we saw many Shearwaters with a torch shortly after dark but no penguins, although penguins with young are common here in late December. There is a basic campsite at the south end of the isthmus on the east side of the road.

3.1e Wader Area
The sandy bay to the west of the isthmus can be seen from the road and is worth a look. We saw **Double-banded Plover, Pacific Gull** and **Caspian Tern** there at low tide.

3.1f Adventure Bay to Lunawanna Road
The road from Adventure Bay, which climbs the side of Mount Mangana before dropping to Lunawanna, is very good for some of the endemics. On the way up the road winds through excellent rainforest; **Strong-billed Honeyeaters** and **Green Rosellas** are common and it was the only place we saw **Scrubtit** on Bruny Island (one by itself brought out by pishing, and one with a party of **Tasmanian Thornbills**). We also saw **Crescent Honeyeater, Beautiful Firetail** and **Olive Whistler** on this road and it was the only place where we heard **Black Currawong** on Bruny Island. The Mount Mangana Track which leads off this road at the summit is also an excellent place for **Scrubtit**. Anywhere along this road where there is good looking habitat is worth checking.

3.1g Cape Bruny
The headland by the lighthouse is good for seawatching; we saw many **Short-tailed Shearwaters** and a few **Shy Albatrosses** in about half an hour.

3.2 Mount Wellington (Map 3.3)

Key Species: **Brown Scrubwren, Scrubtit, Pink Robin**
Mount Wellington is easily reached from south-west Hobart along the Huon Highway. About 6 km from Hobart you get to a place called Fern Tree. On the left is a pub and on the right is a picnic area and a church. The Fern Glade track leads up the side of the church and then off to the right behind the church along a wet gully. We birded along this track until it reached a bitumen road and saw a female **Pink Robin** just behind the church, a fine male **Pink Robin** where the track meets the bitumen road, several **Brown Scrubwren, Scrubtits** and **Bassian Ground-Thrush**. It is possible to see **Black Currawong** in this area. When driving back towards Hobart take the first turn on the left, Pilinger Drive, just after Fern Tree. This road climbs steeply to the summit of Mount Wellington but stop at 'The Springs'

Map 3.3: Mount Wellington

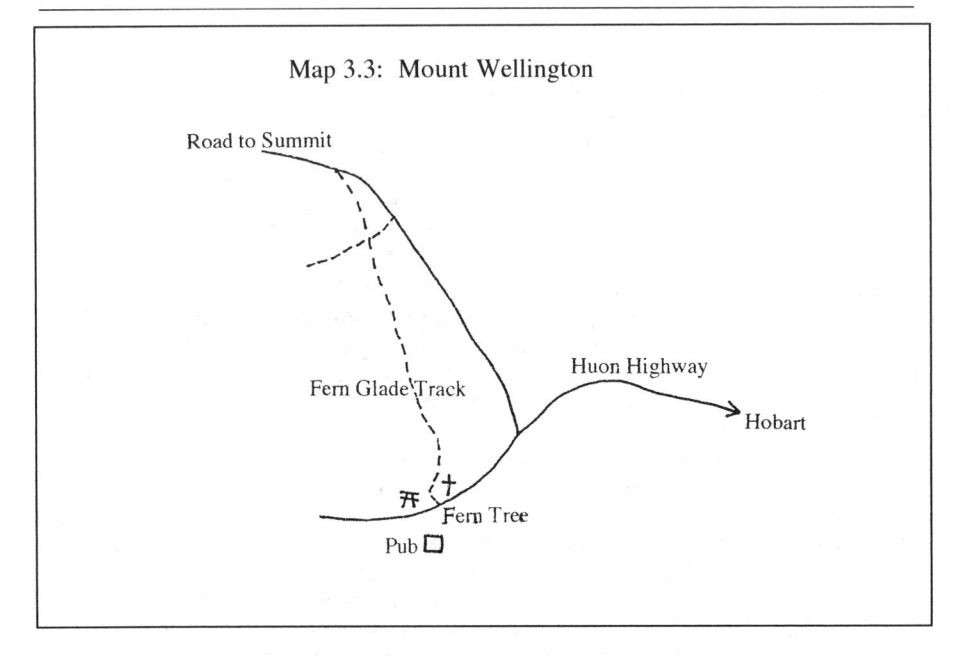

picnic area. About 0.5 km up the road from this area the Lenah Valley track leaves the road on the right; follow this for a short way to look for the currawong. However, if you are going to the north of Tasmania it is not worth wasting time looking for currawongs here as they are very common at Cradle Mountain and Lake St Clair.

3.3 Pittwater Road (Map 3.4)

Key Species: **Masked Owl**
This has been a roosting site for a pair of **Masked Owls** for several years now. It is situated close to Hobart Airport. Drive from the airport towards Sorell and turn right after approximately 3 km into Pittwater Road, towards Seven Mile Beach. After about 400 m stop in a big lay-by on the left hand side of the road. Look straight out from the gate and about 150 m away is a tall tree which has a big hole on a broken limb facing towards you. The owl has been seen roosting in the hole in this tree. Watch from Pittwater Road at dusk, you should not enter the land as it is private. If the owl is roosting here it should appear at the hole before it is fully dark. We had to go back later in the night and then spotlighted one bird close to the road at 3.00 am.

Map 3.4: Pittwater Road

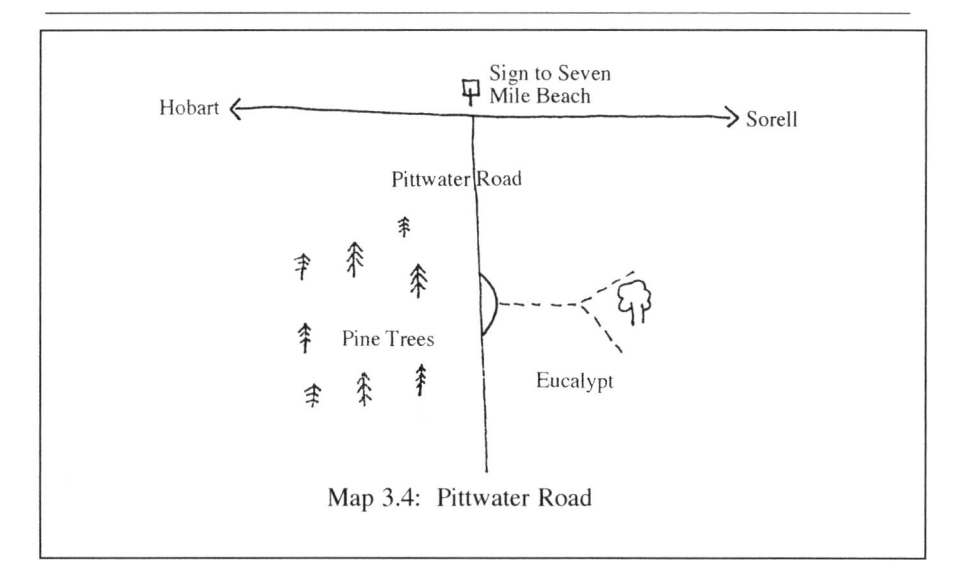

3.4 Maria Island National Park

Key Species: **Hooded Plover, Forty-spotted Pardalote**
This is a very attractive place, unfortunately in the full day that we were on the island it only stopped raining for 20 minutes. The passenger boat to the island leaves from the jetty at Triabunna daily at 10.30 am (at least in the summer, check *Tasmanian Travelways*). It cost us $19.00 return and comes back at 4.30 pm from Maria Island so you would have plenty of time to day twitch **Forty-spotted Pardalote** if on a tight schedule. The crossing takes about one hour. We had to leave early on our second day because of a strong wind warning. The couple who own the boat are very friendly and if there are a group of you it would be well worth asking about chartering the boat for a pelagic. You can camp on Maria Island or stay in the penitentiary, this should be booked in advance by phoning (002) 57 1420. In 1991 the cost was $4.00 per person per night. You must take all your own food and preferably your own stove. All the endemics *except* Scrubtit are common on Maria Island and it has the largest colony of **Forty-spotted Pardalotes** in the world. The best place to look for the pardalotes is the eucalypts by the dam on the Reservoir Circuit Walk (maps are available from the office on Maria Island). The Reservoir Circuit Walk is a round trip of about two hours from Darlington. The pardalotes are high in the trees, especially around the dam, and this is also an excellent area for **Swift Parrots** in summer. We saw **Pink Robin** and **Bassian Ground-Thrush** on the trail, and **Dusky Robin** at the rubbish tip. While out spotlighting we saw **Southern Boobook** and Maria Island is excellent for mammals. **Tasmanian Native-Hens** and **Cape Barren Geese** have been introduced to the Island and are now very common around Darlington. As we left the island there were two **Hooded Plovers** on Darlington Beach, this is a regular place for them.

3.5 Freycinet National Park

This is a scenic national park on the east coast. It is reached by turning south off the Tasman Highway, 11 km south of Bicheno, towards Coles Bay. The area around Hazards Lagoon is good for the Tasmanian race of **Brown Quail**, however we failed to find any. Seawatching from Cape Tourville was good with lots of seabirds passing, including **White-faced Storm-Petrel** (1), a **Giant-Petrel sp**, plus many **Shy Albatrosses**.

3.6 Forest Glen Tea Gardens

Key Species: **Swift Parrot** (October - March)
This is easily the best place to see **Swift Parrots**, but note that they are not present from approximately April to September. The lady who runs the gardens is a real bird lover and has planted blue gums especially for the parrots to feed on. Most of the other Tasmanian endemics are also present here including **Dusky Robin**. The gardens open at 9.00 am, and are well signposted from the Spreyton to Sheffield road, about 3 km from Spreyton. The parrots are numerous and confiding so take a camera.

3.7 Cradle Mountain

Key Species: **Black Currawong, Scrubtit, Striated Calamanthus, Olive Whistler, Pink Robin, Tasmanian Thornbill, Honeyeaters**
This is a really beautiful mountainous national park in the north-west of the island, reached from the C132 road. One of the main attractions is the mammals which can be seen feeding at the back of the Cradle Mountain Lodge on the kitchen scraps which are put out nightly. Numerous possums, two species of quoll and Tasmanian Devils are all regular visitors. Aim to be there at dusk to ensure that you get a good place on the balcony because there are lots of tourists. There is a basic campsite close to the Lodge. **Black Currawongs** are very tame and plentiful around Cradle Mountain Lodge itself; we had a maximum of six on the bonnet of the car! We saw **Swift Parrots** feeding in some flowering trees on the Overland Track about a 45 minute walk from Waldheim Chalet. The bushes around the campsite are good for **Scrubtit, Olive Whistler, Bassian Ground-Thrush** and the endemic honeyeaters. In the alpine grassland along the Overland Track, **Striated Calamanthus** are plentiful. While we were there, leeches were active, even though temperatures were below freezing at night.

3.8 Strahan

Key Species: **Ground Parrot, Beautiful Firetail**
This is an excellent place on the west coast of Tasmania to see **Ground Parrots**. They are easy to find once you have identified the right kind of heathland, this must be not too short and not too long, just so the vegetation goes above your ankles and can be walked through comfortably. Take the road west from Strahan

and turn left towards Wellington Head, drive past the airfield on your right and as you carry on down the dirt track look for the only track on the left which is signposted 'Wests Salmon Fisheries PTY' Private Road. Park by this turn and walk down the private road about 100 m, then head out into the heath on your left; we saw four **Ground Parrots** in this area, all roughly 50 m in from the private road. Also in this heath were **Striated Calamanthus**, **Southern Emuwren** (both common) and **Beautiful Firetails**. If you don't have any success finding the parrots in this particular area, just keep trying other short heathland patches along this road.

3.9 Lake St Clair

Key Species: **Black Currawong, Pink Robin**
The Lake St Clair car-park is full of aggressive **Black Currawongs**. Don't let them rip the sandwiches out of your hands! The woodland along the Overland Track where it skirts the lake itself is also a good area for **Pink Robin**.

3.10 Melaleuca

Key Species: **Orange-bellied Parrot** (summer months), **Beautiful Firetail**
Melaleuca is situated in the remote south-west corner of Tasmania and is the breeding area for **Orange-bellied Parrots**. For anyone visiting Tasmania in the summer and unable to see the birds wintering on the mainland, this represents an easy, though costly, way to view this species. In 1992 the 90 minute flight to Melaleuca with Par Avion cost $180 return from Cambridge Aerodrome in Hobart. Check on the availability, however, as the flights are frequently cancelled or delayed by bad weather. Once at Melaleuca there are two army style huts where you can stay, but take your own food, plus some extra in case your return flight is delayed for several days by the weather. There is an observation hide with a bird table in front of it where the parrots feed daily, both captive reared and truly wild birds are present. **Beautiful Firetails** also use the table and in the nearby bushes **Dusky Robin** and **Olive Whistler** can be seen.

CHAPTER 4

NEW SOUTH WALES

Suberb Lyrebird, one of the most exciting forest inhabitants in coastal New South Wales

Introduction (Map 4.1)
This state is second only to Queensland in terms of time worth spending there. The areas to visit are described roughly south to north in the eastern side of the state, followed by the inland areas. Although completely surrounded by New South Wales, the Australian Capital Territory is treated in a separate chapter following this one.

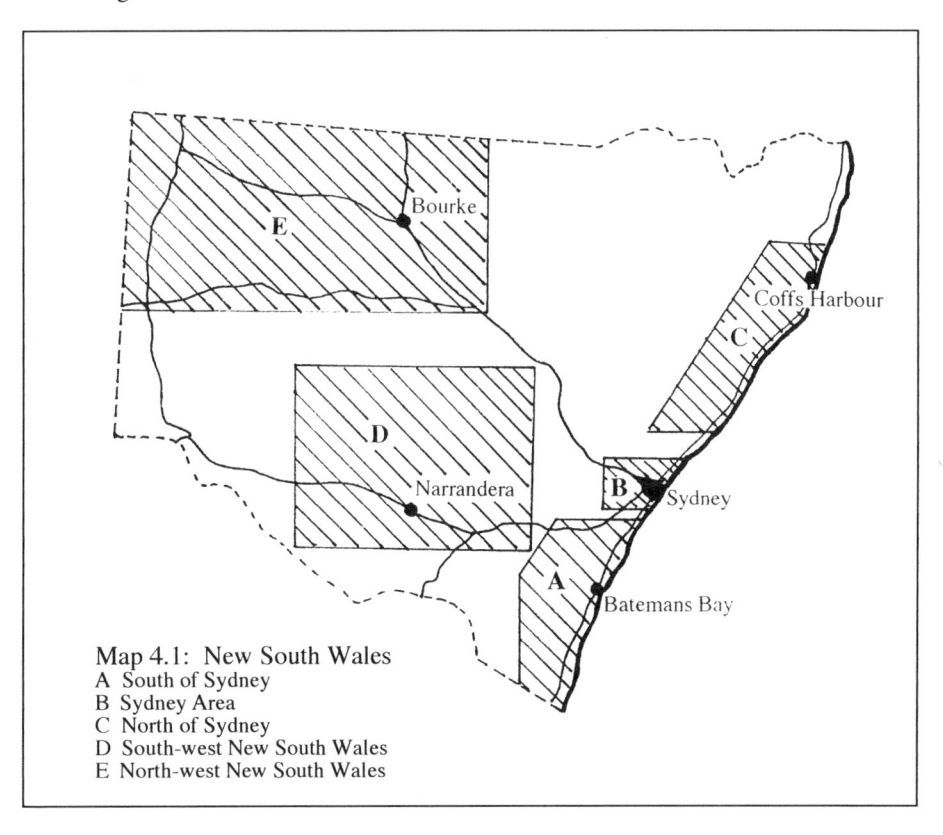

Map 4.1: New South Wales
A South of Sydney
B Sydney Area
C North of Sydney
D South-west New South Wales
E North-west New South Wales

Endemics: Origma, (Relict Raven)
Specialities: Black-backed Bittern, Lewin's Rail, Plains-wanderer, Superb Parrot, Eastern Bristlebird, Pilotbird, Regent Honeyeater, Red-lored Whistler

A South of Sydney (Map 4.2)
The coastal belt south of Wollongong is particularly attractive with its stretches of beaches, fine eucalypt forests and coastal heaths. Be aware, however, that the weather can be bracing during the winter months, although the area is well worth visiting at any time of year. Included in this section is the coastal strip as far west as the Great Dividing Range.

Map 4.2: South of Sydney
1 Barren Grounds Bird Observatory
2 Morton Nat Park
3 Lake George and Lake Bathurst
4 Jervis Bay Nat Park
5 Kioloa Rest Area
6 Nadgee Nature Reserve

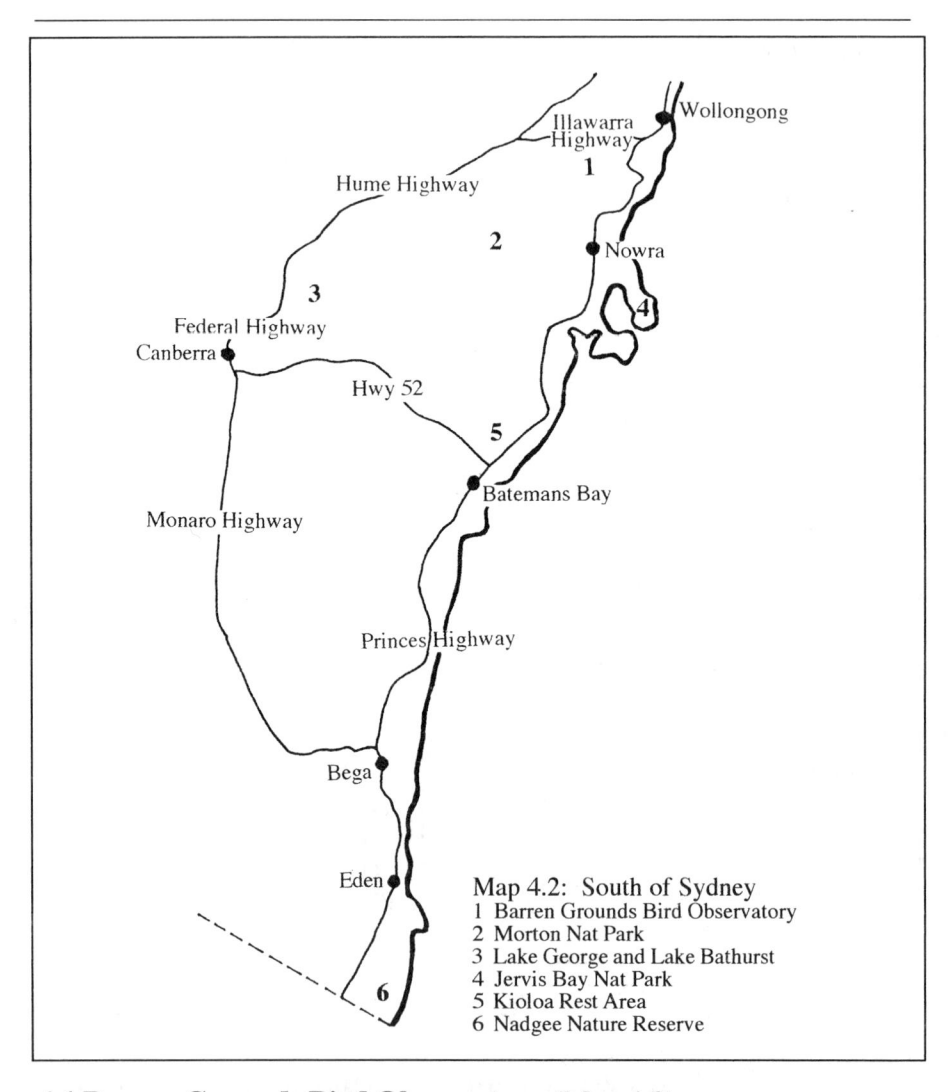

4.1 Barren Grounds Bird Observatory (Map 4.3)

Key Species: **Ground Parrot, Eastern Bristlebird, Southern Emuwren, Chestnut-rumped Hylacola**
Barren Grounds Bird Observatory is a heathland reserve that holds a number of good birds, notably **Ground Parrot** and **Eastern Bristlebird**. Camping is not allowed at Barren Grounds, however you can stay at the observatory or alternatively it is easy to visit on a day trip from Wollongong. It can be reached from the Illawarra Highway. Turn off this highway 4 km to the east of Robertson

Map 4.3: Barren Grounds Bird Observatory

E Eastern Bristlebird
G Ground Parrot
C Chestnut-rumped Hylacola
P Pilotbird

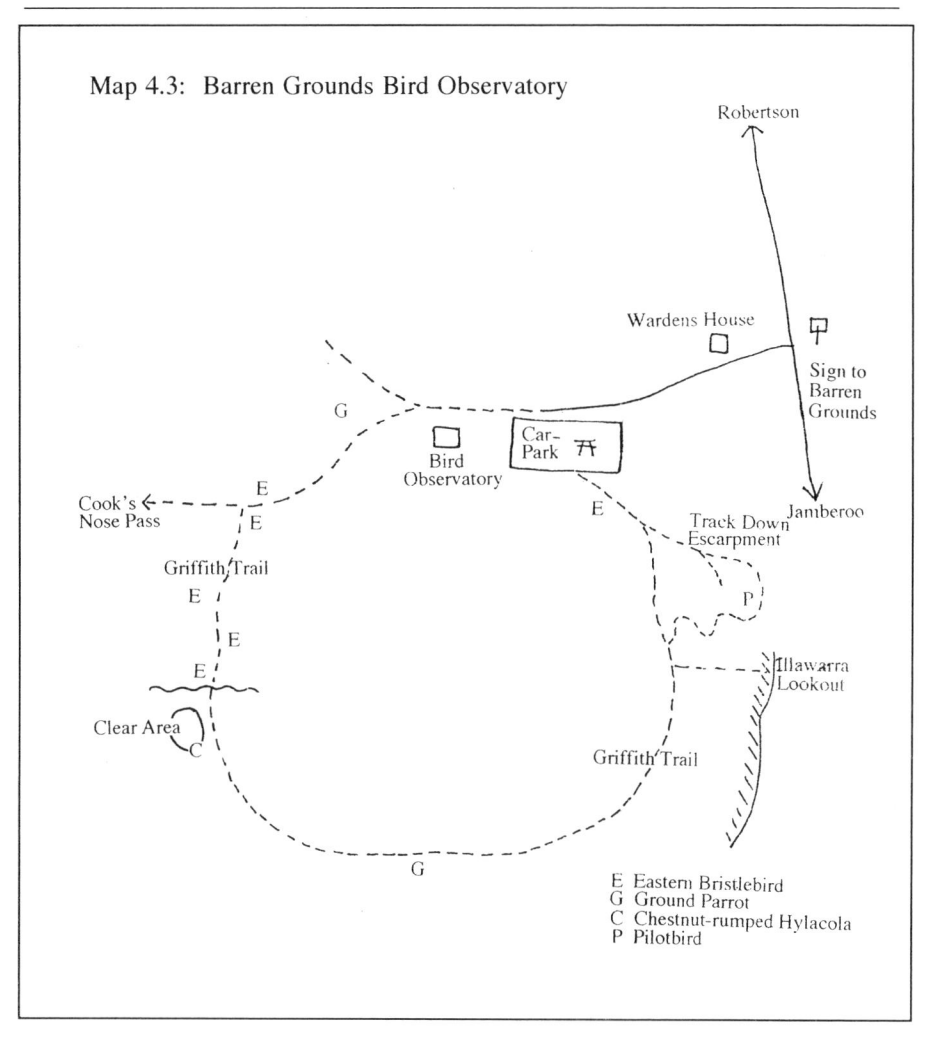

towards Jamberoo, the reserve has a small signpost on the right, 14 km from Robertson and not long after you leave the bitumen. Drive to the car-park then walk past the observatory. **Ground Parrots** occur in the short heathy area to the right, past the observatory; it is important not to leave the tracks and flush them as they are highly endangered and you could be fined. The best way to see them is to help out at the annual census when a line of people walks through the heath, flushing them into a line of mist nets. A census usually takes place in early March and for more information contact the Warden, Barren Grounds Bird Observatory, PO Box 3, Jamberoo NSW 2533 or phone (042) 360 195. If you can't be there on a census date, the best way to see them is to listen for them calling and look for them flying about at dusk. The call is unusual, 3-4 ringing notes, like a bell. We saw them here on two occasions in this way. On another visit we flushed a single bird close to the track along the Griffith Trail. **Eastern Bristlebirds** can be hard to see here, success is very weather dependant. On calm clear days they come out readily onto the tracks and they are certainly easiest in spring when they call a lot more. We saw at least four along the first 500 m of the Griffith Trail in November 1990, the first bird was seen at the very start of the trail. We also heard them at the picnic end of the Griffith Trail, 400 m from the car-park, although they failed to show themselves here due to the strong wind. If you leave the Griffith Trail on the track which goes down the escarpment and eventually loops back, then the woodland you walk through is where **Pilotbirds** are fairly common; we saw a pair easily in November 1990. Illawarra Lookout is good for scanning over the forest below, **Variable Goshawks** and **Topknot Pigeons** are usually around. Just by the turn-off to the lookout, **Southern Emuwrens** are common. **Chestnut-rumped Hylacolas** are found in the short heathy areas; we saw a pair just after the stream on the Griffith Trail, also along here were **Beautiful Firetail**, **Crescent Honeyeater** and **Gang-gang Cockatoo**.

Incidentally, if you carry on towards the coast along the Illawarra Highway; the road winds steeply down the escarpment through Macquarie National Park and this area is excellent for **Superb Lyrebirds**. We drove this section of the road at dawn one morning, on the way to Wollongong, and saw no less than four lyrebirds feeding out in the open on the roadside verges. The track off to the right to Rainbow Falls is good for spotlighting; we saw three **Tawny Frogmouths** along it and heard **Sooty Owl** around the car-park at the end of the track one night.

4.2 Morton National Park (Map 4.4)

Key Species: **White-throated Nightjar** (spring), **Pilotbird**, **Origma**
Morton is a large national park west of Nowra, which covers a huge area and includes several good sites including the most reliable site we know of for **Origma**.
4.2a Fitzroy Falls
To reach these beautiful falls, turn south off the Illawarra Highway 11 km east of Moss Vale towards Kangaroo Valley (signposted). After 19 km you get to the Fitzroy Falls picnic area with an information centre on the left and a car-park on the right and a bit further along on the right a basic campsite. Walking tracks go along both sides of the valley from the falls. On the southern track we saw **Pilotbird** in thick scrub 1 km down the track beyond Valley View, whilst on the northern track we saw another **Pilotbird** in rainforest about 500 m before the Grotto and **Origma** feeding on the streambed from the little footbridge just before the Grotto. Around the falls lookout itself were **Variable Goshawk**, **Gang-gang Cockatoo** and **Crescent Honeyeater**.
4.2b Triabunna Falls
This is a good place for **Origma**, although not as reliable as the following site, which is on the same road. This unsealed road can be rough and unpleasant to drive and leads from the Princes Highway just south of Nowra, through Nerriga to

Tarago, near Lake George. Driving south out of Nowra turn right along Flinders Way. Shortly afterwards you come to a T-junction, turn right here and then just before the entrance to HMAS Albatross turn right again signposted to the domestic airport. This road becomes unsealed after a short distance. At the next T-junction turn right and after travelling about 17 km from this junction there is a car-park on the right hand side for Triabunna Falls. **Origmas** have been seen in this car-park. Alternatively, about 100 m further on the road crosses a stream. Pick your way along the bank heading upstream and look for **Origmas** which regularly feed on boulders in the streambed, we saw a pair in March 1992. **Beautiful Firetails** also occur in the heath here.

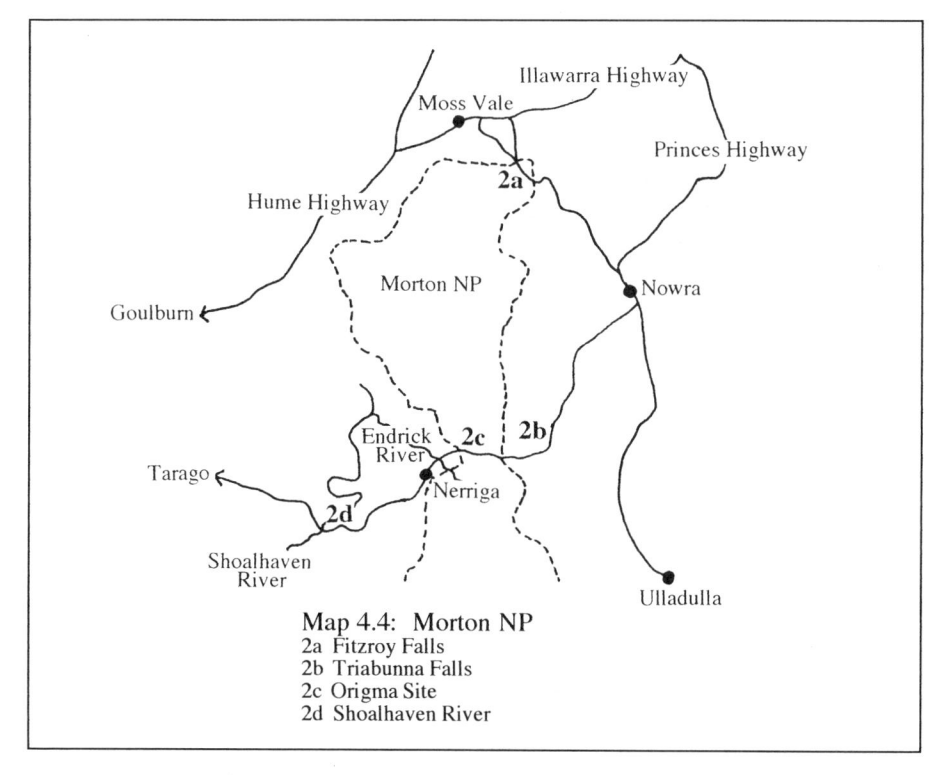

Map 4.4: Morton NP
2a Fitzroy Falls
2b Triabunna Falls
2c Origma Site
2d Shoalhaven River

4.2c Origma Site

This is the best locality we know of to see **Origma**, it is just on the western edge of Morton National Park. Carry on towards Nerriga from Triabunna Falls and after about 21 km you will see on the right a small pull-in and the Morton National Park sign, if you get to the Endrick River you have come too far so double back and look for the pull-in now on the left just before you get to the top of the hill. Park here and walk down the steep slope in front of you on the north side of the road then turn left after a short way onto what is clearly an old road. To your left are some big boulders on which the **Origmas** feed, although we also saw them feeding lower down the slope to the right. If you carry on down the steep slope, the *Casuarina* trees on your right are a roost for **Powerful Owl**, although we only found pellets.

4.2d Shoalhaven River

This is a good site for **White-throated Nightjar**, but only in the spring months, October-December. To get there, drive through Nerriga, then bear right towards Tarago. After about 12 km you get to the Shoalhaven River. Turn around and go back 1 km to an obscure track now on your left. Follow this and turn left at a T-junction after about 300 m to an old bush campsite. From here walk down the steep bank to the river; **White-throated Nightjars** hawk over the river on warm evenings. They have also been seen from the Shoalhaven Crossing. Carrying on further along this road is a good route through to Lakes Bathurst and George and eventually Canberra and the Australian Capital Territory.

4.3 Lake George and Lake Bathurst

Key Species: **Freckled Duck, Banded Lapwing**, waders

These two big lakes close to Canberra are good for **Freckled Duck** and waders. Unfortunately recent politics have made birdwatchers *persona non gratis* at Lake Bathurst, but hopefully the private landowners will allow access in the near future.

4.3a Lake George

This is situated right alongside the Federal Highway between Canberra and Goulburn. Check from the roadside picnic stops for common waterbirds. However, **Freckled Duck** tend to be in the south-west corner and not along the Federal Highway shoreline. To get here, turn off the Federal Highway towards Bungendore, then turn left after a short distance into Lake Road which is a dirt road. Just before you get to the lake there is a pool on the left which is worth checking for waders (we saw **Red-necked Avocet, Marsh Sandpiper** and **Red-kneed Dotterel** in August 1992). Carry on down Lake Road to Lake George itself and check the duck flocks for **Freckled Duck**. Up to three hundred were regularly here, but their numbers fluctuate greatly. It is worth looking for them at any time of the year.

4.3b Lake Bathurst

This lake is certainly better for waders than Lake George but sadly it is currently out of bounds. The best wader spot is reached by driving from Bungendore to Tarago. Go straight on at the 'Loaded Dog' pub cross-roads . Keep going until you can see the lake on your left and park by the second gate. Go through the gate and walk down to the lake shore through another gate. Waders are found along the eastern edge; **Double-banded Plover** is a certainty here in the winter months (May-August). In January-March 1993 we saw **Buff-breasted Sandpiper** (1), also **Pectoral Sandpiper** (6, regular here), **Sharp-tailed Sandpiper** (500), **Red-necked Stint** (600), **Pacific Golden Plover** (15), **Red-capped Plover** and a **Little Curlew**. Most species of Australian duck are found here, e.g. **Blue-billed, Musk, Pink-eared** and **Pacific Black Ducks, Hardhead, Australian Shoveler, Grey** and **Chestnut Teal, Great Crested** and **Hoary-headed Grebes**, summer is best particularly during droughts inland.

There are two points to bear in mind about this site. One, the land has recently been bought so as mentioned earlier it is private, under no circumstances enter the land without permission from the land owners. Canberra Ornithologists Group may be able to help here. Secondly, the area is renowned for its large tiger snake population so be especially careful as you walk down to the shoreline.

The north shore of Lake Bathurst has large boulders and rocks along it which are favoured by other species. To get here drive north from Tarago on the Goulburn road, then turn right onto a dirt track until you get to a big track off on the right. Park here and walk down the big track to the lake shore, then go along the eastern edge of the lake. You should see **White-fronted Chat** here and **Freckled Duck** during the summer months although they are usually sitting well out on the offshore boulders. Check the flocks of **Masked Lapwing** for **Banded Lapwings**, they are usually present but may disappear if the grassland becomes really wet.

4.4 Jervis Bay (Map 4.5)

Key Species: **Eastern Bristlebird**

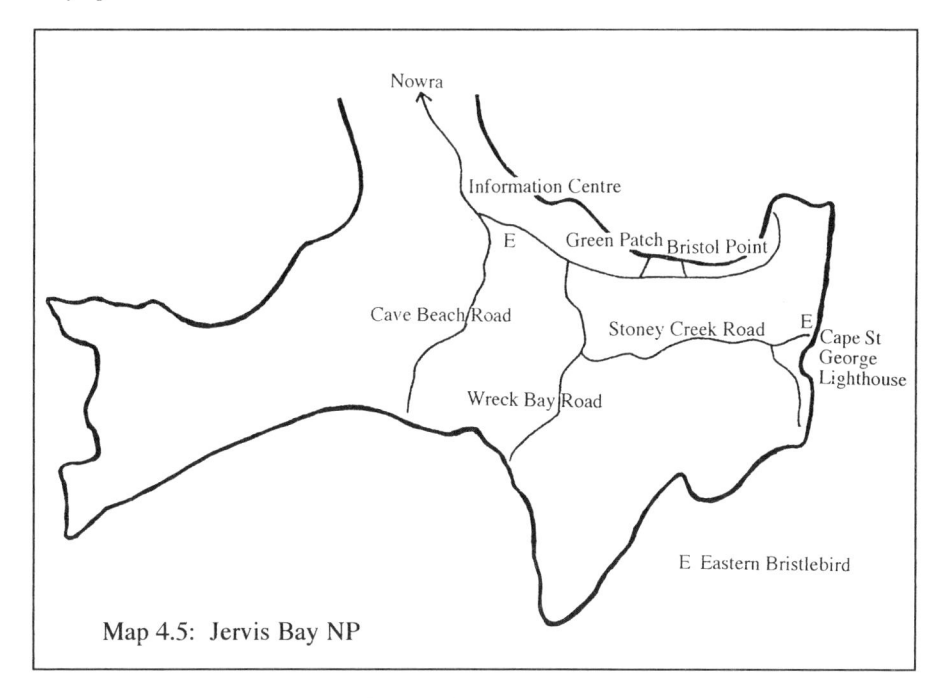

Map 4.5: Jervis Bay NP

Although strictly part of the ACT, Jervis Bay is treated here for simplicity. It is a good place to see **Eastern Bristlebird**, possibly easier than at Barren Grounds. The south arm of the bay is the best birding area, 32 km south-east of Nowra. You pass through a park entrance where an entrance fee is payable, next to it is a useful information centre where excellent campsites can be booked and paid for, also obtain a map of the park here and ask the rangers for bird information. Driving past the centre, along Jervis Bay Road, pull over and park about 100 m past the turn-off to Cave Beach. **Eastern Bristlebirds** regularly cross over the main road here, we heard one singing here in August 1993. The most reliable spot for **Eastern Bristlebird** is reached by continuing down Jervis Bay Road, turning right along Wreck Bay Road then left along Stoney Creek Road. Follow the signs to the car-park at the ruined lighthouse (Cape St. George Lighthouse). Bristlebirds occur around the edge of the car-park and along the tracks between it and the ruined lighthouse. We also recorded **Gang-gang Cockatoo** here. Seawatching from the lighthouse is good in strong onshore winds. If camping overnight in the park the track between Green Patch and Bristol Point campgrounds is good for spotlighting **Powerful Owl**.

4.5 Kioloa Rest Area (Map 4.6)

This is where we found a breeding pair of **Masked Owls**. They were twitched by many people from October 1991 until October 1992 and there must be a good chance that they are still around in the area, basic camping is possible here.

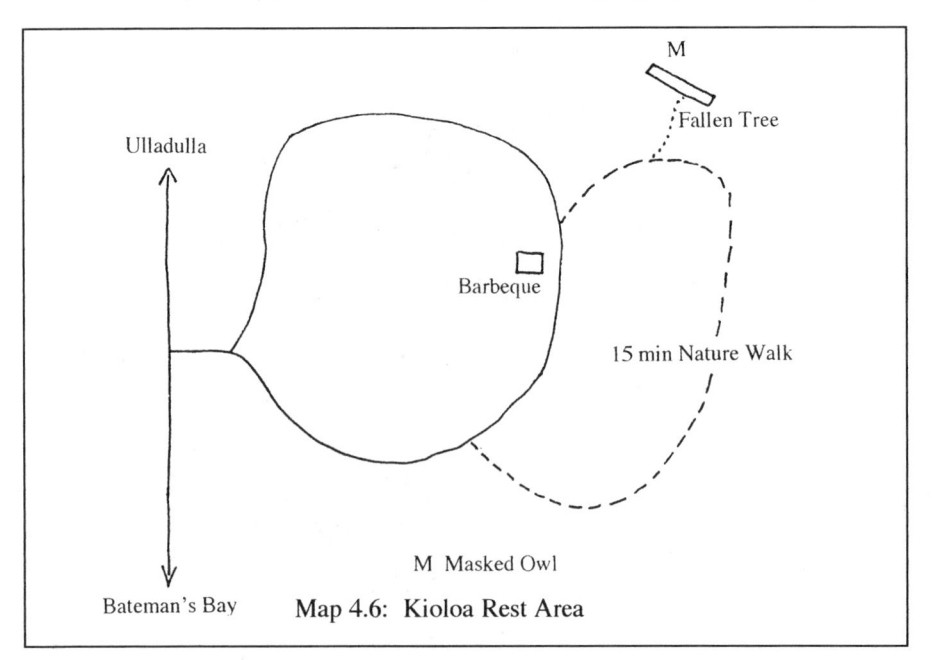

Map 4.6: Kioloa Rest Area

The site itself is on the Princes Highway, north of Batemans Bay. Driving north you should look for the signpost to Kioloa rest area on your right beyond the turn to Durras Lake. Go in here and park near the toilets and take the nature trail track. After about 50 m, cross onto a fallen log and follow it to its end and spotlight the tall trees to the north. The owls were hard to see when we first found them - most people having to wait until just before dawn, but they became very easy to see around Christmas and even easier in July-October 1992 when there was a begging youngster. Obviously a good spotlight is useful.

4.6 Nadgee Nature Reserve (Map 4.7)

Key Species: **Ground Parrot, Blue-winged Parrot, Eastern Bristlebird, Chestnut-rumped Hylacola, Tawny-crowned Honeyeater**
Nadgee Nature Reserve is an excellent area of coastal heathland in the south-east corner of the state. It is primarily a scientific research area, so access is restricted to a maximum of twenty people and must be booked in advance. Write to; The Officer-in-charge, Eden District, Armstrong and Evans Building, Imlay Street Eden, P O Box 186, Eden NSW 2551. Tel (0649) 61434. The weather can be very wet and windy here, so be warned! To get to the reserve, drive south on the Princes Highway from Eden. Turn off east onto a dirt road 24 km south of Eden towards Wonboyn. Turn right after 9 km and keep going a further 9 km until you cross the Merrica River, go through the gates to the ranger station. Register here and drive a further 10 km to the end of the road at Newton's Beach. You can bush camp here, but remember that you must bring all your own food and supplies. Back along the road from the campsite we saw **Chestnut-rumped Hylacola** and several **Brush Bronzewings** feeding on the track in the afternoons. On Newton's Beach itself were several **Hooded Plovers** and on the short heathland by the track, just south from the campsite towards Nadgee River, we saw **Tawny-crowned Honeyeater, Ground Parrot** and **Blue-winged Parrot**. The heathland further south towards Nadgee Point is better for **Ground Parrots** and **Eastern Bristlebirds** and you can bush camp at several places on the way there. A good map of the area is the Nadgee 1:25000 sheet 8823-115.

Other good places to visit in the area include Nullica State Forest and Green Cape. The former is reached by turning west off the Princes Highway 5 km south of Eden, towards Nullica, carry on through Nullica and explore the forestry roads beyond. Both **Masked** and **Sooty Owls** are present in this part of the forest and in summer **White-throated Nightjars** are reasonably common. Green Cape is a superb seawatching vantage point, particularly during strong onshore winds. Turn east off the Princes Highway 19 km south of Eden, follow signposts to the lighthouse and seawatch just below it. We saw **Common Diving-Petrel** (20) and **Royal Albatross** (1 adult) in August 1992 following a south-easterly gale. The heathland adjacent to the road just before the lighthouse has **Eastern Bristlebirds** and **Ground Parrots**. Pelagic trips are regularly run from Eden, see the pelagic section for more details.

Map 4.7: Nadgee Nature Reserve Area

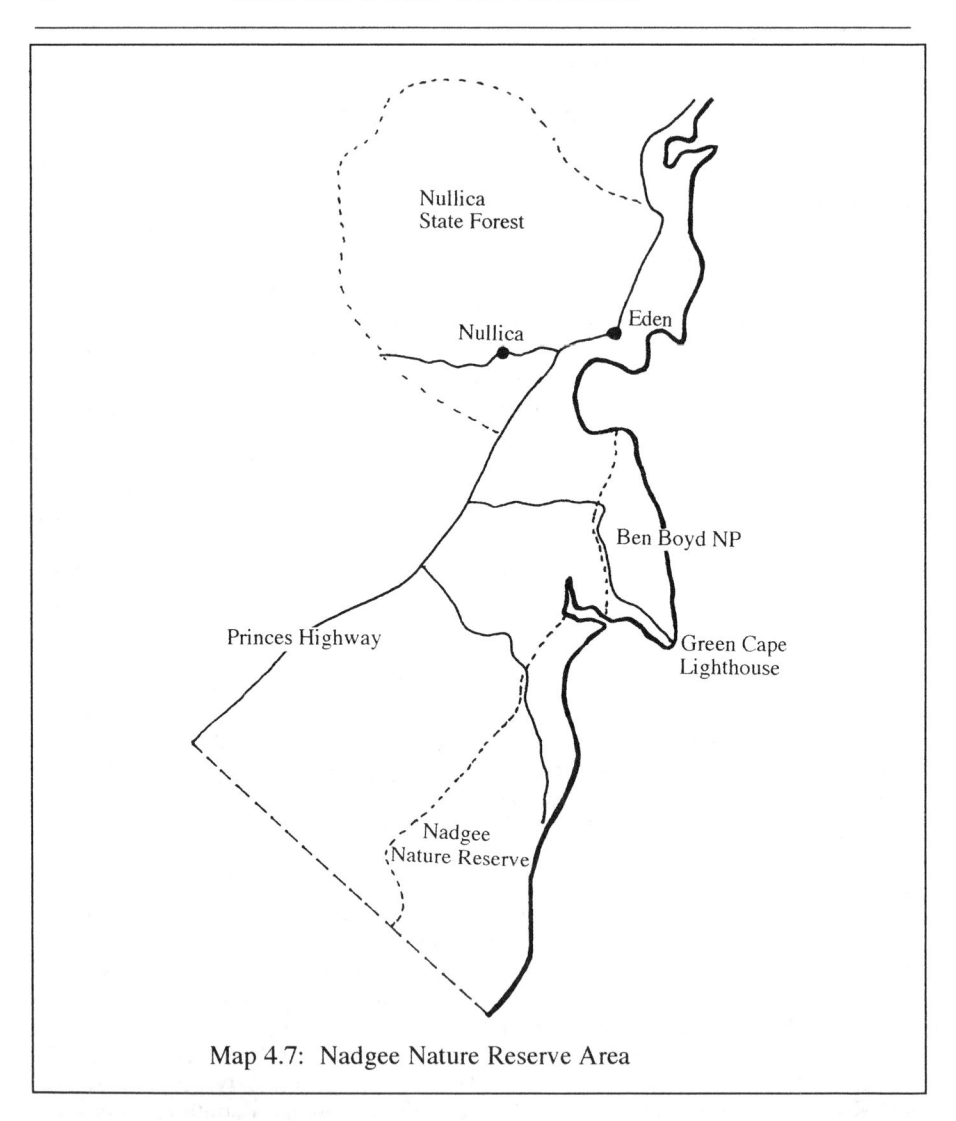

B Sydney Area (Map 4.8)
Sydney makes a good base for doing a number of areas in the south of the state, it is also a good place to meet up with local birders for the latest stake-outs and information. Regular socials are held on the first and third Thursday of each month in the Royal Albert, Reservoir Street, Surry Hills, Sydney. They normally meet around 8.30 pm. There are some good areas around the city which are described below.

SYDNEY AREA 43

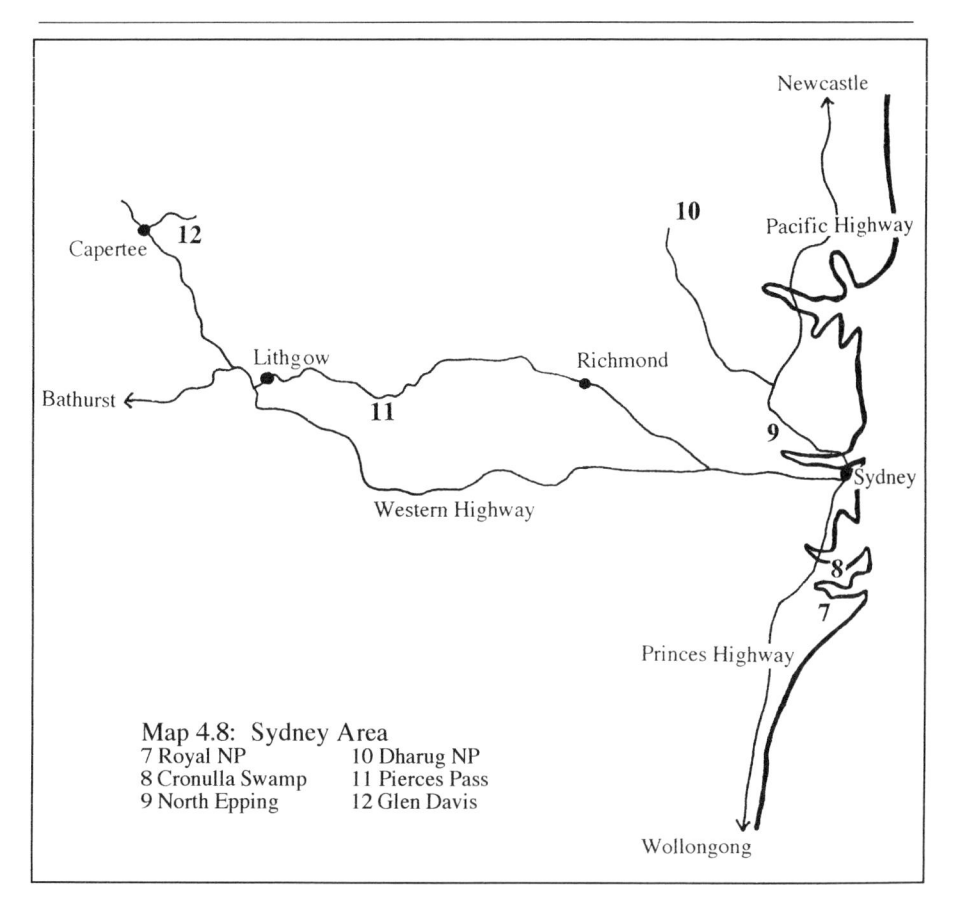

Map 4.8: Sydney Area
7 Royal NP
8 Cronulla Swamp
9 North Epping
10 Dharug NP
11 Pierces Pass
12 Glen Davis

4.7 Royal National Park (Map 4.9)

Key Species: **Powerful Owl, Sooty Owl, Superb Lyrebird**
Although there are no absolutely essential birds to see here, Royal National Park does have an excellent selection of birds. Unfortunately approximately 90% of the park was destroyed in the January 1994 bush fires. Apparently only small patches of rainforest along the rivers now exist. I have given the pre-fire information for the park as hopefully it will quickly regenerate, although you should definitely check with local birders for the latest information. There are three areas to concentrate on, around Audley in the north, the southern end of Lady Carrington Drive and a heath area in the west.
4.7a Audley Area
Drive south from Sydney on the Princes Highway, then turn left towards Audley (it is signposted to the park). A short way down this road is an office where you have to pay an entrance fee ($8). Beyond here, the road crosses the Hacking River to Audley, a short way beyond turn right and cross back over the river. A track

goes off to the right here to Engadine, follow this and check the escarpment on your right for **Origma**. Returning to the bridge, carry on down the road to the car-park at Kookaburra Flat then follow the river for about 100 m to an area of thick trees. **Powerful Owls** regularly roost here. We tried several times but the best we could manage was pellets. In this area we did see **Superb Lyrebird** (tame), **Bassian Ground-Thrush**, **Black-faced Monarch**, **Azure Kingfisher** and **Green Catbird**. The owls have also been found roosting on the opposite side of the river, which is accessible from Lady Carrington Drive.

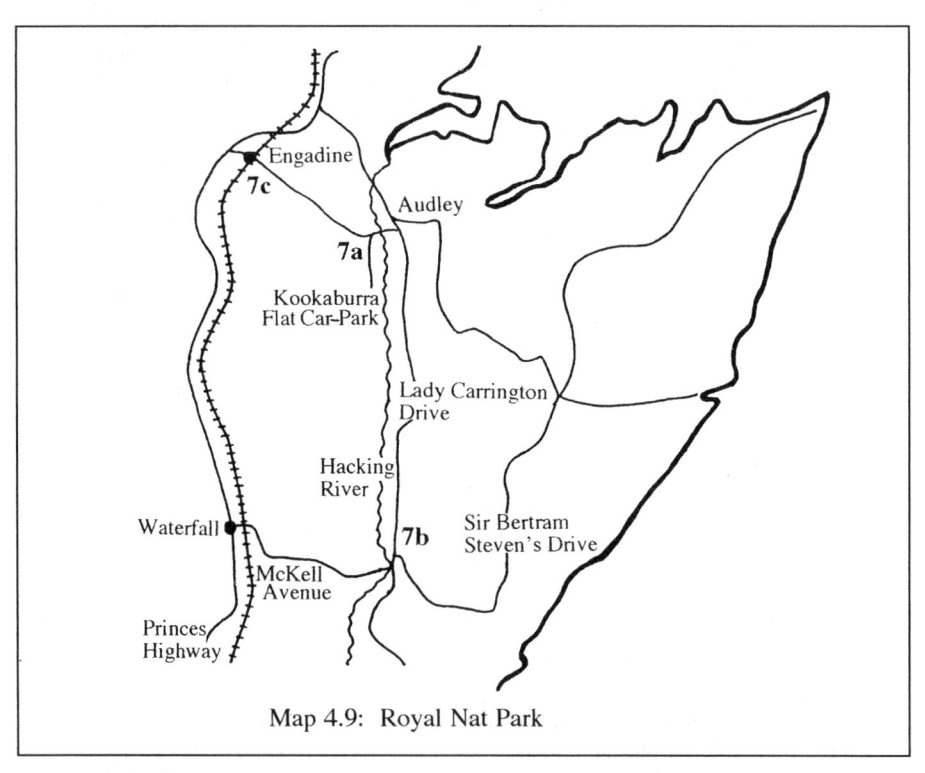

Map 4.9: Royal Nat Park

4.7b Waterfall Area

Turn off the Princes Highway at Waterfall, follow McKell Avenue until you cross the river and turn left onto Sir Bertram Stevens Drive. After less than a kilometre, pull off on the left in a lay-by which has stone entrance walls to a fenced off track. This is the south end of Lady Carrington Drive. This area is mainly known as a place to go spotlighting, but be warned that theft both from and of cars is notorious. Walk down Lady Carrington Drive for about 1-2 km, through some excellent rainforest. **Powerful Owls** occur here, especially the part closer to the lay-by, though I never heard them in four visits. **Sooty Owls** are regularly seen; I heard them on three of my four visits but only managed to spotlight a pair once, about 200 m down the track from the lay-by. The Sooty

Owls here seem to have become accustomed to whistled imitations of their calls so they don't bother to respond now. The best time of year to try for them seems to be August to November. Since the bush fires, they have apparently been recorded further south in the park along Lady Wakehurst Drive, local birders should have more information.

4.7c Heath Area

This good area of heath is behind Engadine Railway Station which is located east of the Princes Highway, south of the Audley Turning. Cross over the railway line on Station Bridge and follow the track into the heath for about 250 m. Birds found here include **Southern Emuwren** (fairly common), **Chestnut-rumped Hylacola, Beautiful Firetail** (rare) and **Tawny-crowned Honeyeater.**

4.8 Cronulla Swamp (Map 4.10)

Key Species: Crakes and **Lewin's Rail**

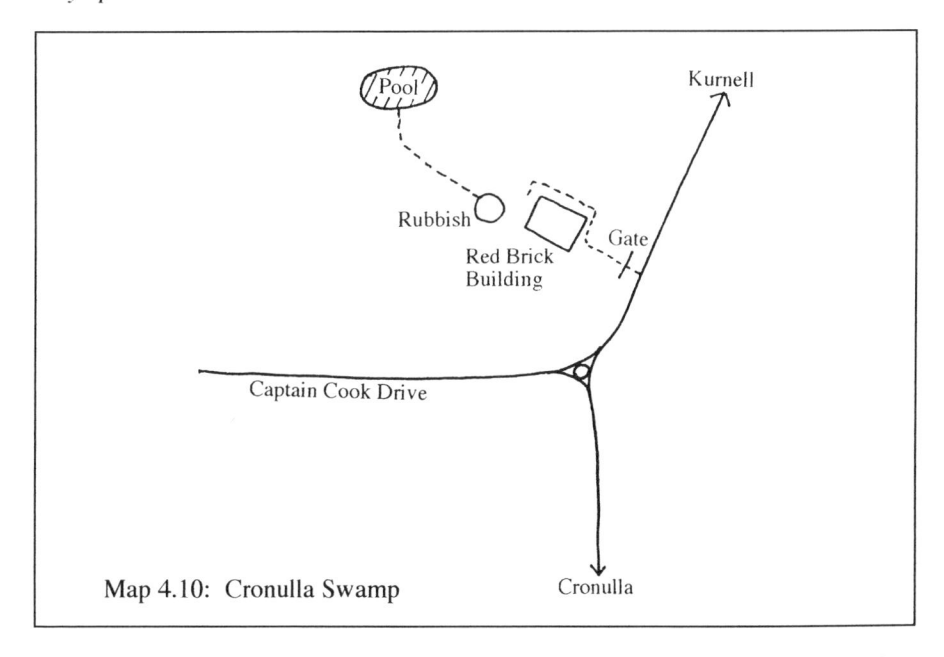

Map 4.10: Cronulla Swamp

Cronulla Swamp is situated south-east of Sydney. It is a good place to see crakes and notably **Lewin's Rail**. The area is best around October until November, after this it unfortunately dries out and is then useless. Check with local birders for the latest information. To get there, drive towards Cronulla along Captain Cook Drive, go past both the public and Cronulla Golf courses on your right and at the roundabout bear left towards Kurnell. Park on the left after about 60 m, walk through the gate, around the edge of a red brick building, then find an obscure track which starts by a pile of rubbish. The track goes through head high reeds then ends up at a small pool. Sit here quietly in the evening and wait for rails and crakes. Apparently if you carry on thrashing through the tall reeds beyond the pool, you have a good chance of flushing **Australasian Bittern** during the summer months. This would not be a pleasant experience however.

4.9 North Epping (Map 4.11)

Key Species: **Powerful Owl**

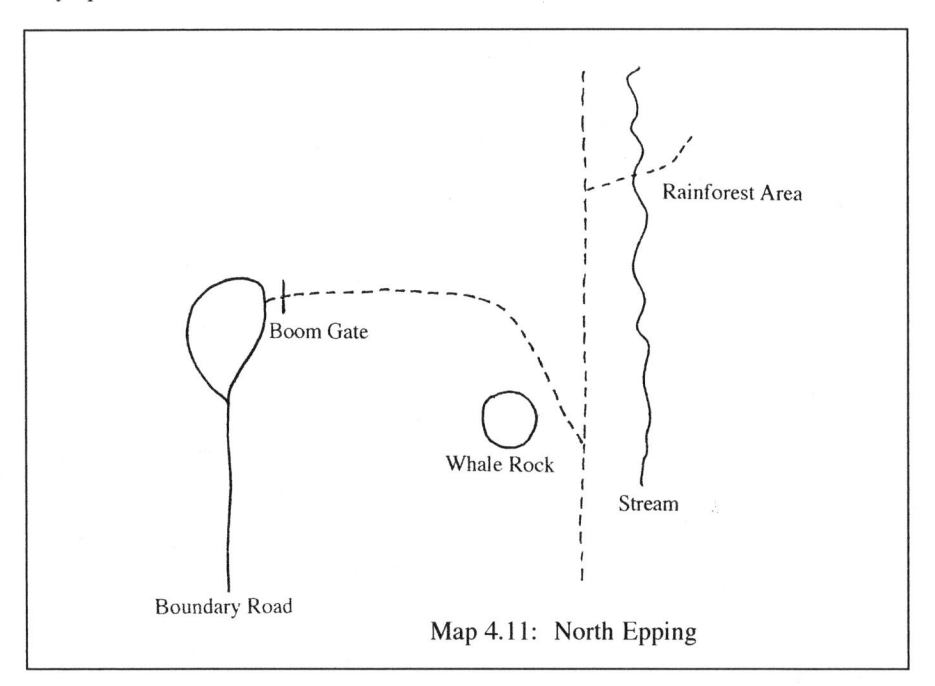

Map 4.11: North Epping

Pennant Hills Park is in the suburb of North Epping in the north of Sydney, close to Macquarie University. It has been a daytime roost for **Powerful Owl** for some years now. Check with the local birders to see if they are still around or are roosting elsewhere. To get there, leave Epping north along Norfolk Road. At the T-junction with Boundary Road, turn left and park at the turn around at the dead end. Walk through the boom gate and turn left past Whale Rock after a couple of hundred metres, look for a small foot track going down the embankment then across the creek. Go over here and check the rainforest patch on the other side. Up to three owls regularly roost here, they can be hard to find when they roost in dense foliage, but often perch lower down on open branches.

SYDNEY AREA 47

4.10 Dharug National Park (Map 4.12)

Key Species: **Lewin's Rail, Glossy Black-Cockatoo, Origma, Spotted Quail-Thrush**

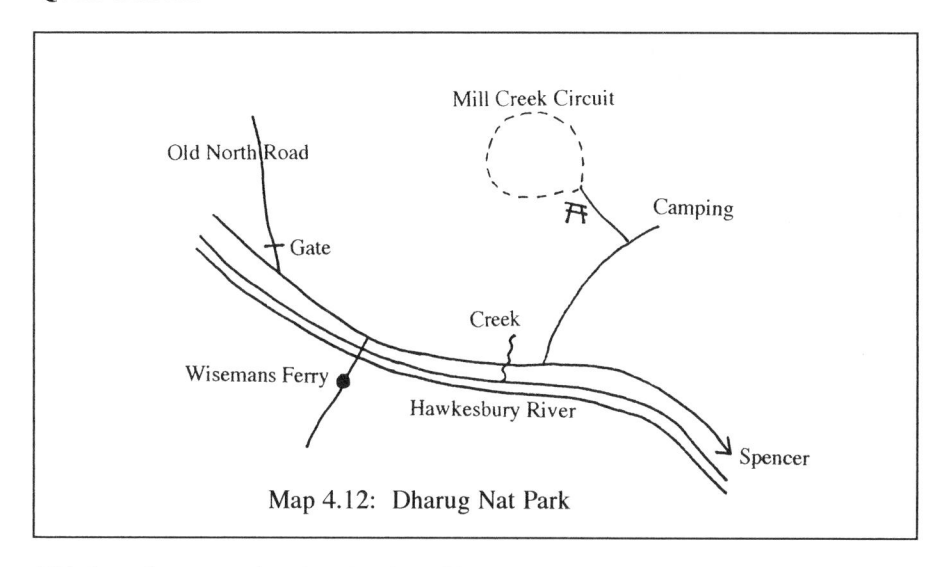

```
                    Mill Creek Circuit
   Old North Road
                                    Camping
        Gate
                    Creek
   Wisemans Ferry
                 Hawkesbury River
                                        Spencer
   Map 4.12: Dharug Nat Park
```

This is a pleasant national park, about 80 km north of Sydney and is as close as you can get to a stake-out for the nomadic **Glossy Black-Cockatoo**. It is also a reliable site for **Lewin's Rail** and **Origma**. Unfortunately this park was also extensively damaged in the January 1994 bush fires. Try to contact local birders for recent information on the state of the park. To get there, drive from Sydney to Wisemans Ferry on the old Northern Road. Take the ferry and once across on the other side of the river turn right and after about 4 km turn left along a track which leads to a picnic area and a good campsite. **Glossy Black-Cockatoos** have been seen on the Mill Creek Circuit walk which starts from the picnic site at the camping ground. They have also been seen flying over the campsite at dawn. We in fact saw them by driving along the road towards Spencer and stopping and scanning. We found three birds feeding in *Casuarinas* right beside this road in April 1991. They can be hard to find because they feed quietly in thick foliage and do not call loudly. The flight call is far carrying, however, similar to that of a Red-tailed Black-Cockatoo. The forest around the picnic site is good for a number of other species, **Brush Cuckoo** in particular is common here (learn the call), also **Superb Lyrebird, Large-billed Scrubwren, Bassian Ground-Thrush** and surprisingly in the tall grass between the campsite and the picnic area we saw **Southern Emuwrens**. The area for Lewin's Rail is as follows, from the campsite return to the road, turn right and stop after a few metres by a bridge over a small tidal creek. Watch from the bridge looking upstream at low tide. **Lewin's Rails** feed out on the mud at the sides of the creek. I saw one bird here in April 1991. For the Origma site you will have to return towards the ferry, but carry on past the ferry turning and after about 1 km you see a track off to the right, blocked off by a gate. This is called the Old North Road, walk up it for about 1 km to an area where the road is built on large sandstone blocks with scree and trees below. **Origmas** are regularly seen on the scree in this section. Carry on further up the track to the dry woodland areas where **Spotted Quail-Thrush** should be found, although it may be a few kilometres.

4.11 Pierces Pass

Key Species: **Pilotbird, Origma**
Situated in the Blue Mountains, Pierces Pass is 23 km beyond Bilpin on the Richmond to Lithgow road. Just after you go around a wide right hand bend, look for the signpost and pull-in on the left (south) side of the road. Park here and walk down a steep track to the picnic area, checking the rocky outcrops for **Origma**. It is worth noting here that the Blue Mountains are well worth visiting and any sandstone outcrops will have Origmas, for example the Jenolan Caves area. To get to the **Pilotbird** area, carry on further down the track to a well vegetated gully just before you go into rainforest. They are reasonably inquisitive and can be pished out. **Chestnut-rumped Hylacola** also occurs here.

4.12 Glen Davis

Key Species: **Turquoise Parrot, Regent Honeyeater, Diamond Firetail, Plum-headed Finch**
This is an excellent area since it covers a range of woodland habitats. It is chiefly noted as a regular site for **Regent Honeyeaters**. They are however very variable in their appearance, being highly dependant on flowering of the yellow box eucalypts; it is best to check with the Sydney birders if any are around. It is also a stake-out for **Plum-headed Finch**. To get to the site, drive west from Sydney on the Great Western Highway, turn north on to Highway 86 to Capertee. At Capertee turn right (east) to Glen Davis. The whole road is good for birding; just stop where the habitat looks good. The best area for **Regent Honeyeaters** is the short section of bitumen on a steep hill about 10 km from Capertee. We saw about twenty birds here in April 1991. Birds were also present and nesting further down the valley from August to December 1992. Further along the road from the bitumen section it crosses a couple of creeks, these are the best areas for **Plum-headed Finch**, we saw three just beyond the second creek, perched on a wire fence in December 1990. At Glen Davis itself is a museum, the trees around here and just before it are good for **Turquoise Parrot**. Other good birds seen along the Glen Davis road were **Brown Quail, Painted Button-Quail, Hooded Robin, Crested Shrike-Tit, Rufous Songlark, Diamond Firetail, Square-tailed Kite, Glossy Black-Cockatoo, Gang-gang Cockatoo, Little Lorikeet, Cicadabird, Origma** (this has been found roosting in the toilet block at the end of the road), **Speckled Warbler** and **Fuscous, Yellow-tufted** and **Black-chinned Honeyeaters**. There is a bush camping area along this road.

C North of Sydney (Map 4.13)

Although there are many good places to go birdwatching to the north of Sydney most of the species of interest are more numerous or easier to see further north. The exceptions are the Rufous Scrub-birds at Barrington Tops and the endemic New England race of Forest Raven, sometimes split as the Relict Raven.

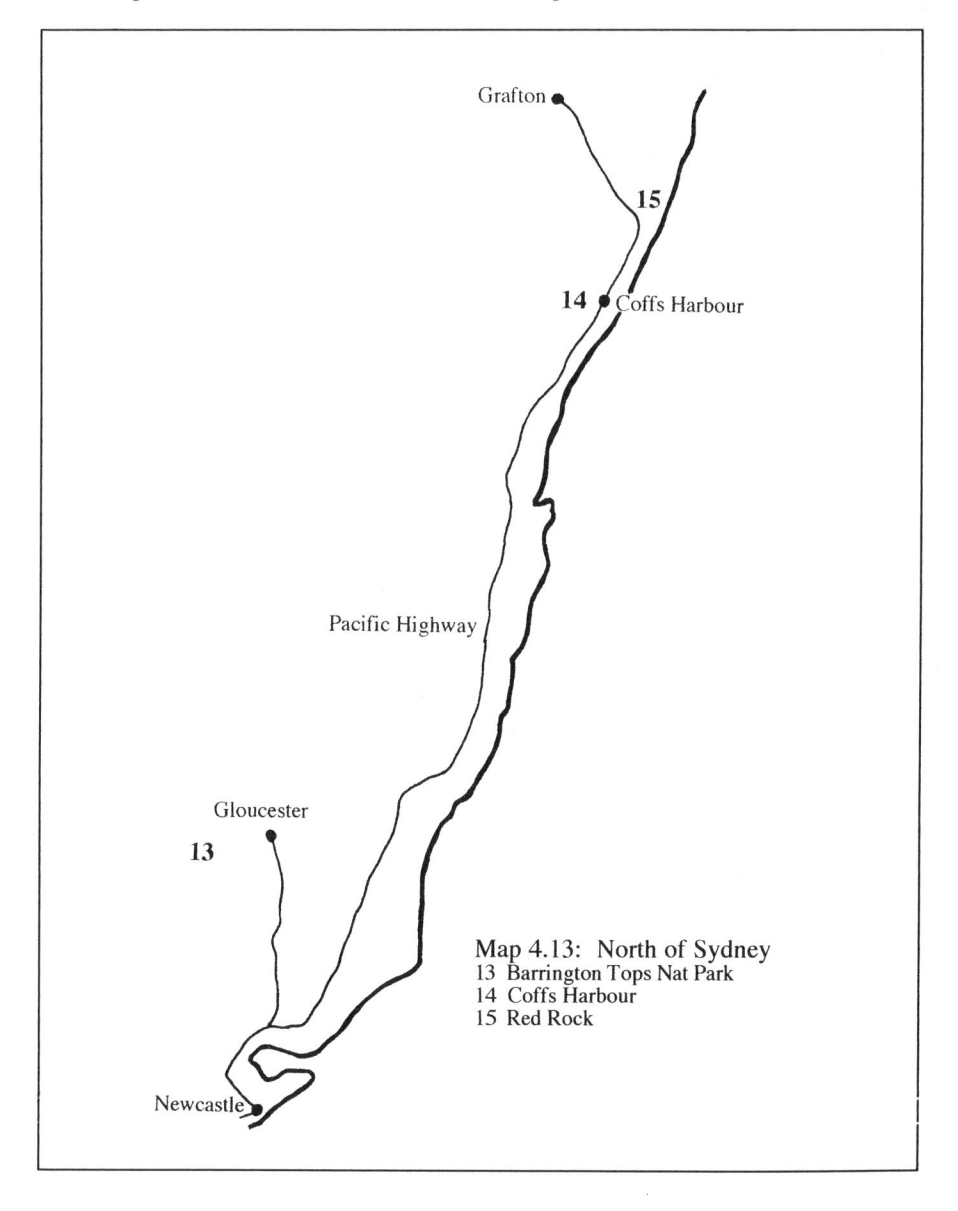

Map 4.13: North of Sydney
13 Barrington Tops Nat Park
14 Coffs Harbour
15 Red Rock

4.13 Barrington Tops

Key Species: **Rufous Scrub-bird, Satin Flycatcher**
This is a rainforest area approximately 100 km north of Newcastle. It is the most southerly point for species such as **Paradise Riflebird**, but more importantly it is noted as a good site for **Rufous Scrub-bird**. For some reason they are easier to see here than at Lamington National Park. The area is also good for **Satin Flycatcher** in the spring. The best area for scrub-birds and general birding is the eastern area of the park, known as Gloucester Tops. To get here, leave Gloucester south on the road to Stratford, but turn right to Faulkland after 6 km. Continue through Berrico then turn right to Invergordon and Gloucester Tops. Whilst driving the latter part of this dirt road, beyond the Kerripit Road turn-off, drive slowly with the windows down listening for scrub-birds. There are several pairs along here, particularly about 100 m before where the road ends. This area is also good for **Rose Robin** and **Bassian Ground-Thrush**. If bush camping overnight, listen out for **Masked Owl** since this is a noted former site for them.

4.14 Coffs Harbour

Key Species: **Pacific Baza** (spring), (**Relict Raven**)
The New England subspecies of Forest Raven may soon be split from the more southern population and called **Relict Raven**. These birds are apparently the commonest corvid around the town of Coffs Harbour but note that Torresian Crow and Australian Raven also occur here. A good place to find them is the road from Coffs Harbour to Armidale *via* Ebor. They occur principally under forest canopy and are best identified by their call, a deep 'caw caw' although not as deep as that of the southern race of Forest Raven, from which they also differ in their relatively longer tail and smaller bill. We saw them along the New England Highway, 9 km north of Armidale. Coffs Harbour itself is an excellent site for **Pacific Baza**, they nest each year in the Botanic Gardens, by the main entrance, but note that they are only around from mid October to late December. Ask the rangers for more information.

4.15 Red Rock Caravan Park

Key Species: **Beach Thick-knee**
This is an excellent site for **Beach Thick-knee** and is an alternative to the sites further north. Turn east off the Pacific Highway 37 km north of Coffs Harbour to Red Rock. Drive 6 km to the end of the road and check the north shore where the river flows into the sea. **Beach Thick-knees** are normally there, a telescope would be useful.

D South-west New South Wales (Map 4.14)

Covering a huge area and a range of habitats, the south-west of the state has many excellent birds including the essential places to see Plains-wanderer, Superb

Parrot, and Red-lored Whistler. Indeed the Deniliquin region is one of the best localities in Australia to catch up with a number of inland specialities.

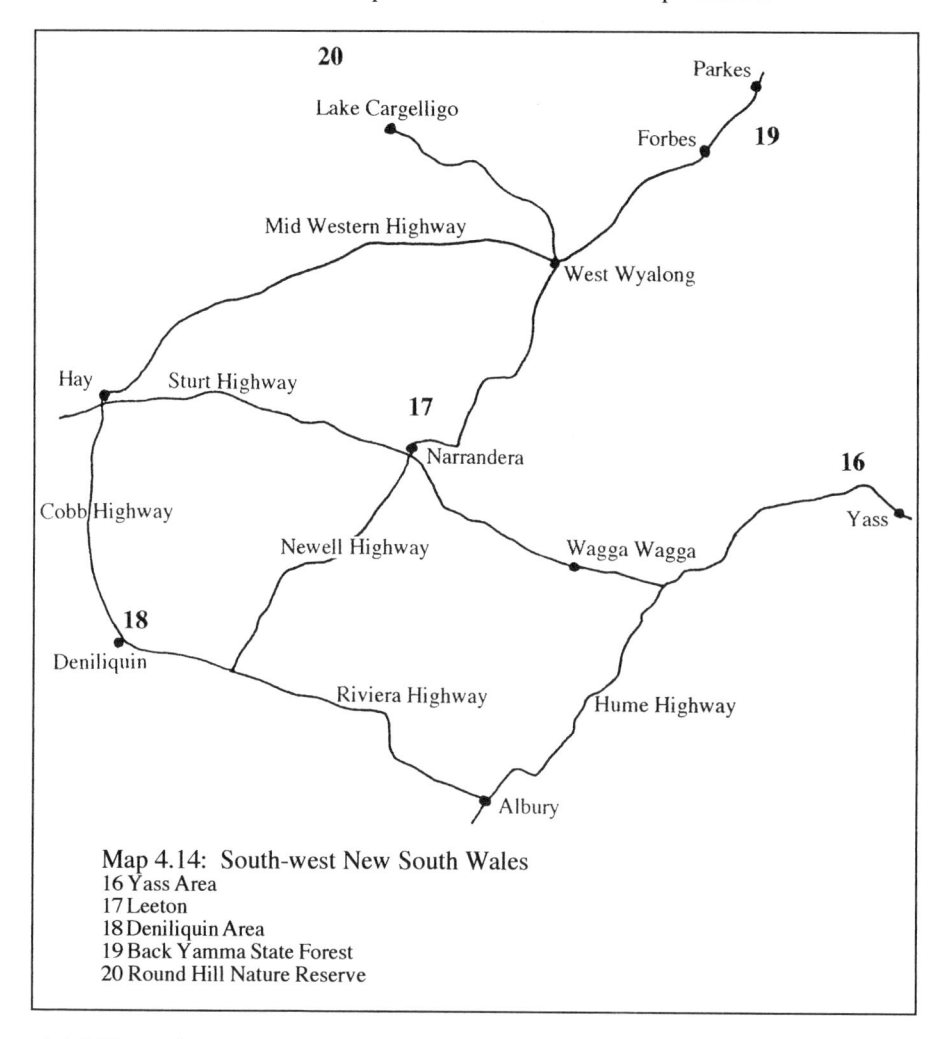

Map 4.14: South-west New South Wales
16 Yass Area
17 Leeton
18 Deniliquin Area
19 Back Yamma State Forest
20 Round Hill Nature Reserve

4.16 Yass Area

Key Species **Superb Parrot** (summer)
The following roads are all reliable places to see **Superb Parrot**, but only in the summer months, late October until February, when they move into the area from further west to feed on grain spills from trucks which use these roads. The best road is the Bowning turn off from the Hume Highway, 14 km west of Yass. Carry on through Binalong and Harden to Temora. Also good is the road 9 km west of

Yass off the Hume Highway through Boorowa to Cowra. The parrots nested along this road, just north of Boorowa in 1992/93, and were particularly numerous in this whole area being also seen on the Olympic Highway south of Young, they also regularly nest near Binalong. Incidentally, Jindalee State Forest which is signposted off the Olympic Highway, just north of Cootamundra is a good place for **Square-tailed Kite** (in spring), **Black-chinned Honeyeater** and **Swift Parrot** (in winter/early spring).

4.17 Leeton Swamp

Key Species: **Freckled Duck, Red-kneed Dotterel**, crakes
Although there are no essential species to see here, Leeton Swamp is a superb wetland particularly during the summer months and can easily be tied in with a visit to Deniliquin. Leeton is 11 km north of the Sturt Highway, not far west of Narrandera. To get to the swamp, drive north out of town then turn right at the second supermarket and follow the road until you see the swamp on the left. Park here and walk around the edge. We saw **Red-kneed Dotterel** (30), **Wood Sandpiper** (6), **Spotless Crake**, **Glossy Ibis**, **Whiskered Tern**, **Freckled Duck** (6), **Red-necked Avocet** and **Plumed Whistling-Duck** (200) in January 1991. Keith Hutton is the resident local birder in Leeton; he regularly finds **Long-toed Stint**, **Painted Snipe** and **Black-backed Bittern** here.

4.18 Deniliquin Area

Key Species: **Australasian Bittern, Black-backed Bittern, Little Button-Quail, Red-chested Button-Quail** (summer), **Black Falcon, Superb Parrot, Plains-wanderer, Banded Lapwing, Painted Honeyeater** (summer), **Gilbert's Whistler**
There are a number of good places to visit in the Deniliquin area which is in southern New South Wales, about nine hours drive from Sydney. Bush camping only is available outside of the town.
4.18a Phil Maher's Spotlighting Trips
It is essential to contact Phil Maher in advance if you wish to go out spotlighting for **Plains-wanderer**. His address is Australian Ornithological Services, P.O.Box 382, Balwyn Victoria 3103, Australia. Tel/Fax +61 03 98176555. Phil is a professional birder so will charge for his services. There are a number of good species which occur in the Deniliquin area which he can probably show you, these include **Superb Parrot** (if you miss it at Gulpa State Forest), **Long-billed Corella**, **Painted Honeyeater** (summer only), **Little Button-Quail** (you will probably see this whilst looking for Plains-wanderer), **Red-chested Button-Quail** (again best seen whilst spotlighting, but it is irregular in occurrence, only in wet years), **Freckled Duck**, **Black Falcon**, **Inland Dotterel**, **Banded Lapwing**, **Australasian** and **Black-backed Bitterns** (Phil usually has both these staked out, the former in rice paddy fields), **Painted Snipe** (irregular) and some crakes and rails. Plus ask him about any other birds you need that occur in this part of the world. In September 1994, **Letter-winged Kites** were breeding

nearby. On our spotlighting trips with Phil we saw **Inland Dotterel, Banded Lapwing, Australian Pratincole, Stubble Quail, Little Button-Quail, Orange Chat, Plains-wanderer** and **Plumed Whistling-Duck**.

4.18b Gulpa State Forest (Map 4.15)
Gulpa State Forest is a reliable site for **Superb Parrot**, though they can get quite scarce in summer. The forest is on the east side of the Cobb Highway between Deniliquin and Mathoura, 18 km south of Deniliquin. Turn east (it is signposted 'Gulpa Island'), and when you get to the fork in the road, just over the creek, bear left along Junction Road. Bear right after 500 m along Langman's Road. We saw a female **Superb Parrot** along this road, about 100 m from the T-junction at the end. When you get to the T-junction, go right and on your left are sand-hills with *Callitris* stands. We saw **Gilbert's Whistler** here, it is also noted for **Superb Parrot**. You can either go back the way you came in or carry on down the road, turn right along Taylors Bridge Road, then right onto Gulpa Creek Road which will bring you back to the first junction. The other good birds we saw here were **Southern Whiteface, Crested Shrike-Tit, Diamond Firetail** and **Little Friarbird**.

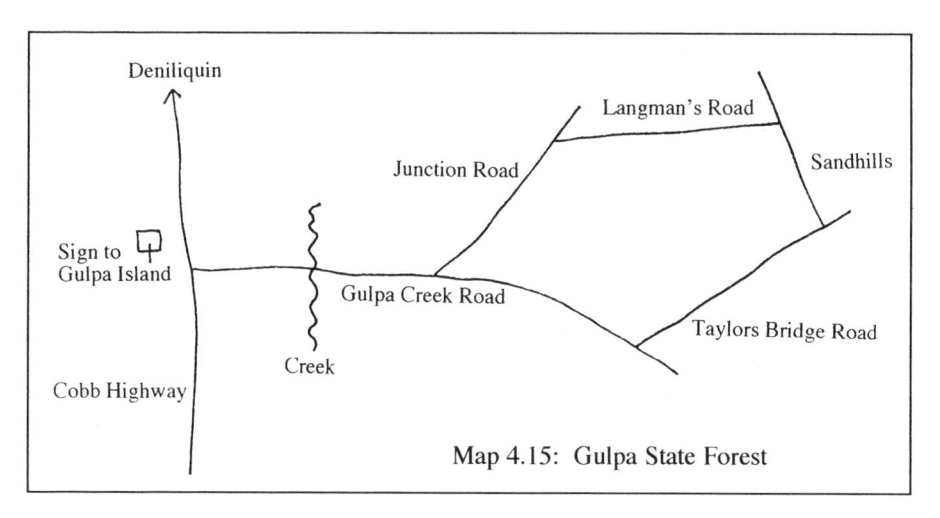

Map 4.15: Gulpa State Forest

4.18c Wildlife Refuge South of Hay
This is a good site for **Painted Honeyeater**, but only in the summer months and they sometimes don't arrive before January. To find the site, leave Deniliquin north on the Cobb Highway towards Hay. Just before the 90 km to Hay green milepost, turn west, follow the track a short distance to a Wildlife Refuge gate. Park here, go through the gate and check the mistletoe affected trees beyond; **Painted Honeyeaters** are easy to find if they are calling - a loud whistled 'Gee-ord-ee' usually in song flight. We saw about six here in early January 1991. Other birds we saw in this area were **Striped Honeyeater, Australian Owlet-Nightjar, Tawny Frogmouth** and **Bush Thick-knee** (the last three all at night). **Black Honeyeater** also occurs if conditions are suitable. Note that

Black Falcons are regularly seen in the Deniliquin area; keep your eyes open along the road to Hay.

4.18d Swamp on Avalon Road

This was a really good swamp, at least in January 1992 when the water was reasonably low with good muddy margins. To get here, leave Deniliquin northeast towards Conargo, but turn right shortly towards Mayrung along Moonee Swamp Road. After 18 km, turn right into Avalon Road, after about 2 km you should see the tops of some reeds on the right hand side, this marks the swamp. Park here and walk to the raised edge of the small dam/swamp. It is worth spending some time viewing from the edge or you can walk all the way around it, the evening is the best time. During six hours spent here in January 1992 we recorded the following; **Black-backed Bittern** (one male), **Australasian Bittern** (1), **Painted Snipe** (4), **Red-kneed Dotterel**, **Black-tailed Native-Hen**, **Spotless Crake**, **Australian Crake**, **Little Grassbird** and **White-fronted Chat**.

4.18e Tuppa Creek Station

We saw about 35 **Superb Parrots** here in January 1992, it was best in the evening, but may not be a regular stake-out. From the above swamp, continue on to the end of Avalon Road, turn right then almost immediately left into Monkanger Road. Carry on along this road to the end, note that we saw several parties of **Long-billed Corellas** along here. At the T-junction at the end, turn left towards Tocumwal, after 7.9 km turn right onto an unsealed track which is marked as a 'No Through Road'. After 2.2 km you come to the turning to Tuppa Creek Station, carry straight on however and we saw the parrots 600 m down here, just as you begin to re-enter eucalyptus woodland.

4.19 Back Yamma State Forest

Key Species: **Turquoise Parrot, Gilbert's Whistler**

Back Yamma State Forest is a good site for **Turquoise Parrot** and is about 350 km west of Sydney. Drive west from Eugowra towards Forbes, but after 5 km, turn right towards Parkes. The state forest is signposted on the left after 12 km. The signpost was largely destroyed when we went so look carefully for it. There is a maze of tracks leading into the forest; the parrots have been seen between 2.8 and 3.8 km along the main track leading in. We saw them as follows; drive straight in for 3.1 km, turn right at the cross-roads and park after 1.2 km. Walk down the track to your right for about 300 m. There are several other good birds to look out for here, **Gilbert's Whistler** (*Callitris* trees), **Diamond Firetail**, **Crested Shrike-Tit**, **Speckled Warbler** and **Hooded Robin**.

4.20 Round Hill Nature Reserve (Map 4.16)

Key Species: Mallee specialities including **Gilbert's Whistler**, *Red-lored Whistler* (spring)

SOUTH-WEST NEW SOUTH WALES

```
Mount Hope ←
                                                    → Euabalong
                        Camping
    RLW

            Old Field


Good driving track
                                        RLW   Guide
                                              Post 43

    RLW  Red-lored Whistler

                                      ↓
                                Lake Cargelligo
```

Map 4.16: Round Hill Nature Reserve

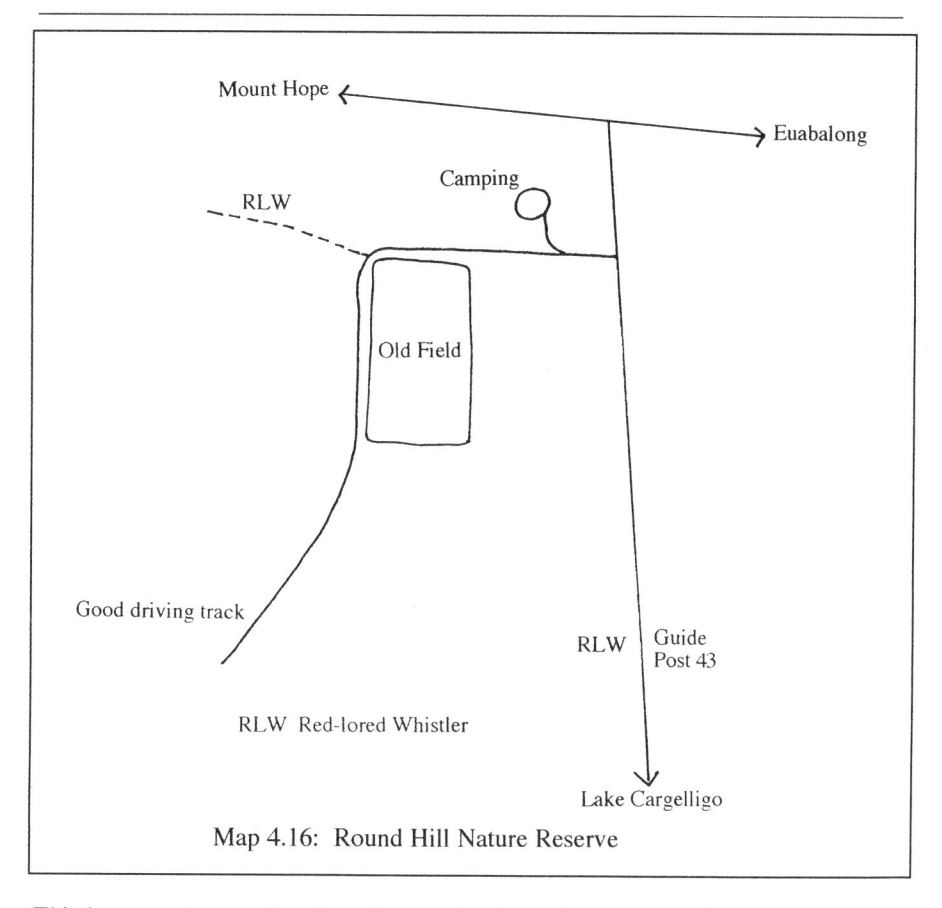

This is a superb area of mallee about a nine hour drive west of Sydney. It is easily the best site to see **Red-lored Whistler**, however, they are only easy to see from late August to October. At other times of the year they do not sing and it is conceivable that they actually leave the area as I know of no-one who has seen them outside of this time, although many have tried. From Lake Cargelligo go north to Euabalong, and turn north-west towards Mount Hope. After 41 km (31 km on dirt), you get to a road junction with a road from Lake Cargelligo. Turn left and after a short distance on your right you will see the nature reserve sign and a track off into the mallee. Drive down this track and after about 300 m a smaller track takes you into a bush camping area. **Southern Scrub-Robin, Shy Hylacola** and **Red-capped Robins** are common around the campground and call mostly at dawn, **Spotted Nightjars** are easy at dusk. Along the main track and in the old field you should see **White-fronted, Yellow-plumed** and **Spiny-cheeked Honeyeaters, Grey-fronted Honeyeater** also occurs. If it has rained heavily a few months earlier, **Black Honeyeater** (on *Eremophila* bushes) and **Little** and **Red-chested Button-Quails** are all found in the old field; we saw both button-quails at Christmas 1990. **Pied Honeyeaters** were displaying here in November 1993. Along the mallee track at the field corner, there are at least two pairs of **Red-lored Whistlers**. Be warned that their usual song, the extended 'chew chew chew chew chew' is almost identical to **Gilbert's Whistler** which also occurs commonly. **Chestnut Quail-Thrush** is common, **Malleefowl** occurs but is hard to find. It is worth driving the track alongside the field; after 16 km you reach a second field which looks better for button-quails. Along the way you pass through excellent mallee where we saw both **Red-lored** and **Gilbert's Whistlers**. Another place to see **Red-lored Whistler** is along the Lake Cargelligo road, look out for the small numbered guideposts, we heard the whistlers calling at guidepost 43 and saw them about 200 m into the mallee. It is worth checking the mulga areas along the road back towards Euabalong. We saw **Mulga Parrot, Mallee Ringneck, Pink Cockatoo, Striped Honeyeater, Spotted Bowerbird, Grey-crowned** and **White-browed Babblers**. **Black-eared Cuckoos** are regularly reported in the park, they are most easily found by call. Clearly the whole place is worth spending a few days in, but take plenty of water, food and fuel; we only saw one vehicle in three days at Christmas 1990. Be careful about straying off the tracks, it is very easy to get lost in the mallee.

E North-west New South Wales (Map 4.17)

This area of New South Wales is true outback country. Journeys to these remote localities should only be undertaken with the proper precautions and visits during the hot summer months are strongly advised against. It is essential to carry all your supplies with you as it is necessary to bush camp at all the sites.

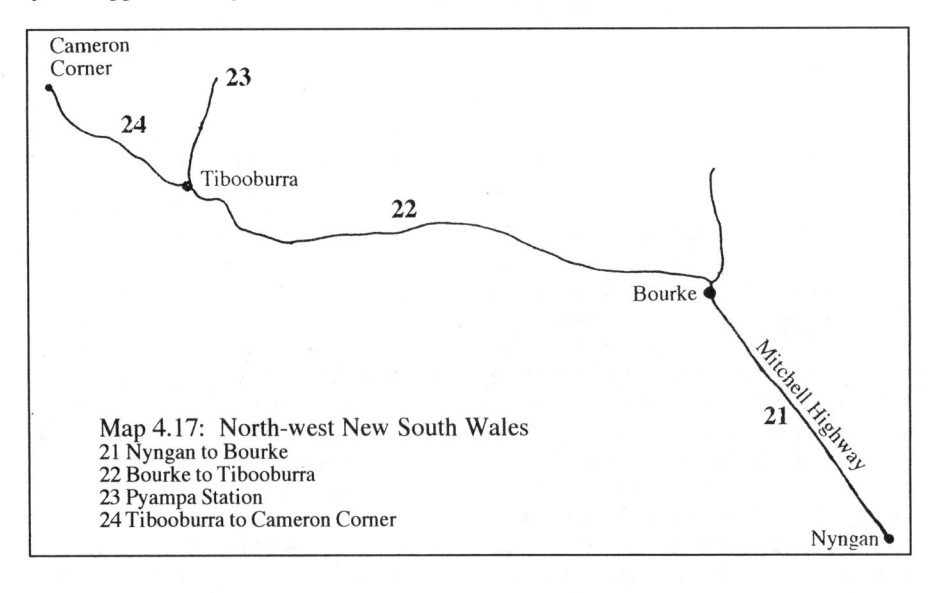

Map 4.17: North-west New South Wales
21 Nyngan to Bourke
22 Bourke to Tibooburra
23 Pyampa Station
24 Tibooburra to Cameron Corner

4.21 Nyngan to Bourke

Key Species: **Black Honeyeater** (spring)
There is a rest area on the Mitchell Highway 100 km south of Bourke which makes an overnight basic camping spot, it is well signposted. Around the rest area we saw **Spotted Bowerbird, Chestnut-crowned Babblers** and **Red-winged Parrots**. The road from Nyngan to Bourke is excellent in the spring for **Black Honeyeaters** (September - November), particularly if it has rained over the winter months. The birds are chiefly attracted by flowering *Eremophila* bushes (also known as emu-bush). These have red tubular shaped flowers with yellow bases and are common along this stretch of road. We drove from the rest area to Bourke in mid October 1992 (incidentally during a drought) stopping at every green triangular 5 km post and searching the surrounding area for the honeyeaters. We eventually found a small party at the 45 km to Bourke post, on the eastern side of the road over the other side of the abandoned railway line. If you are unable to see **Black Honeyeaters** around Alice Springs, then this would be an alternative site but it is only reliable in the spring and numbers of birds vary greatly from year to year. Along here we also saw **Pink Cockatoo, Cockatiel, Mallee Ringneck** and **Bluebonnet**.

4.22 Bourke to Tibooburra

Although unsealed, the road from Bourke to Tibooburra is normally passable to two-wheel drive (2WD) vehicles, provided it is not wet. Fuel is available at Tibooburra, but you should carry enough with you for the 400 km or so from Bourke to Tibooburra. The best birds seen on this road were a pair of **Brolgas** in a pool along the road, **Black-tailed Native-Hen** (1000 in a large salt pan), **Flock Bronzewing** (one male just east of Tibooburra, note that flocks are regularly seen in the vicinity of Tibooburra, and at Pyampa Station) and **Striped Honeyeater** (fairly common).

4.23 Pyampa Station

Key Species: **Grey Grasswren, Orange Chat**
Although Pyampa Station is actually in Queensland, it is treated here for convenience. It is a certain stake-out for **Grey Grasswren**. The deserted Station is on the edge of a large lignum swamp where the grasswrens are very common. To get there proceed as follows; drive north from Tibooburra on the Silver City Highway for 55 km, turning right after 33 km to Wompah Gate. This gate marks the Queensland/New South Wales border. After reaching the gate, continue through it for 5.1 km then turn right on a track towards the disused Pyampa Station (1.9 km from the road and viewable from it). From the station walk north-east out into the swamp (it is usually dry) to the patches of tallest lignum (2-3 km). The birds are common in these patches especially those interspersed with cane grass. They are a relatively easy grasswren to see since, although they are shy, they are inquisitive and will sit up in the lignum to observe you. Interesting

birds we saw in the swamp were **Grey Grasswren** (50), **Orange Chat** (2), **Budgerigar**, and **Chirruping Wedgebill** (2). **Flock Bronzewings** are regularly seen, as is **Grey Falcon**.

4.24 Tibooburra to Cameron Corner

Key Species: **Grey Falcon**
The best birds seen along this road through Sturt National Park were **Chirruping Wedgebill, Budgerigar, Little Button-Quail, Black-breasted Buzzard, Australasian Bushlark, Chestnut-crowned Babbler** and **Diamond Dove**. **Emus** are particularly common here. However, this national park is renowned as perhaps the most reliable place in Australia to see **Grey Falcon**. Keep your eyes open, we were probably just unlucky and didn't see one here. At Cameron Corner you enter South Australia, turn to that section for details of the birding sites in that state.

CHAPTER 5

AUSTRALIAN CAPITAL TERRITORY

Gang-gang Cockatoo, symbol of the Canberra Ornithologist's Group

CHAPTER 5: AUSTRALIAN CAPITAL TERRITORY

Introduction (Map 5.1)

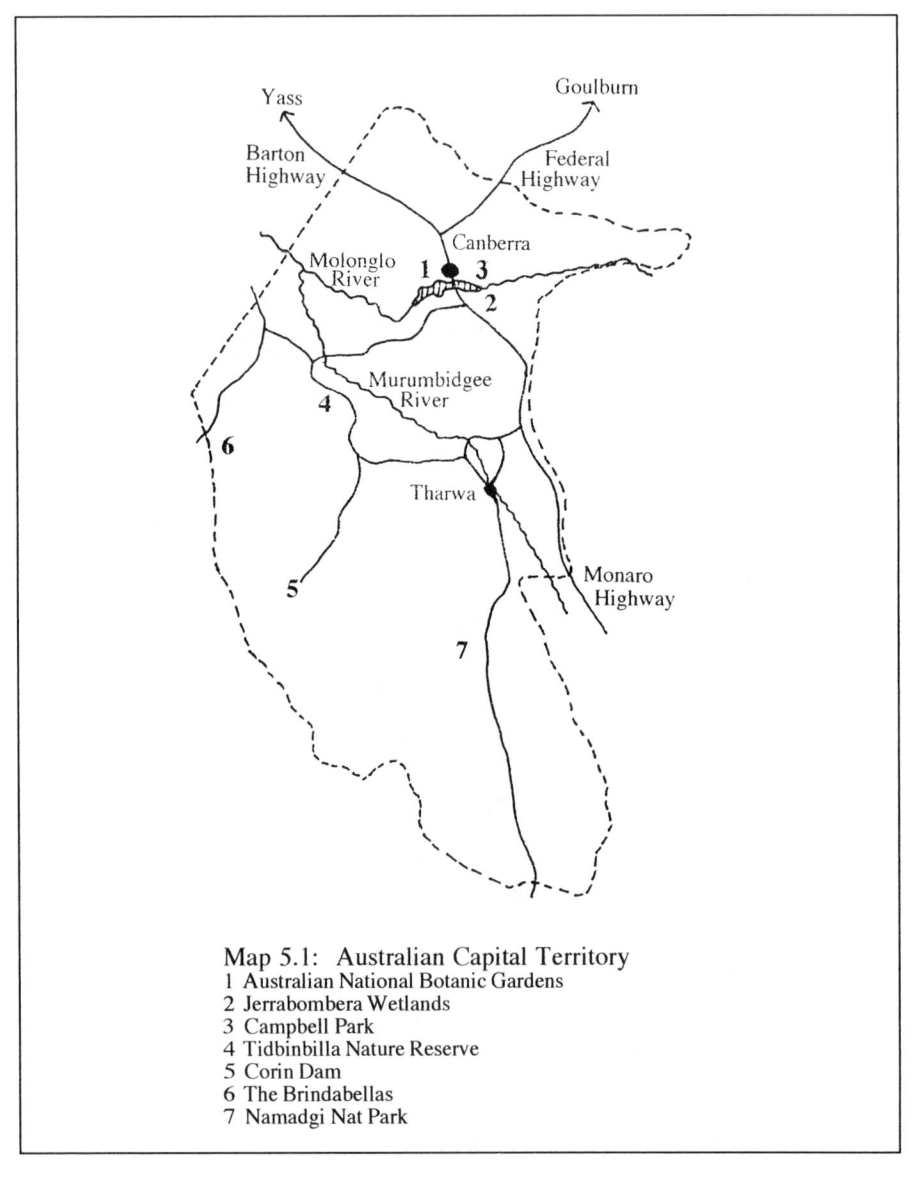

Map 5.1: Australian Capital Territory
1 Australian National Botanic Gardens
2 Jerrabombera Wetlands
3 Campbell Park
4 Tidbinbilla Nature Reserve
5 Corin Dam
6 The Brindabellas
7 Namadgi Nat Park

Although almost completely by-passed by the visiting birder, the Canberra region is a good staging post between Sydney and Melbourne and the city itself makes a good base for exploring the surrounding area. There are a number of species here

AUSTRALIAN CAPITAL TERRITORY

that can prove tricky to see elsewhere and since we spent three years living in Canberra, we know the birding sites deserve a mention. The area is probably best in spring/early summer when migrants are around. A telephone bird information line with latest sightings is run by the Canberra Ornithologists Group. Tel (06) 2475530.

Specialities: Gang-gang Cockatoo, Red-browed Treecreeper, Speckled Warbler

5.1 Australian National Botanic Gardens

Key Species: **Gang-gang Cockatoo, Crescent Honeyeater**
The Australian National Botanic Gardens are well worth a visit. If approaching from the north along the Barton or Federal Highway, drive into the city centre, turn right along Barry Drive, then left into Clunies Ross Street. The gardens are well signposted on your right but note that they are only open 9.00 am to 5.00 pm. There is an information centre where maps can be obtained. During the winter months the Gardens are a stake-out for **Crescent Honeyeater**, the best area being the flowering *Grevillea* bushes at the north-east corner of the Eucalyptus Lawn. Year round the Gardens are a good site for **Gang-gang Cockatoo** and **Common Bronzewing**. The campus of the Australian National University opposite the Botanic Gardens is also excellent for Gang-gangs; they breed in the University House area, at the south end of the campus.

5.2 Jerrabomberra Wetlands

Key Species: Crakes and rails
There is nothing essential here, but these wetlands can be good in the summer months if the main pond (Kelly's Swamp) has dried out and has muddy edges. It is reached from Dairy Flat Road, going north from Fyshwick (it is one-way) on the east side of Canberra. The pond and car-park are off on the left visible from the road, turn off just past the pond into the car-park. There are two hides overlooking the swamp. **Latham's Snipe** is easy to see here each summer, they feed out in the open particularly in the evening. If the water level is down, check along the reed edges for crakes and rails - we saw **Lewin's Rail, Australian, Baillon's** and **Spotless Crakes** over the summers. The sewage ponds across the road and opposite to Kelly's Swamp are good for the common ducks; ask permission at the entrance gate. The usual birds there were **Hoary-headed** and **Australasian Grebes, Hardhead, Grey** and **Chestnut Teal** and **Pink-eared Duck**.

5.3 Campbell Park (Map 5.2)

Key Species: Cuckoos (spring), **Speckled Warbler, Diamond Firetail**
Campbell Park is probably the best area of dry eucalyptus woodland in the Canberra region particularly when the yellowbox trees are flowering, which occurs sporadically. The park is located behind the Australian Defence Force

62 CHAPTER 5: AUSTRALIAN CAPITAL TERRITORY

Offices. From Jerrabomberra Wetlands, carry on along Dairy Flat Road, straight on at the traffic lights and at the following roundabout, then turn left at the T-junction into Fairburn Avenue. Turn right off Fairburn Avenue at the roundabout in Duntroon and follow the road around the side of the car-park to the end. Park here and walk in to the park. The area around the horse gate is especially good, also the 200 m or so beyond this. The park is best in spring/summer when you should get most of the following; **Pallid, Brush, Fan-tailed, Horsfield's Bronze-** and **Shining Bronze-Cuckoos, White-winged Triller, White-throated** and **Western Gerygones** and **Rufous Songlark**. In winter, **Scarlet, Flame** and **Hooded Robins** are here, also **Jacky Winter**, whilst year round the specialities are **Common Bronzewing, Crested Shrike-Tit, Speckled Warbler** (common), **Brown Treecreeper, Brown-headed Honeyeater** and **Diamond Firetail**.

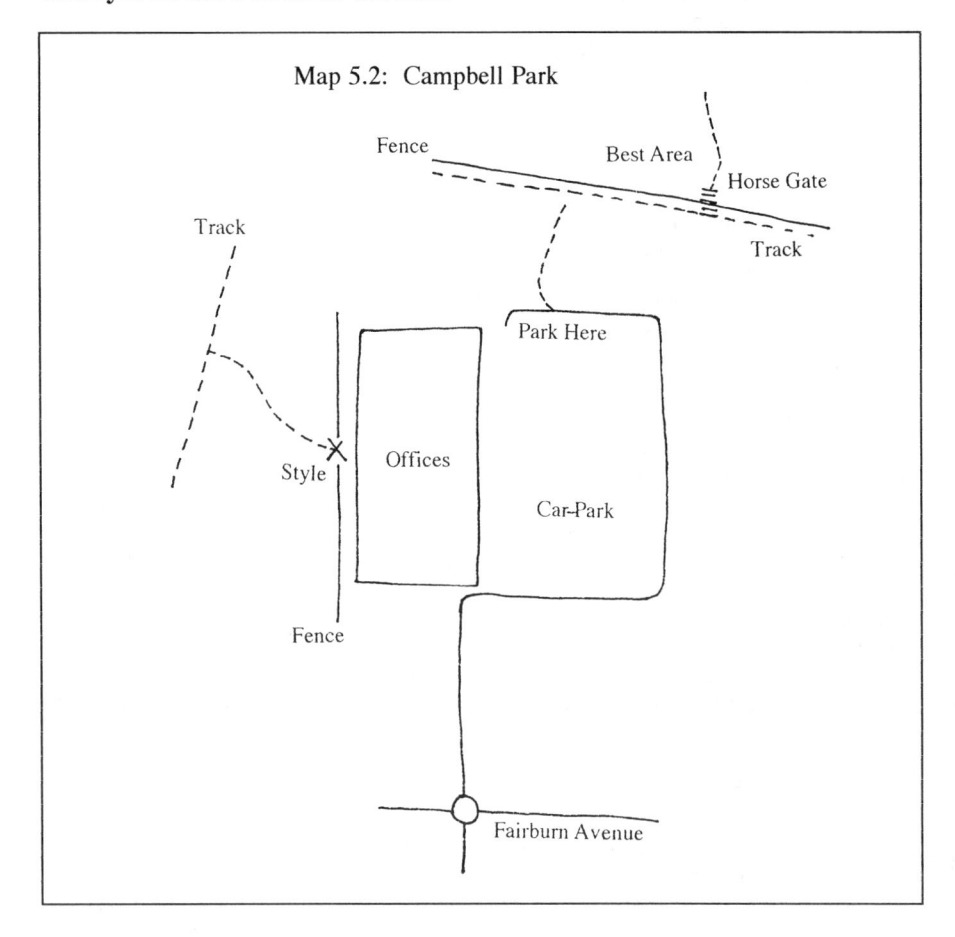

Map 5.2: Campbell Park

5.4 Tidbinbilla Nature Reserve (Map 5.3)

Key Species: **Superb Lyrebird, Red-browed Treecreeper, Satin Flycatcher, Pilotbird**
Tidbinbilla is a really pleasant reserve that provides easy access to the hills and wet sclerophyll forest of the Brindabella Ranges. There are animal enclosures with kangaroos, koalas and wildfowl, but the real attraction for the birdwatcher is the walking trails which abound with good bush birds. The reserve is situated about 40 km to the south-west of Canberra and is easiest to reach by leaving the city to the west along Cotter Road which becomes Paddy River Road then Tidbinbilla Road. Turn south-west off this road through the entrance gate and carry on to the visitor centre.

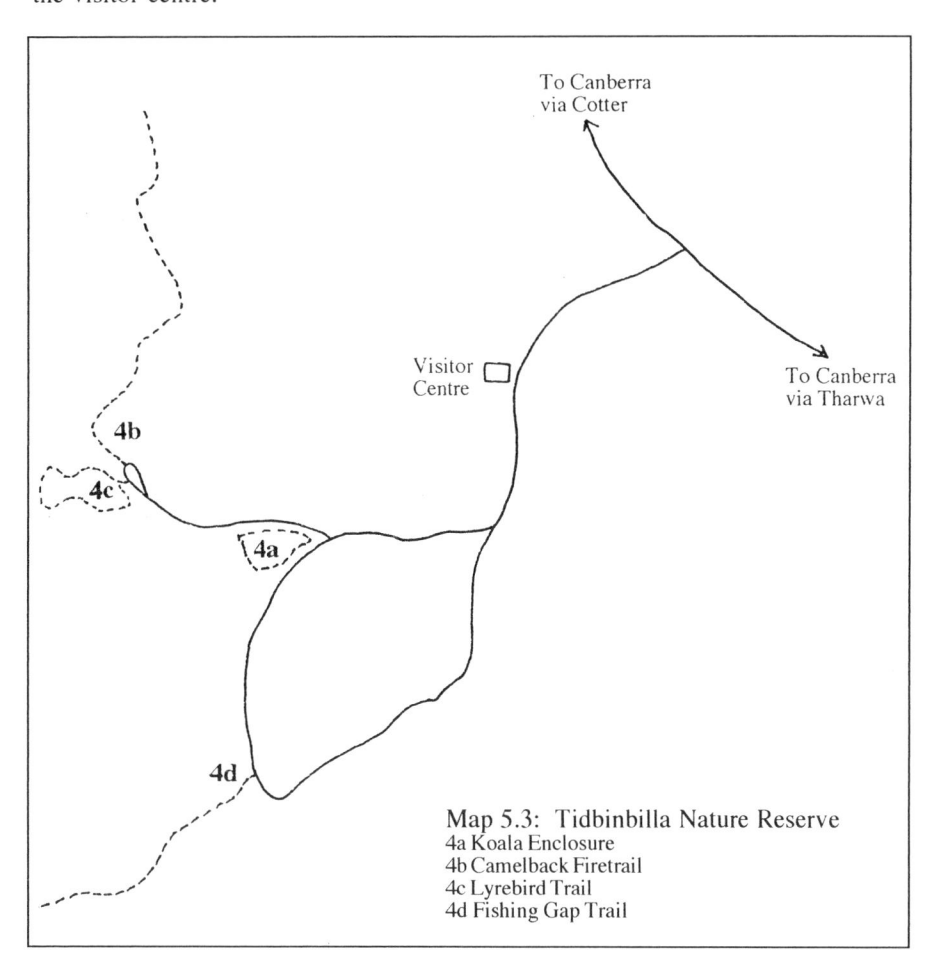

Map 5.3: Tidbinbilla Nature Reserve
4a Koala Enclosure
4b Camelback Firetrail
4c Lyrebird Trail
4d Fishing Gap Trail

CHAPTER 5: AUSTRALIAN CAPITAL TERRITORY

5.4a Koala Enclosure
This has breeding **Satin Flycatchers** (summer only), usually along the roadside. They can usually be seen from the road or if not then try along the tracks inside the enclosure.

5.4b Camelback Firetrail
This runs from the car-park and is a **Spotted Quail-Thrush** site, you have to walk about two hours uphill to get into the right loose litter habitat. Listen for their high-pitched calls, **Brown-headed Honeyeaters** are also in this area.

5.4c Lyrebird Trail
This is probably the best track and is excellent for **Superb Lyrebird**, the 250 m stretch where the track goes along a fern-lined creek always has them, creep along, and try to be the first person along the trail after the park opens. Also along this section, look out for **Pilotbird, Rose Robin** (summer only) and **Bassian Ground-Thrush**. **Pilotbirds** are also found by the very first creek crossing at the start of the trail, along with **Gang-gang Cockatoos**.

5.4d Fishing Gap Firetrail
This is very good for **Red-browed Treecreeper**, particularly the first kilometre. This area is also particularly good for robins; **Scarlet, Flame** and **Eastern Yellow Robins** are all common here.

5.5 Corin Dam

Key Species: **Pilotbird, Olive Whistler**
This is another area of forest close to Tidbinbilla. Turn off Tidbinbilla Road onto Corin Road, and follow this to the dam car-park. Walk the wide track which winds downhill below the dam and look for birds in the forest on your left hand side between the dam and the river. **Pilotbirds** are here year round, but easiest in winter. **Satin Flycatchers** are reasonably common in the summer months, whilst **Olive Whistlers** are found here in the winter months along with **Rose Robins**.

5.6 Namadgi National Park

Key Species: **Spotted Quail-Thrush**
The whole of Namadgi National Park is worth visiting but this site in particular is very good for Spotted Quail-Thrush. The Park is situated about 60 km south of Canberra. From Tharwa (which can be reached along Tidbinbilla Road), drive south along Naas Road and into the national park where you can call at the visitor centre for more information. Carry on into Boboyan Road then turn right into Orroral Road. After about 3 km, turn right into the good Orroral Crossing Campsite. We saw **Spotted Quail-Thrush** on the short loop trail behind the campsite. Further west along Orroral Road, a walking track goes off to the left to Nursery Swamp, this trail is excellent for the quail-thrush; we saw eight mostly on the steep part of the climb up to the swamp.

5.7 The Brindabellas

Key Species: **Pilotbird, Satin Flycatcher** (spring)
The Brindabellas are the mountain ranges to the west of Canberra. Whilst the whole area is good for **Pilotbird** and **Satin Flycatcher** (in spring/summer), the following area is outstanding. Turn right off the Cotter Road just after crossing the Murrumbidgee River, coming from Canberra, and follow the winding road to the T-junction at the end. The farm dam just to the right of this junction is worth checking for common waterbirds such as **Hoary-headed** and **Australasian Grebes**. For the Brindabellas turn left at the T-junction and head west towards Piccadilly Circus. Shortly after where the road becomes unsealed, a track leads off to the left which is worth exploring on foot for **Rose Robin, Satin Flycatcher** and **Cicadabird** (all in summer). Carry on driving uphill towards Piccadilly Circus and park where Blundells Creek Road leaves on your left. Walk down this road and the fern lined stream which eventually joins on your left is good for **Pilotbird**, the trees alongside have **Satin Flycatchers**. This road eventually meets up with Warks Road and around this junction is worth spotlighting for **Powerful Owl**. Returning to your car, carry on uphill to Piccadilly Circus and the whole of the area when you reach the ridge top is excellent for **Gang-gang Cockatoo** and **Flame** and **Scarlet Robins**. On the return trip to Canberra, instead of going back the way you came, as an alternative, carry straight on at the T-junction to Uriarra Crossing. Just after you cross the Murrumbidgee River, park on the left and walk downstream along the river bank. The trees here are the best place near Canberra to find **Yellow Thornbill** and also in summer **Mistletoebird, Rainbow Bee-eater** and **Restless Flycatcher**.

CHAPTER 6

QUEENSLAND

Golden-shouldered Parrot, an endangered parrot found only on Cape York Peninsular

Introduction (Map 6.1)

Queensland is easily the best state for birds in Australia and any time you spend here will not be wasted. I would recommend a minimum of six weeks to really do the sites justice, with less time it would be best to stay in coastal areas.

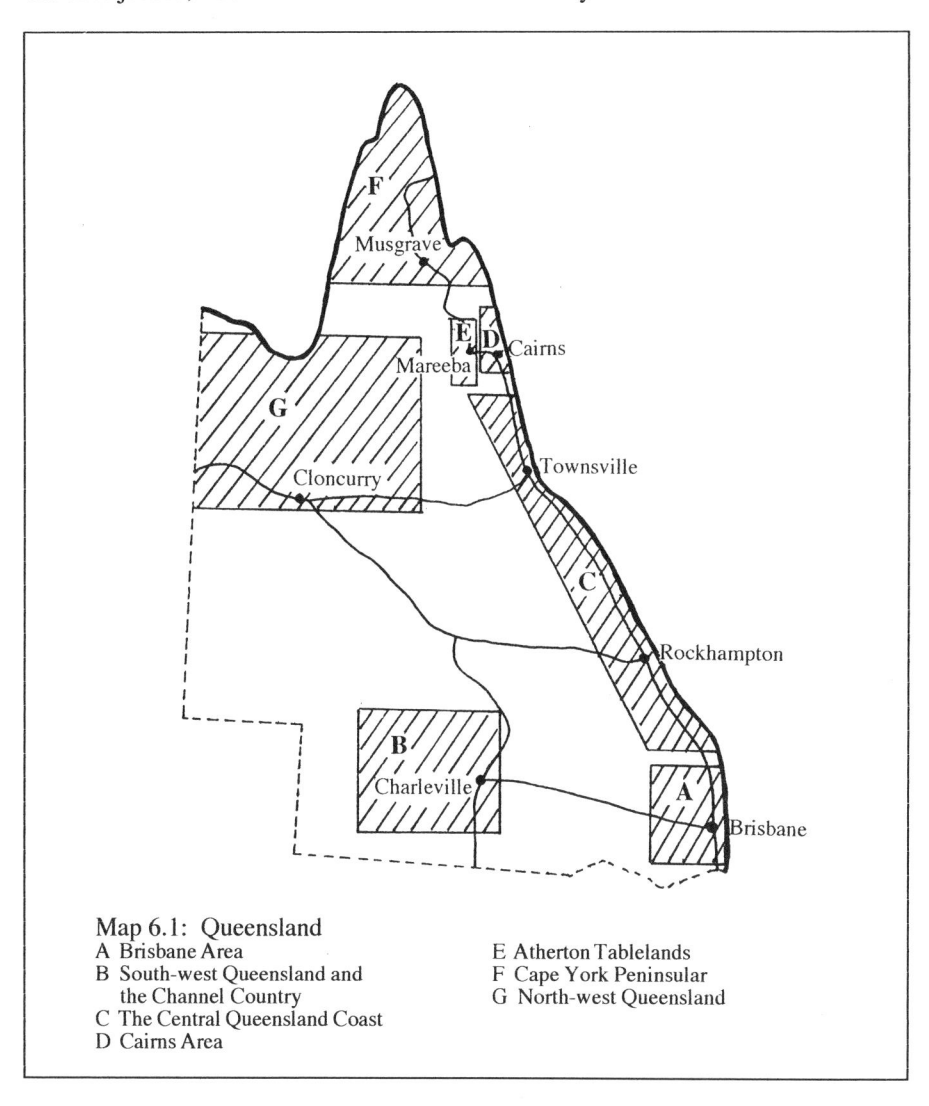

Map 6.1: Queensland
A Brisbane Area
B South-west Queensland and the Channel Country
C The Central Queensland Coast
D Cairns Area
E Atherton Tablelands
F Cape York Peninsular
G North-west Queensland

Endemics: Buff-breasted Button-Quail, Golden-shouldered Parrot, Lesser Sooty Owl, Australian Swiftlet, Tooth-billed Catbird, Golden Bowerbird, (Lovely Fairywren), Fernwren, Atherton Scrubwren, Mountain Thornbill, White-streaked

Honeyeater, Yellow-spotted Honeyeater, Bridled Honeyeater, Eungella Honeyeater, Yellow Honeyeater, Macleay's Honeyeater, Grey-headed Robin, Bower's Shrike-Thrush, Chowchilla, Pied Monarch, Victoria's Riflebird
Specialities: Southern Cassowary, Great Frigatebird, Lesser Frigatebird, Cotton Pygmy-Goose, Australian Brush-Turkey, Black-breasted Button-Quail, Red-necked Crake, Buff-banded Rail, Bush-Hen, Sarus Crane, Wandering Tattler, Beach Thick-knee, Black-naped Tern, Sooty Tern, Bridled Tern, Brown Noddy, Black Noddy, Squatter Pigeon, Wompoo Fruit-Dove, Superb Fruit-Dove, Double-eyed Fig-Parrot, Red-cheeked Parrot, Eclectus Parrot, Palm Cockatoo, Chestnut-breasted Cuckoo, Gould's Bronze-Cuckoo, Channel-billed Cuckoo, Grass Owl, Papuan Frogmouth, Marbled Frogmouth, Yellow-billed Kingfisher, Buff-breasted Paradise-Kingfisher (summer), Red-bellied Pitta (summer), Noisy Pitta, Albert's Lyrebird, Spotted Catbird, Green Catbird, Regent Bowerbird, Fawn-breasted Bowerbird, Tropical Scrubwren, Fairy Gerygone, Green-backed Honeyeater, Graceful Honeyeater, Varied Honeyeater, Mangrove Honeyeater, Tawny-breasted Honeyeater, Brown-backed Honeyeater, Yellow-legged Flycatcher, Pale-yellow Robin, White-faced Robin, Mangrove Robin, Northern Scrub-Robin, Grey Whistler, Hall's Babbler, Black-winged Monarch (summer), Spectacled Monarch, Frilled Monarch, White-eared Monarch, Yellow-breasted Boatbill, Trumpet Manucode, Magnificent Riflebird, Paradise Riflebird, Black-backed Butcherbird, Barred Cuckoo-Shrike, Russet-tailed Ground-Thrush, Metallic Starling (summer), Black-throated Finch, Blue-faced Parrot-Finch, Olive-backed Sunbird

A Brisbane Area (Map 6.2)

The Brisbane area is one of the most pleasant places to go birding in Australia with year round temperatures of about 20-30°C. From a birders point of view, the forests of most interest in the area are the sub-tropical rainforests and there are several species found exclusively in this habitat. There are literally hundreds of excellent birding sites around Brisbane and a selection of the best ones is given below. The City itself makes an excellent base from which to explore. An excellent recording of many of the characteristic birds of this area of Australia has been produced on CD by Dave Stewart entitled 'Voices of the Sub-tropical Rainforest'. Anyone visiting this habitat would be very strongly advised to purchase a copy as I cannot recommend it too highly.

6.1 Manly Yacht Club

Key Species: **Asiatic Dowitcher**
Manly Yacht Club is currently the best high tide roost for waders near Brisbane, particularly during the summer months, although sadly the area is threatened by 'development'. **Asiatic Dowitcher** is a regular occurrence (odd birds being seen most summers), although we dipped at Christmas 1992 when we made several visits. Turn off the Royal Esplanade in Manly towards the gates of the yacht club. Don't go through the gates but instead drive off right over some waste ground and on down the side of the yacht club fence. Park at the end and walk left around the fence towards some pools on the area of wasteland. Hundreds of waders gather

here at high tide. Check the Bar-tailed Godwit flocks for Asiatic Dowitchers. The best birds we saw were **Grey-tailed Tattler, Greater** and **Lesser Sandplovers, Eastern Curlew** and **Red-necked Stint**. Also check Thornside waterfront on the incoming tide for Asiatic Dowitchers. The mangroves here also have **Mangrove Gerygone** and **Mangrove Honeyeater**.

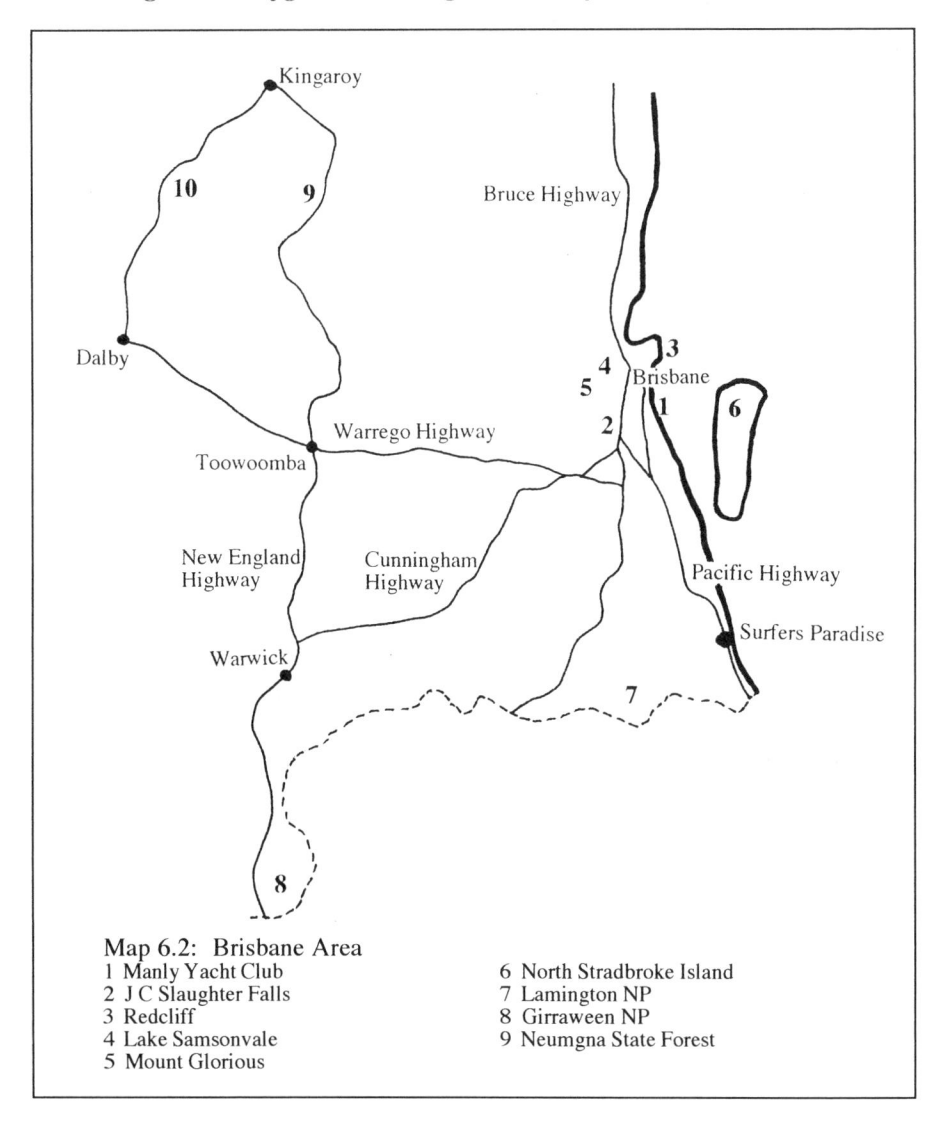

Map 6.2: Brisbane Area
1 Manly Yacht Club
2 J C Slaughter Falls
3 Redcliff
4 Lake Samsonvale
5 Mount Glorious
6 North Stradbroke Island
7 Lamington NP
8 Girraween NP
9 Neumgna State Forest

6.2 J C Slaughter Falls

Key Species: **Powerful Owl, White-throated Nightjar**
This is situated close to Brisbane city centre, on the west side of the city. Turn off the Western Freeway onto the Mount Coot-tha road and then follow the signpost to J C Slaughter Falls. Though good for rainforest species, this is principally known as a spotlighting site. **Powerful Owls** used to nest in a hole in a big tree overlooking the picnic area and were regularly spotlighted there. **White-throated Nightjars** call and fly around the open area at the end of the main path, just on dusk. **Bush Thick-knees** are also found in the short grassy areas.

6.3 Redcliffe

Key Species: **Wandering Tattler**
Redcliffe is a regular mainland site for **Wandering Tattler**, which are uncommon summer visitors to Australia. Turn off the Bruce Highway towards Redcliffe along Anzac Avenue. Shortly after crossing over Oxley Avenue you arrive at a mini roundabout on the sea front at which you go straight on, the road bends sharply right and then left, leading down to a car-park next to the sea. Check the rocks just off shore, it is best at high tide when the tattlers are pushed closer towards the coast. If you dip here, other good sites are the breakwater at Caloundra, about 1.5 hours drive north of Brisbane and Port Cartwright (rocks on the west side of the Point), again north of Brisbane.

6.4 Lake Samsonvale

Key Species: **Blue-breasted Quail, Red-backed Button-Quail**
Lake Samsonvale is a private lake about 30 km to the north-west of Brisbane for which permission to visit should be obtained from the Brisbane Waterboard. It can be a highly unpleasant place to go birding with head-high tall wet grass. It does, however, always have both **Blue-breasted Quail** and **Red-backed Button-Quail**, although the origin of Blue-breasted Quail in most of Australia must be open to questioning as many birds have been released for shooting purposes over the years. To get to the best area, drive south from Dayboro towards Samford, after about 9 km turn left onto Postman's Track. Follow the track to its end at a locked gate. Walk from here along the track through tall grasslands towards the lake shore. We found it a waste of time to try and walk through the tall grass and eventually saw a **Red-backed Button-Quail** on the edge of the main track by walking one on each side of the track. We also saw **Brown Quail** and along the lake shore **Latham's Snipe** in December 1992.

6.5 Mount Glorious

Key Species: **Marbled Frogmouth, Sooty Owl, Russet-tailed Ground-Thrush**

Mount Glorious is a superb area situated not far west of the city centre and incorporating Maiala Nat Park which includes some good rainforest patches as well as dry eucalyptus woodlands. To get there drive west out of the city along Highway 31, through The Gap and up the Mount Glorious Road. Carry on up the steep escarpment, first passing the turning to Bellbird Grove on your right, then keep going through Mount Nebo (which has a large **Bell Miner** colony) to Mount Glorious. Go through the village of Mount Glorious and park at the picnic site on the right hand side. From the picnic area take the first right into Brown's Road, walk down here for about 0.5 km until just past a 'pedestrians crossing' warning sign, where there is a walking track on the left. Walk down the steep track until you get to some wooden bridges. This is a good area for **Sooty Owl**, we saw a juvenile just before the first wooden bridge in December 1992. It was constantly begging for food so it was not hard to hear the bird, however it was difficult to spotlight because it was so high up in the canopy. We also heard at least six **Marbled Frogmouths** calling around here on the same date, but did not attempt to spotlight them. During the day this track is fairly good, we saw **Noisy Pitta, Russet-tailed** and **Bassian Ground-Thrushes, Rufous Shrike-Thrush** and **Pale-yellow Robin**. The track just before the picnic site on the other side of the road is good for fruit-doves if the figs are fruiting, usually during the summer months. We saw **White-headed** and **Topknot Pigeons, Brown Cuckoo-Dove** and **Wompoo** and **Rose-crowned Fruit-Doves**. Also here were **Noisy Pitta, Spectacled Monarch, Paradise Riflebird** and **Pacific Baza**. Bellbird Grove is worth a visit. Park in the car-park and walk up the dirt road on the left for about 2 km to the top of the ridge. **Spotted Quail-Thrushes** are found here, they favour the steep slopes just below the road on either side of the ridge.

6.6 North Stradbroke Island

Key Species: **Wandering Tattler**, seabirds
This island is reached by passenger ferry from either Cleveland (bookings Tel (07) 2862666) or Redland (bookings Tel (07) 3582122) to Dunwich, it is renowned as a place for seawatching. The place to look from is Point Lookout, which is about 20 km from Dunwich. Obviously it is good during or just after strong easterly winds with **White-necked Petrel** and **Streaked Shearwater** regularly recorded during the summer months. It is best after cyclones with **Tropicbirds, Grey Ternlet** and **White Tern** all recorded. The rocks below the lighthouse are a stake-out for **Wandering Tattler**.

6.7 Lamington National Park (Map 6.3)

Key Species: **Sooty Owl, Marbled Frogmouth, Black-breasted Button-Quail, Albert's Lyrebird, Rufous Scrub-bird, Eastern Bristlebird**
Lamington National Park is certainly the premier sub-tropical rainforest birding locality in southern Queensland. There are numerous hand tame parrots and even bowerbirds to be found all around the guest house of O'Reilly's on the northern side of the park. Aim to spend a minimum of three days at Lamington in order to

really do the place justice. It was amongst our most favourite localities we visited in Australia. Situated on the New South Wales-Queensland border, the O'Reilly's end of Lamington National Park is reached from the north *via* Canungra, which is approximately 100 km south of Brisbane. Both **Scaly-breasted Lorikeet** and **Pale-headed Rosella** are common in Canungra village. It is approximately 35 km on a slow winding road from Canungra to the world famous O'Reilly's Guest house. Ask for Peter O'Reilly at O'Reilly's, he is very friendly and extremely helpful for information. There is an excellent campsite on the right just before you reach the end of the road or you can stay at O'Reilly's itself. Both places need booking, particularly during school holidays. For the campsite phone (075) 440634 (2.00 to 4.00 pm) and for O'Reilly's phone (075) 440644. There is also an information centre, shop and cafe here.

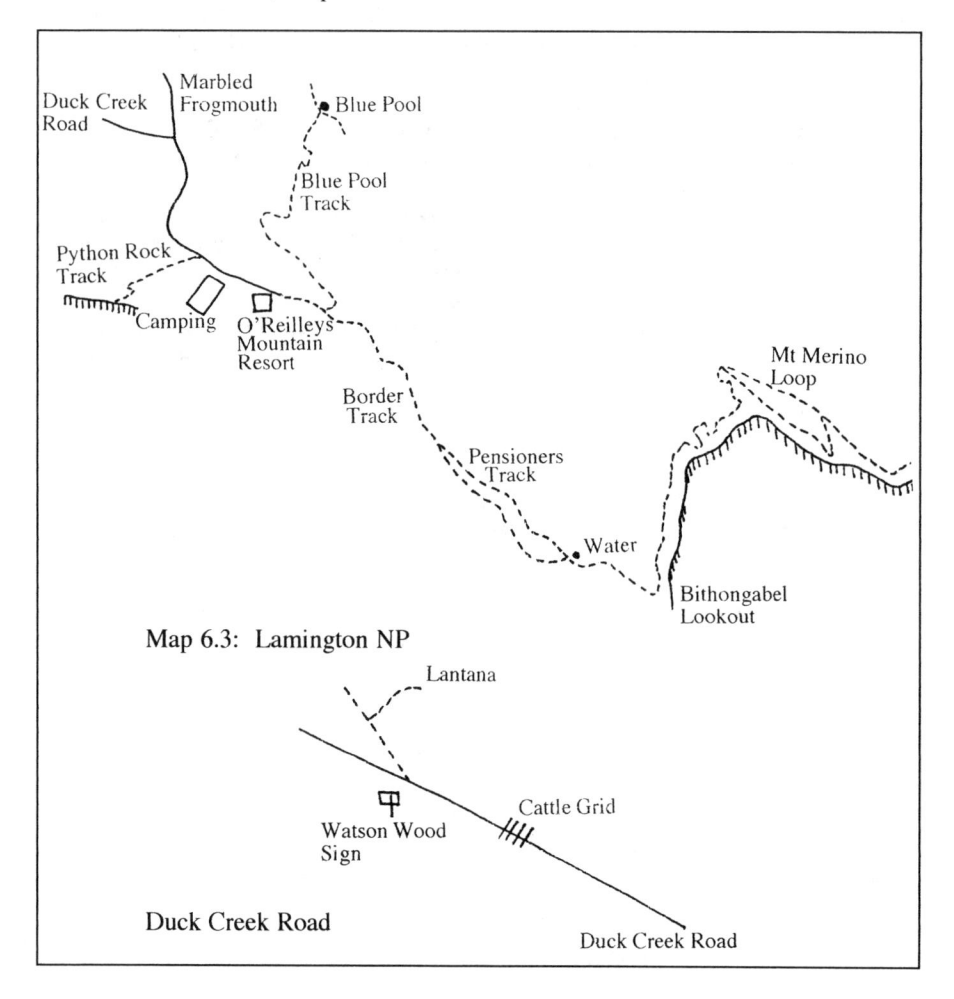

Map 6.3: Lamington NP

All of the excellent forest trails will produce birds. The following notes give some idea which areas are best for certain species. The Pensioners Track is the best trail for **Albert's Lyrebird**, and although shy they can easily be seen by observers used to looking for rainforest skulkers. They sometimes make a loud, distinctive, frog-like croaking before beginning to sing and the song is not as varied or full of mimicry as that of the Superb Lyrebird. Usually the dry leaf litter makes it easy to pick up feeding birds even when they are not calling. We saw several on or near the Pensioners Track in the daytime, and in the evening found two roosting in trees right over the Track. We also saw birds on the Border Track alongside Mount Merino, on the Blue Pool Track and in the rainforest along Duck Creek Road. The Python Rock Trail is also a regular place to find this species at dawn.

In late April we found the Mount Merino loop to be the best place to see **Rufous Scrub-bird**. It is about a 2 h walk from O'Reilly's to the end of the Pensioners Track and anywhere from there on scrub-birds can be found in the Antarctic Beech forest. The birds from the 'water 20 m' sign to the start of the cliff have been taped out by birders in the past, and consequently do not respond well to taping/pishing. The birds around the Mount Merino Loop, however, are less used to birders and can be more easily pished out. The key to successful pishing is to conceal yourself in the undergrowth where you can see a patch of the forest floor 2 m or so away and then to begin pishing as loudly as possible. It is also important to keep going for at least 10 minutes, the scrub-birds only appeared after other birds had lost interest. They run about very close, one even ran into my hand-held tape recorder as I was trying to tape it! Pishing also often starts the birds singing. The best place we found to see the birds is the very small campsite on the track over Mount Merino, this is the only area on the short bit of track where you could camp; it is about 4 m long and 2 m wide and along the edge of it is a log; kneel down behind this and look in a hole in the undergrowth at some small moss covered logs. By focusing our binoculars on these mossy logs and pishing very loudly we were able to get excellent views of a scrub-bird as it went berserk singing at us - it ran frequently up and down the mossy logs to get between its' song-posts. At one time it was singing simultaneously with a bird behind us - possibly this campsite marks the boundary of two territories. On six occasions pishing we saw three scrub-birds in April, however the best time of year to find this species is October to December when they breed, but only if it has been raining.

Regent and **Satin Bowerbirds** are common in the rainforest all around O'Reilly's, they regularly sit on tree tops around the campsite. In the early morning birds often visit the area just outside O'Reilly's to be hand fed fruit. **Noisy Pittas** are not hard to see just inside the entrance to the Border Track, we also saw them along the Mount Merino Loop, the Blue Pool Track and the Python Rock Track. This latter track is one of the best for **Paradise Riflebird**, listen for their loud harsh grating call and also listen for them picking at Staghorn ferns high on the trees. Other places we saw this species were the button-quail site (see later), the feeding table outside O'Reilly's and at the start of the Blue Pool Track.

Other birds you should find around the entrance to the Border Trail are **Green Catbird**, **Brown Cuckoo-Dove**, **Wompoo** and **Rose-crowned Fruit-Doves** (if there are fruiting figs around), **Logrunner**, **Bassian Ground-Thrush**, **Russet-tailed Ground-Thrush** (less common than Bassian although they seem more numerous at lower altitudes, e.g. the Blue Pool Track once you've dropped down to the pool, also try Duck Creek Road around the turn off and along the main roadsides in the evening) and **Pale-yellow Robin** (found around creek crossings along the walking trails). The campsite is a good place to get birds flying over, we saw **Variable Goshawk**, **Topknot** and **White-headed Pigeons**.

There are two other areas worth visiting near O'Reilly's. The first of these is a reliable site for **Marbled Frogmouth**. Drive back towards Canungra from O'Reilly's. Shortly after you pass Duck Creek Road, you come out of the rainforest for the first time and on your right hand side are eucalyptus trees. After 300 m or so you re-enter the rainforest. A pair of **Marbled Frogmouths** is resident here just inside the rainforest, and we saw them easily in November 1991 and again in January 1993. This species is also regularly reported where the road flattens out about 1 km down Duck Creek Road. The second area is a place to find **Black-breasted Button-Quail** and **Eastern Bristlebird**. Drive down Duck Creek Road (be careful as this is only a four-wheel drive (4WD) track when wet because it is steep and slippery) and after 7.7 km park just past the cattle grid and look for an obscure track off to the right by the Watson's Wood sign. A foot-track leads off this down the slope into an area of *Lantana*, creep along this, checking out any rustling in the leaves. We saw three male **Black-breasted Button-Quails**, **Paradise Riflebird**, **White-eared Monarch** and **Varied Triller** here. Duck Creek Road itself is also a fairly reliable site for **Glossy Black-Cockatoos** and it is also a good place to see **Red-browed Treecreeper**, in the eucalyptus trees. If you drive further down Duck Creek Road there is a turning on the right which almost doubles back on itself. Park here and walk down this track for about 1 km to a dry creek signposted 'Bristlebird Creek'. Appropriately enough this is the area to find **Eastern Bristlebird**, although they can be very elusive and it is best to try early morning. Finally, ask at O'Reilly's about any recent **Sooty Owl** sightings, we heard them just at the start of the Pensioners Track and they are regularly reported around the Duck Creek Road turn-off and along the Canungra Road about 2 km from the campsite.

6.8 Girraween National Park (Map 6.4)

Key Species: **Turquoise Parrot, Plum-headed Finch**
Girraween National Park is reached by turning east off the New England Highway between Tenterfield and Stanthorpe signposted to Storm King Dam. Drive into the park and turn left into the excellent Bald Rock Creek camping area. The open eucalyptus woodland along the Link Circuit trail from here is good for **Chestnut-rumped Hylacola** and **Yellow-tufted Honeyeater**, whilst the Junction Track also starting here is good for **Turquoise Parrot**, **Spotted Quail-Thrush** and

BRISBANE AREA 75

Diamond Firetail. At the road junction beyond the HQ, turn left onto the old Wallangarra road. This is another good area for **Turquoise Parrot** and **Plum-headed Finch.**

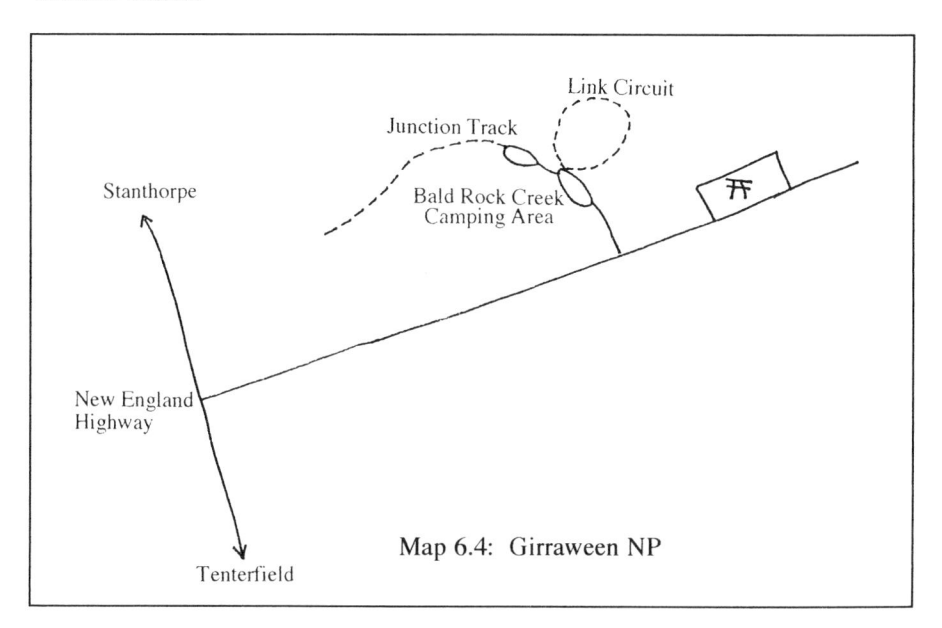

Map 6.4: Girraween NP

6.9 Neumgna State Forest (Map 6.5)

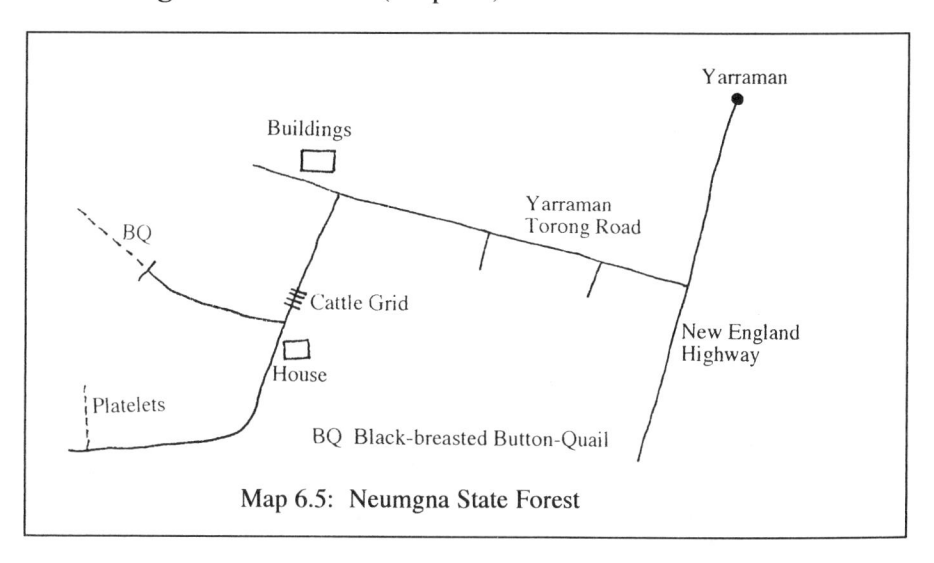

Map 6.5: Neumgna State Forest

Key Species: **Black-breasted Button-Quail**

Neumgna State Forest is situated close to Yarraman, about 2.5 hours drive north-west of Brisbane. From Yarraman, head south-west on the New England Highway then turn right after 2 km along Yarraman Tarong Road. After 800 m the bitumen ends just before some buildings. Turn left, cross a cattle grid, and turn right down a short dead end (see map). Whilst parked here, we saw a female **Black-breasted Button-Quail** cross the track beyond the barbed wire fence. We went in and had excellent views of it on the ground. Another place which had numerous platelets was the next track off to the right beyond the house. Bush camping only is available.

6.10 Bunya Mountains National Park (Map 6.6)

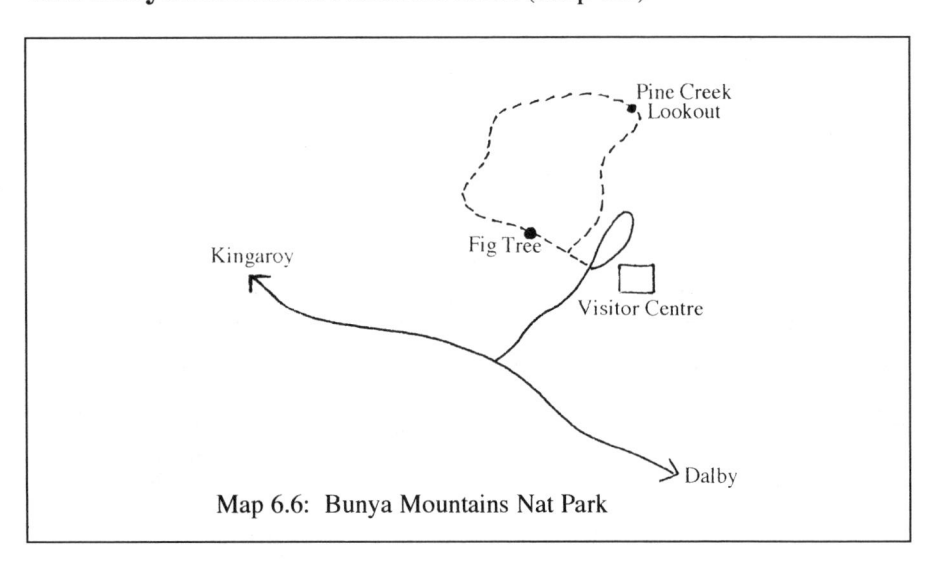

Map 6.6: Bunya Mountains Nat Park

Key Species: **Sooty Owl**
Bunya Mountains National Park is another sub-tropical rainforest area, situated about 65 km south-west of Kingaroy and approximately 3 hours drive from Brisbane. The birds are essentially the same as those found at Lamington National Park. The main attraction however is a regular daytime roost for Sooty Owl which has been in use for some time now and hopefully will still be around for some years to come. The quickest way to the Bunya Mountains from Brisbane is to drive west on the Warrego Highway through Toowoomba, turn right at Jondaryan and carry on to Quinalow. The road climbs steeply after here to the top of the escarpment. Turn right to Dandabah and park in the car-park at the end next to the excellent campsite. Take the Scenic Circuit which starts behind the ranger station. If you go around this clockwise, after about 300 m the track goes right through a large, open, hollow fig tree. Stand underneath and look directly

upwards inside the tree and you should see a **Sooty Owl** roosting about 30 m up. The birds have roosted in this tree regularly, despite the large numbers of noisy tourists walking the trail but note that the roost is not used every day. We birded all the way around the rest of the circuit. The best birds seen were **Rose Robin** (6, but note that they are altitudinal migrants and commonest here in spring and autumn), **Regent Bowerbird** (6) and **Paradise Riflebird**. There are several other rainforest walks which would be worth trying.

B South-west Queensland and the Channel Country (Map 6.7)

The Channel Country is an extremely remote area about seven hours drive west of Windorah. We visited it in the spring in early September 1991, primarily to see Letter-winged Kites, which were present in large numbers then (following a population explosion of Long-haired Rats); this is anyway the stronghold area for this species. The kites are only viewable during rat plagues but you should check with birders on their current status before venturing there because of the remoteness and dangers of visiting this region. Access is *via* the Diamantina Developmental Road west of Windorah which is unsealed after about 100 km and although rough and sandy in many places we did manage it in a two wheel drive car. Note that the road would be impassable in wet weather. The main problem, apart from the danger of getting bogged down in sand, is the deep wheel ruts made by trucks which use the route; in a car it is very easy to bottom out and a good ground clearance is essential. Unless you have very up to date information about the whereabouts of the kites, plus permission from the relevant cattle station the birds are on, the only reason to go west of Windorah would be to cut through to the Birdsville Track and South Australia but note that this link road has the reputation of being rougher than the Birdsville Track itself. The turning is 115 km west of Windorah, and the arid plains along this section of road are good for **Australian Pratincole**, **Inland Dotterel** and **Gibber Chat**, which you should see from the car. It is worth spending some time to the east of Windorah in order to see Hall's Babbler, even if you do not plan to travel to Birdsville.

6.11 Sixty-three km West of Charleville

At this particular spot the road crosses over a small creek, if there are still pools of water left in the creek bed then it is worth spending some time here in order to see good numbers of honeyeaters and parrots drinking in the late afternoon and early morning. We bush camped here and saw **Grey-headed Honeyeater** (2), **Pink Cockatoo** and **Red-winged Parrot**.

6.12 Eighty-four km East of Windorah

Key Species: **Hall's Babbler, Australian Owlet-Nightjar, White-browed Treecreeper**

CHAPTER 6: QUEENSLAND

Map 6.7: South-west Queensland and the Channel Country
11 63 km west of Charleville
12 84 km east of Windorah
13 Lake Bindegolly
14 Eulo Bore

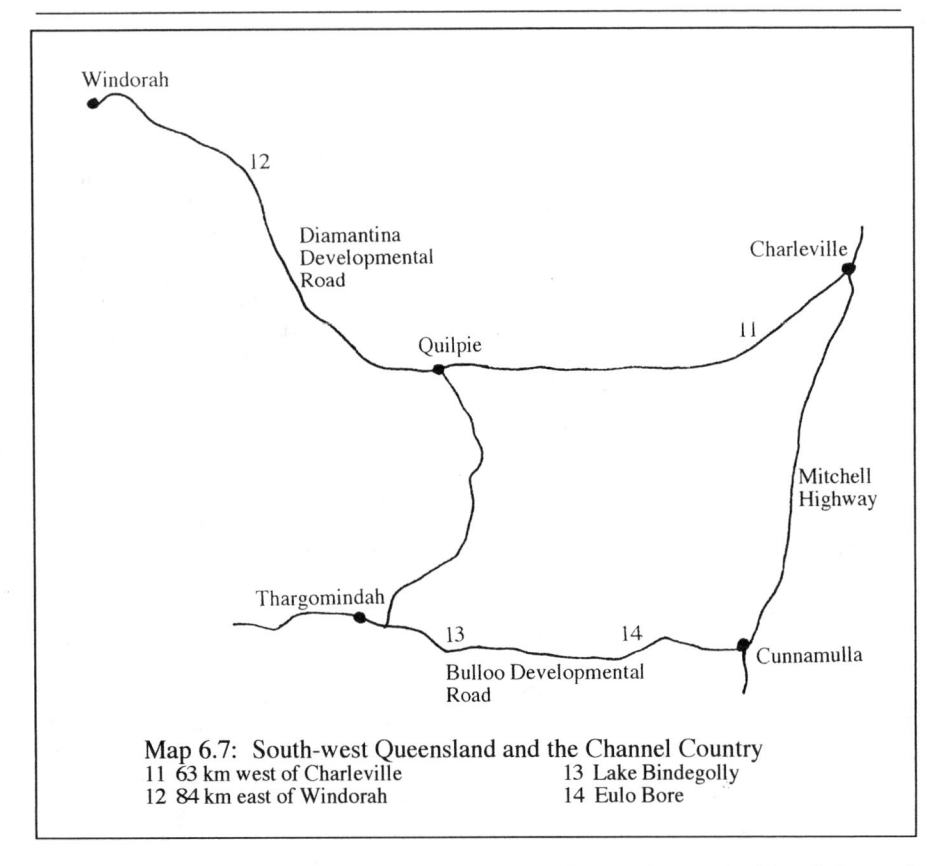

This is a well known reliable site for Hall's Babbler on the north side of the road between Quilpie and Windorah, 161 km west of the former. Park by the firebreaks which run out at right angles to the road and make your way down past the overhead power lines to a dry creek bed. Walk along the creek until you find **Hall's Babbler** and **White-browed Treecreeper** both of which occur in the thick mulga here, although we also saw the former in mulga underneath the power lines themselves. We bush camped overnight and also saw **Australian Owlet-Nightjar** and **Bourke's Parrot**. This seems a particularly good place for the former and birds will often follow you around during the daytime. Try tapping on any trees with suitable roosting hollows in them.

6.13 Lake Bindegolly

Key Species: **Freckled Duck, Blue-billed Duck, Baillon's Crake, Grey Falcon**

This lake is about 70 km west of Eulo and although it can dry up from time to time, there are usually plenty of water birds here, making it well worth a visit.

From the bridge and the telegraph pole bridge (centre section missing) we saw **Baillon's Crake** (26), **Australian Crake** (23), **Spotless Crake** (1), **Rufous Night-Heron, Blue-billed Duck** and **Freckled Duck** (2). The samphire area along the west shore is a reliable locality for **Orange Chat** (we saw three), also in this area were **Black-tailed Native-Hen** (20) and **Red-kneed Dotterel**. **Grey** and **Black Falcons** are regularly recorded at this site and the road between here and Eulo is good for **Ground Cuckoo-Shrike**.

6.14 Eulo Bore

Key Species: **Bourke's Parrot, Spotted Bowerbird, Hall's Babbler, Chestnut-breasted Quail-Thrush**
This is a water bore located about 15 km east of Eulo (it is known locally as nine mile bore). Just look for the raised bore sides on the north side of the road as you drive along. It is a well known site for **Bourke's Parrot** which drink from the lower pool, especially in the morning and it is a thoroughly recommended area in which to bush camp. We saw **Bourke's Parrot** (5), **Spotted Bowerbird** (3, they drink from the top pool in the afternoon) and **Plum-headed Finch** (2). Also in this area are **Mulga Parrot, Black-eared Cuckoo, Grey-headed Honeyeater, Ground Cuckoo-Shrike** and **White-browed Treecreeper** plus many commoner species. The area of Coomunda Homestead, 1 km west of Eulo and also the area between Eulo and the bore all hold **Hall's** and **Chestnut-crowned Babblers** and **Chestnut-breasted Quail-Thrush**. A good place for the latter species is the small ridge with telegraph posts on it to the south side of the road, 2.5 km to the east of the bore. This species is also fairly easy to see as you drive the roads in this area; we saw them between Eulo and Quilpie and 2 km west of Quilpie. **Hall's Babbler** has been seen in the thick mulga area to the south of the road; try the mulga 150 m behind telegraph post No 270, just east of the bore.

C The Central Queensland Coast (Map 6.8)

There are a number of good places worth visiting on this long stretch of coast between Cairns and Brisbane. Essential is Eungella National Park west of Mackay which holds the endemic, recently described, Eungella Honeyeater.

6.15 Cooloola National Park (Map 6.9)

Key Species: **Ground Parrot, Grass Owl**
Situated to the east of Gympie, this national park has a good area of heathland. Drive towards Rainbow Beach on Tin Can Bay Road, 17 km before Rainbow Beach, turn south onto Cooloola Way . After 2-3 km, where the power lines cross the road, turn left along a firebreak and stop by a wooden bridge after 1 km. The dry heath on the left and right has **Ground Parrot, Blue-breasted Quail** and **Southern Emuwren**. Further along the firebreak, there is a track off to the right and a sign saying 'Road Closed to Traffic'. Walk down here 200 m and the area to your right is a good place for **Grass Owls** at dusk. **Ground Parrots**

also occur in the heath here. There is a good campsite at the park headquarters at Freshwater Bay.

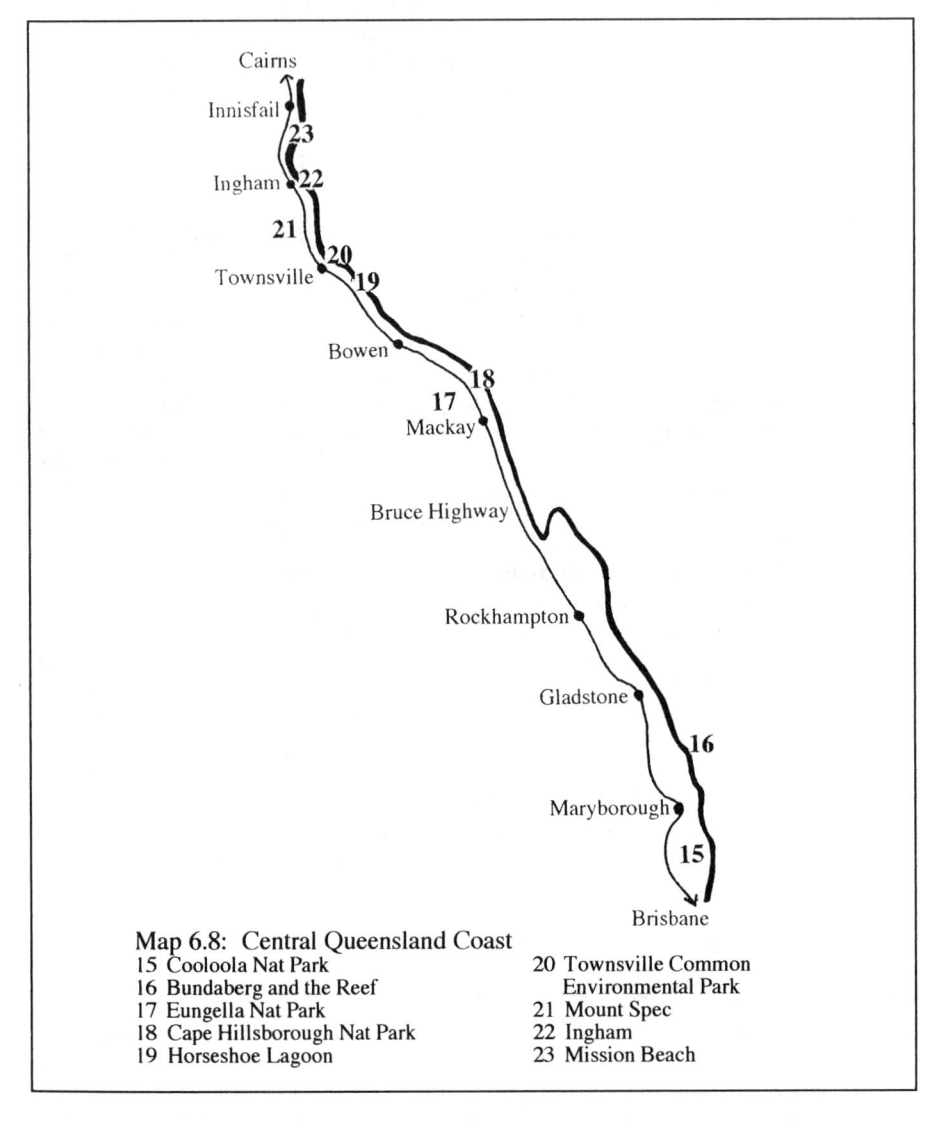

Map 6.8: Central Queensland Coast
15 Cooloola Nat Park
16 Bundaberg and the Reef
17 Eungella Nat Park
18 Cape Hillsborough Nat Park
19 Horseshoe Lagoon
20 Townsville Common Environmental Park
21 Mount Spec
22 Ingham
23 Mission Beach

6.16 Bundaberg and the Reef

Key Species: **Black** and **Brown Noddies, Roseate Tern, Red-tailed Tropicbird** (Lady Elliot only), **Bridled Tern**

CENTRAL QUEENSLAND COAST

The town of Bundaberg is situated about 370 km or four hours drive north of Brisbane and is the most southerly place to gain access to the Great Barrier Reef. There are two ways to visit the Reef, either go on a boat, the 'Lady Musgrave' which leaves four days a week from Burnett Heads Tourist jetty and visits Lady Musgrave Island, details from any Queensland Tourist Centre or phone (071) 52 90 11 or fly to Lady Elliot Island (booked through travel agents) which can be expensive, although we got a special fare of $95 return including lunch and snorkelling gear.

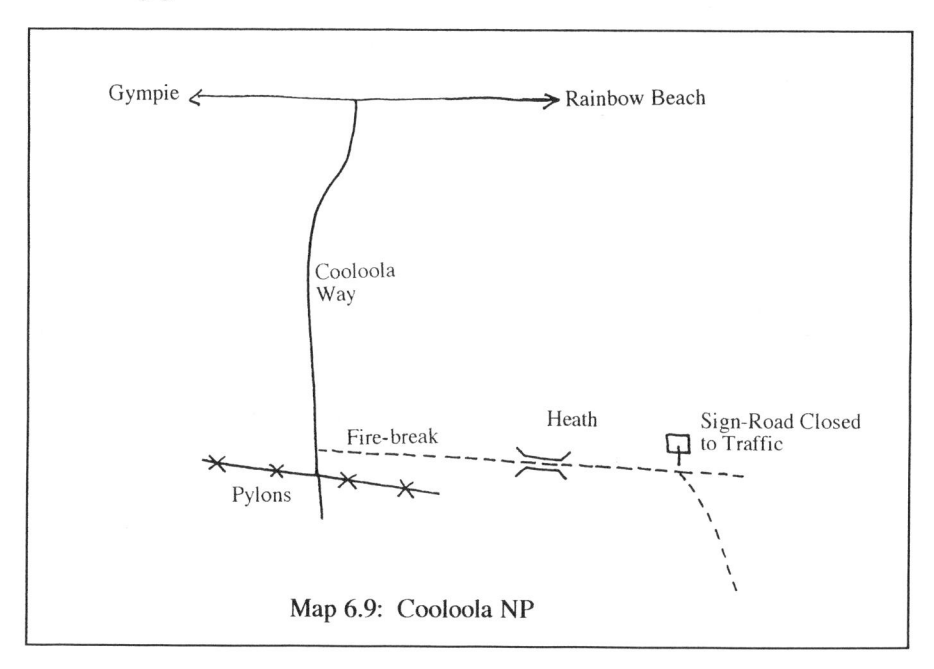

Map 6.9: Cooloola NP

I went to Lady Musgrave Island in March and most of the breeding seabirds had left. The best birds were **Fluttering Shearwater**, **Black Noddy** (common), **Black-naped Tern, Brown Booby** and **Buff-banded Rail**. Note that you do not normally get Sooty Terns this far south, although they are common off Cairns.

Much better for birds was Lady Elliot Island which we visited as a day trip in mid-November. At this time of year all the breeding seabirds are present, the best birds seen were **Bridled Tern, Black Noddy, Brown Noddy, Roseate** and **Black-naped Terns** (all fairly common), **Lesser Frigatebird** (common) **Great Frigatebird** (2), **Red-tailed Tropicbird** (breeds here, best December to March), **Brown Booby, Buff-banded Rail** (tame) and **Silver-eye**. Just walk around the perimeter of the island for the birds. Note that the beach with breeding Roseate Terns is normally roped off.

On the mainland, at Bundaberg Airport whilst waiting for the flight we saw **Little** and **Scaly-breasted Lorikeets** in flowering eucalypts at the back of the airport building. Burnett Heads from where the Lady Musgrave boat leaves has a good area of mangroves. To get there, drive the 15 km from Bundaberg to Burnett Heads, carry on through the town to the harbour and on your left is an area of mangroves on the south shore of the Burnett River. Loud pishing is very effective and the easiest way of seeing the birds here. We saw **Mangrove Honeyeater**, **Mangrove Gerygone** (both common), **Rainbow Bee-eater**, **Caspian Tern**, **Osprey**, **Brahminy Kite** and **Collared Kingfisher**. On the rocks around the harbour check for waders such as **Terek Sandpiper**, **Grey-tailed Tattler**, **Whimbrel** and **Greenshank**.

6.17 Eungella National Park

*Key Species: **Eungella Honeyeater***
Eungella National Park is high up in the hills to the west of Mackay. The best location for finding Eungella Honeyeaters is not actually in the park itself, but to get there drive west from Mackay *via* Marian to Eungella (83 km). When you reach the top of the steep escarpment, bear right onto Dalrymple Road and follow it for 16 km then turn left down Chelmans Road and follow this to where it ends at a forestry gate. Park here and walk through the gate, following the overgrown track. We saw a pair of **Eungella Honeyeaters** fairly easily about 200 m along here; they reacted well to pishing. (In the summer months, try Range Road View Point for this species; see the Bird Finding Guide entry). Also along this track we saw **Regent Bowerbird**. It is worth noting that a 'Sooty' Owl was seen here by Mike Entwhistle in 1986 although it has never been established which species of Sooty Owl was involved since the two were not split in those days. Eungella is supposed to be in a gap separating the distribution of the two species so further study is needed and sightings here with details should be reported to the RAOU. The national park itself can be reached by returning along Dalrymple Road to the top of the escarpment, and instead of going back to Mackay, carry straight on to the good Broken River Campsite. Around here we saw **Cicadabird** and **Barred Cuckoo-Shrike**. There is a viewing platform built over a pool in the Broken River where Duck-billed Platypuses are very tame and unconcerned by the activities of noisy kids above them, although apparently recently there has been rather a lot of cattle disturbance to this pool.

6.18 Cape Hillsborough National Park

Cape Hillsborough National Park is signposted from the Bruce Highway, 50 km north of Mackay. There is a basic campsite. Birds recorded include **Beach Thick-knee** (Smalleys Beach), **Bush Thick-knee**, **Large-billed Gerygone**, **Mangrove Honeyeater**, **Superb**, **Rose-crowned** and **Wompoo Fruit-Doves** and **White-eared Monarch** (in rainforest along the Hidden Valley circuit).

6.19 Horseshoe Lagoon

Key Species: **Cotton Pygmy-Goose**
This Lagoon is on the east side of the Bruce Highway between Townsville and Ayr, and it is signposted from the Highway. Coming from Townsville, turn left just before the sign, drive down the road and you will see the lagoon on the right hand side. If you ask permission at the farm, there should be no problem going across the fields for a closer look. We saw **Plumed** and **Wandering Whistling-Ducks**, **Green** and **Cotton Pygmy-Geese**, **Comb-crested Jacana**, **Black-necked Stork**, **Sharp-tailed** and **Marsh Sandpipers**, **Whiskered Tern** and **Crimson Finch**.

6.20 Townsville Town Common Environmental Park

Key Species: Waterbirds including **Cotton Pygmy-Goose**
This is a huge wetland area just north of Townsville on Cape Pallarenda Road, near Rowes Bay. It is particularly good in the dry season (April to July) when hundreds of waterbirds are concentrated here and it is renowned as a site of international importance. **Cotton Pygmy-Geese** can be found year round on the Borrow Pits and other notable birds in the area include **Wandering Whistling-Duck**, **Pacific Baza**, **Bush Thick-knee**, **Brown-backed** and **Yellow Honeyeaters**. You should check about access and other details from the Queensland Parks and Wildlife Service in Marlow Street in Pallarenda but note that camping is not allowed here.

6.21 Mount Spec National Park

Key Species: **Macleay's Honeyeater, Victoria's Riflebird, Chowchilla, Fernwren**
Mount Spec National Park is another excellent area of rainforest and the most southerly place to find several Atherton Tableland specialities. Turn west off the Bruce Highway approximately 60 km north of Townsville to Paluma. Wind up the steep hill until you reach Paluma, about 18 km, where there is an Art Gallery run by two local birders, Cliff and Dawn Frith. They can probably help you with local information, notably the location of a **Golden Bowerbird** bower. There is one near the track down to Birthday Creek Falls. Also in Paluma is the Ivy Cottage Tea Gardens which is famous for the tame birds which land on the table to share your cream tea. These include **Bridled** and **Macleay's Honeyeaters**, **Victoria's Riflebird** and **Spotted Catbird**. At the bottom of the garden is a rainforest trail which is good for **Bower's Shrike-Thrush**, **Chowchilla** and **Grey-headed Robin**. Nearby, Witts Lookout Trail is good for rainforest species, notably **Fernwren** and **Chowchilla**. Both **Lesser Sooty Owl** and **Papuan Frogmouth** occur, the former has been spotlighted at McClelland's Lookout, the latter is often present at the lower junction of the 'Loop' at night. Along the road just past Paluma we saw a **Red-necked Rail** which ran across the road and also **Tooth-billed Catbird** and **Barred Cuckoo-Shrike** in fruiting

trees. On the road back to the Bruce Highway look for **Noisy Pitta, Pied Monarch, Bassian Ground-Thrush** (race *cuneata*), **Mountain Thornbill, Fairy Gerygone, Scarlet Honeyeater** and **White-headed Pigeon** in wooded areas. Basic camping is allowed by the Loop picnic area.

6.22 Ingham

Key Species: **Masked Owl, Grass Owl**
Ingham is the home of John Young who is a professional birder so will charge for his services. If you are interested in going out with him, just ask in Ingham for his current address. His speciality is nightbirds and he will be able to show you **Masked, Grass, Rufous** and **Lesser Sooty Owls**. You can search yourself for **Barn, Masked** and **Grass Owls** by driving the roads around Ingham at night; the birds hunt in recently cut paddocks. Try driving at night along wooded roads west of Trebonne for **Masked Owl**. Wallaman Falls National Park which is 40 km west of Trebonne is supposed to be good for **Southern Cassowary** and **Lesser Sooty Owl**; look for them both around the campsite.

6.23 Mission Beach

Key Species: **Southern Cassowary**
Mission Beach is about 150 km south of Cairns and is reached by turning east at El Arish on the Bruce Highway. There are many warning signs about cassowaries crossing the roads all around the area. We found a current good site by driving into Mission Beach and asking local people where cassowaries have been seen recently. As you drive from Mission Beach towards Tully, you have to turn left at a T-junction and shortly afterwards there is a signpost and an unsealed track to a waterhole. Go down this track, park at the end and walk to the waterhole. We saw an adult **Southern Cassowary** plus chick in the rainforest on the other side of the pool. The birds also cross over the track to the waterhole regularly. Another good place to try is on the road from El Arish to Mission Beach. Shortly after you cross Lacey's Creek, you will see a signpost 'Licuala State Forest' on the right hand side. The walking track beyond is a good place for cassowaries, particularly in the early morning. There is also a good range of rainforest birds in the Mission Beach area including **Little Kingfisher, Noisy Pitta, Barred Cuckoo-Shrike** (in fruiting fig-trees), **Double-eyed Fig-Parrot, Orange-footed Scrubfowl, Wompoo Fruit-Dove, Yellow-breasted Boatbill, White-eared Monarch, Lemon-bellied Flycatcher** and **Tooth-billed Catbird**. Try spotlighting for **Rufous Owl** in the car-park at Lacey's Creek, on the left hand side just after you cross the creek coming from El Arish. There are several hotels and caravan parks in Mission Beach.

D Cairns Area (Map 6.10)

Cairns is a small town in the tropical north and it makes an excellent centre for really exploring the diverse habitats to be found in this region from coastal mangroves to the Atherton Tablelands. There are many sites which are all readily

CAIRNS AREA

accessible from Cairns and if possible, at least two weeks should be spent in this part of Australia. It is a good idea to get a map of Cairns itself from the Tourist Information Office.

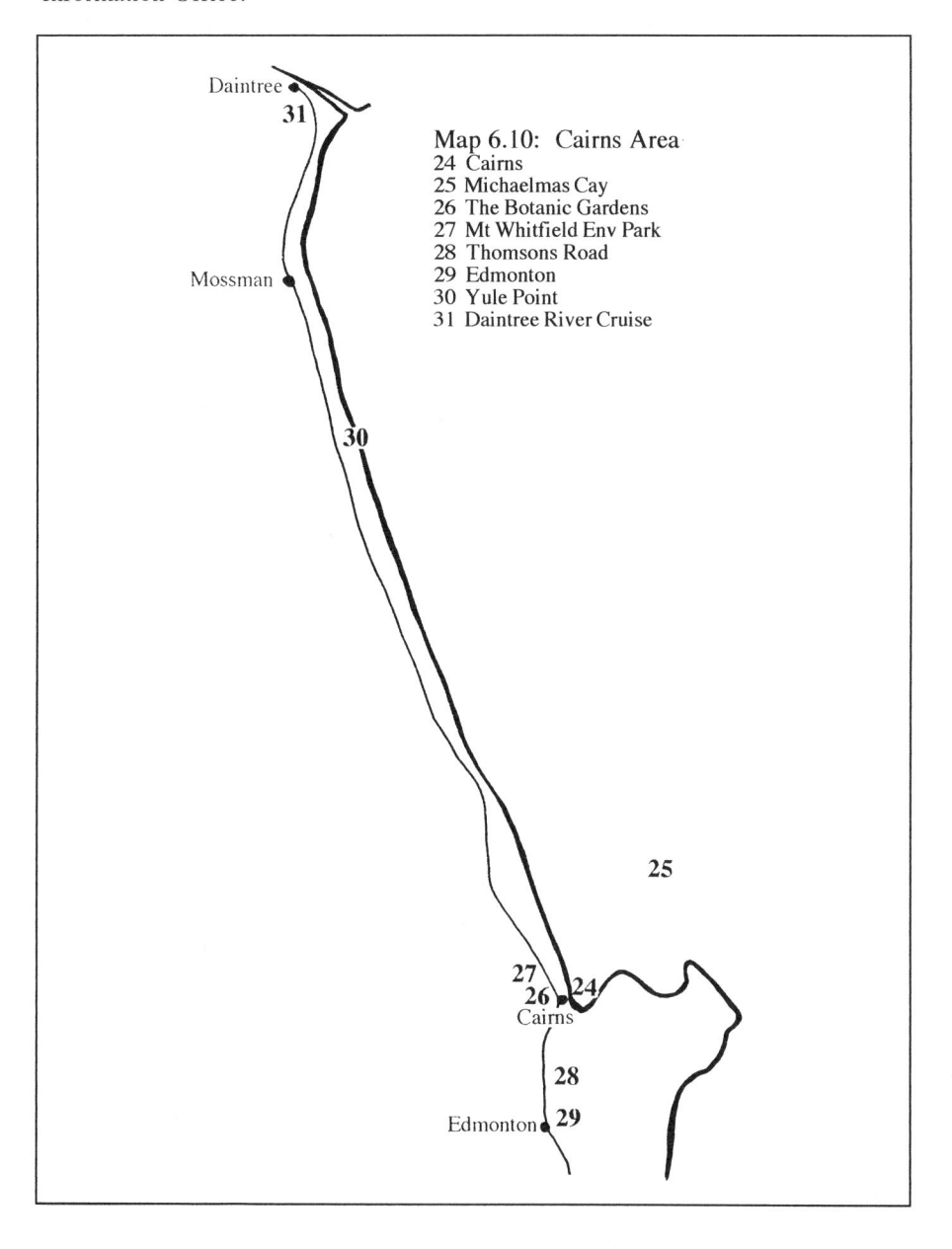

Map 6.10: Cairns Area
24 Cairns
25 Michaelmas Cay
26 The Botanic Gardens
27 Mt Whitfield Env Park
28 Thomsons Road
29 Edmonton
30 Yule Point
31 Daintree River Cruise

6.24 Cairns Esplanade

Key Species: Waders, **Double-eyed Fig-Parrot**
The muddy beach area that can be viewed from the main esplanade in Cairns is excellent for many species of wader, particularly on an incoming tide. Many rarities have been seen here in the past and if you are watching birds, John Crowhurst is almost sure to find you. He is the council gardener and tends the park adjacent to the esplanade. He is usually wearing an orange council shirt and a straw hat. As well as information on waders, he is a mine of information on all the local specialities in the Cairns area. The best waders we saw here were **Greater** and **Lesser Sandplovers, Eastern Curlew, Grey-tailed Tattler, Broad-billed, Sharp-tailed** and **Terek Sandpipers, Black-tailed Godwit** and **Red** and **Great Knots**. **Double-eyed Fig-Parrots** are regularly seen in the fig trees in the adjacent park. Sadly the Esplanade is under very serious threat of 'redevelopment'.

6.25 The Great Barrier Reef

Key Species: **Great Frigatebird, Sooty Tern, Black Noddy, Brown Noddy**
Trips out to the Barrier Reef can be booked from the Tourist Information Office in Cairns which is at the south end of the Esplanade. The best area to visit for breeding seabirds is Michaelmas Cay. We went in late December with a boat called 'Sea Star II' which visits Michaelmas Cay for a couple of hours, then goes on to Hastings Reef for snorkelling. Note that when snorkelling it is highly advisable to wear an old tee-shirt and sun-block to prevent sunburn. The snorkelling gear is provided. The captain of the Sea Star II is keen on birds and can show you the breeding species at Michaelmas Cay. These are **Brown Noddy** (several thousand pairs), **Black Noddy** (very few pairs, be prepared to search for some time through the Brown Noddy flocks), **Sooty Tern** (common), **Black-naped Tern** (a few), **Lesser-crested Tern, Brown Booby** and **Masked Booby** which occasionally rest with the Brown Boobies on the Cay. On the way out, you should see **Bridled Terns** not far offshore and keep a look-out for tropicbirds which are occasionally seen. Both **Great** and **Lesser Frigatebirds** are present. The Sea Star II takes a full day and is excellent value for money. Many of the larger boats only go as far as Green Island which is not really far enough out to see breeding seabirds. Green Island does however have **Rose-crowned Fruit-Dove, Torresian Imperial-Pigeon** (summer only), **Wandering Tattler**, plus some people maintain the population of **Silver-eyes** present are actually **Pale White-eyes**.

6.26 Cairns Botanic Gardens (Map 6.11)

Key Species: **Papuan Frogmouth, Red-necked Rail, White-browed Crake, Little Kingfisher, Metallic Starling, Brown-backed Honeyeater**
The Botanic Gardens are an excellent area in central Cairns, particularly good at dawn and dusk. They are reached from the Captain Cook Highway, drive north

along Sheridan Street (the Captain Cook Highway), turn left into Collins Avenue and the entrance to the Botanic Gardens is on the left hand side. There is always a regular nest stake-out/roosting site for **Papuan Frogmouth** in central Cairns. When we were there it was close to the Gardens but ask John Crowhurst for the current directions. The whole Botanic Gardens area is good for **Pacific Baza, Double-eyed Fig-Parrot, Metallic Starling** (*except* February to April), **Graceful, Yellow, Yellow-spotted** and **Brown-backed Honeyeaters.** Creep along the Centenary Board walk at dusk and look for **Red-necked Rail** and **White-browed Crake.** We saw one Red-necked Rail actually underneath the board walk. The Saltwater and Freshwater Pools regularly have **Little Kingfisher** around the edge and **Mangrove Robin** occurs in the mangroves bordering the central channel.

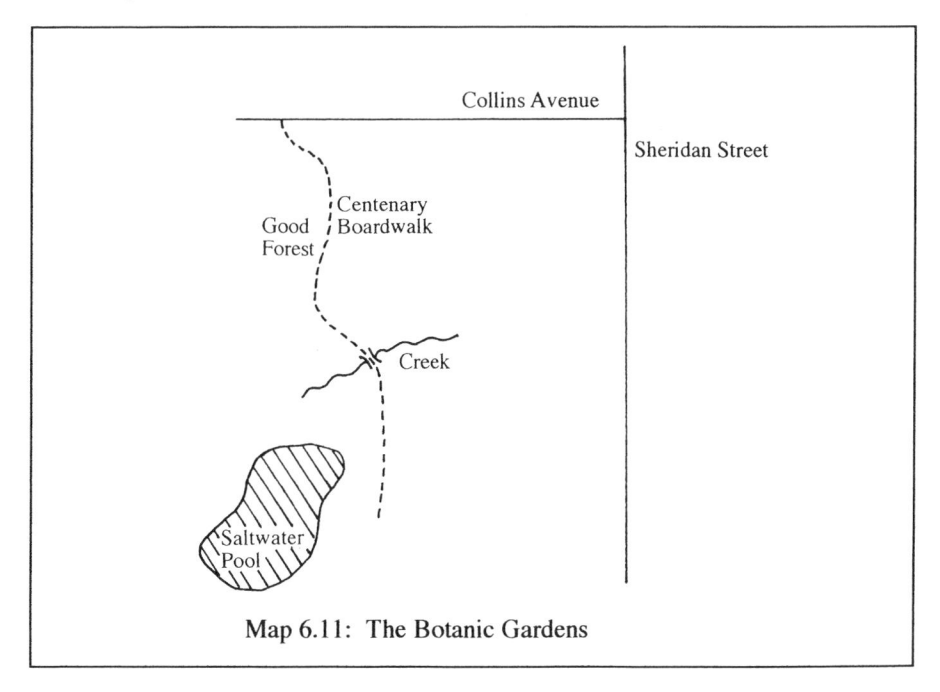

Map 6.11: The Botanic Gardens

6.27 Mount Whitfield Environmental Park

Key Species: **Lovely Fairywren**
The entrance to this park is marked on the north side of Collins Avenue, just before you get to Macdonnel Street and the Botanic Gardens. Take the Blue Arrow Circuit track up Mount Whitfield to the top then down the other side into the rainforest. **Buff-breasted Paradise-Kingfishers** are common in summer along with **Noisy Pitta, Wompoo** and **Superb Fruit-Doves** and **Pied Monarch** and also **Lovely Fairywren.** Sadly the last Southern Cassowary

which lived in this park was recently killed by local dogs. This caused outrage in the local newspapers and the owner was prosecuted and the dogs destroyed.

6.28 Thomsons Road, Edmonton (Map 6.12)

Key Species: **Little Kingfisher, Mangrove Robin**
Thomsons Road is a left turn off the Bruce Highway if driving south, less than 10 km from Cairns. Follow the road down and park opposite the speedway, take a track on the left just beside a building which leads to the bank of a mangrove-fringed creek. Sit here and scan the small area of mangroves for **Mangrove Robin** which feed on the mud at low tide. They can be easily pished or whistled in, the call is a down slurred whistle. Also present here are **Varied Honeyeater, Little Kingfisher, Olive-backed Sunbird, Graceful Honeyeater, Varied Triller, Australian Koel, Shining Flycatcher** and **Buff-banded Rail**. Close to Cairns Airport is a similar area of mangroves with a well signposted boardwalk which is worth checking for **Little Kingfisher** and **Varied Honeyeater**.

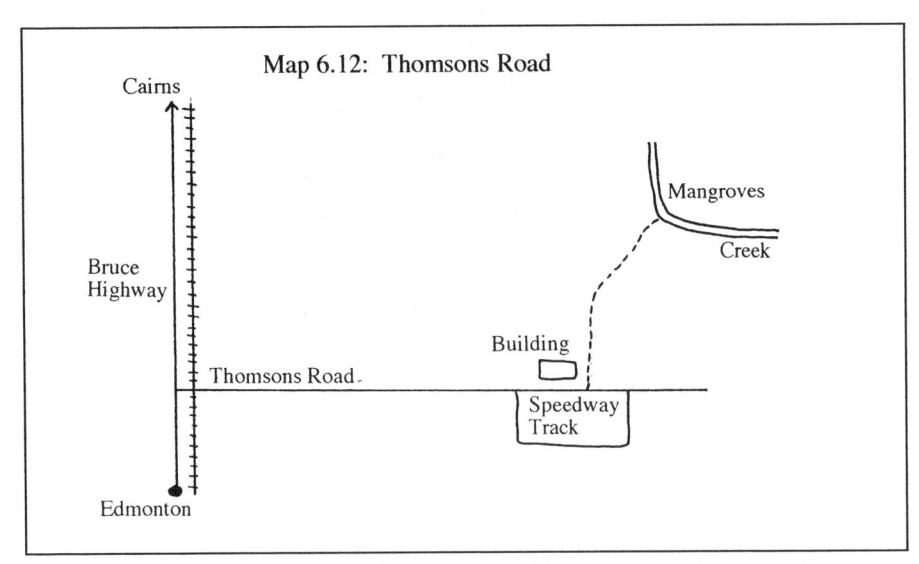

Map 6.12: Thomsons Road

6.29 Edmonton and Yarrabah Turf Farms

Key Species: **Little Curlew, Oriental Plover, Oriental Pratincole, Yellow Wagtail** (all present in summer only)
These turf farms are excellent places for grassland species during the Austral summer months. Edmonton or 'Everdale' Turf Farm is found just off the Bruce Highway south of Edmonton. Just after Wright Creek turn left on Hill Road and go 1.1 km to the farm. Check the short grass for waders; we saw **Little Whimbrel** (20) and **Sharp-tailed Sandpiper** (100). Further south on the

Bruce Highway take the road signposted to Yarrabah. A short way along this road you will see a turf farm on the left hand side. As long as you keep to the edges of the fields and well out of the way of any workers it is possible to birdwatch here. We found this farm to be better than the Edmonton one. The highlights were **Oriental Plover** (3), **Oriental Pratincole, Australian Pratincole, Australian Swiftlet** (common), **Little Curlew, Pacific Golden Plover** and **Sharp-tailed Sandpiper** and **Yellow Wagtail.** At the nearby signposted Crocodile Farm, the first pool on the right after the shop is a stake-out for **White-browed Crake.**

6.30 Yule Point

Key Species: **Beach Thick-knee**
To get to Yule Point drive north from Cairns on the Captain Cook Highway. The point itself is not signposted, but it is just north of Pebbly Beach which is signposted and approximately 20 km south of Mossman, Yule Point is the only large area of mangroves that you will see from the Highway. Pull off by the mangroves and walk through them down to the beach. Walk north along the beach on the edge of the mangroves until you find the **Beach Thick-knees.** We saw one after about a 1 km walk. Low tide is best, otherwise it is hard to pick your way through the mangroves to the beach. Check the mangroves for **Varied Honeyeater** and **Large-billed Gerygone** and the beach for other waders.

6.31 Daintree River Cruises

Key Species: **Little Kingfisher, Large-billed Gerygone**
This is a short tourist boat trip on the Daintree River run by Chris Dahlberg who also runs the Red Mill House Bed and Breakfast in Daintree village. The cruises depart daily at 6.30 am and 9.30 am from Daintree Jetty and last about two hours. The early morning cruise is obviously the best for birding. Booking agents are Barney Booth, Daintree General Store (Tel 986 146) or Denise Collins, Red Mill House (Tel 986 169). From the boat we saw a **Papuan Frogmouth** roosting in the mangroves, **Mangrove Robin** (6, pished out when we were close to the mangroves, **Large-billed Gerygone, Little Kingfisher** (seen virtually every trip) and **Azure Kingfisher.** In the winter months, **Great-billed Heron** is seen on most trips and it is still possible in the summer months but much less likely. Saltwater crocodiles are also regularly seen.

E The Atherton Tablelands (Map 6.13)

This is an excellent area of rainforest centred around the town of Atherton. There are a number of important sites to visit in order to see all the Atherton specialities. Driving along the roads, particularly the Kennedy Highway in the early morning is supposed to be a good way to see **Bush-Hen,** however **Buff-banded Rails** are very numerous along the roadsides at this time and it is difficult to get good views of birds scuttling back into the undergrowth.

Map 6.13: Atherton Tablelands
32 The Crater Nat Park
33 Hastie's Swamp
34 Lake Eacham and Lake Barrine
35 Cathedral Fig Tree
36 Nardellos Lagoon
37 Tinaroo Creek Road
38 Pickford Road
39 Big Mitchell Creek
40 Mt Lewis and Julatten
41 Abattoir Swamp
42 Mt Carbine Road
43 Mt Molloy

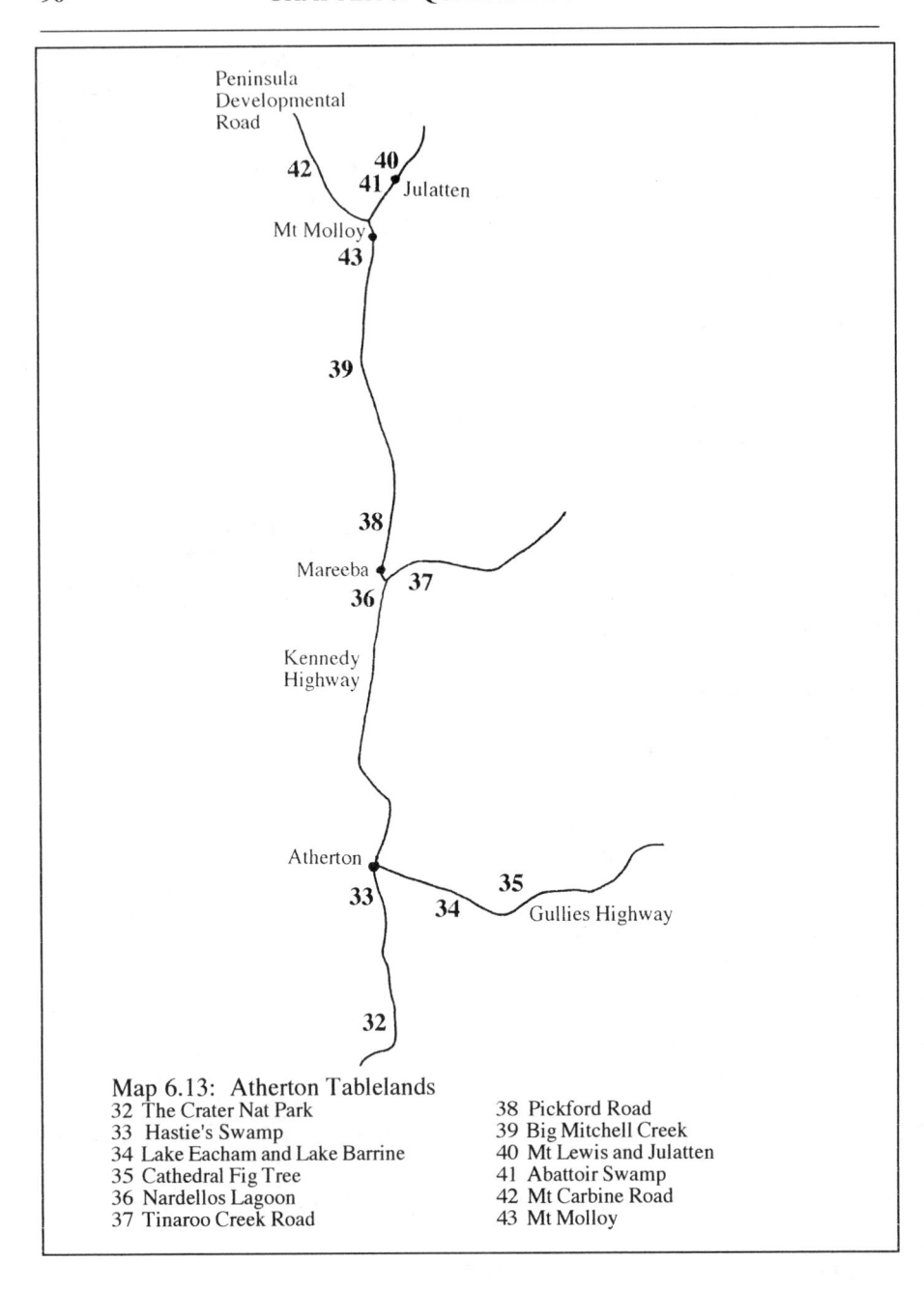

ATHERTON TABLELANDS 91

6.32 The Crater National Park (Map 6.14)

The Crater National Park is signposted from the Kennedy Highway, about 20 km south of Atherton. The road between the highway and the car-park is good for birding with **Tooth-billed Catbird**, **Golden Bowerbird**, and **Barred Cuckoo-Shrike** (if there are fruiting trees). **Grey-headed Robins** and **Bridled Honeyeaters** are common in the car-park. From the car-park, take the track towards the crater. On the left just after the second bridge leave the track and search up the gully for ground feeders such as **Atherton Scrubwren**, **Chowchilla** and **Fernwren** as well as **Victoria's Riflebird** and **Mountain Thornbill**. Spotlighting here is good for mammals and **Lesser Sooty Owl** has been seen here although we only heard them. Close by there is a **Golden Bowerbird** site but note that the bower is only tended during the summer months; at other times of the year you may have to wait hours for the male to show up. Drive from the Crater National Park car-park a further 2.5 km south along the Kennedy Highway then turn right into a small gravel parking area. Take the track leading from the parking area. About 300 m from the start of the track (about 75 m beyond a fallen log across the trail), look for a very obscure overgrown track leading off to the right. Follow this for ~40 m to the bower. This male is quite tame and used to people. Bush camping is possible at the Crater National Park although you should obtain a permit from the Queensland National Parks and Wildlife Service at Lake Eacham.

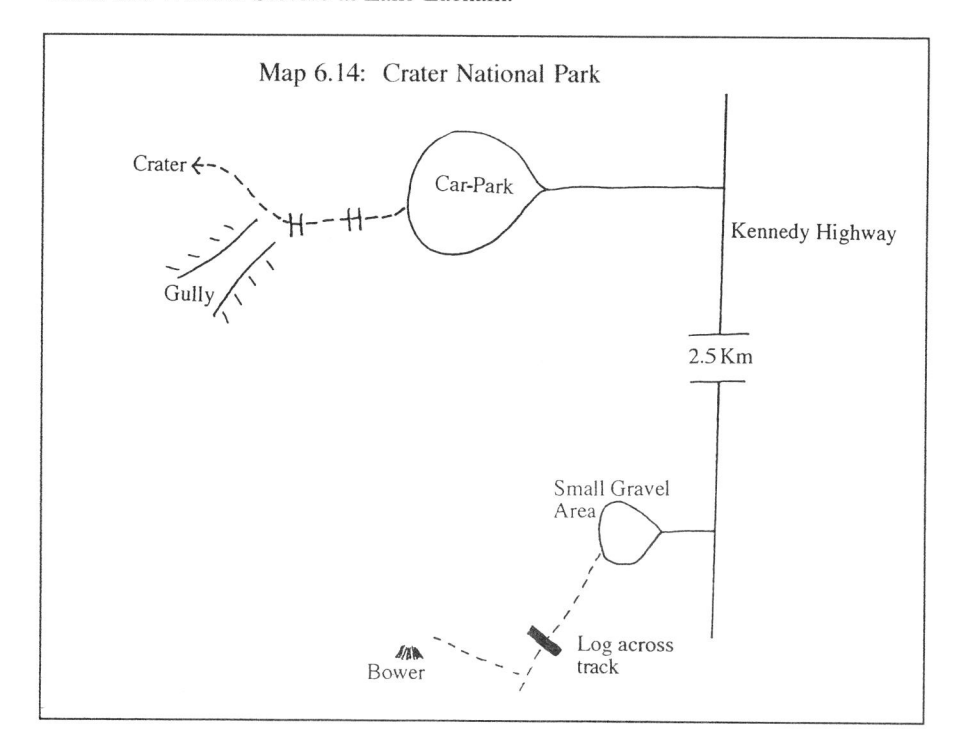

Map 6.14: Crater National Park

6.33 Hasties Swamp

Key Species: **Sarus Crane, Bush-Hen**
Hasties Swamp is situated south of Atherton. Leave Atherton on the Kennedy Highway and turn right into Hasties Road. Turn left off this into Koci Road and you will see the swamp on the right as you get to a dead end. **Sarus Cranes** regularly roost here at dusk although not if the swamp has dried up. If this is the case, try nearby Bromfield Swamp which is situated 6 km south of Malanda viewable from the Malanda to Upper Barron road. We did see two **Bush-Hens** at Hasties, however, which walked about on the road in the early morning whilst we watched from the car. Also present are **Buff-banded Rails**.

6.34 Lake Eacham and Lake Barrine

Both of these lakes are signposted off the Gillies Highway. We saw **Tooth-billed Catbird** and **Grey-headed Robin** at Lake Eacham and **Wandering Whistling-Duck** at Lake Barrine. Lake Eacham is a good area for **Pacific Baza** - try asking the rangers who see them regularly around the work shed. There is no camping at either site.

6.35 The Cathedral Fig Tree

This enormous fig tree is well signposted from the Gillies Highway along the Danbulla Forest Drive. It is a good place for pigeons if it is fruiting and also for **Bower's Shrike-Thrush** and **Pied Monarch** in the rainforest around the base of the tree.

6.36 Nardellos Lagoon

This is a large lagoon situated to the west of the Kennedy Highway, south of Mareeba. It is visible from the road and regularly holds **Cotton** and **Green Pygmy-Geese**.

6.37 Tinaroo Creek Road (Map 6.15)

Key Species: **Black Bittern, Squatter Pigeon**
For this site, turn south off the Kennedy Highway just east of Mareeba into Tinaroo Creek Road and drive along it until the bitumen ends at a cross-roads. **Squatter Pigeons** are regularly here in the early morning (best to stay in the car). Turn left at the cross-roads and on the left hand side of the track we found **Black-throated Finches** nest building beside some tall termite mounds. If you go straight on at the cross-roads, just beyond the cattle grid is another place where **Squatter Pigeons** are regularly seen feeding on the short grass on the right hand side. The track to the right at the cross-roads soon crosses a stream, walk down this stream and look for **Black Bittern** (we saw two). Other birds in this area include **Yellow Honeyeater**, **Red-backed Fairywren**, **Pheasant Coucal**,

Blue-winged Kookaburra, Channel-billed Cuckoo (common) and Silver-crowned Friarbird. Another place to try for Squatter Pigeon is on the short grassy lawn in the grounds of the Agricultural College you pass on Tinaroo Creek Road. Both Cranes are regularly found further along Henry Hannam Drive.

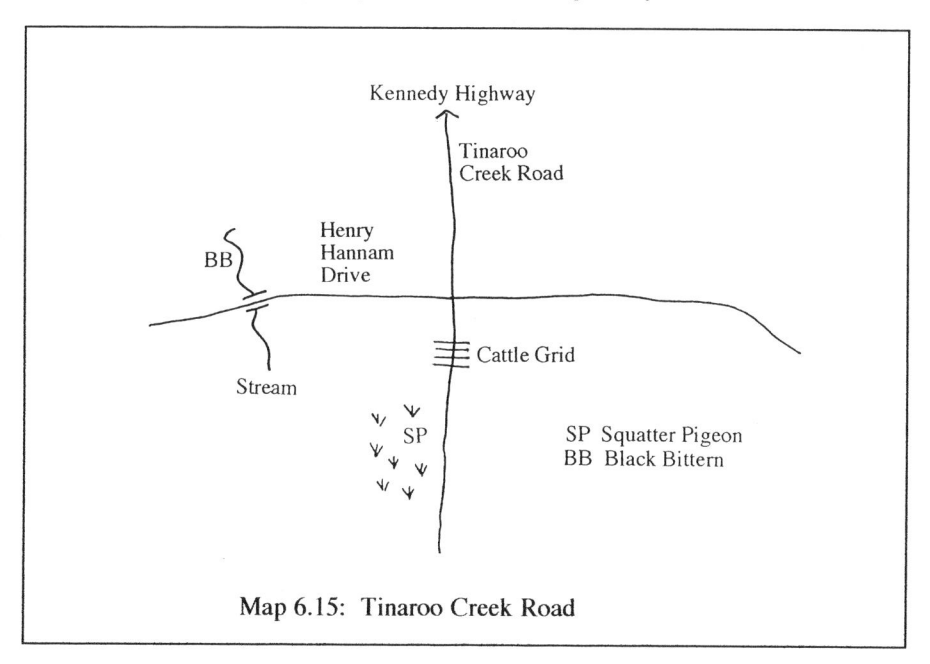

Map 6.15: Tinaroo Creek Road

6.38 Pickford Road

Key Species: **Black-throated Finch**
Pickford Road is signposted 3 km south of Biboohra on the Mareeba to Mount Molloy road, after 1 km there is a waterhole on the right hand side where **Black-throated Finches** regularly come to drink. If it is dry, search the surrounding fields and hedges for them. They have been seen in a fenced compound in a large horse paddock just north of this area.

6.39 Big Mitchell Creek

Key Species: **White-browed Robin**
This creek is signposted along the Mareeba to Mount Molloy road about 20 km north of Mareeba. Park by the bridge and walk west along the (usually) dry creek bed for **White-browed Robin** and other dry country birds. **Red Goshawk** is reputedly in this area. A **Great Bowerbird** bower is on the west side of the road, on the south side of the creek, about 50 m in.

6.40 Mount Lewis and the Julatten Area (Map 6.16)

Key Species: **Lesser Sooty Owl, Barking Owl, Masked Owl, Grass Owl, Red-necked Rail, Pied Monarch, White-eared Monarch, Yellow-breasted Boatbill, Bower's Shrike-Thrush, Chowchilla, Fernwren, Atherton Scrubwren, Mountain Thornbill, Bridled** and **Macleay's Honeyeaters, Victoria's Riflebird, Golden Bowerbird, Tooth-billed Catbird, Spotted Catbird,** *Blue-faced Parrot-Finch*

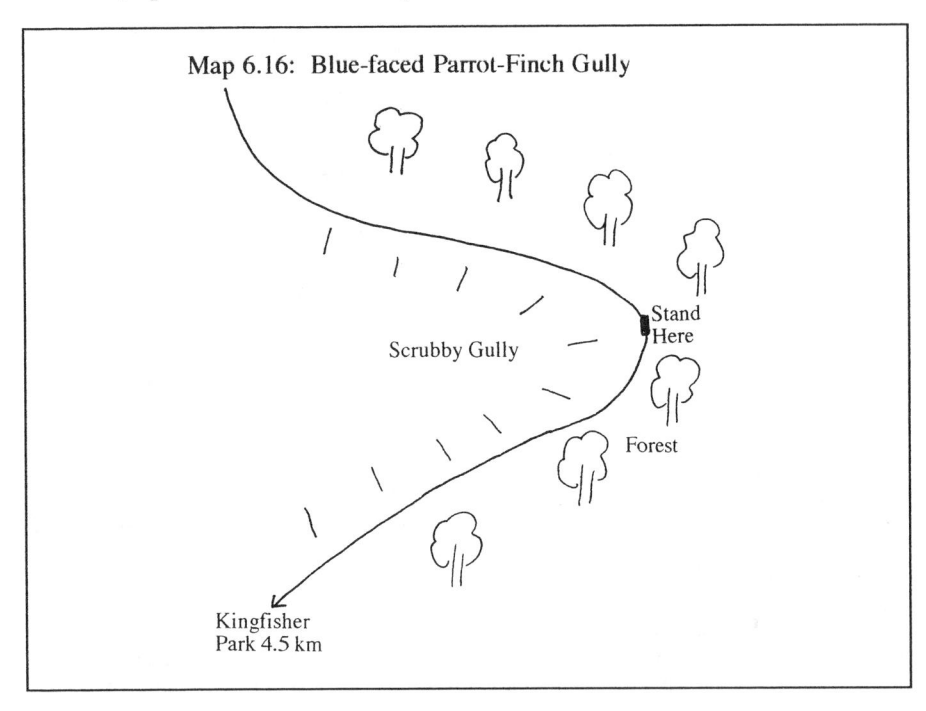

Map 6.16: Blue-faced Parrot-Finch Gully

Scrubby Gully

Stand Here

Forest

Kingfisher Park 4.5 km

This is an absolutely superb area where the *only* place to stay is Kingfisher Park which is situated off the Mossman to Mount Molloy road and is well marked. It is run by Geoff and Sandra Nicholson and you can either camp or hire a room. Geoff is a keen birder and knows all the local sites. An amazing variety of species occur either in the Park or the surrounding area. Geoff is also a bit of a spotlighting expert (he makes a small charge for spotlighting or day trips). **Barking** and **Lesser Sooty Owls** are always around and he can tell you if **Rufous, Grass** or **Masked Owls** are currently being seen. In the Park itself is a pool in the orchard which has **Red-necked Rails**, these are best seen at dusk (good with a spotlight). Around Kingfisher Park you should find **Pied Monarch, White-eared Monarch** and **Yellow-breasted Boatbill** (all fairly common if you learn their calls), **Red-necked Rail, Pacific Baza, Buff-breasted Paradise-Kingfisher** (summer only), **Macleay's Honeyeater, Wompoo** and

Superb Fruit-Doves, Bush Thick-knee (they roost on the rockery of the house opposite), *etc*. Spotlighting at night here we saw **Lesser Sooty Owl** (2), **Barking Owl** and **Papuan Frogmouth**.

The road up Mount Lewis is signposted from the main road, north of the Park. This is the most reliable site in Australia for **Blue-faced Parrot-Finch**, although they are readily seen overseas. One site for them was about 3 km along the road. There is a gully on the left hand side of a sharp bend 300 m before the state forest sign. Stand at the apex of this sharp left hand bend and view down the gully. Don't wander about or try to go down the gully as you will scare the birds off. It is best to be there when the sun hits the gully in the late morning. Listen for the call, a very high 'tsit' usually as a double note. The birds tend to fly in calling and perch in full view on top of a bush for several seconds before dropping down to cover. This is also a good spot for **Pied** and **White-eared Monarchs** and **Yellow-breasted Boatbill**. Note that **Chestnut-breasted Cuckoo** has also been seen here; check out any Fan-tailed Cuckoo type calls. A second site for **Blue-faced Parrot-Finch** is higher up the mountain when you get to a clearing, approximately 14 km from Kingfisher Park. There is now a **Golden Bowerbird** bower on one side of this clearing. The finches are regularly seen here in the early morning feeding near *Lantana* bushes, usually in the company of **Red-browed Firetails**. A track leads off to the left from this clearing through excellent rainforest. It is a good place for most of the Atherton specialities. We saw **Grey-headed Robin, Bower's Shrike-Thrush, Pied Monarch, Yellow-breasted Boatbill, Chowchilla, Fernwren, Atherton Scrubwren, Mountain Thornbill, Bridled Honeyeater, Victoria's Riflebird, Tooth-billed Catbird** and **Spotted Catbird** here. The road carries on past this clearing for another 30 km or so and this is the best place to go spotlighting. We went out with Geoff one night and saw **Lesser Sooty Owl** (perched in a roadside tree), **Southern Boobook** (of the 'red' race) and **Variable Goshawk** (they often roost in trees over the road so are easily picked up spotlighting). It is well worth spending at least two days in this area.

6.41 Abattoir Swamp

Key Species: **White-browed Crake**
Drive from Kingfisher Park towards Mount Molloy and turn left into McDougalls Road. Stop after 2 km just after you go over a creek where there is a pool on the right. **White-browed Crakes** regularly come out onto the lily pads to feed here, although when we visited this pond had dried up so Geoff took us to a private swamp nearby where we able to see at least three crakes.

6.42 Mount Carbine Road

This is the road which eventually leads up Cape York. Drive along it in the early morning checking the roadside edges for **Squatter Pigeon, Australian Bustard**, and **Black-throated Finch**.

6.43 Mount Molloy (Map 6.17)

Key Species: **Buff-breasted Button-Quail**
Head south out of Mount Molloy then turn right after a short distance into Bakers Road. You soon cross over Dairy Creek where it is worth looking for **White-browed Robin** in creekside vegetation. Follow the dirt road several kms until you pass the fourth cattle grid. Shortly after this is a short dead end track to your right and a bit further on another track off to the right. **Buff-breasted Button-Quails** are found between these two tracks. We eventually flushed a pair of near the top of the small hill where they favour the patches of open, thinner grass. Good flight views of one bird were obtained by repeatedly flushing it. Lloyd Nielson who lives in Mount Molloy has found a nest here on at least two occasions; he can be contacted for the most recent information through Geoff at Kingfisher Park. Surrounding areas with longer denser grass hold **Painted Button-Quail** so beware! Also in the area we saw a pair of **Bush Thick-knees**.

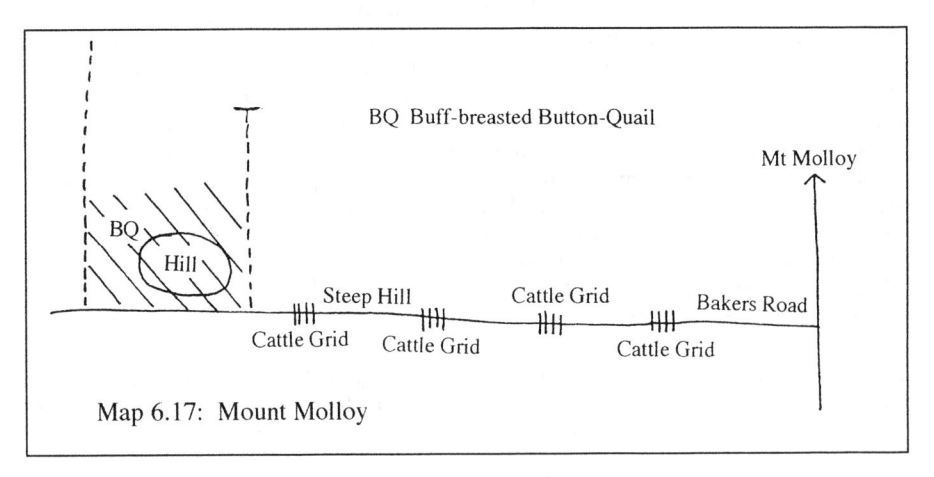

Map 6.17: Mount Molloy

F Cape York Peninsula (Map 6.18)

There are approximately 20 species of birds which are confined to the Cape York Peninsula. However, only two of these, Golden-shouldered Parrot and White-streaked Honeyeater, are actually endemic to the area, the rest also occur in New Guinea and many are widespread in other regions. Unfortunately it is not possible to see all the Cape York specialities in one visit. This is because two species, Golden-shouldered Parrot and Black-backed Butcherbird are found in the arid area in the south of the peninsula and it is only possible to drive there during the dry season (May to November) when two other species, Red-bellied Pitta and Black-winged Monarch, are wintering in New Guinea. These latter species migrate to Cape York in the wet season (December to April) to breed when the Peninsula Developmental Road will be impassable. Thus, if you are visiting Cape York in the wet season, it will be necessary to fly in, in which case you will miss the parrot and butcherbird. During this season all the other specialities can then be found at one place, Iron Range National Park and it is certainly worth making the effort to visit this park.

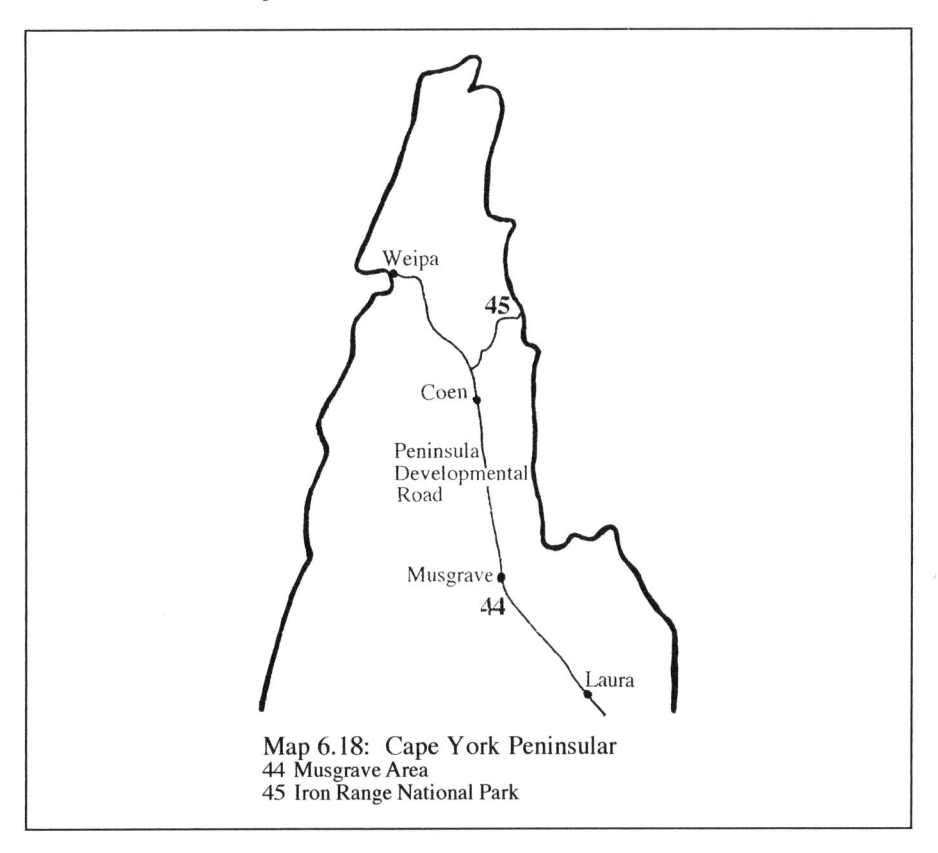

Map 6.18: Cape York Peninsular
44 Musgrave Area
45 Iron Range National Park

6.44 Musgrave Area (Map 6.19)

*Key Species: **Golden-shouldered Parrot, Black-backed Butcherbird***
Musgrave Station is approximately 310 km north of Mount Molloy along the Peninsula Developmental Road. This road should only be attempted during the dry season since during the wet season, the Morehead River floods cutting off the road for up to three months. Even during the dry season this road is extremely rough, depending on how recently it has been graded. Beyond Lakeland the road is unsealed and can be very rough, although we managed to drive it in our Kingswood stationwagon in October 1993 however, it cost us a tyre and our front number plate as well as a dent in the back when our back end slid away on a sharp, corrugated downhill bend. Beware of very deep bull dust patches particularly on small rises. The usual rules to remote travel apply; take plenty of water, fuel (supplies can be bought at Lakeland and Laura), jerry cans and food and let

someone know where you are going. Check before hand with the RACQ in Cairns on the road conditions, particularly if you are in a 2WD. The locals regarded the road as being in good condition but even so it took us seven hours of bumping along to reach Artemis Station.

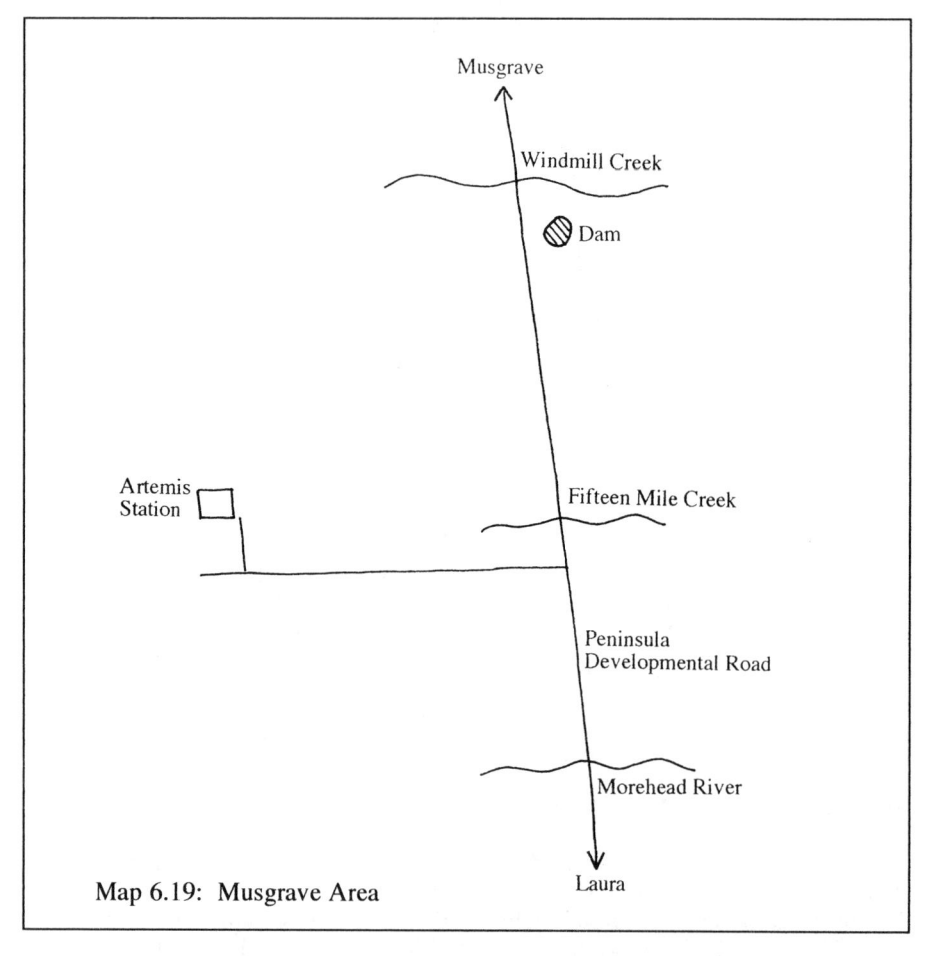

Map 6.19: Musgrave Area

To maximise your chances of seeing the parrots you should go as late as possible in the dry season (late August to November) when the birds will be coming in to drink at regular waterholes. It is also a good idea to contact the RAOU in Victoria who are currently involved in a research project on the parrot. Stephen Garnett is the person to speak to, and he may be interested to know if you can spare a few days to look for birds at other waterholes in the area. The best place to look for the parrots is around Windmill Creek, about 16 km before Musgrave and approximately 17 km beyond the Morehead River. On the right hand side of the road is a farm dam just before Windmill Creek itself. This is a regular dry season drinking dam but they could be using other nearby dams so it is essential to obtain the latest information before you go. In early October we bush camped here and saw about 25 **Golden-shouldered Parrots** coming in to drink, although only two were adult males. They flew in about an hour after dawn, drank for about 30 minutes then dispersed to feed on the ground about 300 m from the dam. Also around the dam we saw **Blue-winged Kookaburra, Red-winged Parrot, Pale-headed Rosella, Great Bowerbird, Little Friarbird, Yellow** and **Banded Honeyeaters**. It is essential to make sure you are at the dam at dawn. About 7 km south of Windmill Creek is Fifteen Mile Creek, and just beyond to the south is a turning to the west marked by an oil drum. This leads after about 1 km to Artemis Station on the right hand side. This station is run by the Shepherds and Sue Shepherd knows all about the parrots and will no doubt help you to find the birds if you get stuck. Please remember that this is private property and they are busy people, so only disturb them if you really are failing. The birds are regularly seen along the roadside between Fifteen Mile Creek and Musgrave, although the farm dams are your best bet. The other Cape York speciality in this area is **Black-backed Butcherbird** and these are fairly common along the roadside once you get north of Laura. **Pied Butcherbirds** are reasonably common here too so check carefully.

6.45 Iron Range National Park (Map 6.20)

Key Species: **Marbled Frogmouth, Rufous Owl, Double-eyed Fig-Parrot, Red-cheeked Parrot, Eclectus Parrot, Palm Cockatoo, Buff-breasted Paradise-Kingfisher** (December to March), *Yellow-billed Kingfisher, Chestnut-breasted Cuckoo, Superb Fruit-Dove, Red-bellied Pitta* (December to March), *Northern Scrub-Robin, Green-backed Honeyeater, Tawny-breasted Honeyeater, White-streaked Honeyeater,* **Fawn-breasted Bowerbird**, *White-faced Robin,* **White-eared Monarch, Frilled Monarch, Black-winged Monarch** (December to March), *Yellow-legged Flycatcher, Tropical Scrubwren, Trumpet Manucode, Magnificent Riflebird*

Iron Range National Park is situated high on the Cape York Peninsula, about 500 km north of Cairns. To get there you can either drive during the dry season, although even then a 4WD is necessary beyond the Morehead River, or you can fly with Flight West from Cairns, this is expensive, it was $154 each way in 1991. The advantage of flying is that you can get to Iron Range National Park in the wet season, when the two summer visitors come across from New Guinea to breed. Both arrive mid-late November and depart about April and, incidentally, both are relatively easy to see in New Guinea and elsewhere. We flew to Iron Range for a week over Christmas 1991. The flight from Cairns arrives at Lockhart River Airport. Just by the airport is a mission hospital and several kilometres away is the Lockhart River Township to the south and the Portland Roads township to the north. The main birding site is in the national park, around the turn off to Coen, it is about 12 km north of the airport located along the road to Portland Roads.

CHAPTER 6: QUEENSLAND

Map 6.20: Iron Range National Park

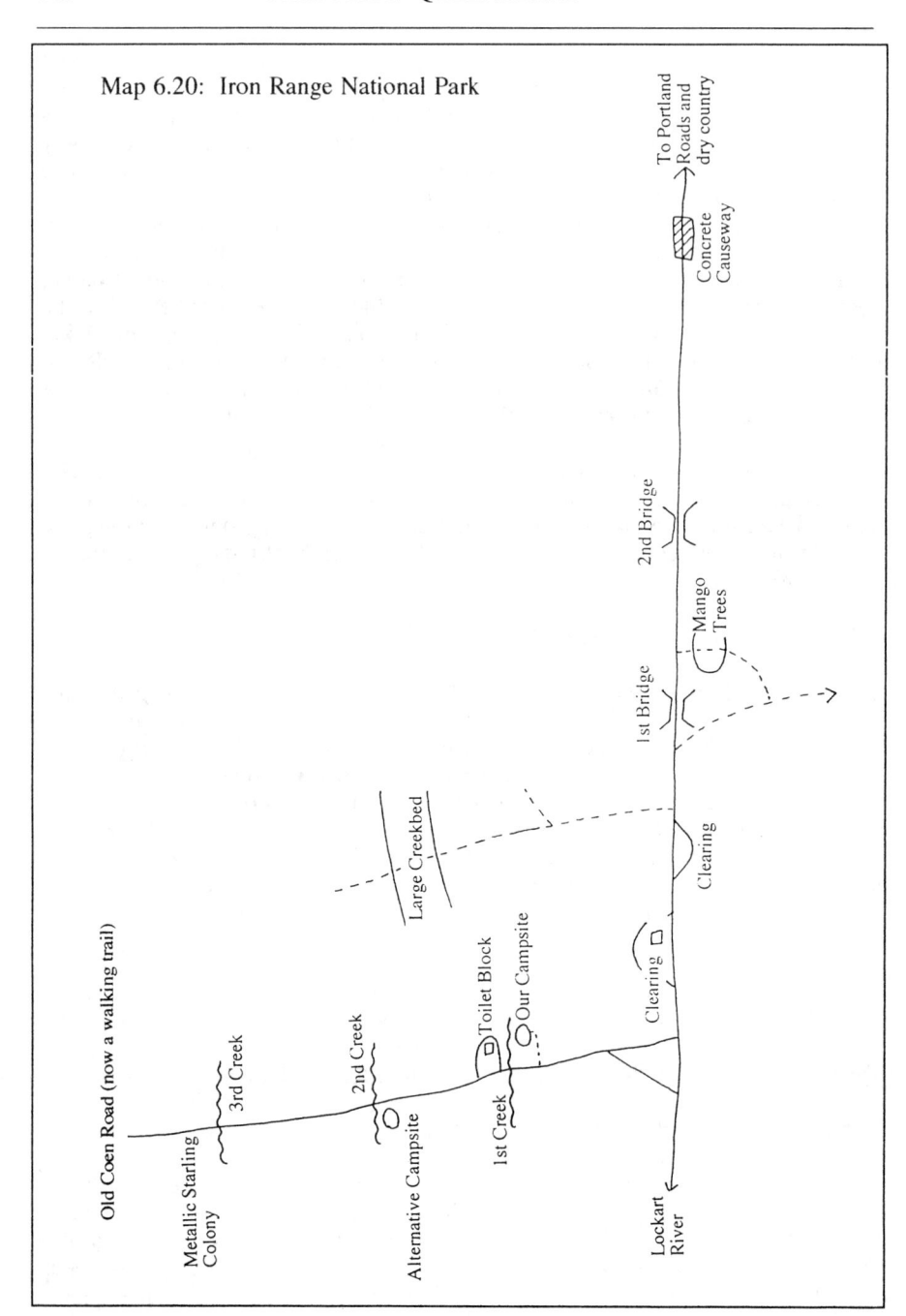

There are several ways to get there from the airport. You can decide to walk in which case you will pass the rangers house about 5.5 km from the airport. If he is around, there is a good chance he will give you a lift down to the turn off, otherwise it could be a hard slog. Alternatively there is sometimes a 'bush taxi' service from Lockhart River Airport; to book, phone Geoff or Helen Pope (070) 607193. Note that there is a new road coming in on the left, so that the Coen Road turn-off is now the second road on the left, 12 km from the airport. There are no facilities at Iron Range National Park, so where you bush camp will depend on how much water is around, there is always running water available from one of the three creeks along the Coen Road. We camped under the trees on the right just before the first creek crossing. This creek contained large pools of rainwater for drinking, although we always sterilised this water before drinking it. The second creek crossing is apparently a permanent water source; you can camp under the trees on the left just before this creek and we drank water straight from this stream with no ill effects. You should take all your own food although there is apparently a very basic store in Lockhart River Aboriginal Community, but to get there without a vehicle would take a day and would not be much fun. Whilst we were there, the mango trees were loaded with ripe fruit which made for excellent eating. You can expect rain anytime from December and although we hardly experienced any, the following year at the same time there was a cyclone in the area. It is probably wise to take a tarpaulin to put over your tent to give some protection in the event of torrential rain. Late on in the wet season, when all the creeks are full, crocodiles may be present and if you get down to the coast, don't go paddling in the sea for the same reason. Leeches may also be present in the forest although we had absolutely no problem with them and saw none, presumably because of the dry conditions. It is a good idea to take plenty of mosquito repellent, anti-fungal cream and antiseptic cream with you. Snakes are quite numerous and be very careful when spotlighting at night as they often come out onto the road after dark. Do not to go under trees which have Metallic Starling colonies in them as you can get infected by mites which get under your skin and can be a problem for several months.

All the birds are fairly straightforward to find, particularly if you have learned the calls beforehand by listening to the 'Birds of Iron Range' tape produced by R. J. Swaby and available from the RAOU. The area to concentrate on is the rainforest patches around the turn off itself and along the Portland Road. All the specialities can be seen here except the two dry country species, White-streaked Honeyeater and Fawn-breasted Bowerbird for which you will have to walk further towards Portland Roads. The best birds we recorded were as follows **Marbled Frogmouth** (2 spotlighted along Portland Road but commonly heard calling after dark), **Rufous Owl** (several heard, spotlighted on Portland Road), **Double-eyed Fig-Parrot** (rainforest edge), **Red-cheeked Parrot** (noisy and frequently seen in flight over Portland Road), **Eclectus Parrot** (noisy and conspicuous in flight), **Palm Cockatoo** (easiest to see around the causeway), **Buff-breasted Paradise-Kingfisher** (common), **Little Kingfisher, Yellow-billed Kingfisher** (2 seen, but frequently heard), **Chestnut-breasted Cuckoo** (fairly common but often perch high up), **Superb Fruit-Dove** (common), **Wompoo** and **Rose-**

crowned **Fruit-Doves**, **Red-bellied Pitta** (common and heard calling even at night, they frequently call from high up in trees), **Noisy Pitta** (fairly common), **Northern Scrub-Robin** (fairly common), **Green-backed Honeyeater** (around the toilet block), **Tawny-breasted Honeyeater** (common), **White-streaked Honeyeater** (around the causeway, but nomadic and seen wherever there are flowering eucalypt trees), **Fawn-breasted Bowerbird** (dry country up to 3 km beyond the causeway), **Great Bowerbird** (dry country), **White-faced Robin** (common), **White-eared Monarch**, **Frilled Monarch** (rainforest edges), **Black-winged Monarch** (rainforest edge), **Yellow-legged Flycatcher** (roadside rainforest, scarce), **Lemon-bellied Flycatcher**, **Broad-billed Flycatcher**, **Lovely Fairywren** (tree falls), **Tropical Scrubwren** (tree falls), **Trumpet Manucode** (fruiting trees), **Magnificent Riflebird** (common), and **White-browed Robin** (1). **Southern Cassowary** also occurs at Iron Range and is usually seen around the causeway. The mangroves at Portland Roads, some 25 km further beyond the Coen turn-off hold **Red-headed Honeyeater**, **Lesser** and **Great Frigatebirds**. Finally, there have been several sightings of **Buff-breasted Button-Quail** in the area, both in tall grasslands around the airfield and in the rainforest edges along the roadsides but they are notoriously difficult to see and may only be present in the dry season.

G North-west Queensland and the Gulf Country (Map 6.21)

If you are driving from Cairns westwards towards the Northern Territory there are a number of places which can be taken in *en route* and, although there are no essential birds to see, the journey outlined below takes you to the best sites for both White-breasted Whistler and Carpentarian Grasswren.

6.46 Georgetown Area (Map 6.22)

Key Species: **Squatter Pigeon, Black-throated Finch**

Georgetown is about 700 km south-west of Atherton, 150 km west of where the Gulf Developmental Road leaves the Kennedy Highway. Cumberland Dam, just to the west of Georgetown is famed as an excellent drinking hole particularly for finches. Drive west from Georgetown on the Gulf Developmental Road and just past the 20 km to Georgetown sign on the opposite carriageway, turn left along a dirt track towards a big chimney which is viewable from the road. Pass a small pool on your right and park at the head of the large dam. This makes an excellent camping area. Check the waters edge, particularly around the dam itself, and also the eucalypts in the dry streambed. **Pictorella Mannikin** and **Gouldian Finches** are regular here around February to April. We saw the following in October; **Squatter Pigeon**, both along the roadside between Mount Surprise and Georgetown and at Cumberland Dam, **Australian Bustard, Brolga, Cockatiel, Budgerigar, Red-winged Parrot, Pale-headed Rosella, Blue-winged Kookaburra, Yellow-tinted** and **Rufous-throated Honeyeaters, Black-throated, Masked** and **Plum-headed Finches** (the latter rare this far north-west).

Map 6.21: North-west Queensland and the Gulf Country
46 Georgetown Area
47 Karumba
48 Cloncurry
49 Mount Isa
50 Lady Loretta Project Road

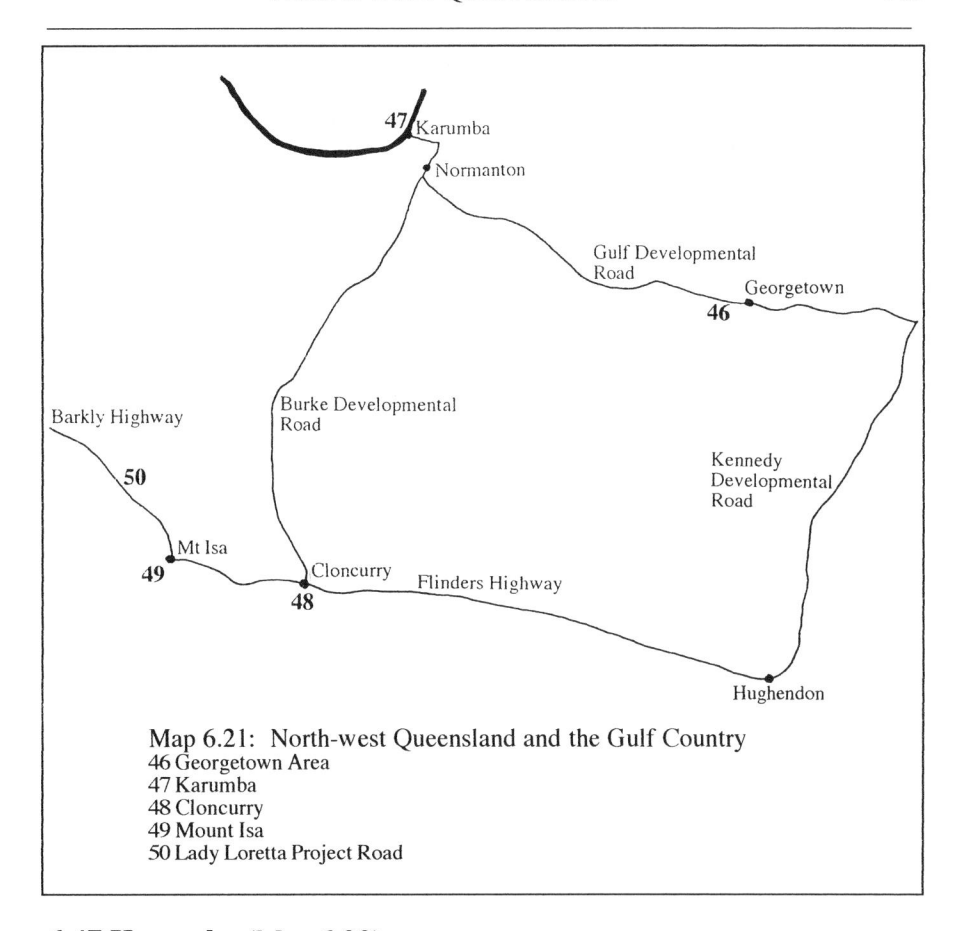

6.47 Karumba (Map 6.23)

Key Species: **White-breasted Whistler**
Karumba is rather a detour from Normanton, but well worth a visit as the mangroves here are an excellent place to see **White-breasted Whistler**, particularly as this species seems to have disappeared from many of its former haunts further west. Just east of Normanton, the Matilda Highway crosses a causeway and the pools on either side of the road hold a few birds, we saw **Brolga**, **Sarus Crane**, **Red-necked Avocet** (4) and **Marsh Sandpiper**. Past this, the Matilda Highway crosses a huge flat open plain where parties of both species of cranes feed. Also in this area, **Australian Pratincoles** are common, mostly sat on or next to the roadside. Just before you enter Karumba the tall grass area adjacent to the Highway is an excellent place to find **Zitting Cisticola**. Once at Karumba, turn right at the T-junction, drive past the school and down to the foreshore. Walk east along the edge of the mangroves, taking care to look out

for crocodiles and the state of the tide. This was the most productive area of mangroves when we visited and we recorded the following **White-breasted Whistler** (fairly common), **Red-headed Honeyeater**, **Zitting Cisticola**, **Broad-billed Flycatcher**, **Mangrove Gerygone**, **Yellow White-eye**, and **Little Bronze-Cuckoo**. The mangroves at the west end of town had similar species but were less accessible, we saw **Red-backed Kingfisher** and **Australian Bustard**. **Mangrove Robin** and also **Mangrove Golden Whistler** have been recorded at Karumba, the latter favours the larger mangrove trees, whilst White-breasted Whistlers occur in the smaller ones. We did not see Mangrove Golden Whistler here, it is much easier further west in the Northern Territory (see that section for details). Note that we also saw a **Rufous Whistler** in the mangroves at Karumba. There is an excellent caravan park and campsite in Karumba itself where we saw at least three **Barking Owls** at night.

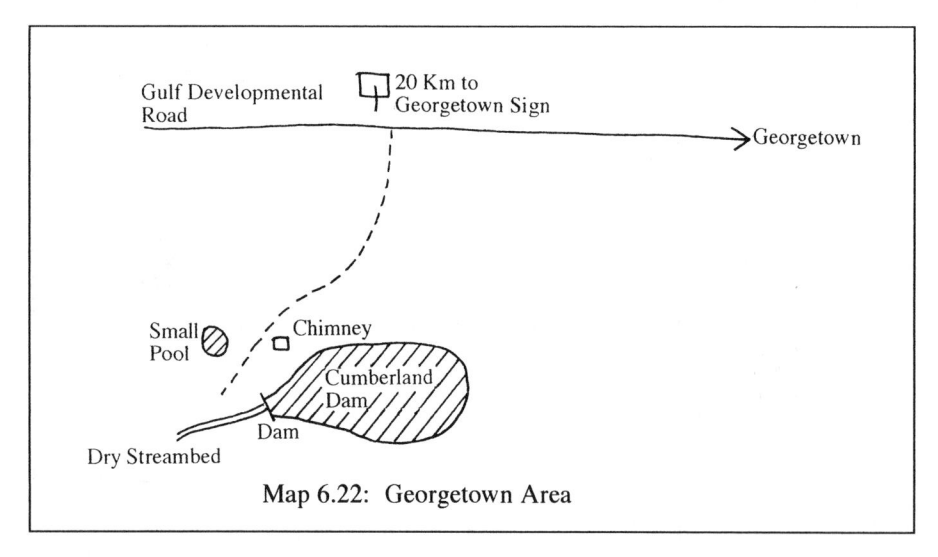

Map 6.22: Georgetown Area

6.48 Cloncurry

Key Species: Night Parrot!!!
Turn south off the Barkly Highway 9 km west of Cloncurry towards Duchess. At least two **Night Parrots** were reliably seen along the road in 1993 and according to local people, there are several around in the area! The sighting was 37 km along this road on the unsealed section of the track between Malbon and Duchess, two birds were feeding at night under a spinifex bush. One day somebody will be lucky again!

Map 6.23: Karumba

Sea

Mangroves

School

Matilda Highway

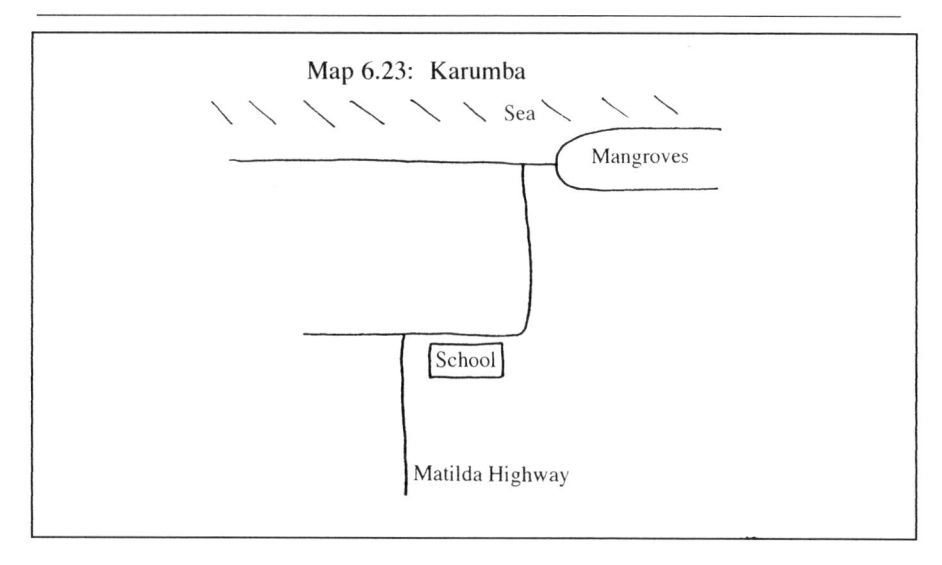

6.49 Mount Isa (Map 6.24)

Key Species: **Dusky Grasswren**
Mount Isa is a famous, sweltering, mining town and well worth visiting in order to see the isolated Queensland race of **Dusky Grasswren** which is easy to see close to the town. Leave Mount Isa southwards on the Diamantina Developmental Road and after 13 km pull off on the right hand side, just before you cross Mica Creek. Check the rocky hills to your right for the grasswrens. We recorded **Dusky Grasswren** (3), **Painted Firetail** (5) and **Little Woodswallow** here. In the dry creekbed were **Grey-headed Honeyeaters** and **Pied Honeyeater** has been recorded here in the past.

6.50 Lady Loretta Project Road

Key Species: **'Cloncurry' Ringneck, Carpentarian Grasswren, Golden-backed Honeyeater**
This is easily the most accessible place to see the recently discovered **Carpentarian Grasswrens** near Mount Isa. They are apparently an isolated population from those near Boroloola and their habitat is certainly very different and they may yet prove to be a distinct species, although further study is needed. One can only hope that Australia's taxonomists will wake up to the fact that the study of birds can be undertaken without the need to go shooting them out of existence. Worries about this kind of behaviour happening here meant that this site was kept secret for some time. To reach the site, drive north out of Mount Isa on the Barkly Highway and after 66 km turn right, just before the 120 km to Camooweal sign, onto a dirt road marked to Lady Loretta Project. Drive along this road to two dry creek crossings at 7.8 km and 8.2 km from the turning. The

grasswrens are on the east side of the road between the two creeks in the tallest spinifex patches. In this area we saw **Carpentarian Grasswrens** (3, along the creek at 8.2 km), **Spinifexbird, 'Cloncurry' Ringneck** and **Golden-backed Honeyeater**. Carpentarian Grasswren is reputedly the shiest of all grasswrens, so be prepared to put some time in looking for them, and be patient. It took us an evening plus a full morning to find them and they were very shy, although inquisitive. Bush camping only is possible here.

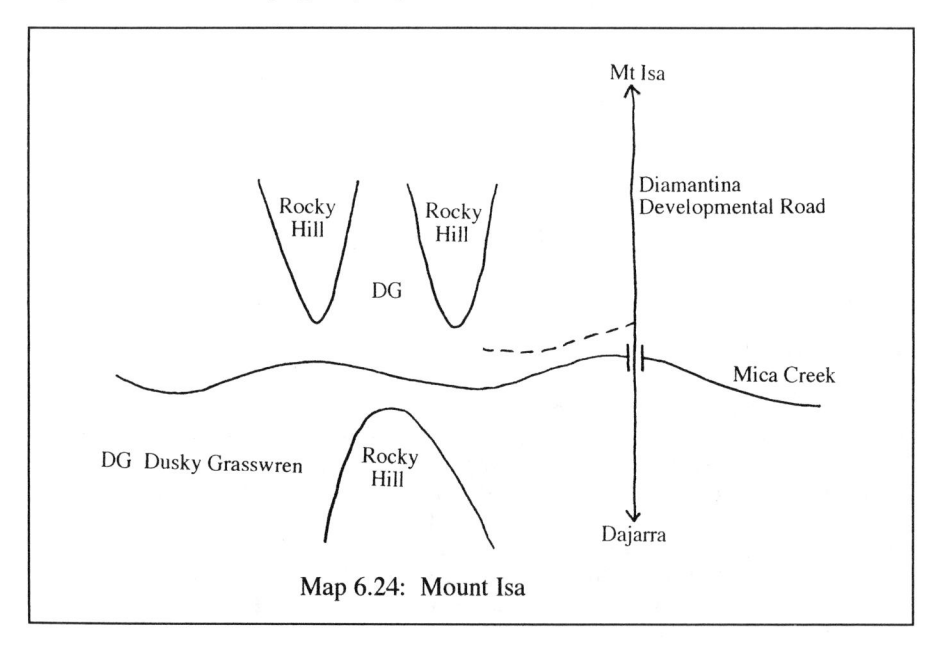

Map 6.24: Mount Isa

CHAPTER 7

NORTHERN TERRITORY

Rainbow Pitta, a delightful Pitta, found only in the Top End of Australia

CHAPTER 7: NORTHERN TERRITORY

Introduction (Map 7.1)
The Northern Territory is a huge area with habitat ranging from true red outback to tropical rainforests and coastal mangroves. This makes for some of the most challenging and exciting birding in Australia.

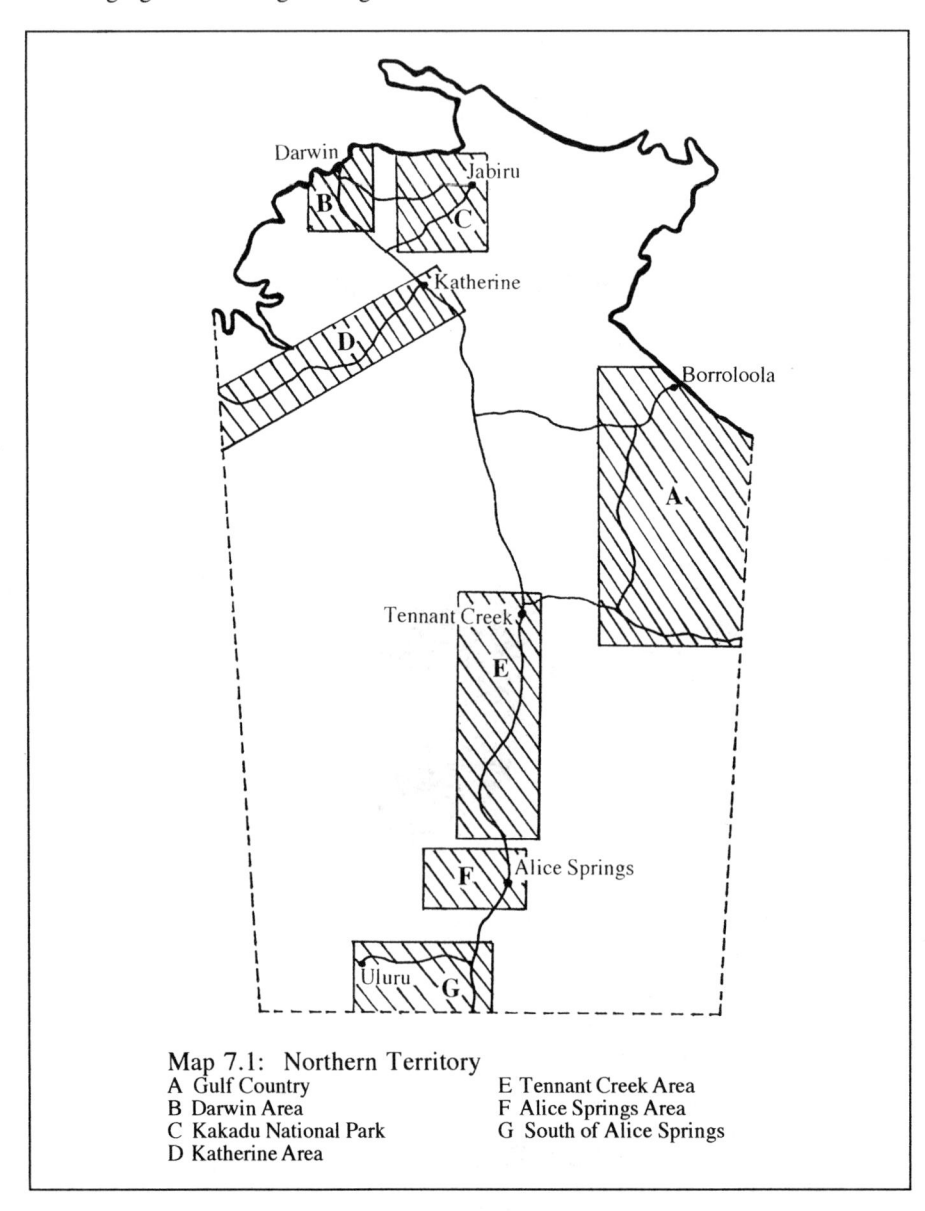

Map 7.1: Northern Territory
A Gulf Country
B Darwin Area
C Kakadu National Park
D Katherine Area
E Tennant Creek Area
F Alice Springs Area
G South of Alice Springs

Endemics: Chestnut-quilled Rock-Partridge, Black-banded Fruit-Dove, Hooded Parrot, White-throated Grasswren, Brown Whistler
Specialities: Pied Heron, Green Pygmy-Goose, Black-breasted Buzzard, Red Goshawk, Blue-breasted Quail, Red-backed Button-Quail, Chestnut-backed Button-Quail, Swinhoe's Snipe (summer), Flock Bronzewing, Partridge Pigeon, Varied Lorikeet, Rainbow Pitta, Great Bowerbird, Purple-crowned Fairywren, Rufous-crowned Fairywren, Green-backed Gerygone, White-lined Honeyeater, Rufous-banded Honeyeater, Grey Honeyeater

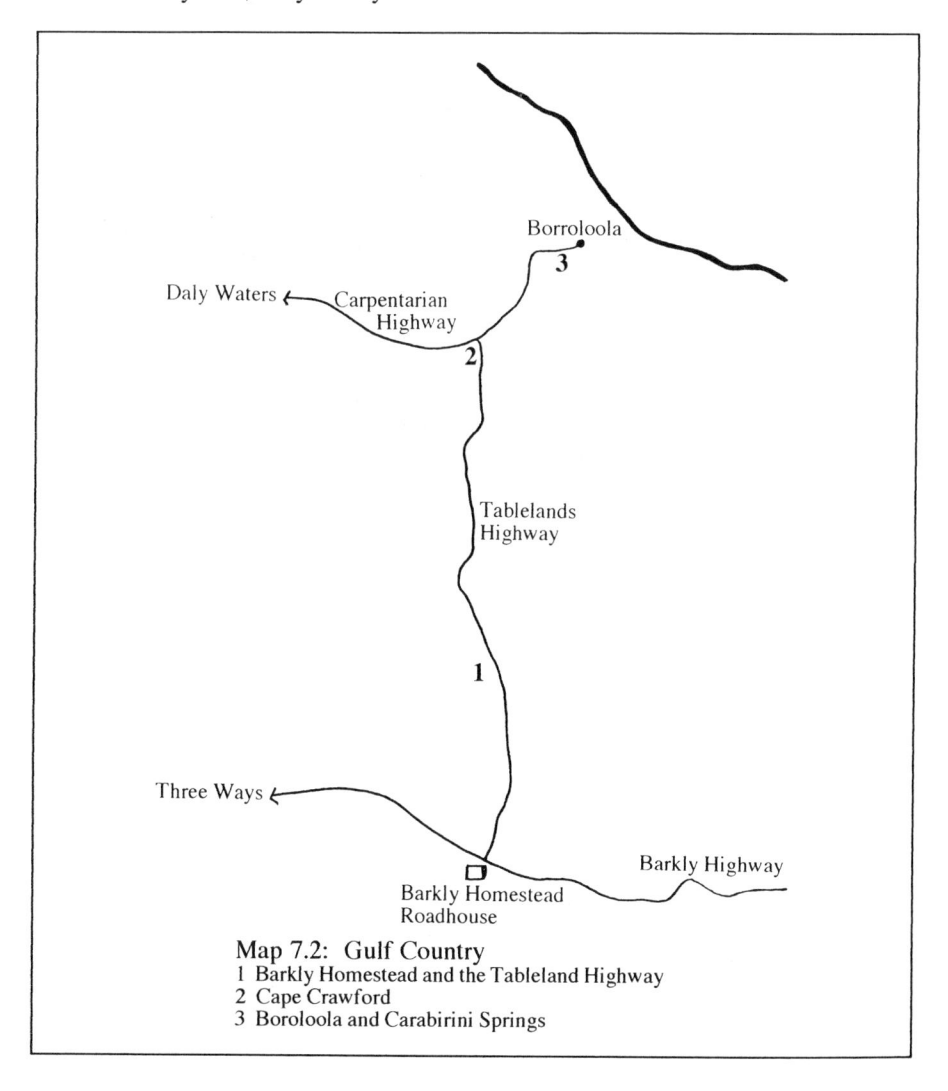

Map 7.2: Gulf Country
1 Barkly Homestead and the Tableland Highway
2 Cape Crawford
3 Boroloola and Carabirini Springs

A The Gulf Region (Map 7.2)

The Gulf Region is a large area of land covering parts of Queensland and the Northern Territory, that is somewhat ignored by the visiting birder. However there are several important birding sites to visit.

7.1 Barkly Homestead and the Tableland Highway

Key Species: **Black Falcon, Letter-winged Kite, Flock Bronzewing, Red-chested Button-Quail, Yellow Chat**

We drove to Barkly Homestead from Mount Isa along the Barkly Highway. This highway crosses the flat grassy tablelands and is good for raptors, we recorded **Black Falcon** (2) and several **Spotted Harriers** on the journey. Any of the water bores along this road are worth bush camping by, to see if **Flock Bronzewings** come in to drink in the evening or early morning; this species is highly nomadic but should be somewhere in the area, you just have to be lucky. We turned north at Barkly Homestead along the Tableland Highway and after 50 km we found a **Letter-winged Kite** just by the Alroy Downs station turn off. We drove slowly up the highway in the late afternoon and found another 22 kites in the next 10 km of road, many actually sat on the tarmac! We camped at the roadside here and next morning saw 32 **Letter-winged Kites** in the area. This region is well known as a regular haunt of this species and it is well worth driving the Tableland Highway in the late afternoon / early evening. Both **Yellow Chat** and **Flock Bronzewing** have been seen at the water bore close to the road 21 km north of the Playford River crossing, and the latter has been seen at the bore on the east side of the highway, 5.7 km north of the turn-off to Elliot. A driveable track leads 1 km to the water bore just before the floodway. Check the surrounding grassland for **Red-chested Button-Quail**. Other birds we saw on the drive from Alroy Downs to Cape Crawford included **Black Falcon** (1), **Australian Pratincole** (6), **Spotted Harrier** (4), **Ground Cuckoo-Shrike** (6) plus many **Budgerigars**. When you cross the McArthur River, just south of Cape Crawford, it is worth stopping and checking the trees alongside the bridge, we saw a few common species such as **Blue-Winged Kookaburra, White-gaped** and **Yellow-tinted Honeyeaters** and **Long-tailed** and **Crimson Finches**.

7.2 Cape Crawford

Water sprinklers on the grass around the petrol station at Cape Crawford attract a good variety of birds coming to drink. Some of the birds we recorded in mid October 1993 were **Spinifex Pigeon** (2), **Silver-crowned** and **Little Friarbirds, Great Bowerbird, Red-collared Lorikeet, Banded, Yellow-tinted, Blue-faced, Golden-backed** and **Rufous-throated Honeyeaters, White-winged Triller, Double-barred** and **Long-tailed Finches** and **Collared Sparrowhawk**.

7.3 Boroloola and Caranbirini Springs (Map 7.3)

Key Species: **Carpentarian Grasswren, Sandstone Shrike-Thrush**
This area, 40 km before Boroloola on the Carpentaria Highway was formerly the only readily accessible site to see **Carpentarian Grasswren**, before their discovery near Mount Isa (see section 6.50). Although we failed to see them here it was the only place that we saw **Sandstone Shrike-Thrush**. After you pass the Boroloola 40 km post you first cross a floodway, then a cattle grid after about 500 m. Park here and follow the fence at right angles to the road and up the first escarpment. Carry on to the second escarpment and wide valley and check the rocky spinifex boulders. Take a compass and water as it is very easy to get lost. Some people see the grasswrens easily, but others struggle, we saw no sign of them although we only looked briefly. Birds we saw in the area were **Sandstone Shrike-Thrush, Spinifex Pigeon, Spotted Nightjar,** and **Little Button-Quail.**

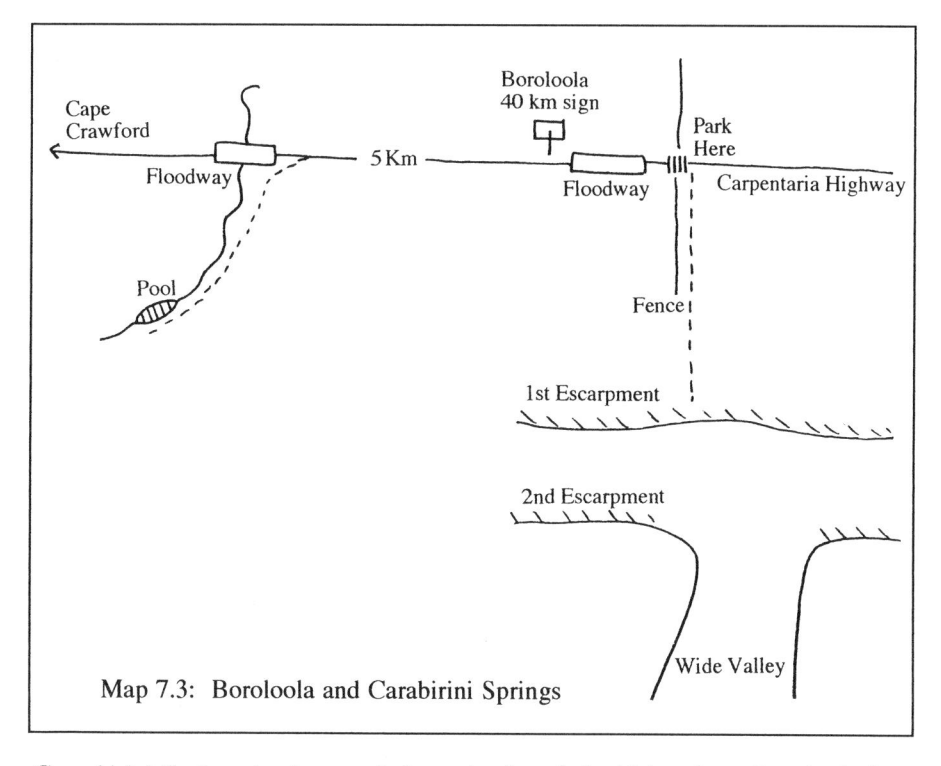

Map 7.3: Boroloola and Carabirini Springs

Caranbirini Springs is also worth investigating, it is 45 km from Boroloola just after you cross the floodway on the Carpentaria Highway coming from Cape Crawford. A dirt track goes off to the south, walk along this and view the springs to your right. Unfortunately cattle have smashed down most of the waterside vegetation making it no longer attractive to Lilac-crowned Fairywrens. The roadside signpost has also disappeared. We did see a good selection of commoner birds here however, such as the following, **Brolga, Rufous Night-Heron, Green Pygmy-Goose, White-throated, Yellow-tinted, Banded** and **White-gaped Honeyeaters, Little Friarbird, Great Bowerbird, Australian Hobby, Common Bronzewing, Northern Rosella, Blue-winged Kookaburra** and **Brown Quail**. In addition, this is a fairly good dry season drinking pool for finches including **Gouldian Finch** and **Pictorella Mannikin**. Bush camping only is available.

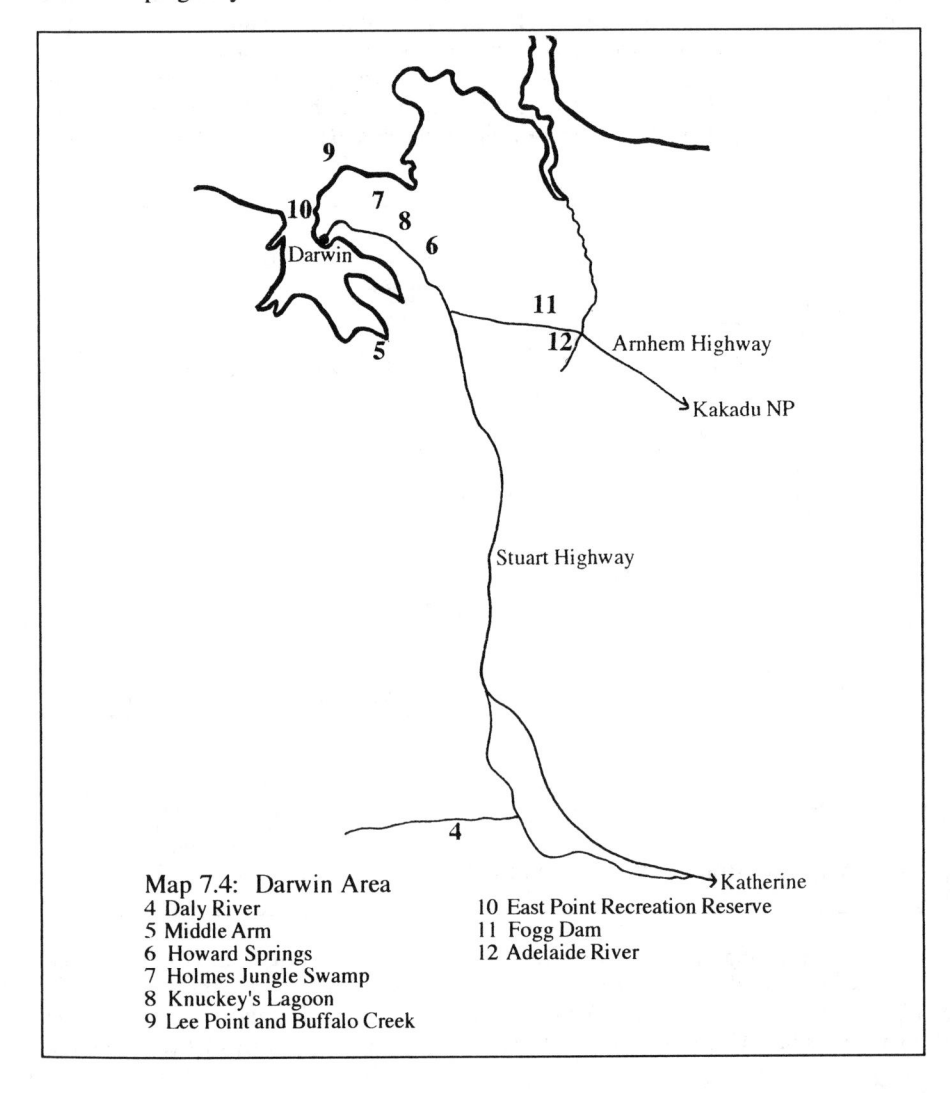

Map 7.4: Darwin Area
4 Daly River
5 Middle Arm
6 Howard Springs
7 Holmes Jungle Swamp
8 Knuckey's Lagoon
9 Lee Point and Buffalo Creek
10 East Point Recreation Reserve
11 Fogg Dam
12 Adelaide River

B Darwin Area (Map 7.4)

Darwin and the immediate vicinity of the city has many excellent birding sites making it a good base from which to explore. Indeed, in late spring, when we were there, nearly every football pitch, even roadside verges, has a flock of Little Curlews on it. Oriental Plovers similarly occur in big numbers at this time of year. This part of Australia is where you probably stand the greatest chance of finding a rarity - indeed whilst we were there an Elegant Imperial-Pigeon, a bird from the Aru Islands of Indonesia, was discovered in the suburb of Nightcliff, where we were actually staying. Unfortunately we didn't hear of its discovery until we had driven to Alice Springs! More than a year later the bird was still present, and according to local people had been for some time, so check with local birders if it is still about when you visit. Some of the better places to visit near the city are given below.

7.4 Daly River (Map 7.5)

Key Species: **Rufous Owl**

Unfortunately, when we visited this site we were hit by the heaviest thunderstorm I have ever experienced and we didn't see the owl, however, it was seen here shortly afterwards. Turn off the Stuart Highway 116 km south of Darwin at Adelaide River towards Daly River. Turn right after 33 km on the road to Daly River and stop after 10 km when you cross the Adelaide River. The remnant rainforest south of the bridge has a **Rufous Owl** which regularly calls from the isolated tree next to the road and can be easily spotlighted. We dipped but did see **Varied Lorikeet** (40), **Bush Thick-knee** (1), **Tawny Frogmouth** (1) and heard **Australian Owlet-Nightjar**.

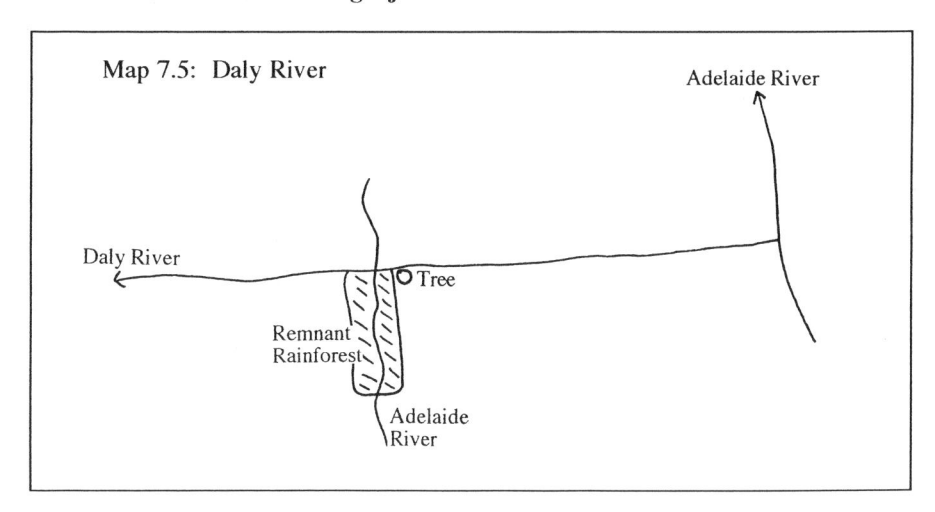

Map 7.5: Daly River

7.5 Middle Arm

Key Species: **Great-billed Heron, Chestnut Rail**
This is without doubt the easiest place to see both **Great-billed Heron** and **Chestnut Rail**, although a telescope may be necessary. Leave Darwin south on the Stuart Highway and turn right after 46 km signposted to Berry Springs. After 2 km turn right onto the dirt road to Middle Arm. When you get to the crossroads go straight on. The road between here and the boat ramp is good for **Partridge Pigeons** in the early morning. We found the best technique at Middle Arm was to sit on the boat ramp with a mounted telescope and wait. We spent almost two days here but were rewarded with superb views of a **Chestnut Rail** as it crossed the boat ramp twice only feet away from us. Apart from this individual we only saw them feeding out on the mud on the opposite bank at low tide. Eventually a **Great-billed Heron** appeared on our side of the inlet then flew over to the far bank and began fishing along it. Whilst waiting we saw the following species of note, **Little** (1), **Azure** and **Collared Kingfishers**, **Red-headed Honeyeater**, **Broad-billed** (1) and **Shining Flycatchers**, **Large-billed Gerygone**, **Black Butcherbird** and **Varied Lorikeet** (30). We camped close to the boat ramp and at dusk saw several **Large-tailed Nightjars** and a **Bush Thick-knee**.

7.6 Howard Springs Nature Park (Map 7.6)

Key Species: **Rainbow Pitta**

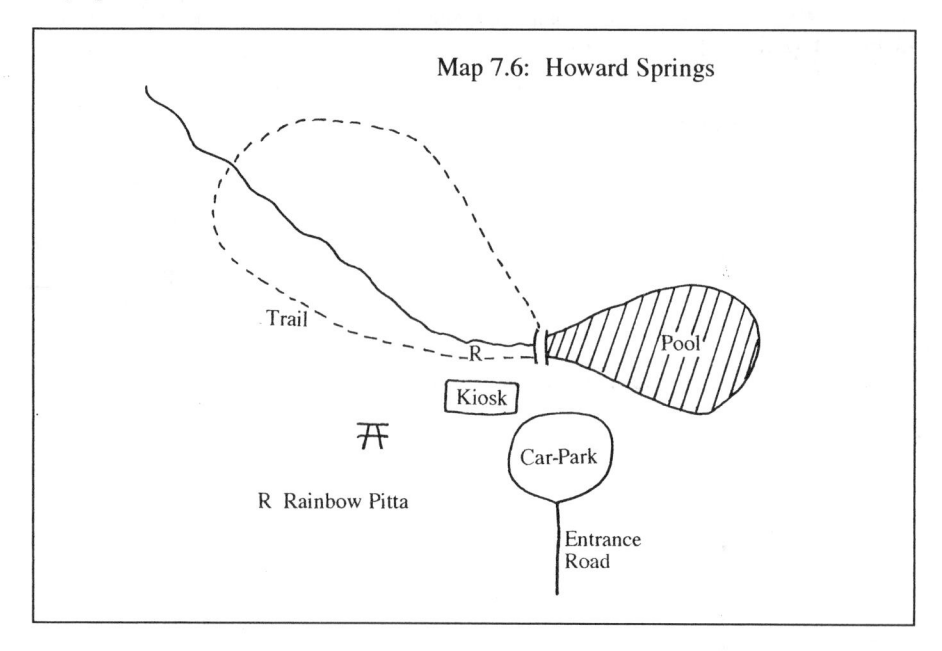

Map 7.6: Howard Springs

R Rainbow Pitta

Howard Springs is most noted as *the* place to see **Rainbow Pitta**. The birds are tame and confined to the tiny patches of rainforest around the springs. The nature park is well signposted off the Stuart Highway 30 km east of Darwin. Follow the signs to the car-park and turning circle at the end. Take the walking track which goes around the edge of the rainforest beside the stream. The pittas occur mainly close to the footbridge and are easily seen. Keep a look out for other rainforest species. We saw **Rainbow Pitta** (2), **Varied Triller, Orange-footed Scrubfowl, Shining Flycatcher, Blue-winged Kookaburra, Yellow Oriole** and **Forest** and **Azure Kingfishers**. **Rufous Owl** is said to occur although you are not allowed to stay overnight in the park and **Black Bitterns** are often seen around the lake at dusk.

7.7 Holmes Jungle Swamp (Map 7.7)

Key Species: **Red-backed Button-Quail, Blue-breasted Quail**

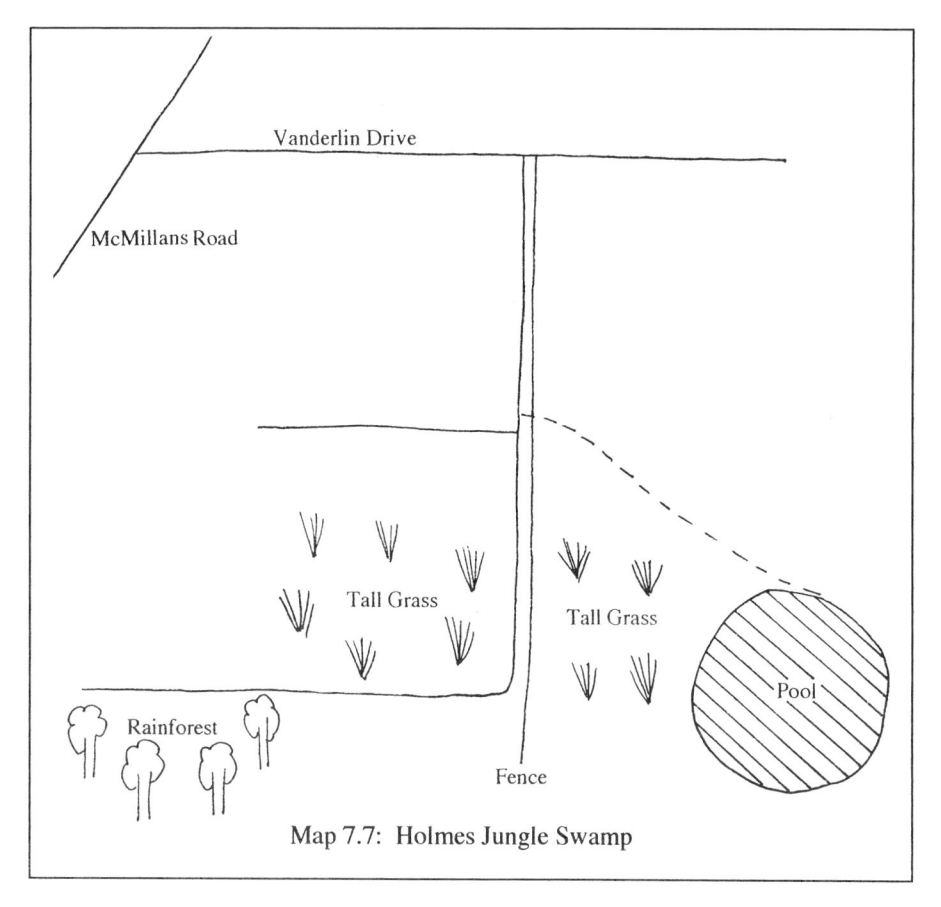

Map 7.7: Holmes Jungle Swamp

Not the most inspiring place to go birding, but about the only place where **Red-backed Button-Quails** are resident. Turn east off the Stuart Highway onto MacMillans Road, in the suburb of Karama. At the roundabout, turn right along Vanderlin Drive then after 1 km turn right along the dirt track which is signposted to the swamp. After 2.5 km, the road does a very sharp right hand bend. Park here and check the areas of tall grass to your right and also the other side of the fence. We eventually flushed the following, **Blue-breasted Quail** (1+), **Brown Quail** (10) and **Red-Backed Button-Quail**. Also **Tawny Frogmouth** (1) and **Zitting Cisticola** (5). A driveable track led to a drying up pool the other side of the fence which was good for waders, **Red-necked Stint** (1), **Sharp-tailed Sandpiper** (2), and **Pacific Golden Plover** (2) were all present as well as hundreds of **Magpie Geese**.

7.8 Knuckey's Lagoon (Map 7.8)

Key Species: **Swinhoe's Snipe** (Austral summer)
Knuckey's Lagoon is a small marsh, known locally as the best spot for **Swinhoe's Snipe**, **Garganey** and **Yellow Wagtail**, all three are annual arriving in early to mid November, although we saw none of them in late October 1993. Turn off the Stuart Highway between Darwin and Palmerston into Lagoon Road. Look for the marsh on your right hand side which is easily visible from Lagoon Road, before you get to Secrett Road. Walk down to the waters edge and tramp around for snipe *etc*. Birds we recorded included **Little Curlew** (50), **Sharp-tailed Sandpiper** (10), **Australian Pratincole** (10), **Common Sandpiper** (2), **Tawny Grassbird**, **Zitting Cisticola**, **Radjah Shelduck**, **Black-necked Stork** (2) and **Australasian Bushlark**.

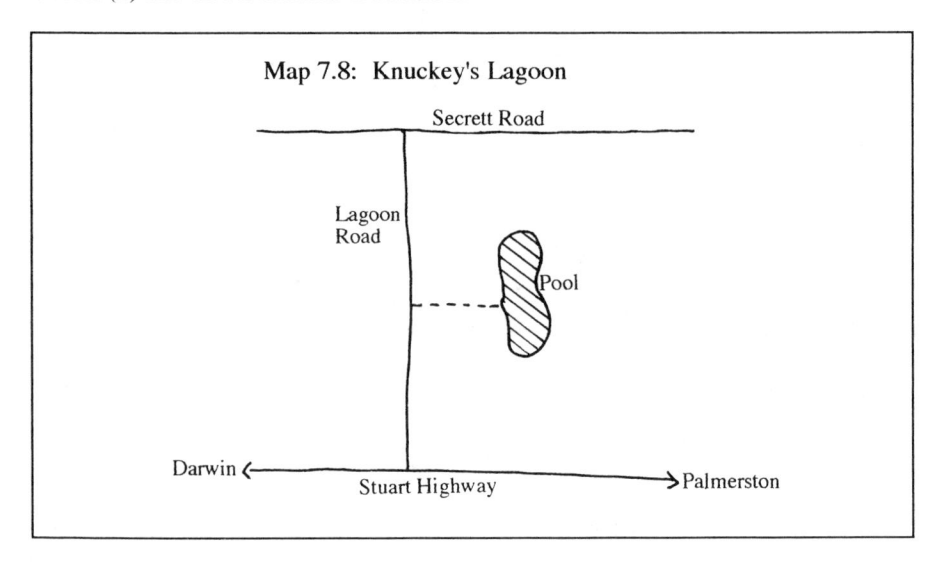

Map 7.8: Knuckey's Lagoon

7.9 Lee Point and Buffalo Creek

Key Species: **Oriental Plover** (October/November)
Lee Point Road is a turning off MacMillans Road. Follow the road and check the short grassy RAAF fields with radio masts on them (after you pass Fitzmaurice Road) for Oriental Plovers which are regularly seen here on migration. Buffalo Creek is a right turning 1 km south of Lee Point itself. Follow the road to the car-park and boat ramp. We saw a pair of **Chestnut Rails** in the mangroves opposite this boat ramp and in bushes around the car-park were **Green-backed Gerygone** (1), **Grey Whistler** (3, race *simplex*), **Varied Triller** (2) and **Yellow White-eye**. On the beach we saw **Black-tailed Godwit** (30), **Great Knot** (30), **Greenshank** (1), **Pacific Golden Plover** (2), **Grey Plover** (1) and **Eastern Curlew** (10). The mangroves around here are one of the few sites where **White-breasted Whistlers** have been seen in recent years.

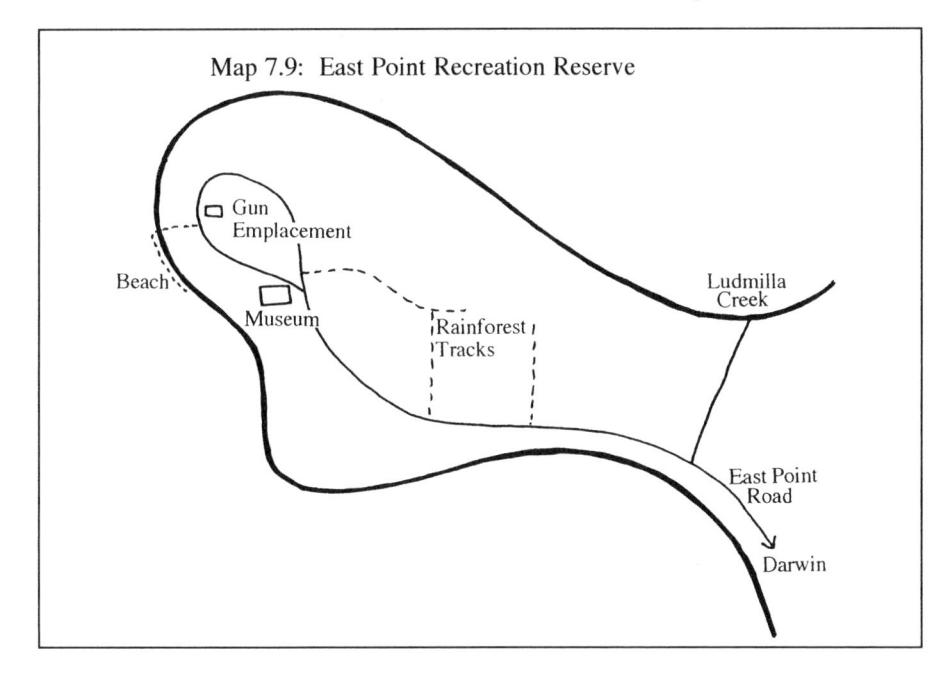

Map 7.9: East Point Recreation Reserve

7.10 East Point Recreation Reserve (Map 7.9)

Key Species: **Green-backed Gerygone**
This reserve is reached from Darwin by driving north along Gilruth Avenue then turning left along East Point Road. Stop in the car-parks and explore the rainforest tracks, **Green-backed Gerygones** are common and have a strange reeling song, we also recorded **Rose-crowned Fruit-Dove** and **Rainbow Pitta** here. The walking track below the gun emplacement along the beach is a good site

for **Beach Thick-knee**. The mangroves at Ludmilla Creek Boatyard are also worth a look for birds such as **Red-headed** and **Rufous-banded Honeyeaters**, **Collared Kingfisher** and **Little Bronze Cuckoo**.

7.11 Fogg Dam

Key Species: **Rose-crowned Fruit-Dove**
Fogg Dam is an excellent wetland area, it is well signposted off the Arnhem Highway, about 32 km east if its junction with the Stuart Highway. Drive to the car-park and either explore the marsh from the top of the dam wall on foot or by car. The forest walk signposted from the car-park is also worth doing and is a very reliable locality for **Rose-crowned Fruit-Dove**. In the wetland area we recorded the following, **Magpie Goose** (1000's), **White-browed Crake** (1), **Common**, **Wood** (1) and **Marsh Sandpipers**, **Little Curlew** (30), **Green Pygmy-Goose**, **Radjah Shelduck**, **Wandering Whistling-Duck**, **Whiskered Tern**, **Comb-crested Jacana**, **Egrets**, **Straw-necked** and **Australian Ibises**, **Golden-headed Cisticola** and **Crimson Finch**. Whilst along the rainforest walk we saw **Rainbow Pitta** (2), **Rose-crowned Fruit-Dove** (2) and **Lemon-bellied Flycatchers**, it is also a good site for **Broad-billed Flycatcher**. Also worth visiting is Leaning Tree Lagoon, situated about 20 kilometres further east and well signposted off the Arnhem Highway. This lagoon has **Red-backed Button-Quail** in the grass around the fringes of the lagoon and is good for waders and waterfowl, including regular **Garganey** in early summer. Camping is not allowed.

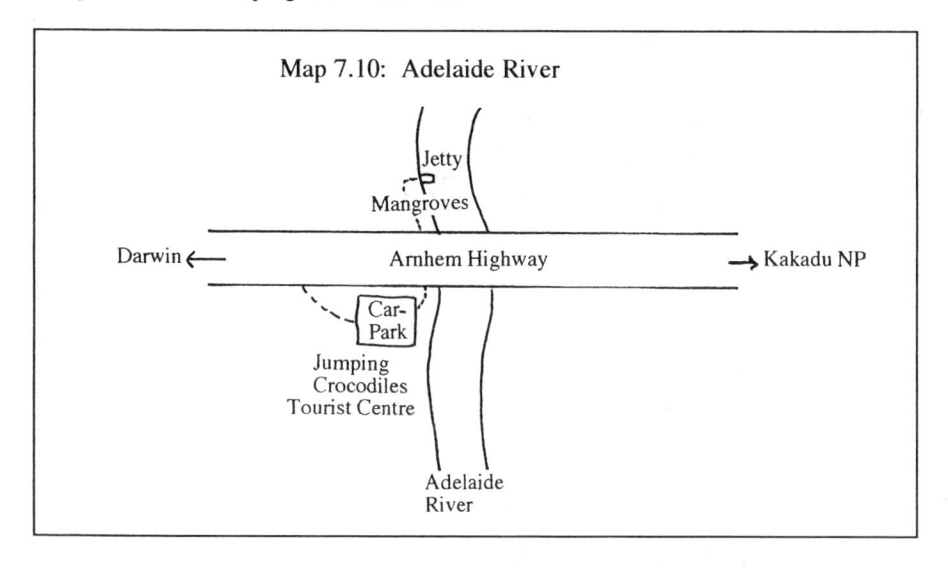

Map 7.10: Adelaide River

7.12 Adelaide River (Map 7.10)

Key Species: **Mangrove Golden Whistler**
The mosquitoes here are both numerous and very vicious, probably the worst we encountered in Australia. The site is 33 km east of where the Arnhem Highway joins the Stuart Highway. Park in the 'Jumping Crocodiles Tourist Centre' carpark and bird the mangroves on the other side of the road, either from the bridge itself or the path that runs under it. If the track to the landing stage is open, this gives the best access to the mangroves, however, the mosquitoes are at their worst here. We recorded the following **Rufous-banded Honeyeater, Restless, Shining, Broad-billed** (1) and **Lemon-bellied Flycatchers, Little Bronze Cuckoo, White-browed Crake** (1), **Yellow Oriole, Mistletoebird, Varied Triller** (1) and **Mangrove Golden Whistler** (1). In addition **Great-billed Heron** has been seen flying along the river here, and you might try one of the river cruises to look for them.

C Kakadu National Park (Map 7.11)

Kakadu National Park is world famous, noted for its aboriginal paintings and sacred sites, it is also the best area to get to grips with the Arnhem Land specialities and also excellent for waterbirds and crocodiles. The main park headquarters is located 2.5 km south of Jabiru on the Kakadu Highway, but there are two entrance stations, one is on the Arnhem Highway about 43 km west of Kakadu Holiday Village and the other is on the Kakadu Highway about 59 km from Pine Creek. There is a park entrance fee of $10 per person per week payable at either entrance station where you should also find out information about the various campsites and road conditions. Many roads will be impassable in the wet season so a visit in the dry season is recommended, we visited in late October 1993. The whole park is good for the elusive Red Goshawk; indeed this is their major stronghold. They nest and hunt mainly in rainforest along large rivers such as the Wildman and West Alligator Rivers. Despite spending six days and seeing fourteen species of raptor in the park, we never connected with a Red Goshawk, although apparently they are considerably easier to see in July/August when they occasionally display over the treetops. Try quizzing the rangers in Kakadu for recent sites, but don't expect to get far. The following are the most important bird sites in the park to visit.

7.13 Arnhem Highway

The Arnhem Highway is reputed to cross through the best areas to see **Red Goshawk**. We completely failed. Good areas are supposed to be where the road crosses the various branches of the West Alligator River and also the Wildman River crossings. We tried camping at Two Mile Hole campsite, just east of the entrance station, to look for this species, but saw little there except the following; **Australasian Koel, Varied Lorikeet** (120), **Torresian Imperial-Pigeon, Shining Bronze** and **Pallid Cuckoos.** Around the entrance gates of the CSIRO research station at Kapalga (you are not allowed in there under any circumstances) we saw **Black-tailed Treecreeper** (2) and **Partridge Pigeon** (5). Also along the highway we saw **Brown Goshawk** (2), **Australian Hobby** (2), **Black-breasted Buzzard** (1), **Little Eagle, Brahminy, Whistling** and **Black Kites** and **Spotted harrier** (1).

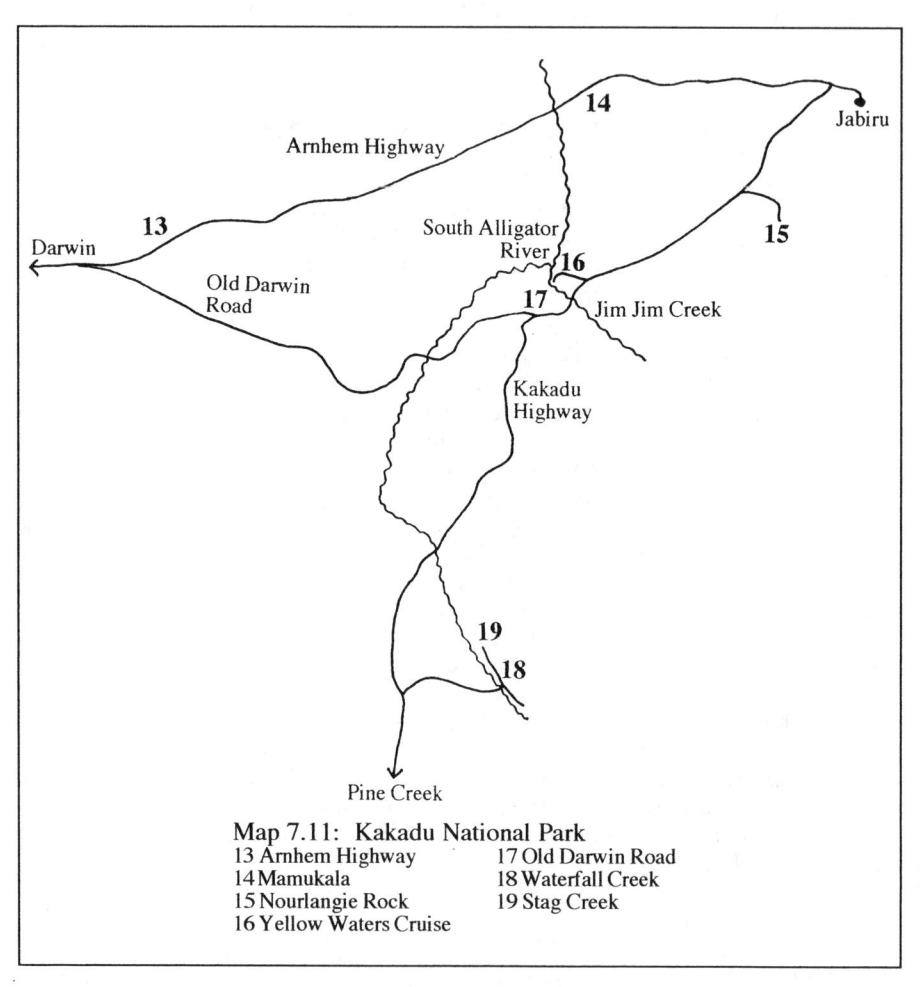

Map 7.11: Kakadu National Park
13 Arnhem Highway
14 Mamukala
15 Nourlangie Rock
16 Yellow Waters Cruise
17 Old Darwin Road
18 Waterfall Creek
19 Stag Creek

7.14 Mamukala

Mamukala has an observation building and hide overlooking a large wetland area. It is well signposted, 31 km west of Jabiru on the Arnhem Highway. When we visited in late October 1993, the wetlands there had completely dried up, however on the grassy plains in front of the hide we saw **Little Curlew** (40), **Oriental Plover** (5), **Pacific Golden Plover** (1) and **Australian Pratincole** (40). In bushes around the hides we saw **Lemon-bellied Flycatcher** (2), **White-throated Gerygone** and **Australian Hobby**.

7.15 Nourlangie Rock

Key Species: **White-lined Honeyeater, Partridge Pigeon**
Well signposted off the Kakadu Highway, this is a well known tourist spot where you can see some spectacular aboriginal rock paintings. We walked to the Ambangbang Rock Shelter and saw several **White-lined Honeyeaters** in bushes by the main gallery. These birds were clearly used to people and quite tame, allowing excellent views. This area is also good for **Banded Fruit-Dove**, apparently they occur high up above Nourlangie Rock on a marked trail, but I have no other details, ask the rangers if in difficulty. The Kakadu Highway between the Nourlangie Rock turn off and the park headquarters visitor centre is good for **Partridge Pigeons** which feed on the roadside in the late afternoon. Also look for them feeding on the lawns of the visitor centre and west along the Arnhem Highway.

7.16 Yellow Waters Boat Cruises

Key Species: Waterbirds
These cruises are the best way to observe some of the huge numbers of waterfowl that occur in Kakadu, they are also an excellent way to get close up views of Salt Water Crocodiles. Turn off the Kakadu Highway and drive to Gagudju, Cooinda Lodge where there is also an excellent campground. For those not wishing to camp elsewhere in the park, Cooinda Lodge is the best place to base yourself. Boats can be booked here but it is necessary to do so at least one day in advance and for birds it is best to go on the early morning cruise. The cruises cost around $25.00 per person and take you round a series of billabongs where the waterfowl congregate in the dry season. In late October 1993 we recorded the following, **Magpie Goose, Green Pygmy-Goose, Wandering** (50) and **Plumed** (20) **Whistling-Ducks, Australian Darter, Striated, Rufous Night-, Pacific, Pied** and **White-faced Herons, Great, Intermediate, Little** and **Cattle Egrets, Black-necked Stork, Little Pied** and **Great Cormorants, Glossy** and **Sacred Ibises, Royal Spoonbill, Australasian Grebe, Radjah Shelduck, Whistling Kite, White-bellied Sea-Eagle, Comb-crested Jacana, Whiskered Tern, Pheasant Coucal, Azure, Forest** and **Sacred Kingfishers, Yellow Oriole, Leaden** and **Shining Flycatchers**, and best of all, a male **Flock Bronzewing** which circled low over the boat several times. In addition, **Little Kingfisher** and **Great-billed Heron** have both been regularly seen on this cruise in the past. Where the Kakadu Highway crosses Jim-Jim Creek is also worth stopping to explore, we saw several of the above species plus **Straw-necked Ibis, Bar-breasted** and **Rufous-throated Honeyeaters** from the bridge.

7.17 Old Darwin Road (Map 7.12)

Key Species: **Chestnut-backed Button-Quail**
This area is easily the most reliable place to find **Chestnut-backed Button-Quail** in Kakadu as they seem to be resident here. 8.5 km south of Yellow Waters is where the Old Darwin (dirt) Road turns off the Kakadu Highway. Walk down the churned up old road and search the area to the north, up to 300 m in from the road. The key to finding the button-quails is to look for recent platelets. The birds prefer areas of unburned under storey with a mix of open ground and grassy patches. Once you have found an area like this with platelets, just keep marching around until you flush a bird. It took us about 1 hour to do this. They tend to fly about 100 m and run just after they land. By quickly following up a flushed bird you should be able to get views of it on the ground; this took a further two hours to achieve. Whilst at this site we recorded the following, **Chestnut-backed Button-Quail** (4), **Brown Quail** (7), **Black-tailed Treecreeper**, **Black-breasted Buzzard** (1), and **Forest Kingfisher**.

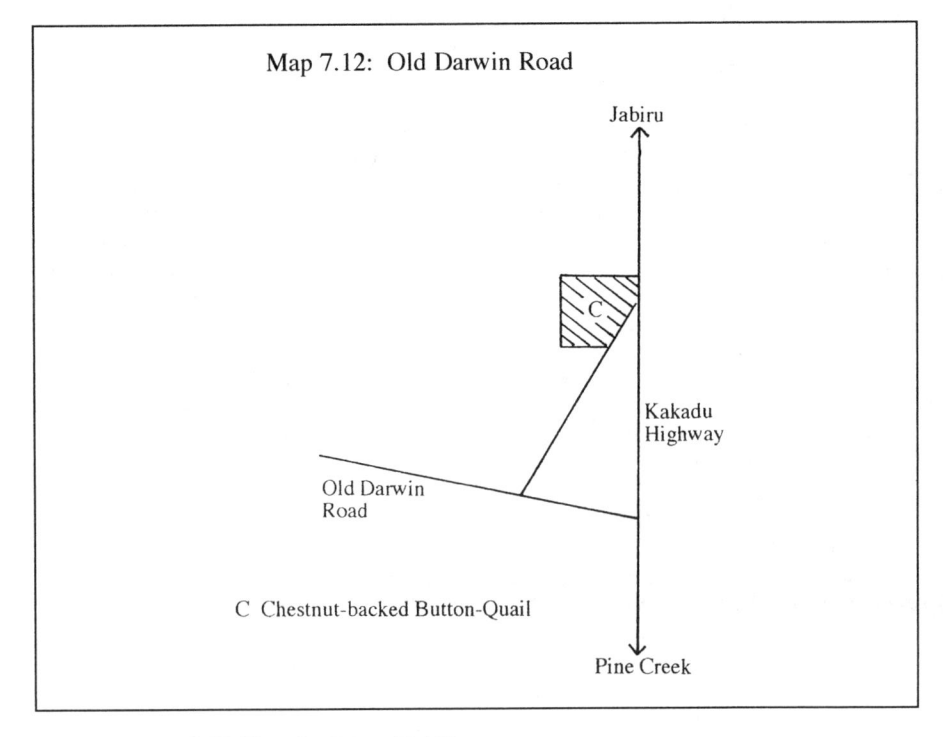

Map 7.12: Old Darwin Road

Jabiru

Kakadu Highway

Old Darwin Road

C Chestnut-backed Button-Quail

Pine Creek

7.18 Waterfall Creek (Map 7.13)

Key Species: **White-throated Grasswren**, **Chestnut-quilled Rock-Pigeon**

Map 7.13: Waterfall Creek

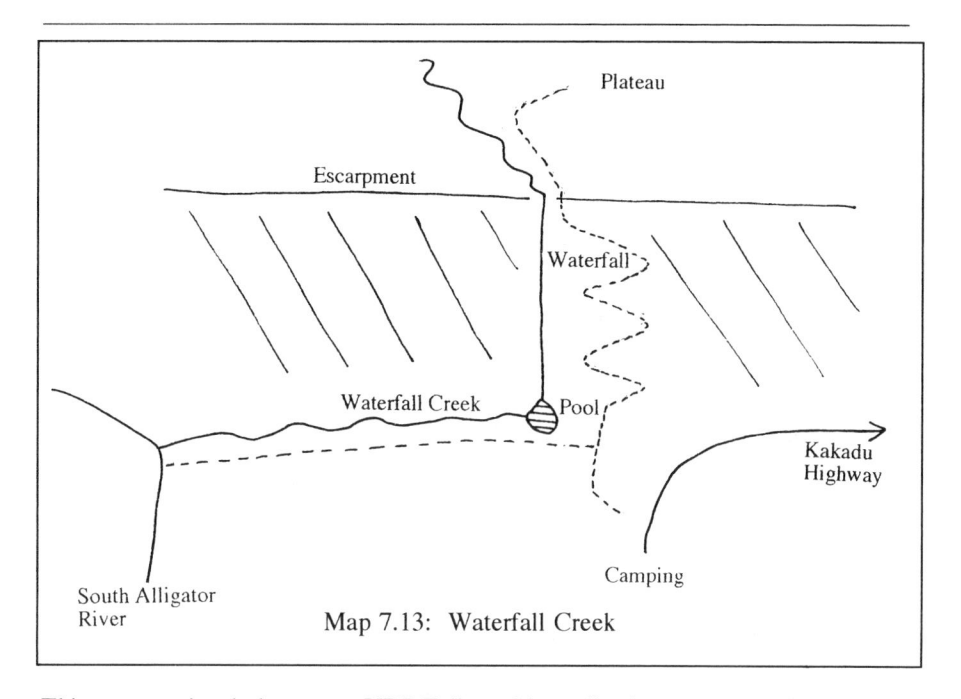

This was previously known as UDP Falls and is easily the most accessible place to see the beautiful **White-throated Grasswren**. Turn left at the T-junction where the Kakadu Highway meets Pine Creek Road, 89 km south of the Yellow Waters turn and follow the dirt road to a T-junction after 26 km. Turn left to Waterfall Creek, a further 11 km to the north. Good camping is available here at the foot of the waterfall and escarpment. To see the grasswrens it is necessary to climb the steep track (to the right of the falls as you look at them) up to the top of the waterfall. From the falls, carry on about 100 m along the track then climb up the rocky escarpment to your right (there is no track). Scramble up as best you can and check the plateau areas with spinifex clumps. We first heard a pair of grasswrens singing then saw them just this side of the wide valley, opposite a distinct pale sandstone rock face and indeed this is a regular area in which to find them. They are not terribly shy as grasswrens go. Whilst scrambling around the plateau you should find **Chestnut-quilled Rock-Pigeons**, we saw three. Also at the top of the waterfall we saw, **Banded Honeyeater, Black-tailed Treecreeper** and a pair of **Pacific Bazas**. Take plenty of water with you as it gets very hot and take care whilst scrambling on the rocks. Around the campsite at night **Bush Thick-knees** are easily whistled in and along the dry Waterfall Creek spotlight for **Rufous** and **Barking Owls**. The walk along this creek as far as the South Alligator River (approximately 1 km) in the day time is good; we saw **Partridge Pigeon** (2), **White-browed Robin** (1), **Forest Kingfisher, Blue-winged Kookaburra, Northern Rosella, Masked Finch** and **Great**

Bowerbird. In addition, **Great-billed Heron** has been seen at the point where you get to the river.

7.19 Stag Creek (Map 7.14)

Key Species: **Banded Fruit-Dove**
From the campground at Waterfall Creek, drive 7.8 km back along the road until you cross a bridge over a dry creek. Note that there is no signpost indicating the name of the creek on the roadside. Follow the stream bed eastwards past a mining spoil heap on your left, then an old mine shaft on your right. Pick your way along the boulders of the stream bed until you reach a large fig tree overhanging the river adjacent to a very large rock outcrop. **Banded Fruit-Doves** will be seen either feeding in this tree or in fig trees further upstream, just carry on until you find them, although they are mainly present in the early morning. Also along this walk you should find **White-lined Honeyeaters** (we saw two), also **White-browed Robin** (1), **Weebill** (race *flavescens*), **Variegated Fairywren** (race *rogersi*), plus some commoner honeyeaters, **Dusky**, **White-throated**, **White-gaped** and **Brown Honeyeaters**. **Rainbow Pitta** has also been seen here. Returning from here to the Kakadu Highway, just where you cross Kanbolgie Creek there is a basic campsite around which **Rufous Owl** has regularly been spotlighted in riverside trees.

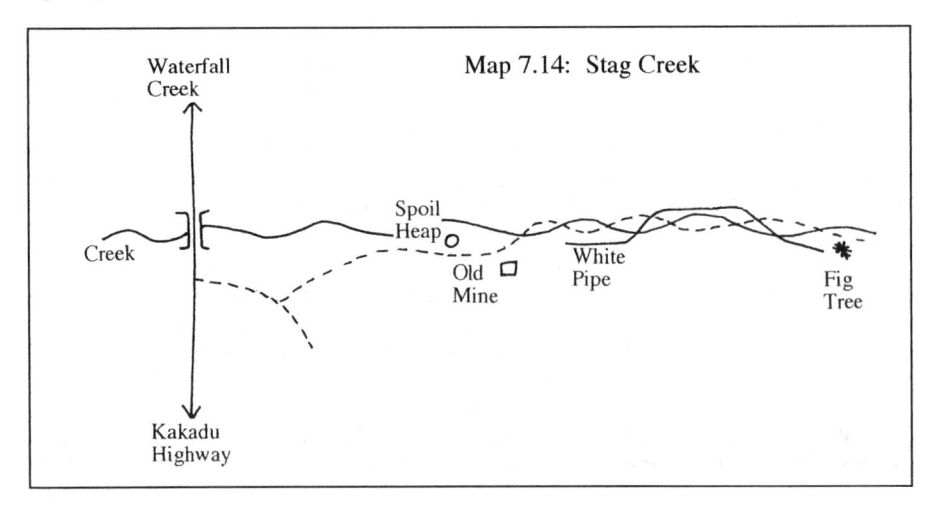

D Katherine (Map 7.15)

There are several places worth visiting in the vicinity of Katherine, most notably it is the best area to find Hooded Parrots which can be hard to find in Kakadu.

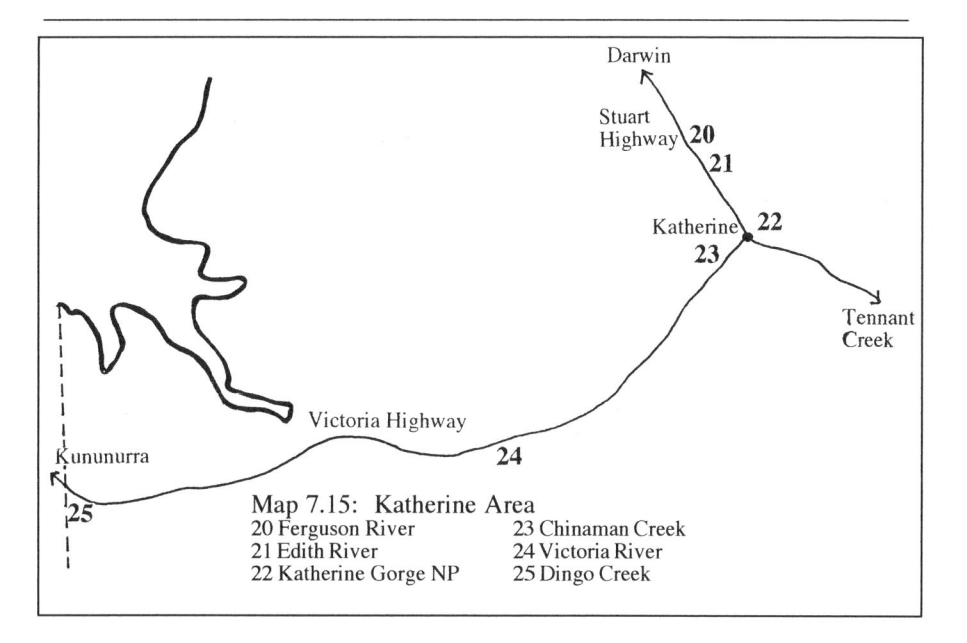

Map 7.15: Katherine Area
20 Ferguson River
21 Edith River
22 Katherine Gorge NP
23 Chinaman Creek
24 Victoria River
25 Dingo Creek

7.20 Fergusson River (Map 7.16)

Key Species: **Hooded Parrot, Gouldian Finch**
In the dry season there are several permanent water pools along the Fergusson River and it is here where we found **Hooded Parrots** after finding that the Chinaman Creek site had dried up. Early morning is best for birds coming into drink. Park by the bridge where the Stuart Highway crosses the Fergusson River, about 60 km north of Katherine. Pick your way down to the dry river bed and walk east upstream until you find the water pools. We found two large pools just beyond the second old bridge, the parrots drank at the rocky one furthest upstream, flying in about an hour after dawn. We saw, **Hooded Parrot** (100), **Bar-breasted** and **Rufous-throated Honeyeaters, Black Bittern** (1), **Rufous Night-Heron, Collared Sparrowhawk, Long-tailed, Double-barred** and **Crimson Finches. Gouldian Finches** are also regularly recorded here.

7.21 Edith River (Map 7.17)

Key Species: **Chestnut-backed Button-Quail**
Drive north from Katherine on the Stuart Highway for about 45 km until you cross over the Edith River. Two km beyond this, turn right onto a dirt track across an old railway line and stop after 5 km where there is a gravel pit set back about 10 m from the track. On the left is a rather bare open ridge; check this and other bare areas nearby for **Chestnut-backed Button-Quail**. They are very difficult to find on the ground, but follow up quickly after you flush one and there

CHAPTER 7: NORTHERN TERRITORY

is a good chance you will see it on the ground. **Hooded Parrot** and **Gouldian Finch** have been seen a further 5 km down the dirt track.

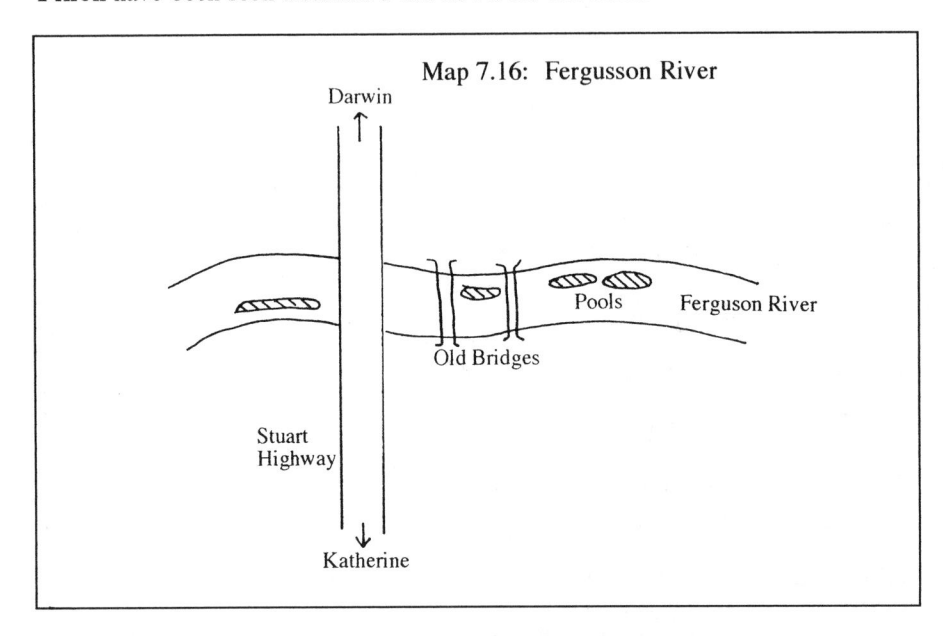

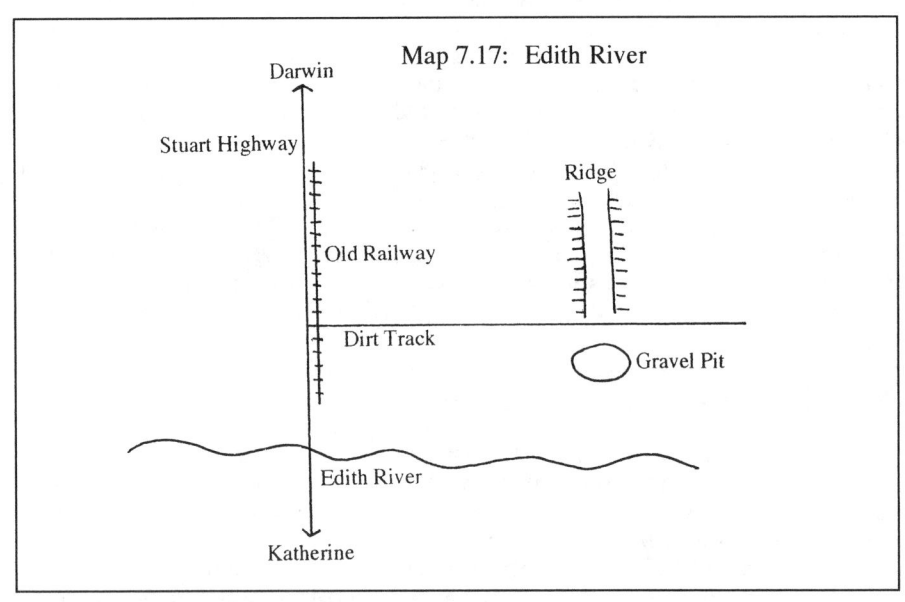

Map 7.16: Fergusson River

Map 7.17: Edith River

7.22 Katherine Gorge National Park

Katherine Gorge is a spectacularly scenic national park, and worth a visit for this alone, since all the most interesting birds here are easier to see elsewhere. The rangers at the visitors centre were exceedingly helpful with information and if you are having trouble finding **Gouldian Finches** at one of the sites mentioned in this guide, ask them here about possible access to the private Mount Todd area where this species has been studied for several years. The gorge is signposted from Katherine town centre and is 23 km to the north-east of the town. Around the carpark and picnic area there are good numbers of tame Great Bowerbirds with their bowers. A walk from the visitors centre to Seventeen Mile Creek is recommended for commoner bush birds such as **Northern Rosella, Red-backed Kingfisher, Lemon-bellied Flycatcher, Bar-breasted** and **Banded Honeyeaters, Olive-backed** and **Yellow Orioles**. There is a good campsite and a caravan park nearby.

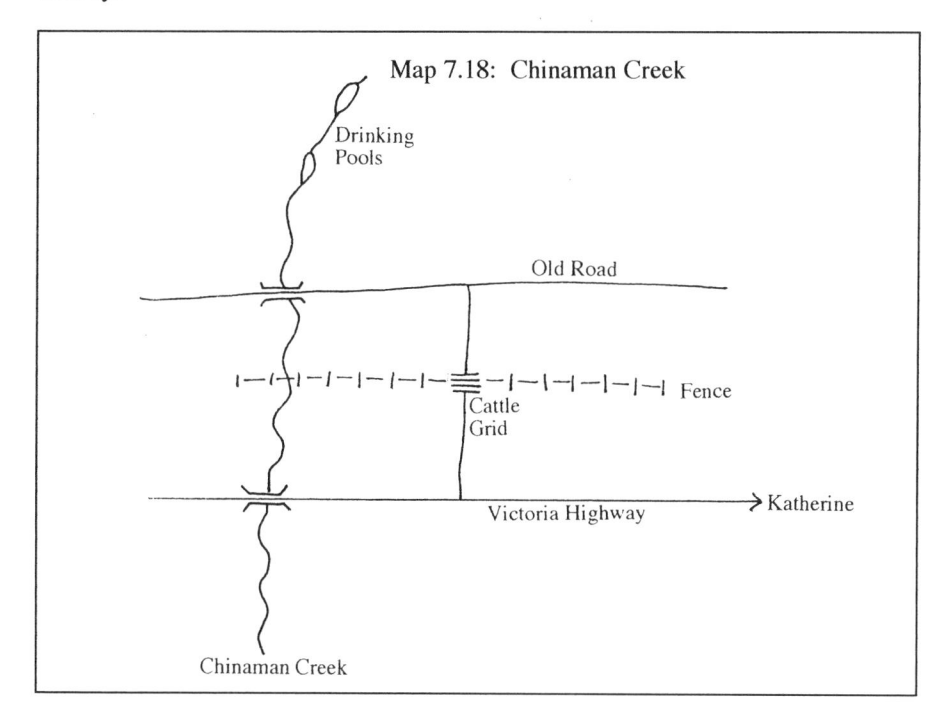

Map 7.18: Chinaman Creek

7.23 Chinaman Creek (Map 7.18)

Key Species: **Hooded Parrot, Gouldian Finch**
This is one of the best sites for **Hooded Parrot**. Leave Katherine south-west on the Victoria Highway, and after 16 km you cross Chinaman Creek. About 150 m before this, take the dirt track on the right and follow it across a cattle grid and on

to the old road. Park here and walk north along the dry creek bed until you come to a drinking pool just by a sharp left hand bend in the creek. Sit quietly where you can see the pool at first light and be patient. A good selection of birds should come in to drink and will normally include both **Hooded Parrot** and **Gouldian Finch**. When we visited in mid October 1993 the pool had dried up and we didn't see either species, although both had been present just a month earlier.

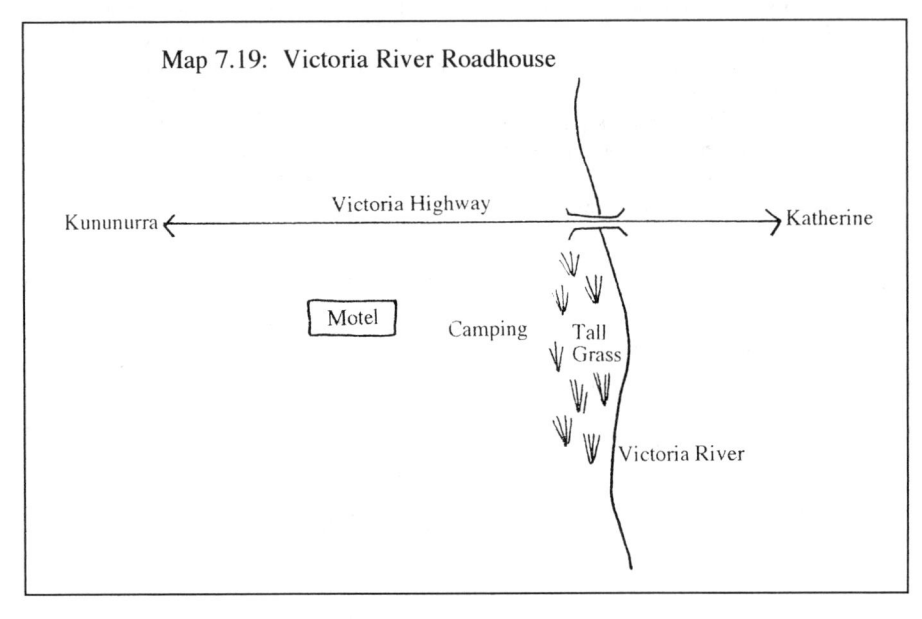

Map 7.19: Victoria River Roadhouse

7.24 Victoria River Roadhouse (Map 7.19)

Key Species: **White-quilled Rock-Pigeon**, **Barking Owl**, *Lilac-crowned Fairywren*, **Sandstone Shrike-Thrush**

The Victoria River Roadhouse is situated on the Victoria Highway 194 km south-west of Katherine and is the easiest place to observe the exquisite **Lilac-crowned Fairywren**. Coming from Katherine, there is a petrol station, motel and excellent campsite on the left hand side just after you cross over the Victoria River. The tall grass between the campsite and the river is brilliant for the fairywren, a good time is in the early morning when the wrens come up to preen and sing from the top of the grass heads. They respond very well to pishing and squeaking. Around the campground and river we saw the following, **Grey Falcon** (1), incredibly one bird flew over the campground whilst we were eating breakfast giving excellent views. Several other people have recorded it in the vicinity so keep your eyes open. About 10 minutes later a **Black Falcon** came right through the campground, **Radjah Shelduck, Little Corella, Red-tailed Black-Cockatoo, Banded, Bar-breasted, Brown** and **White-gaped Honeyeaters, Double-barred Finch, Red-collared Lorikeet,** and **Blue-**

winged Kookaburra. At night a family party of **Barking Owls** regularly come and sit on the petrol pumps where they have been fed on steak for several years. Ask in the roadhouse about them.

Just west of the roadhouse is a track up the escarpment that is good for **White-quilled Rock-Pigeon**. Drive west along the Victoria Highway, pull off into a car-park after 2 km and take the path up to the lookout. Leave the track at post 4 and walk right along the top of the escarpment where you will find the rock-pigeons, we saw three. Further up the trail look for **Sandstone Shrike-Thrush** just before the lookout. In the tall grass opposite the car-park we saw **Lilac-crowned Fairywren** (2), **Star Finch** (1) and **Silver-crowned Friarbird**. Additionally, we saw five **Ground Cuckoo-Shrikes** on the road between Katherine and Victoria Roadhouse.

7.25 Dingo Creek

Key Species: **Gouldian Finch**
Dingo Creek is a dry season drinking hole for finches, notably **Gouldian Finch**. The Victoria Highway crosses this small signposted creek 56 km east of Kununurra, about 15 km from the WA border. Walk south down the stream bed for about 300 m until you find a small drinking pool. It was unfortunately dried up when we visited in mid October 1993. On a different occasion in July 1992 there was still a small pool which attracted birds in the early morning. Wait here in the early morning and be patient. We recorded **Gouldian** (3), **Masked** (6), **Double-barred** and **Long-tailed Finches**, **Red-collared Lorikeet**, **Brown Goshawk** and **Blue-winged Kookaburra**.

E Tennant Creek Area (Map 7.20)

This area is largely ignored by the visiting birder since it lies in between the true outback and the tropical north. There are a couple of places worth stopping however, if only to break the monotony of the long journey from Darwin to Alice Springs.

7.26 Tennant Creek

Key Species: **Grey-fronted Honeyeater**
Turn west off the Stuart Highway 5 km north of Tennant Creek, 100 m north of the Mary Ann Dam junction. Follow the track to the second creek crossing and search the large spinifex clumps. **Rufous-crowned Emuwrens** occur here, although we failed to find any, we did see **Spinifexbird** (2), **Painted Firetail** (2), **Grey-fronted Honeyeater** and **White-winged Fairywren**. Bush camping only is possible at the site although you could stay in the town itself.

Map 7.20: Tennant Creek Area

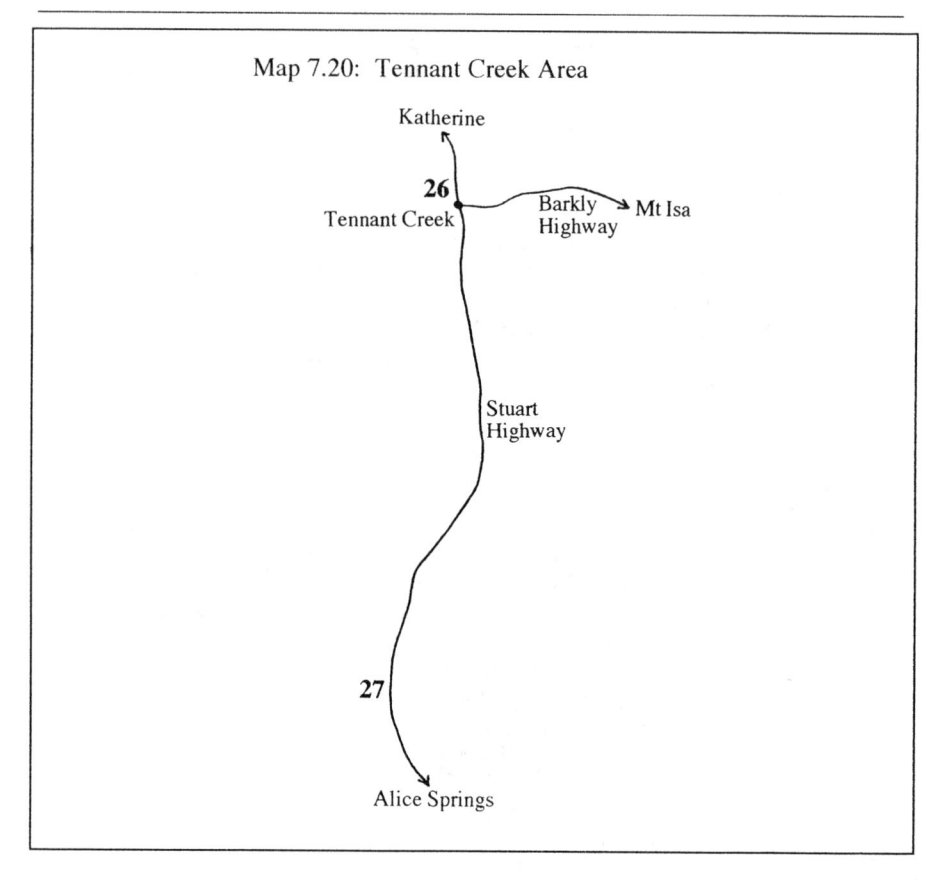

7.27 Tennant Creek to Alice Springs

Along the drive from Tennant Creek to Alice Springs we saw **Red-backed Kingfisher** (3), **Budgerigar**, **White-backed Swallow** and **Black-breasted Buzzard** (2). An area of flowering *Eremophila* bushes 104 km north of Alice proved very productive with **Pied** (20), **Black** (10) and **White-fronted Honeyeaters**, **Crimson Chat**, **Horsfield's Bronze-Cuckoo**, **Masked Woodswallow**, **White-winged Triller** and **Rufous Songlark**, but obviously this site will depend on conditions at the time of your visit. We were lucky to be visiting roughly six weeks after heavy rain around Alice Springs.

F Alice Springs Area (Map 7.21)

Truly in the red centre of Australia, there are a few excellent birds to be found in the vicinity of Alice Springs plus it is well worth visiting the incomparable Ayers Rock.

Map 7.21: Alice Springs Area
28 Kunoth Well
29 Simpson's Gap
30 Ellery Creek Big Hole
31 Ormiston Gorge NP

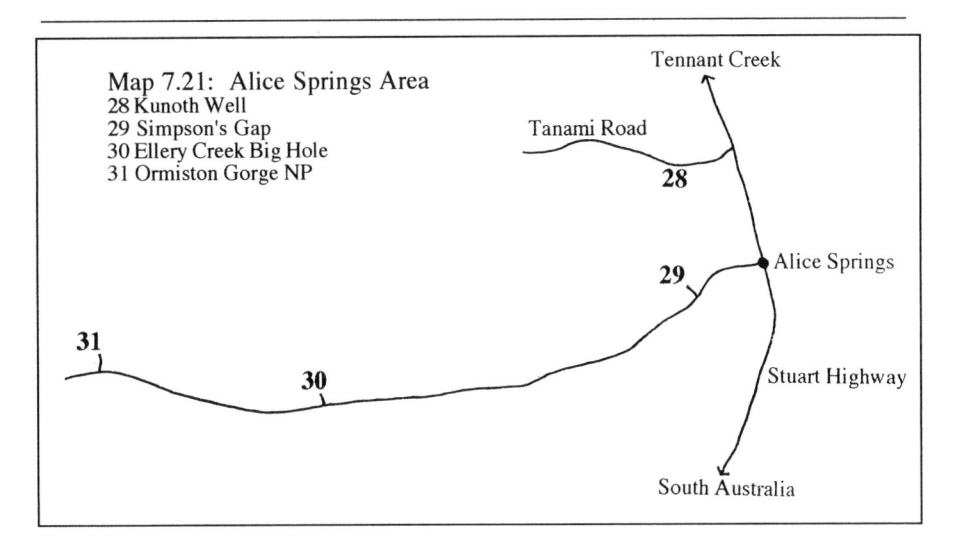

7.28 Kunoth Well (Map 7.22)

Key Species: Grey Honeyeater, **Slaty-backed Thornbill**
This is the only reliable stake-out for the elusive and nomadic **Grey Honeyeater**, however, you may have to search hard to find it as they are very inconspicuous. Turn west off the Stuart Highway 21 km north of Alice Springs on to the Tanami Road and after about 30 km you will see a windmill and small track leading to it on your left, on the right is an old signpost 'Kunoth Well'. The small dam next to this windmill is worth checking, we saw **Pacific Heron** (1), **Black-tailed Native-Hen** (70), **Black-fronted Dotterel, Pink Cockatoo** and **Brown Songlark**. The main area for **Grey Honeyeater** is reached by taking the dirt track signposted to 'Hamilton Downs Youth Camp' just 500 m beyond the well on the left and searching the mulga on the right hand side of the track up to 5 km from the junction. Bush camping only is possible at this site although it could be covered from Alice Springs quite comfortably. On my first visit, in July 1992, we parked 4.3 km down the track and incredibly found a pair of Grey Honeyeaters nest building about 300 m in from the track within ten minutes. We were able to obtain prolonged views of them. Other birds in the area on this visit included **Slaty-backed** and **Chestnut-rumped Thornbills, Splendid Fairywren, White-browed Babbler** and **Ground Cuckoo-Shrike** (1). On the second occasion in November 1993 the whole area was a mass of colourful flowers following heavy rain in the region some two months earlier. The best birds we recorded then were **Little Button-Quail** (40), **Diamond Dove, Bourke's Parrot** (10), **Pallid** and **Horsfield's Bronze-Cuckoos, Red-backed Kingfisher, Red-capped** and **Hooded Robins, Grey-crowned** and **White-browed Babblers, Rufous Songlark, Splendid Fairywren, Western Gerygone, Inland, Chestnut-rumped** and **Slaty-backed Thornbills, White-browed Treecreeper** (3), **White-fronted** (10), **Grey** (1) and **Pied**

Honeyeaters and **Crimson Chat** (100), plus many commoner species. In addition, on the bare open area on the left hand side of the track 5 km from the junction were **Spotted Harrier** (1), **Inland Dotterel** (29) and **Banded Lapwing** (3). **Black-eared Cuckoo** is regularly seen at Kunoth Well.

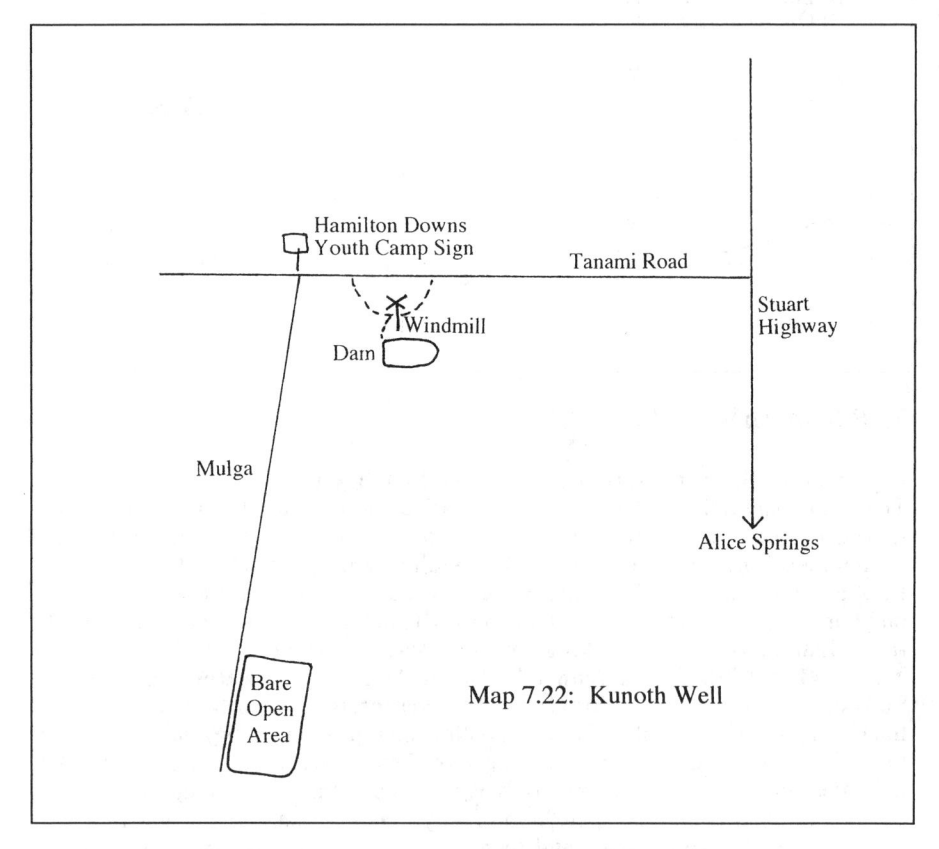

Map 7.22: Kunoth Well

7.29 Simpson's Gap

Key Species: **Dusky Grasswren**
Simpson's Gap is the first in a series of excellent national parks situated to the west of Alice Springs in the Macdonnell Ranges, Simpson's Gap is the easiest place to see **Dusky Grasswren**. Leave Alice Springs westwards on Larapinta Drive signposted to Hermannsburg. Simpson's Gap National Park is on the right hand side after 16 km. Park in the car-park and walk to the gorge. **Dusky Grasswrens** are found on the steep rocky slope on your left hand side as you walk towards the gorge. They are so used to tourists here that they are tame and can sometimes be seen hopping along the foot path. The pool in the gorge is a drinking hole for **Painted Firetails**, early morning is best before large numbers

of tourists arrive. Birds we encountered around the gorge included **Peregrine** (2), **Little Woodswallow, Chestnut-rumped** and **Inland Thornbills, Grey-headed Honeyeater** and **Dusky Grasswren** (4). In addition **Grey Falcon, Red-browed Pardalote** and **Golden-backed Honeyeater** have been seen here in the past. Note that camping is not allowed here.

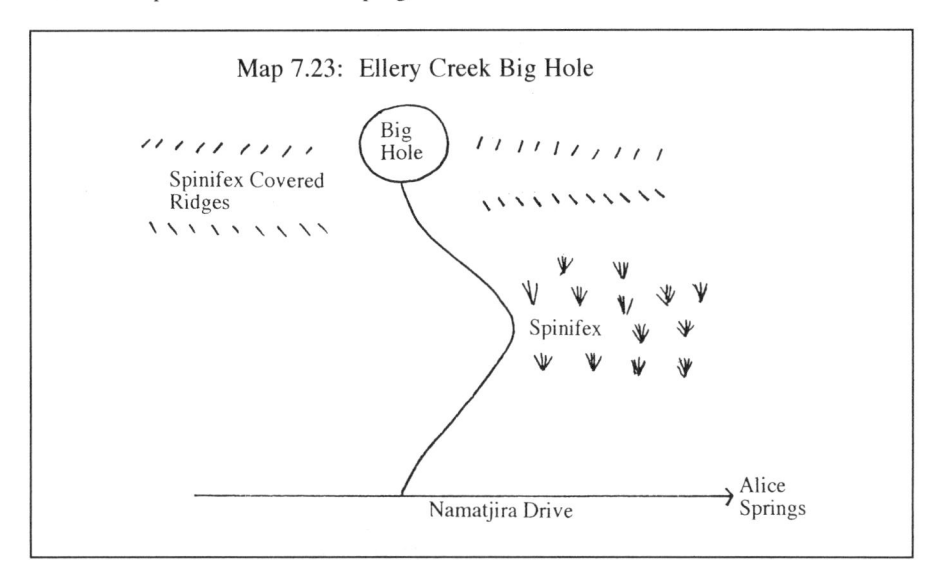

Map 7.23: Ellery Creek Big Hole

7.30 Ellery Creek Big Hole Nature Park (Map 7.23)

Key Species: **Rufous-crowned Emuwren, Spinifexbird**
This is a delightful place with some excellent stands of spinifex where the extremely skulking **Rufous-crowned Emuwren** can be found. It is about 90 km west of Alice Springs along Namatjira Drive, bear right onto this road off Larapinta Drive 46 km west of Alice Springs. On the short track to the waterhole you cross a dry creek bed then shortly afterwards is a sharp left hand bend where a spinifex covered plain stretches out on the right hand side. Park here and search the largest clumps of spinifex. In July 1992 we found a female **Pied Honeyeater** here also **Spinifexbird** (4), **Grey-headed** and **Black Honeyeaters, Black-faced Woodswallow, Red-browed Pardalote, Rufous-crowned Emuwren** (3), **Little Button-Quail** and **White-winged Fairywren**. The waterhole itself makes a pleasant swimming and camping spot. The rocky spinifex covered ridges running west from the car-park are also a good place to look for the emuwren.

7.31 Ormiston Gorge and Pound National Park (Map 7.24)

Key Species: **Spinifex Pigeon, Rufous-crowned Emuwren, Black Honeyeater, Painted Firetail**

CHAPTER 7: NORTHERN TERRITORY

Map 7.24: Ormiston Gorge and Pound NP

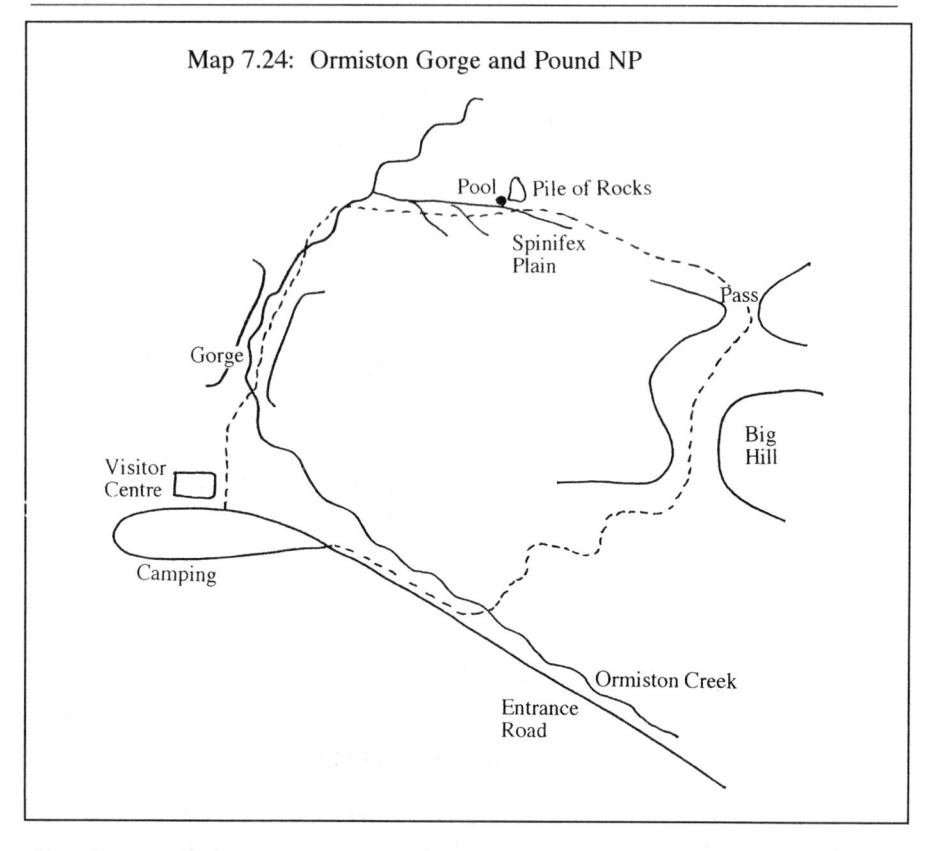

A really wonderful national park with some truly spectacular scenery and some excellent birding. It is probably the easiest place to find the elusive **Rufous-crowned Emuwren**. There is a good campsite, but bring your own drinking water. The turn off to the park is 41 km further west than Ellery Creek along the Namatjira Drive. We spent three days here in early November 1993 when the daytime temperature was around 38 °C. Take plenty of water with you particularly if doing the Ormiston Gorge Pound Walk. Around the campsite and pools in the gorge were **Diamond Dove** (20), **Spinifex Pigeon** (30, the birds here are tame and can be hand fed in the campground), **Ringneck Parrot** (5), **Budgerigar** (100's, this is a very reliable locality for this species), **Rufous Songlark**, **Australian Owlet-Nightjar** (1), **Red-browed Pardalote**, and **Western Bowerbird** (2, this is a very reliable locality for this species, they frequent trees around the campsite). The Ormiston Gorge Pound Walk takes about three hours. From the road you first wind up a steep slope where **Dusky Grasswrens** are plentiful, you then enter a spinifex covered valley with a big hill to your right. **Rufous-crowned Emuwren** and **Spinifexbird** are both found in this valley, however, if you carry on you climb to a pass between the hills and below you is a vast spinifex plain. Near the track, about half way across this plain (*c*. 300 m from the first river crossing) there is a small pile of rocks and opposite it a tiny drinking pool in a dry creek bed. Although the pool is not visible from the track listen for the activity of **Zebra Finches** which regularly drink there to help you locate it. **Painted Firetails** regularly drink at this pool. Further on, between two dry creek beds we saw a pair of **Rufous-crowned Emuwrens**. The whole Ormiston area is good for **Black** and sometimes **Pied Honeyeaters**. It is a good place to try for the former if the surrounding countryside is not covered in flowering bushes as they tend to retreat to the Macdonnell Ranges at such times.

G South of Alice (Map 7.25)

Although not essential to visit from a birding point of view, the opportunity to visit Ayers Rock should not be missed and this area can be very productive if it has recently rained.

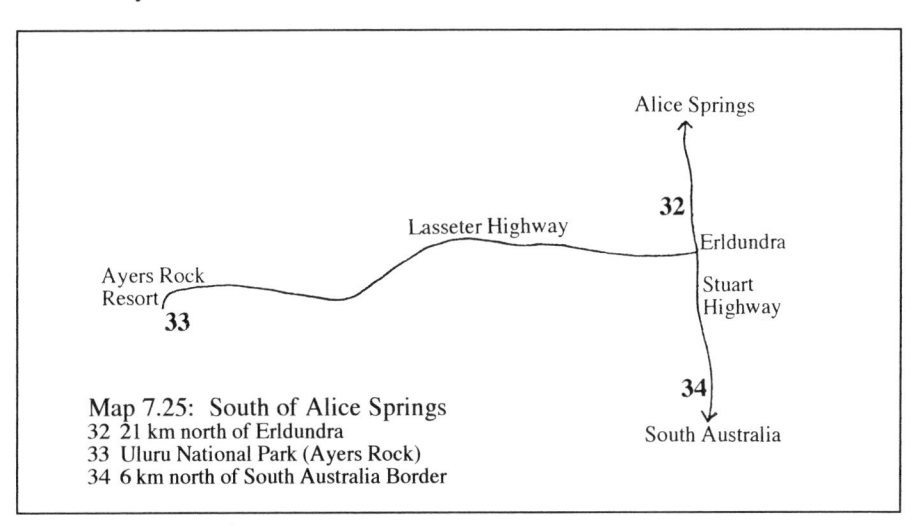

Map 7.25: South of Alice Springs
32 21 km north of Erldundra
33 Uluru National Park (Ayers Rock)
34 6 km north of South Australia Border

7.32 Twenty-one km North of Erldunda (Map 7.26)

Key Species: **Banded Whiteface**
Roughly 200 km south of Alice Springs on the Stuart Highway is the Erldunda Service Station. Twenty-one km north of this is a place that has proven very reliable for seeing **Banded Whiteface**. The habitat is mostly open bare ground. However look out on the west side of the road for two isolated trees about 50 m from the road. They are the only trees for miles and are just north of the Kulgera 95 km, Alice Springs 180 km post. A faint track leads off the highway here, walk along this and on your left is a shallow depression with some low bushes in it. The whitefaces are usually here although we found them in some bushes 100 m to the west of the depression. Although it looks like a moonscape it is nevertheless good

for birds and we saw **Orange Chat** (6), **Crimson Chat** (6), **Banded Whiteface** (6), **Southern Whiteface** (7), **Cinnamon Quail-Thrush** (3) and **Chiming Wedgebill** (1). Around Erldunda Service Station itself was a pair of **Pink Cockatoos** and **White-backed Swallows** were common along the Lasseter Highway from here to Ayers Rock, mostly around road cuttings.

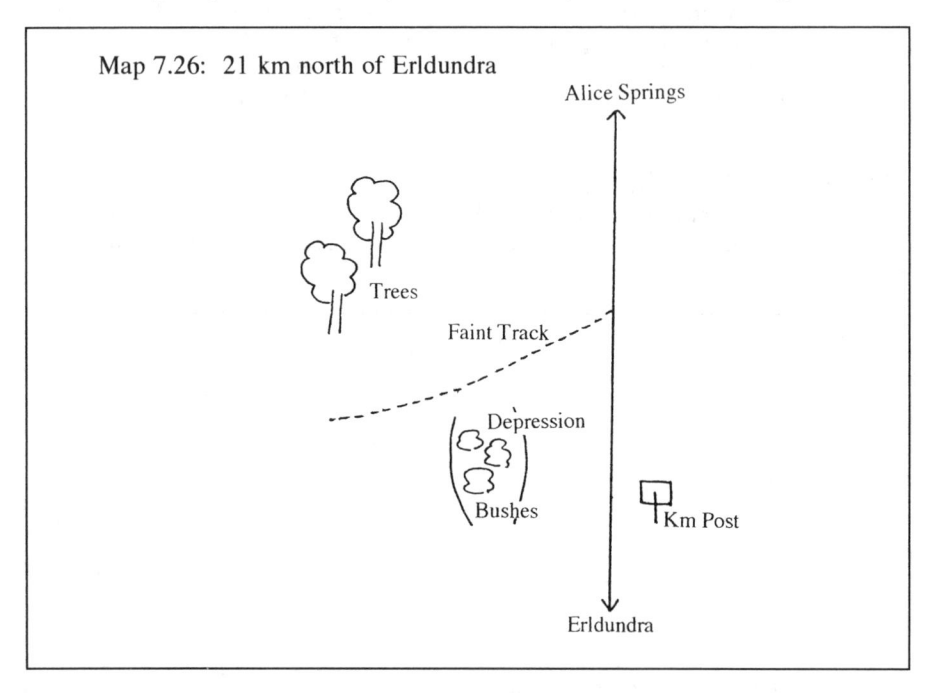

Map 7.26: 21 km north of Erldundra

7.33 Ayers Rock or Uluru National Park (Map 7.27)

Key Species: **Striated Grasswren, Banded Whiteface**
Well worth the long detour from the Stuart Highway, Ayers Rock or Uluru as it is nowadays called is truly impressive, although somewhat spoiled by the unnatural greenery of the tourist village, shops and bus loads of tourists. There is a $10.00 per person entrance fee and excellent although expensive camping facilities and even hotels are available. A view of the Rock at either dawn or dusk will long be remembered. Of course the main reason for visiting the park is to see the superb *whitei* race of **Striated Grasswren**. Park in the sunset viewing car-park and search the spinifex up to 100 m behind the car-park on the opposite side of the road. We saw very little else of note here although if conditions are right, this is a good place to see **Black** and **Pied Honeyeaters**. The park itself is a good place for **Banded Whiteface** if you fail to see them north of Erldunda, but the key to finding them here is to look for the correct habitat. The birds nest and frequent areas which have been recently burned, not the charcoal blackened areas, but places which were burned about twelve months previously and are now strongly

regenerating. Since controlled burning of small areas is part of the park management strategy, it is a good idea to ask a ranger to point out an area which fits the requirement. In 1991 a pair was found nesting in the burned area just beyond the park checkpoint where the first sandy track leads off the road to the left. The birds were quite obvious since they would frequently sit on top of the bushes calling and even song flighting.

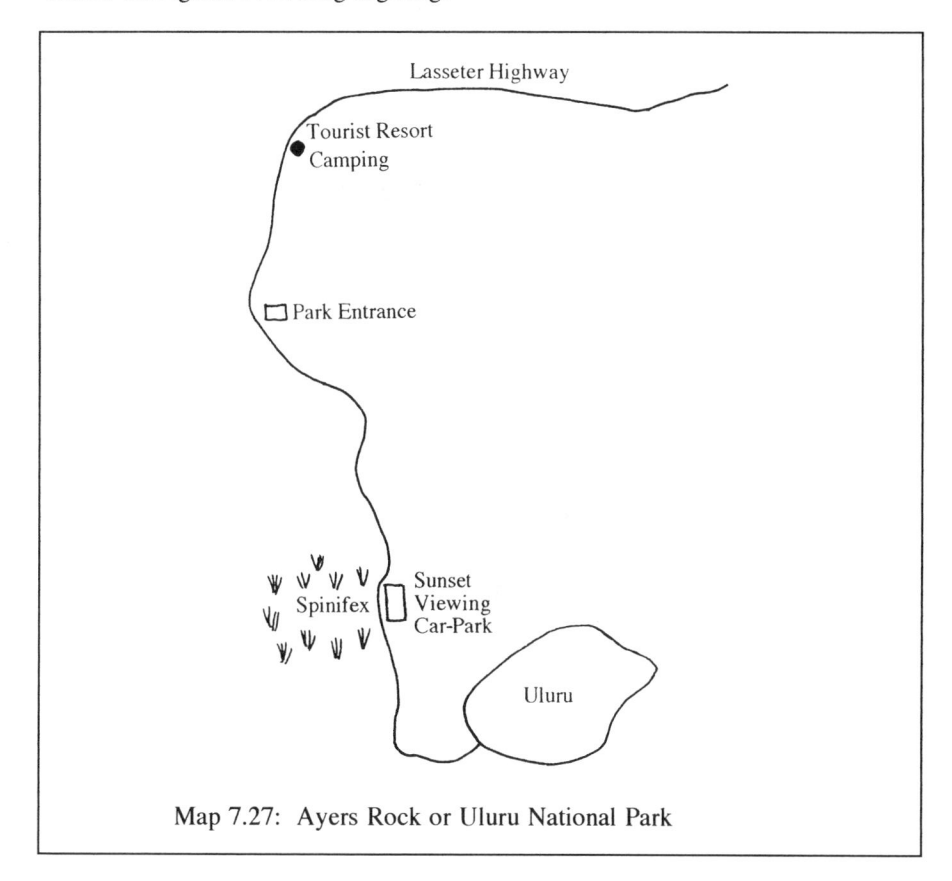

Map 7.27: Ayers Rock or Uluru National Park

7.34 Six km North of South Australia State Border

We saw relatively few birds on the drive south from Erldunda to South Australia, however we did camp next to the Stuart Highway just 6 km north of the border and found a few birds in the scrubby bushes 200 m west of the highway. These included **Western Bowerbird** (1), **Chiming Wedgebill** (common), **Crimson Chat**, **White-browed Babbler** and **Masked Woodswallow**.

CHAPTER 8

WESTERN AUSTRALIA

Western Spinebill, an attractive honeyeater that is found only in the south-west corner of Australia.

Introduction (Map 8.1)

Western Australia covers a large portion of Australia, however, despite its size there are relatively few endemics compared to the rest of the country. The majority of these endemics are in the south-west corner of the state with the other main area being the Kimberleys, home to the rare Black Grasswren. Between these two areas there are relatively few important birds unless you are planning an expedition along the Canning Stock Route for Princess Parrot.

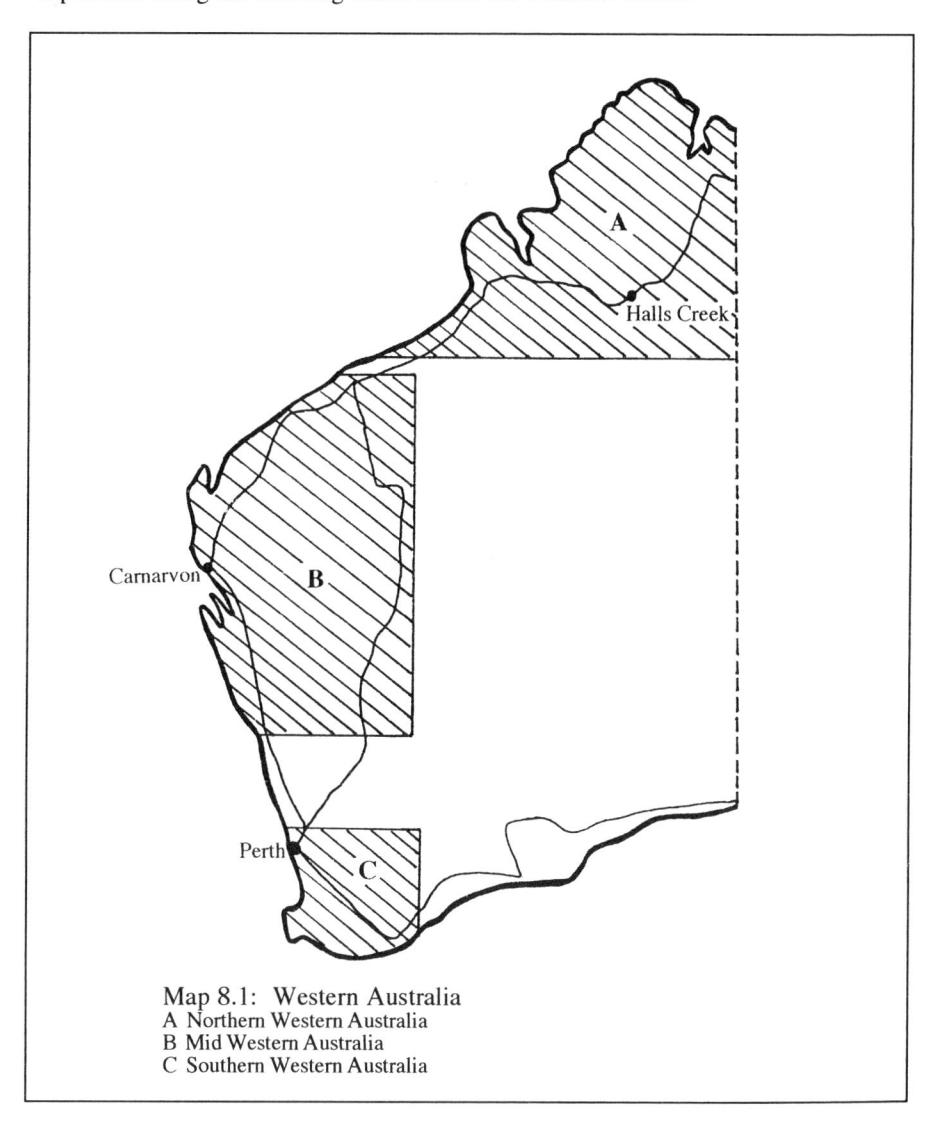

Map 8.1: Western Australia
A Northern Western Australia
B Mid Western Australia
C Southern Western Australia

CHAPTER 8: WESTERN AUSTRALIA

Endemics: Red-capped Parrot, Western Rosella, White-tailed Black-Cockatoo, Long-billed Black-Cockatoo, Western Corella, Noisy Scrub-bird, Red-winged Fairywren, Black Grasswren, Western Bristlebird, Western Thornbill, Dusky Gerygone, Western Spinebill, (Little Wattlebird), (Brown-tailed Flycatcher), White-breasted Robin, Red-eared Firetail
Specialities: Asiatic Dowitcher (summer), Princess Parrot, Rufous Treecreeper, Western Yellow Robin, Mangrove Fantail, Yellow-rumped Mannikin, Pictorella Mannikin

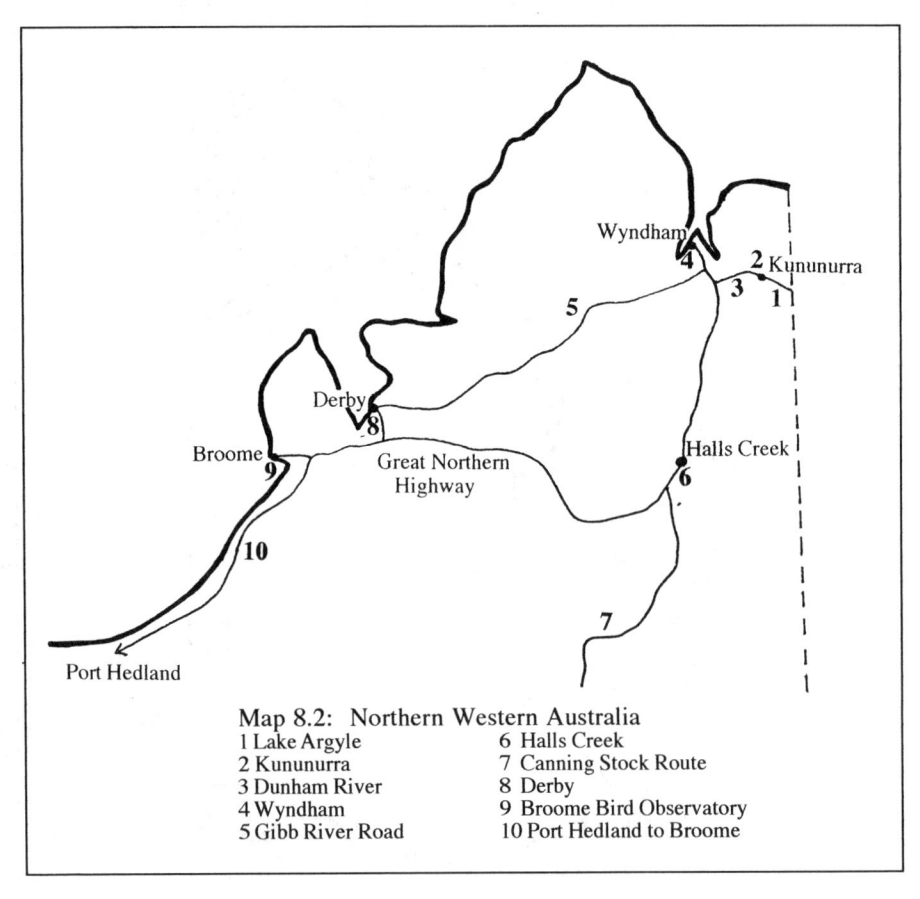

Map 8.2: Northern Western Australia
1 Lake Argyle
2 Kununurra
3 Dunham River
4 Wyndham
5 Gibb River Road
6 Halls Creek
7 Canning Stock Route
8 Derby
9 Broome Bird Observatory
10 Port Hedland to Broome

A Northern Western Australia (Map 8.2)

Although relatively few birds are found exclusively in this part of Australia, it does include some spectacular scenery in the Kimberleys and the Bungle-Bungles. Distances between sites are vast and a reliable vehicle is essential to cover this part of the continent. Kununurra makes an excellent base from which to explore the surrounding area. There is an excellent campsite and caravan park on the shores of Lake Kununurra on the south side of the Duncan Highway.

8.1 Lake Argyle

Key Species: **Yellow Chat, Pictorella Mannikin**
To reach the best area of shoreline around Lake Argyle, turn south off the Victoria Highway 40 km east of Kununurra, just before the border of Western Australia with Northern Territory, along Golden Gate Drive. This is a rough 19 km track that is passable with care in a 2WD vehicle, although you may need to do some road maintenance on the dry creek bed crossings. In the dry season, the tall dry grass along the track has literally hundreds of **Pictorella Mannikins** about 10 km from the highway. We also saw a **Black-breasted Buzzard** and flushed some **Red-chested Button-Quail** in this grassland. The woodland at the start of the track has **Black-tailed Treecreepers** and **Varied Lorikeets**. After 19 km you reach the lake shore; walk to your right along the shore checking the dead trees and branches which are favoured perches for **Yellow Chats**. We saw three feeding on the short wet grassy areas and they have bred here at least two years running. Water birds abound, the best we saw were as follows, **Magpie Goose, Wandering Whistling Duck, Radjah Shelduck, Green Pygmy-Goose, Brolga, Australian Pratincole** and **Marsh Sandpiper**. Nearby it is worth camping at Keep River National Park, just over the border in the Northern Territory. The walking track from the main campsite to the sandstone escarpment is an excellent place to find **White-quilled Rock-Pigeon**.

8.2 Kununurra (Map 8.3)

Key Species: **Yellow-rumped Mannikin**
The irrigation fields to the north of the town are very good for finches, and in particular this is the best site in Australia for **Yellow-rumped Mannikin**. Turn north off the Victoria Highway at the west end of town into Ivanhoe Road, signposted to Ivanhoe Crossing. Park by the third irrigation channel you cross and walk west along the north side of the channel checking the reed beds and small pool. We visited this site in 1992 and 1993 and on both occasions **Yellow-rumped Mannikins** were common. Other birds recorded here were **Chestnut-breasted x Yellow-rumped Mannikin** hybrids (2), **Pictorella Mannikin** (2), **Star** and **Crimson Finches**.

Celebrity Tree Park, adjacent to Kimberly-land Holiday Caravan Park on the shores of Lily Creek Lagoon in town makes a pleasant picnic stop. In the park we saw **Star Finches** and **Banded Honeyeaters**.

Hidden Valley National Park is on the outskirts at the east end of town. Turn off the Victoria Highway into Weaber Plain Road, then right into Barringtonia Avenue then left into Hidden Valley Road. Follow to the car-park at the end and explore the walking trails for **White-quilled Rock-Pigeon** and **Sandstone Shrike-Thrush**.

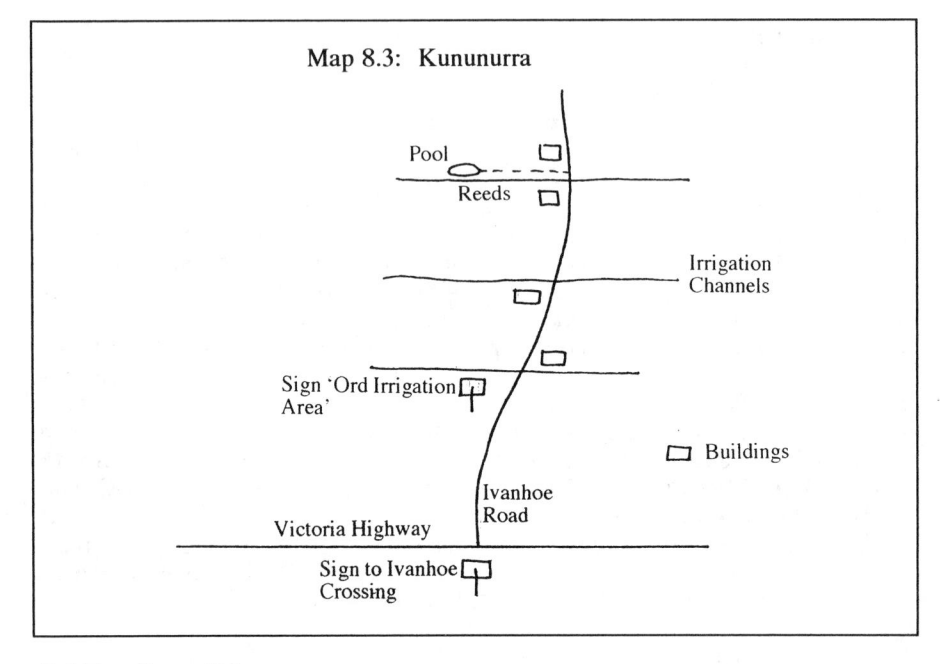

```
Map 8.3: Kununurra
```
(map showing Pool, Reeds, Irrigation Channels, Sign 'Ord Irrigation Area', Buildings, Ivanhoe Road, Victoria Highway, Sign to Ivanhoe Crossing)

8.3 Dunham River

Key Species: **White-browed Robin**
This site is about 8 km west of Kununurra where the Victoria Highway crosses the Dunham River. Check the riverside forest on the west bank of the river, on the south side of the road for **White-browed Robin** (race *cerviniventris*). We saw one here very easily, they react well to pishing.

8.4 Wyndham

Key Species: **Gouldian Finch**
Three Mile (Wyndham) Caravan Park is signposted from the main road through Wyndham, along Baker Street. Not only can you camp or stay in a caravan there, but during the dry season a large number of birds are attracted to the water sprinklers used on the grass and to the pools in the creek alongside the park. Notably, this is probably the most reliable site in the dry season to see **Gouldian Finch**. We visited in late October 1993 and recorded the following birds of note; **Gouldian** (5), **Long-tailed, Masked, Star, Double-barred** and **Zebra Finches, Spinifex Pigeon** (common), **Rufous-throated** and **Yellow-tinted Honeyeaters**. It is also a regular site for **Black-eared Cuckoo**.

Map 8.4a: Mount Elizabeth Black Grasswren Site

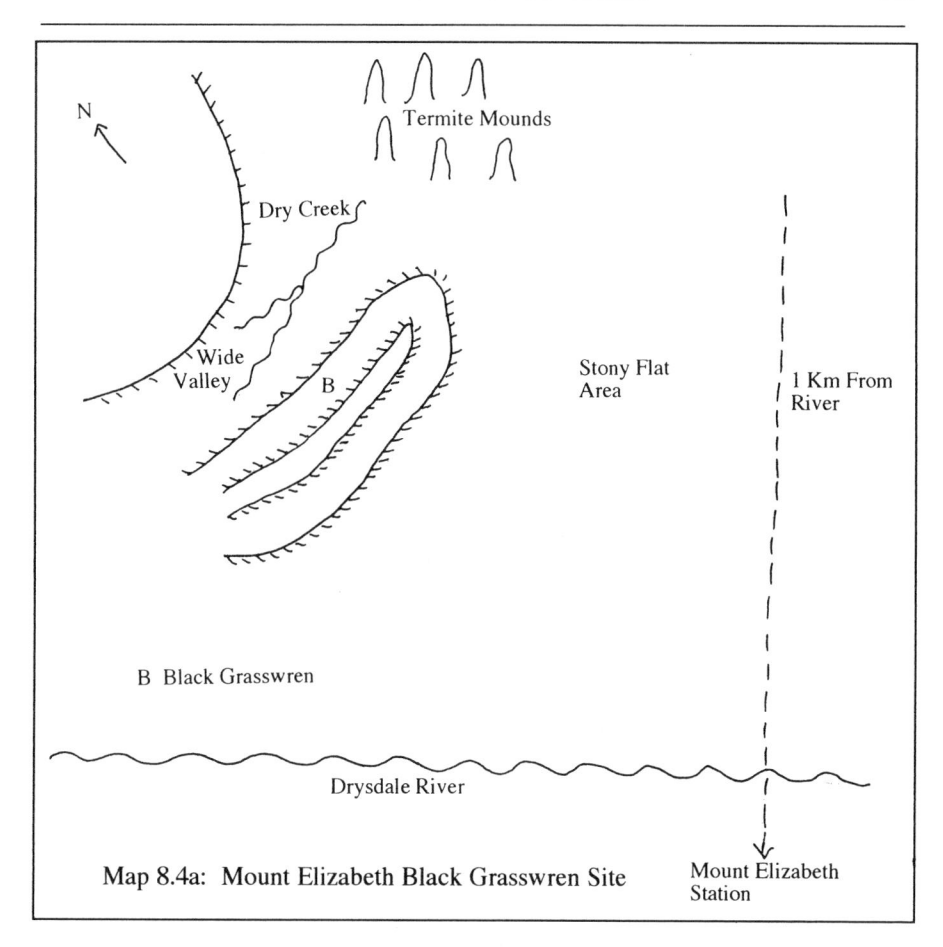

8.5 The Gibb River Road (Maps 8.4a and 8.4b)

Key Species: **Red Goshawk,** *Black Grasswren*
This road provides access to the remote Kimberley region of northern Western Australia, home of the shy, elusive **Black Grasswren**. Unfortunately, the road has the reputation for being the roughest in Australia, and is thus not for the faint hearted. It runs from Derby in the west to Kununurra in the east and it should not be attempted in the wet season (December to April) when apart from the shocking daytime temperatures, the roads may also be flooded and impassable for months at a time. Seeing Black Grasswren thus provides a considerable logistical problem for the travelling birder. There are several strategies for getting to one of the sites and at all places it will be necessary to bush camp.
8.5a Mount Elizabeth Station With a 2WD, the best option is to drive east from Derby to Mount Elizabeth Station, a distance of 338 km (the first 62 km of

which are sealed) to the station turn off from where it is 30 km to the station itself. Mount Elizabeth Station is run by the Lacey family, and if you telephone them in advance, (Tel (091) 914 644) you can arrange for Peter Lacey to take you in his 4WD to where he has a party of grasswrens living on his property. The site is about 50 km north-west of the station and it takes about 90 minutes drive to get there. Get Peter to drop you off and pick you up a couple of days later; you don't want to dip! Take plenty of food with you, although water should be available there. This service will cost about $200 depending on how many of you go. The grasswrens live on a high boulder covered plateau at the eastern end of a rocky outcrop; Peter can point out the place when you get there. Other good birds you should see whilst looking for the grasswrens are **White-quilled Rock-Pigeon**, **Sandstone Shrike-Thrush** and **Green-backed Gerygone**.
On the way to Mount Elizabeth you will pass Mount Barnet Station, fuel is available here but it is a good idea to check in advance that they have your type available (Tel (091) 917 007). You can camp close to the station at Manning Gorge. This is in itself a good birding site. There is a track marked by tinnies hanging from the trees that leads from campground No 2 to the gorge. Follow this to the north end of the gorge then pick your way through the riverside vegetation to see **Black Bittern**. **Red Goshawk** is regularly seen hunting over this gorge, whilst the rocky plateau above the falls is a former site for **Black Grasswren**. Scramble up the plateau from near the campground and check any fairywren flocks carefully. A few Black Grasswrens are still present in this locality, unfortunately however the population here was decimated by a big fire. The few remaining in the area are exceedingly shy so don't count on seeing this species here. You should find **Sandstone Shrike-Thrush** and **White-quilled Rock-Pigeon** however. Take a compass up here as it is very easy to get yourself lost.
Having seen the grasswrens at Mount Elizabeth you will be faced with a dilemma, either to return to Derby, which will mean a huge detour, or to continue east along the Gibb River Road. The eastern section of the road is notoriously rough, much worse than the western end and in a 2WD vehicle it will take at least two days of driving. A major obstacle is the Pentecost River Crossing just 57 km before the junction with the Great Northern Highway. This is about 200 m long across the tidal river and is very rocky and difficult without the clearance of a 4WD. Obviously local knowledge of the road conditions should be sought, but it is also a good idea to contact the Main Roads Department for information (Tel (091) 911 133). Fuel is available from Durack River Station or Home Valley Station. Along this section of the road we recorded **Australian Bustard** (11) and **Pictorella Mannikin** (10).
8.5b Mitchell Falls and Plateau This place can only be reached by 4WD because of the high ground clearance needed. The best area for **Black Grasswren** is Mitchell Falls which is reached from the Kalumburu Road. The Kalumburu turn-off is 248 km from the eastern end of the Gibb River Road and 419 km from Derby. Fifty-nine km north of the junction is Drysdale River Homestead which has a store and fuel (Tel (091) 614 326), 103 km beyond this, turn left towards Mitchell Plateau, then after 70 km turn off to Mitchell Falls which is signposted. This final 14 km of track was the roughest part of the whole

road and took almost an hour to drive. Once at the car-park, cross the dry Mertens Creek stream bed and follow the obscure track off to the left, marked with coloured tapes in the trees. It takes about one hour to walk to the spectacular falls. The grasswrens have been seen around the top of the main waterfall, although we failed to find them here. On the walk down you will pass Mertens Falls on your left; this is another grasswren site although all we saw here of interest was **White-quilled Rock-Pigeons**; check the rocky areas at the head of the falls. Also on this walk we saw a party of **Partridge Pigeons** and flushed what was probably **Chestnut-backed Button-Quail** (they are fairly common in this area). **Green-backed Gerygone** and **Red Goshawk** also occur. The area where we eventually found and had good views of Black Grasswrens was only about 200 m from the car-park; cross over Mertens Creek and head straight on at right angles to the waterfall track to an area of boulders with spinifex clumps. The birds were reasonably tame and confiding once located by call. We visited this site in late October 1993 when the daytime temperatures were already up to 45 °C so take plenty of water with you (we were drinking about five litres each per day). If the unthinkable happens and you cannot find the grasswrens at Mitchell Falls, do not panic! Return to the main track and drive north a further 19 km then turn left to Surveyors Pool which is 6 km down a rough track. The grasswrens are fairly common on the rocky boulders around the pool.

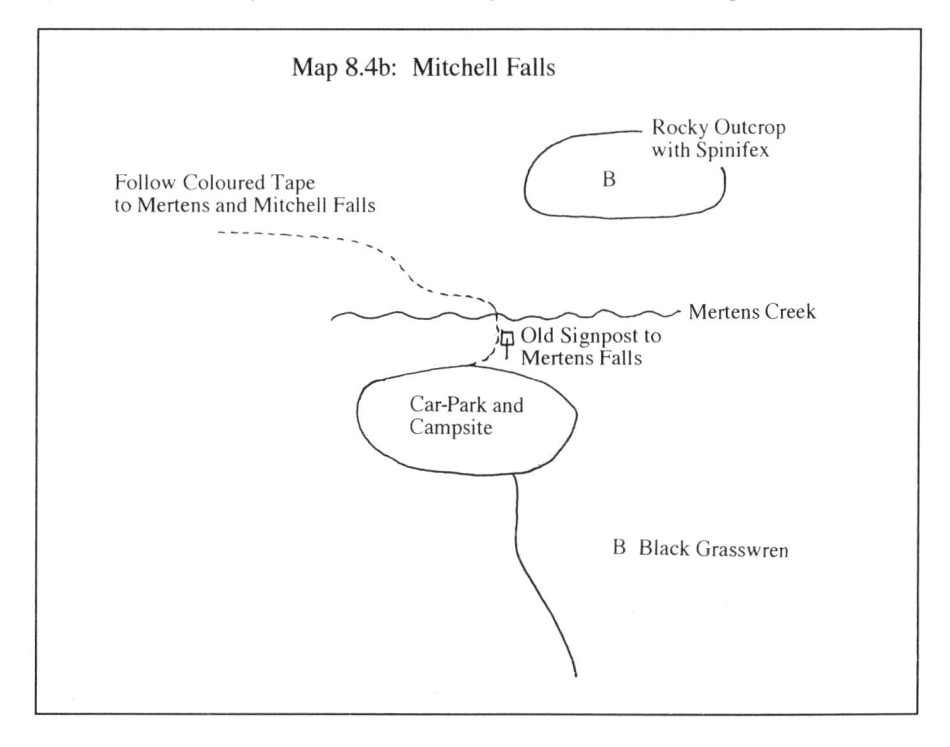

Map 8.4b: Mitchell Falls

Follow Coloured Tape to Mertens and Mitchell Falls

Rocky Outcrop with Spinifex

B

Mertens Creek

Old Signpost to Mertens Falls

Car-Park and Campsite

B Black Grasswren

We visited Mitchell Falls in a small Suzuki 4WD hired from Hertz in Kununurra. There is a fairly steep charge per kilometre with 4WD hire, and many companies will not allow their smaller vehicles into the Kimberleys. The total cost for a three day hire was $462 plus fuel, rather expensive but a superb and beautiful area and Black Grasswren is a brilliant bird! For the latest information on the Kimberly region, 4WD hire, and also an invaluable travellers guide to the Gibb River and Kalumburu Roads, try any of the following tourist/visitor centres in Wyndham ((091) 611 054), Derby ((091) 911 426), Kununurra ((091) 681 177), or Broome ((091) 922 222). Many 4WD tours also visit Mitchell Falls and Surveyor's Pool, so you could possibly go on one of these to see the grasswren, they cost around $370 per person, details from any of the visitors centres.

8.6 Halls Creek

Key Species: **Grey-fronted Honeyeater, Painted Firetail**
Halls Creek makes a good place to stop if you are driving the Great Northern Highway from Kununurra to Derby. It is also the starting off point for the Canning Stock Route. The best area for bird watching is known as China Wall and is reached by leaving Halls Creek south-east on the Duncan Highway, China Wall is signposted on the left after approximately 5 km. Go through the gate and on to the car-park. Below the car-park is a stream which is a morning drinking site for **Painted Firetails**, whilst in the riverside scrub we saw **Red-browed Pardalote** (1), **Golden-backed Honeyeater** and **Grey-fronted Honeyeater** (common).

8.7 The Canning Stock Route

Key Species: **Princess Parrot**
This is without doubt one of the most remote places on earth and can only be attempted in a reliable 4WD, one that is able to cope with crossing sand dunes. You must carry all your own food, water and vehicle spare parts. Ideally at least two vehicles should be travelling in convoy in case one breaks down. The Stock Route itself runs for some 1600 km, crossing the Great Sandy Desert from Halls Creek in the north to Kalgoorlie in the south. The track is only a vehicle widths wide and crosses big sand dunes, about two every kilometre for hundreds of kilometres. The track is the only reliable place in Australia to see the exquisite **Princess Parrot**. In recent years up to several hundred have been recorded down the track each July. They are probably present at other times of the year, but this is the only sensible time to attempt the Route since it gets unbelievably hot in summer. The parrots are highly nomadic but can usually be found between 400 and 500 km from Halls Creek, you just have to drive along keeping your eyes open. An excellent detailed map of the Route is available from motoring organisations; basically it follows an old cattle driving route, going from one well to the next. Some of these wells have drinkable water in them, however you still need to take huge amounts with you in case of a breakdown. A radio is a good idea, although it may be useless if you have an electrical failure. We carried a

satellite beacon to enable us to alert passing aircraft in case of difficulty. We saw relatively few birds along the track until we found approximately 120 **Princess Parrots** feeding on seeds on the tops of sand dunes 2 km north of well No 40, not far before reaching Lake Tobin. The birds were incredibly noisy and conspicuous, especially in the early morning. During the heat of the day they would sit silently in eucalyptus trees so make sure you examine each tree thoroughly whilst searching for the birds. Other birds seen *en route* included **Painted Firetails, Grey-fronted Honeyeaters** and **Spotted Nightjar**, all around the natural rock waterhole in the Bredon Hills. **Bourke's Parrots** were seen around Koranya Homestead, about 150 km south of Halls Creek just past Wolf Creek Crater National Park. Fuel is available from the store here but you should carry enough fuel for at least 1500 km and remember that you will burn it up more quickly during slow sand driving. We spent four days doing a return trip from Koranya to Lake Tobin. We found a small party of parrots on the afternoon of our second day and camped that night with them. Next morning the sky was filled with the sight and sound of at least 120 birds. If you try for this species, take care and good luck!

8.8 Derby

Key Species: Mangrove specialities, (**Brown-tailed Flycatcher**)
Derby is at the west end of the Kimberleys and therefore could be the starting off point for a trip along the Gibb River Road. It also has mangroves close to the town and is the most accessible area to see **Brown-tailed Flycatcher**, although this is usually now regarded as a race of Lemon-breasted Flycatcher. Leave Derby south-westwards along the causeway to the new jetty. Take the last turning on the left before the jetty to the boat ramp and check the mangroves opposite the ramp. Also check the mangroves adjacent to the jetty. In addition to the flycatcher, other birds here include **White-breasted Whistler, Dusky** and **Mangrove Gerygones, Mangrove Fantail, Yellow White-eye** and **Broad-billed Flycatcher.**

8.9 Broome Bird Observatory

Key Species: **Asiatic Dowitcher** (Austral summer)
Although mainly known as a superb area for waders, which migrate here for the Austral summer, many are nevertheless present year round. The observatory area is also very good for mangrove species such as **Mangrove Golden** and **White-breasted Whistlers.** The observatory is run by the RAOU and it is situated on the shores of Roebuck Bay, south of Broome. Turn south off the Great Northern Highway 9 km before Broome on to the All Weather Road. After 10 km, turn left at the T-junction and the observatory is on the left after 6 km. The wardens can advise on the best areas for roosting waders at high tide, most notable of which are **Asiatic Dowitchers** which occur in some numbers every year. It is possible to camp or stay in chalets at the observatory and it is certainly worth giving the wardens a ring if you are about in the vicinity, for example, a **Grey Falcon** spent

several months in the area in 1992/3. For bookings, either write to The Warden, Broome Bird Observatory, Crab Creek Road, PO Box 1313, Broome WA 6725 or telephone (091) 935 600. Barred Creek, some 44 km north of Broome is another mangrove site for **Brown-tailed Flycatcher**. Obtain local directions from town.

8.10 Port Hedland to Broome

This stretch of road is very good for **Australian Bustard**.

B Mid Western Australia (Map 8.5)

It is important to pick up Dusky Gerygone north of Perth, particularly if like us you don't intend to drive all the way around the coast from Perth to Darwin. The other important bird to get is Western Corella, formerly the race *pastinator* of Little Corella. We found this species along the south bank of the Swan River, close to where Brearly Avenue joins the Eastern Highway near the airport, although the birds here may be introduced. Offshore from Geraldton lie the Abrolhos Islands which have a wealth of breeding seabirds including **Lesser Noddy**. Unfortunately it is only possible to visit these islands with an expensive boat charter, although it may be possible to find a fishing boat going out that way.

8.11 Point Samson Mangroves

Key Species: **Mangrove Golden** and **White-breasted Whistlers**, **Dusky Gerygone**

This is an excellent mangrove area. Drive north from Roebourne towards Point Samson. After you have gone through Wickham, shortly before Point Samson, you cross a bridge over a wide inlet. The mangroves here are excellent and are best at high tide, pish at those on the east side of the bridge for **Mangrove Golden** and **White-breasted Whistlers**, **Mangrove Fantail**, **Mangrove Robin**, **Collared Kingfisher**, **Dusky Gerygone** and **Yellow White-eye**.

8.12 Maitland River and Mairee Pool

This site is signposted off the North West Coastal Highway about 60 km west of Roebourne, the turn is north of the bridge over the Maitland River on the south side of the highway. Check the small reed fringed pool just east of the bridge for **Black Bittern**. Around the basic campsite, look for **Painted Firetail** and **Star Finch**.

MID WESTERN AUSTRALIA

Map 8.5: Mid Western Australia
11 Point Samson Mangroves
12 Maitland River and Mairee Pool
13 Cape Range National Park
14 Carnarvon Area
15 New Beach
16 Denham and Monkey Mia
17 Mount Magnet Area

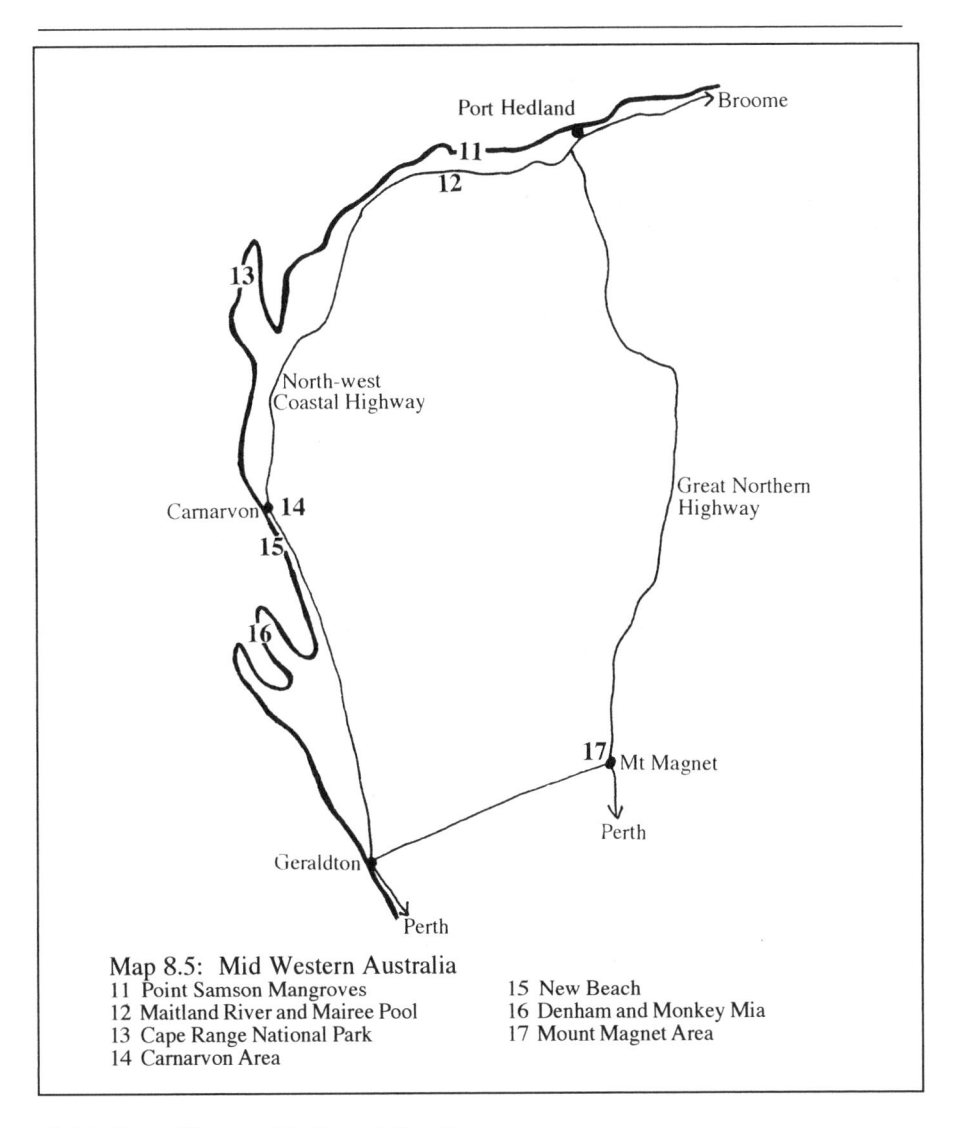

8.13 Cape Range National Park

Cape Range National Park is a good area to birdwatch. Although it has no key species, it is nevertheless a good place to see **Rufous-crowned Emuwren** and there is a good chance of **Pied Honeyeater**. Leave the North West Coastal Highway at Minilya Roadhouse and head north towards Exmouth. Turn west, north of Learmonth along Charles Knife Road (which is good for the western race of **Spinifex Pigeon, Painted Firetail, Masked** and **Little Woodswallows**).

The main birding area, however, is along Shothole Canyon Road. Check the area around the second creek crossing beyond the first car-park; this is a good area for **Rufous-crowned Emuwren** (in the largest spinifex clumps, they are very skulking), **Painted Firetail** (in rocky areas), **Spinifexbird, Red-backed Kingfisher, Red-browed Pardalote** and **Black-eared Cuckoo**. The area 100 m behind the information board at the park entrance is the territory of a **Western Bowerbird** - ask the rangers. There is also a good mangrove area in the park; drive south from the entrance for about 6 km to the mouth of Mangrove Creek. **White-breasted Whistler, Dusky Gerygone, Mangrove Fantail** and **Yellow White-eye** all occur here. Basic camping is possible here.

8.14 Carnarvon Area

On the main road coming into Carnarvon check for **Red-backed Kingfisher** on roadside telegraph wires. In Carnarvon itself, about 2 km south-west of the town centre is the fishing boat harbour, follow the road signs to the harbour. There are quite a few mangroves at the harbour mouth and **Dusky Gerygone** can be seen easily here by pishing. At low tide there is a large area of mud flats with lots of waders including **Great Knot, Terek Sandpiper, Lesser Sandplover** and **Grey-Tailed Tattler**, also **Osprey**. There is also a huge tern flock on the beach, mostly **Crested** but also **Lesser Crested, Gull-Billed, Caspian, Common, Whiskered** and **Fairy Terns**. Another good area near Carnarvon is Rocky Pool. This is reached by turning right off the main highway 7 km north of Carnarvon onto the unsealed road to Gascoyne Junction. The pool is 5 km down a left turn about 38 km along this road and is signposted. **Chiming Wedgebills** were common along this road, also **Redthroats** and **White-winged Fairywrens**. We also saw a party of about fifteen **Crimson Chats**. At the pool itself there was little apart from hundreds of **Little Corellas**.

8.15 New Beach

Key Species: **Dusky Gerygone, Orange Chat, Slender-billed Thornbill**
This is a left turn signposted off the North West Coastal Highway about 40 km south of Carnarvon. New Beach is down 9 km of unsealed road and is an area of fairly extensive mangroves where bush camping is possible. Walk south and bird in the samphire scrub and mangroves. We saw **Dusky Gerygone, Mangrove Fantail** and lots of **Yellow White-eyes**. In the surrounding scrub we saw **Orange Chat** (3), **Elegant Parrot** (1), **Brahminy Kite** and **Slender-billed Thornbill**, this is a good stake-out for the latter.

8.16 Denham and Monkey Mia (Map 8.6)

Key Species: **Chiming Wedgebill, Pied Honeyeater, Thick-billed Grasswren**

Map 8.6: Denham and Monkey Mia

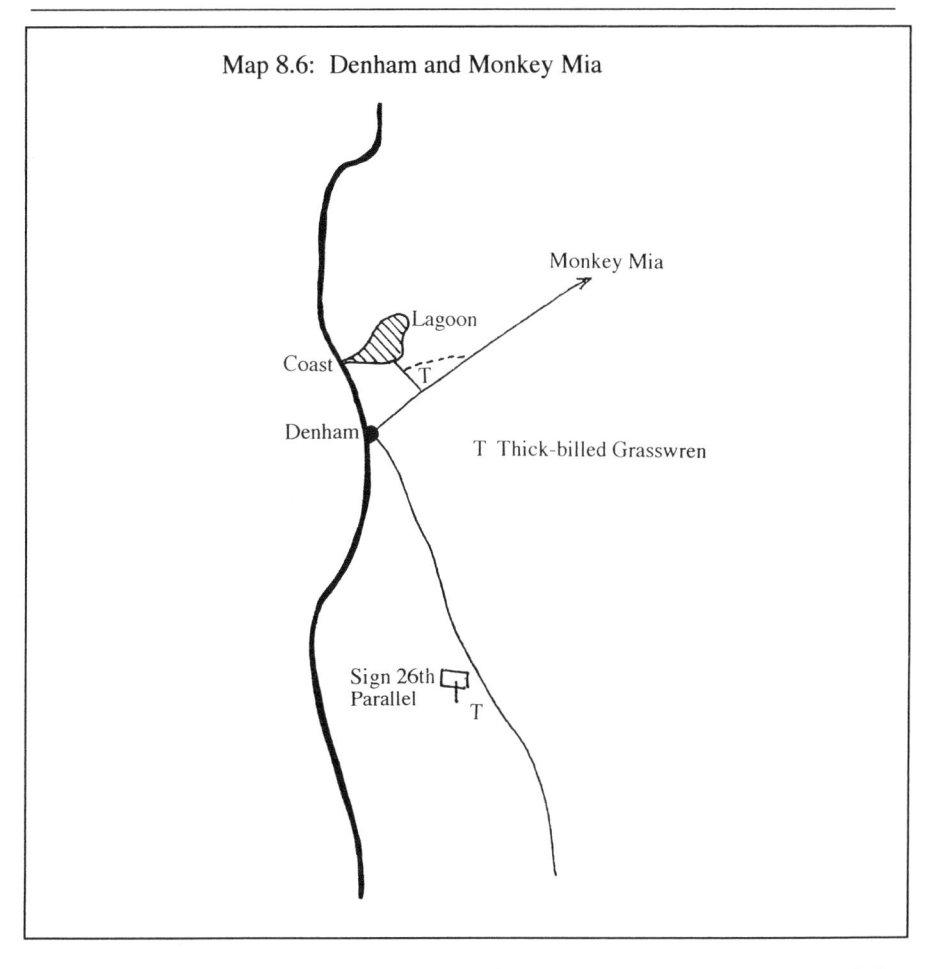

Both these places are on the Peron Peninsula. The Peron Peninsula is one of the most reliable sites in Australia for **Pied Honeyeater**, they will be common if it has rained recently in the area and the bushes are flowering. Denham is about 130 km from the main North West Coastal Highway, the turn off is at the Overlander Roadhouse, which is approximately 700 km north of Perth. The peninsula is excellent for **Thick-billed Grasswrens**. There are two good areas for them, the first is in the bushes around the 26th parallel sign, 10 km before you get to Denham. The second is just as you come out of Denham on the road to Monkey Mia, take a left turn signposted to the Lagoon; just past the first (right hand) bend a track goes off to the right. The start of the track has been blocked off by the raised sides of the lagoon road (making the track hard to find in the dark). The track itself is a vehicle width wide and straight and joins up with the road to Monkey Mia after about 300 m. The grasswrens hop across this track at dawn and dusk. We saw three just after dawn at the Monkey Mia end of the track. In the surrounding scrub **Chiming Wedgebills** were common and easy to see. Continue down to the lagoon, walk round on the left shore and follow the outlet down to the sea. The sides of the outlet are lined with small mangroves where we saw **Mangrove Fantail** and **Yellow White-eye**. At the sea were lots of waders including **Grey-tailed Tattler**. Continue from Denham to the famous dolphin feeding attraction at Monkey Mia. The resort is very well signposted and it is also possible to camp here. By walking right along the beach from the dolphins at Monkey Mia we saw lots of waders on a sandy spit. In the bushes just past a fence across the beach, was an adult **Black-eared Cuckoo**. This was the only one we ever succeeded in seeing in Australia. On the drive back towards the Overlander Roadhouse we saw **Australian Bustard** (3) right beside the road (about 60 km from Denham in an area in which **Emus** were very common).

8.17 Mount Magnet Area

Key Species: **Chestnut-breasted Quail-Thrush, Grey Honeyeater, Slaty-backed Thornbill**

This is a huge area of mulga country along the Great Northern Highway beginning at Dalwallinu all the way to Mount Magnet, some 600 km from Perth, and it is easy to bush camp anywhere out of sight of the road. We drove along stopping whenever we saw birds and checking the surrounding scrub. The best area is just around Mount Magnet itself, where it is possible to stay in motels, and the road west to Geraldton passing through Yalgoo. *En route* the best birds we saw were **Red-tailed Black-Cockatoo** (a flock of about two hundred) and **Slaty-backed Thornbill**. Just out of Mount Magnet on the road signposted to Cue, there is a 'golf course' on either side of the road and a parking area on the left hand side of the road. Park here and work the scrubby bushes on the right hand side of the road around the edge of the golf course. This is a good **Chestnut-breasted Quail-Thrush** site, we saw a pair here and also a pair of **Western Bowerbirds**. About 10 km west of Mount Magnet on the road to Yalgoo we saw a party of **Bourke's Parrots** feeding by the roadside and also **Chestnut-breasted Quail-Thrush**. One km west of Yalgoo we saw two **Redthroats** in roadside scrub. The mulga here is a stake-out for **Grey Honeyeater**, apparently they are easier in the spring but it doesn't seem to be as reliable a site as Alice Springs (see section 7.28).

C Southern Western Australia (Map 8.7)

There are a number of birds endemic to the south-western corner of the continent which includes some of the rarest birds in Australia. These are White-tailed Black-Cockatoo, Long-billed Black-Cockatoo, Red-capped Parrot; Western Corella, Western Rosella, Noisy Scrub-bird, White-breasted Robin, Red-winged Fairywren, Western Bristlebird, Western Thornbill, Western Spinebill, and Red-eared Firetail. Four other species, Rufous Treecreeper, Blue-breasted Fairywren, Western Whipbird and Western Yellow Robin are only found in the south-western corner and in a limited part of South Australia so it is well worth spending time tracking these down when you are visiting the south-west. The climate around Perth and to the north is notoriously hot during the summer months but around Albany it has a reputation for being wet, windy and cold, especially during the winter months. This can make locating the skulking specialities at Two Peoples Bay difficult even though this is their main breeding season and you should allow enough time in your itinerary to allow for bad weather in the region.

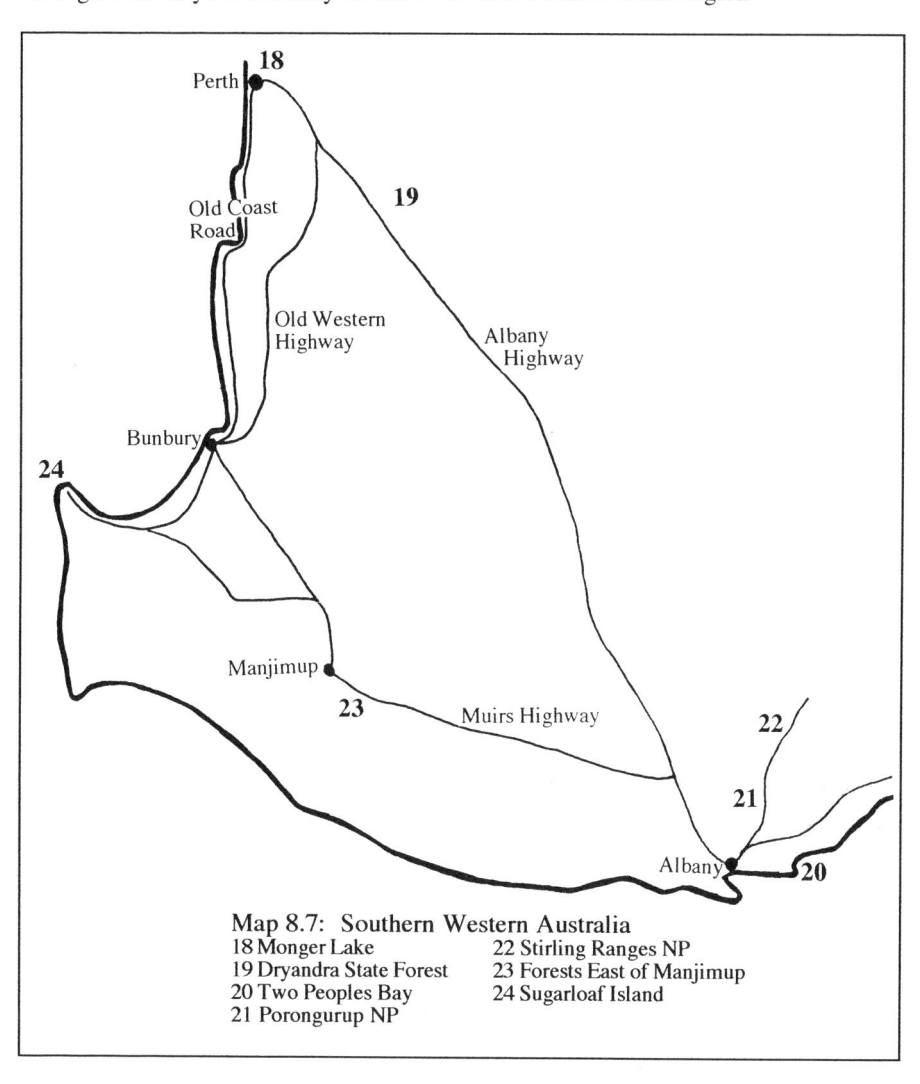

Map 8.7: Southern Western Australia
18 Monger Lake
19 Dryandra State Forest
20 Two Peoples Bay
21 Porongurup NP
22 Stirling Ranges NP
23 Forests East of Manjimup
24 Sugarloaf Island

8.18 Monger Lake

Key Species: **Western Corella**
Located just north-west of Perth city centre, there are car-parks for Monger Lake just west of the Mitchell Freeway. Check the lake for waterbirds especially **Blue-billed Duck** and the trees at the southern end for **Western Corella**. If you dip here, there is a small, declining population of the corella 150 km further north along the Midlands Road between Moora and Dongara. Check agricultural land off to the west as you drive along. Be warned that in such a huge area they can be hard to find, but are easiest to see at dawn and dusk as they fly to and from their roosting sites. Another good place to try is Perup Nature Reserve, located 40 km north-east of Manjimup.

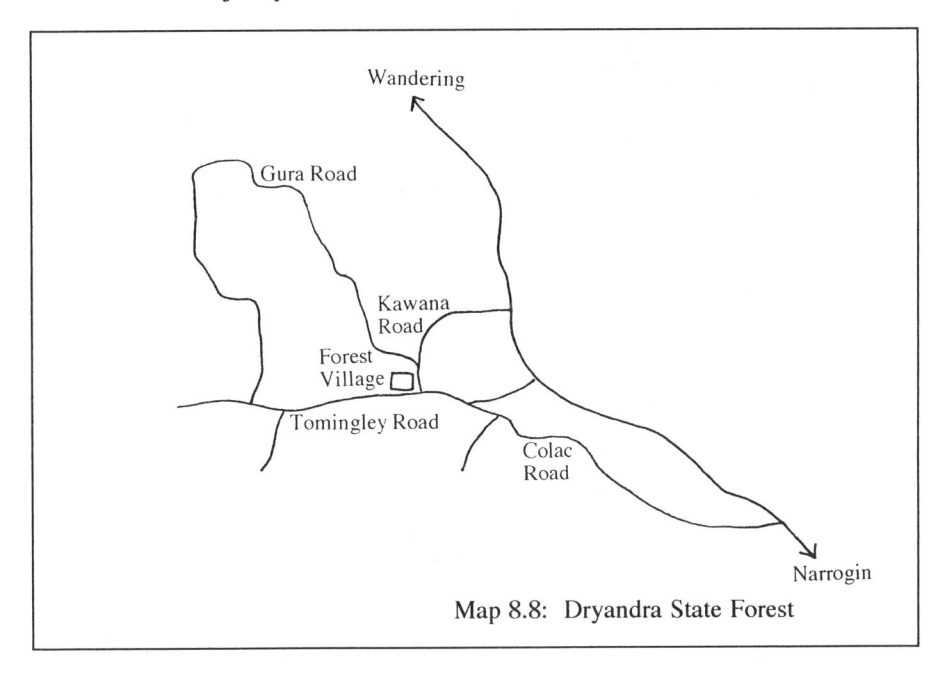

Map 8.8: Dryandra State Forest

8.19 Dryandra State Forest (Map 8.8)

Key Species: **Blue-breasted Fairywren, Crested Shrike-Tit** (race *leucogaster*)
To get to Dryandra State Forest, turn off the Albany Highway at North Bannister 95 km south-east of Perth towards Wandering, 2 km beyond Wandering turn left to Pingelly and after 18 km turn right towards Narrogin. The forest is well signposted off to the right after 25 km. Follow Kawana Road, a dirt track in to the Forest Village. It is mainly a dry eucalyptus forest and the area is excellent for **Blue-Breasted Fairywren**; we saw several groups around the Forest

Village and along the Gura Road. Along the Gura Road you will find **Western Spinebills**. Along the other forest tracks we also saw **Rufous Treecreeper, Western Rosella** and **Painted Button-Quail**. Other birds in the area are **Port Lincoln Ringneck** 'the twenty eight race', **Bush Thick-knee, Regent Parrot, Elegant Parrot, Western Yellow Robin**, and **Grey Currawong**. This is also a good place for the rather rare western race of **Crested Shrike-Tit** and this is also the best place to see the charming, diurnal numbat. It is also worth checking the bushland opposite the caravan park in the nearby town of Narrogin which is a good site for **White-tailed Black-Cockatoo, Regent Parrot** and **Tawny-crowned Honeyeater**. This is the closest place to stay as you are not permitted to camp in the park.

8.20 Two Peoples Bay (Map 8.9)

Key Species: **Noisy Scrub-bird, Western Bristlebird, Western Whipbird, Red-eared Firetail, (Little Wattlebird), White-breasted Robin, Red-winged Fairywren, Rock Parrot**

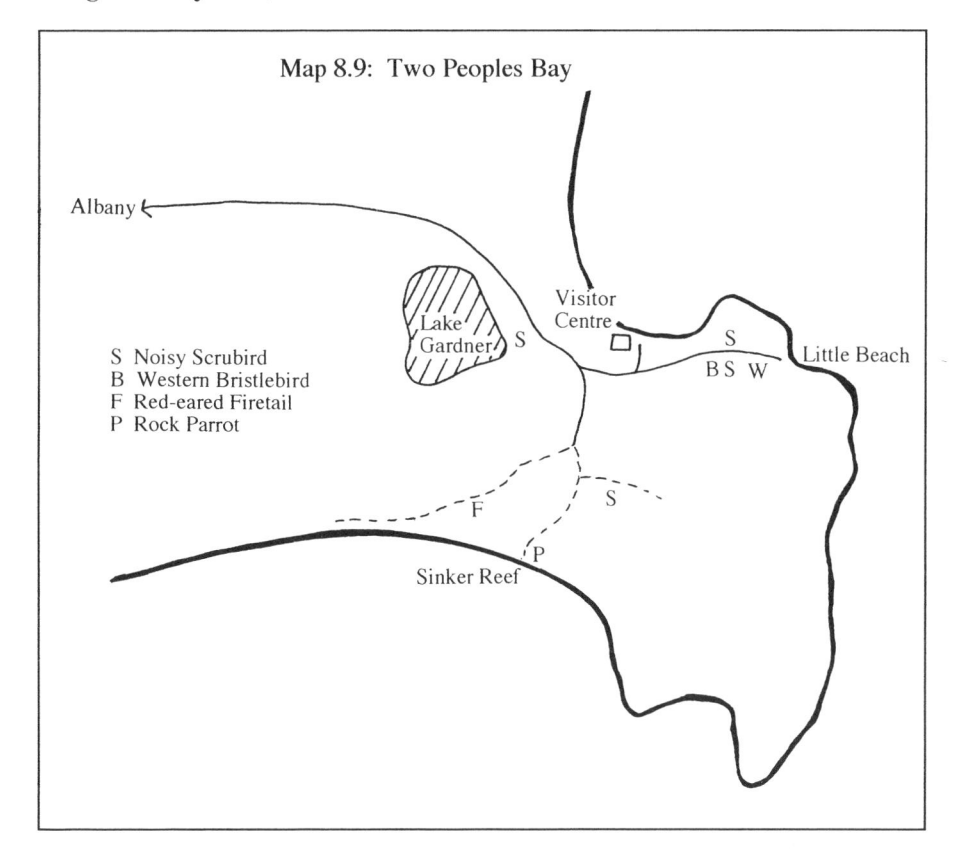

Winter is best for Two Peoples Bay, the most essential site in south-west Australia. It is reached from Albany, drive east along the South Coast Highway and turn right just before King River, then left at the T-junction and left again onto the unsealed track signposted to Two Peoples Bay after about 10 km. You are not allowed to sleep at Two Peoples Bay - we bush camped at the side of the entrance road near where it joins the sealed road to Nanarup. Alternatively you could stay in Albany. **Western Bristlebirds** are mainly found on the firebreaks above Little Beach car-park; we saw one here which was exceptionally tame and hopped past us on the open sand only 1 m away, around the toilets at Little Beach is also an excellent area for them. **Western Whipbirds** are also in the heathland here, we failed to see any but up to six were singing around Little Beach car-park (including one in the turn around on one occasion). **Noisy Scrub-birds** can be heard singing everywhere. Two were in the Little Beach area - both hard to see! Around Lake Gardener is another good place to hear (but not see!) them - the habitat is very dense. The warden was extremely helpful and gave us a private site where they often crossed a track - I saw three here in about 10 mins including one female. Along the heathland walking tracks you will certainly hear this species and occasionally a bird will hop up into a bare bush to sing. Like Rufous Scrub-birds in the east, the birds are very inquisitive and will often come out to investigate very loud pishing and this is a highly recommended way of finding this species. Of the other specialities of the area, **White-breasted Robins** are plentiful around the car-park, **Red-capped Parrots** and **Red-winged Fairywrens** are both reasonably common. We also saw **Rock Parrot** (1), **Red-eared Firetail** (2), **Rufous Calamanthus**, **Western Spinebill** and **Little Wattlebird** as indicated on the map. Also on the road between Two Peoples Bay and Albany, where it crosses the Kalgan River estuary is a good place for **Banded Stilts**.

8.21 Porongurup National Park (Map 8.10)

Key Species: **Rufous Treecreeper**
This national park is about 45 km north-east of Albany *via* Chester Pass Road and Napier, turn north-west towards Mount Barker, then left after about 7 km into Bolganup Road. Follow to the main car-park and picnic area at the end. **Rufous Treecreepers** are very common and tame around the main picnic area, called Tree in the Rock. We also saw **Western Thornbill**, **Red-eared Firetails** (3 near the toilet block), **Blue-breasted Fairywren** and there were lots of **Purple-crowned Lorikeets** around the car-park feeding on the flowering eucalyptus trees. **Western Rosellas** and **White-breasted Robins** were seen a short way along the track to Nancy Peak. We also encountered a party of eight **Long-billed Black-Cockatoos** on the way out to Stirling Ranges National Park about 1 km or so from the turn into Porongurup National Park along the Mount Barker to Porongurup road. Unfortunately, camping is not permitted at this national park, although nearby you could stay at Karri Bank Chalets.

Map 8.10: Porongurup NP

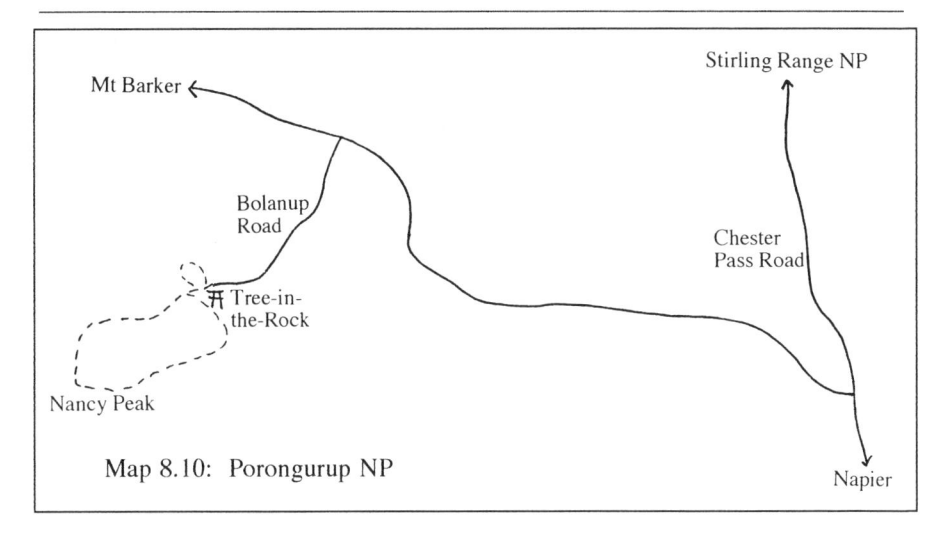

8.22 Stirling Ranges National Park (Map 8.11)

Key Species: **Western Yellow Robin, Western Thornbill, White-tailed Black-Cockatoo**
To get to Stirling Ranges National Park, carry on north-east along Chester Pass Road from Porongurup. The (good) campsite and ranger station are signposted on the left. The clearing opposite this ranger station is an excellent place for **Western Yellow Robin**; ask inside for precise details. **White-tailed Black-Cockatoos** are fairly common here and a large group was actually roosting in the campground at Moingup Springs rangers station when we visited. The roadside verge from Porongurup National Park to Stirling Ranges National Park was really excellent for parrots in the late afternoon. We saw good numbers of **Red-capped Parrots, Western Rosellas, Ringneck Parrots,** and **Elegant Parrots**. Bluff Knoll can be reached by turning south off Chester Pass Road just where it leaves the park; it is well signposted. It is supposed to be a good site for **Western Whipbird** but unfortunately it had been completely burnt out when we visited, but should have regenerated by now so should still hold this species. Try the caravan park opposite the turning to Bluff Knoll for **Western Yellow Robin**.

Map 8.11: Stirling Ranges National Park

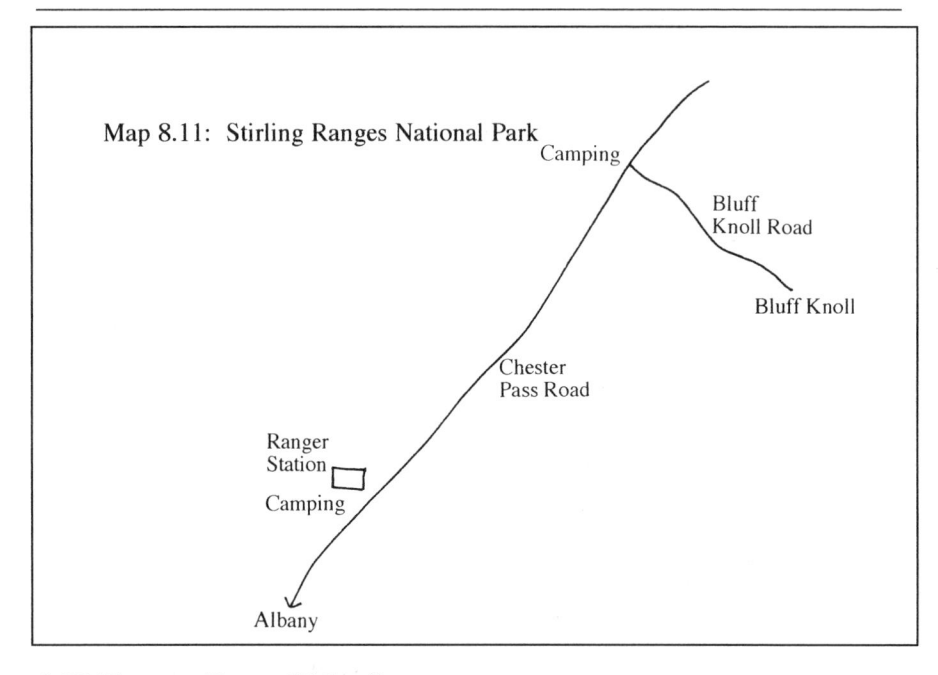

8.23 Forests East of Manjimup

We made several roadside stops along the road to Manjimup looking for **Western Yellow Robin** and eventually found one feeding on the roadside verge about 90 km east of Manjimup.

8.24 Sugarloaf Island

Key Species: **Red-tailed Tropicbird**
Situated about 3 km before the tip of Cape Naturaliste on the west coast, the island is signposted from the lighthouse road. Drive to the car-park and view the island from the nearby viewpoint. It has a breeding colony of **Red-tailed Tropicbirds** during the summer months and a few are supposed to hang around all year although we failed to see any. The roadside trees near to the entrance of the park are often frequented by **Long-billed Black-Cockatoos** in summer, particularly in the evenings.

CHAPTER 9

SOUTH AUSTRALIA

Chestnut-breasted Whiteface, the only bird endemic to South Australia and an exceedingly rare and local species.

CHAPTER 9: SOUTH AUSTRALIA

Introduction (Map 9.1)

South Australia is a large dry state and most people tend to spend time doing the Birdsville and Strzelecki Tracks and rather ignore the rich coastal sites that hold many good species. The excellent saltworks at Adelaide is definitely worth visiting however as this is one of the best wader sites in Australia.

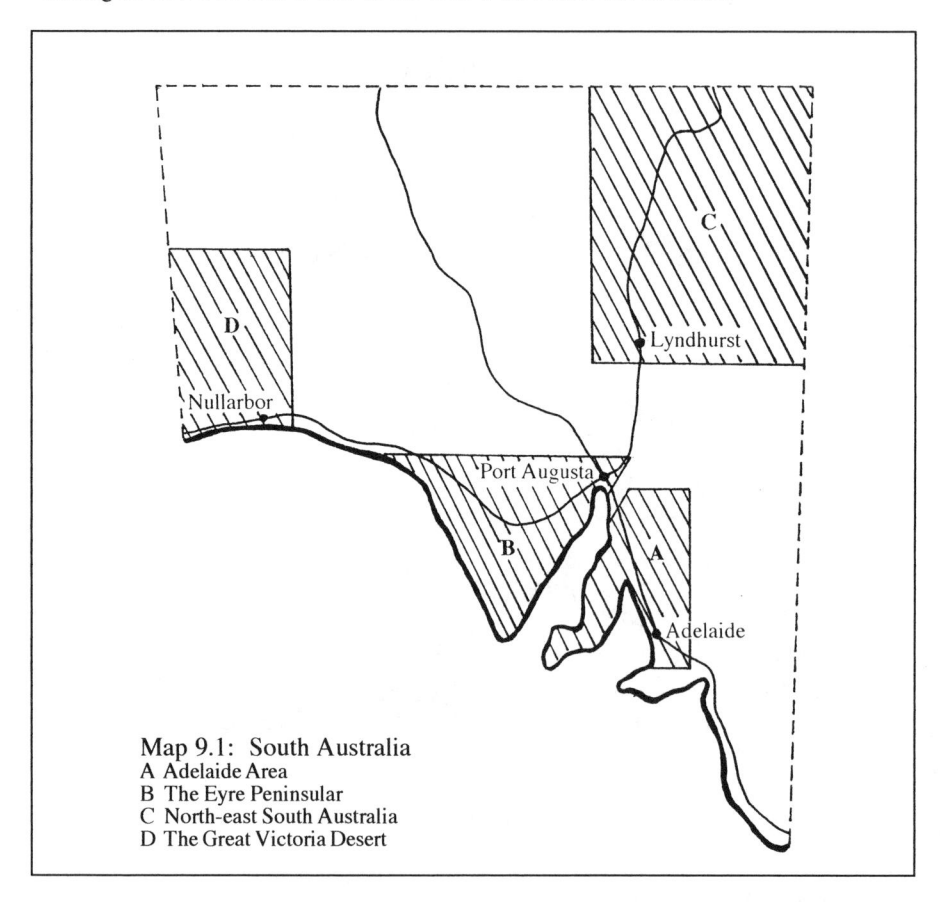

Map 9.1: South Australia
A Adelaide Area
B The Eyre Peninsular
C North-east South Australia
D The Great Victoria Desert

Endemic: Chestnut-breasted Whiteface
Specialities: Cape Barren Goose, Scarlet-chested Parrot, Eyrean Grasswren, Gibber Chat

A Adelaide Area (Map 9.2)

There are several good places to go birding here and Adelaide city would make a good base for exploring many of them.

Map 9.2: Adelaide Area
1 Adelaide ICI Saltworks
2 Port Gawler and Port Prime
3 Mount Remarkable National Park
4 Innes National Park
5 Bool Lagoon

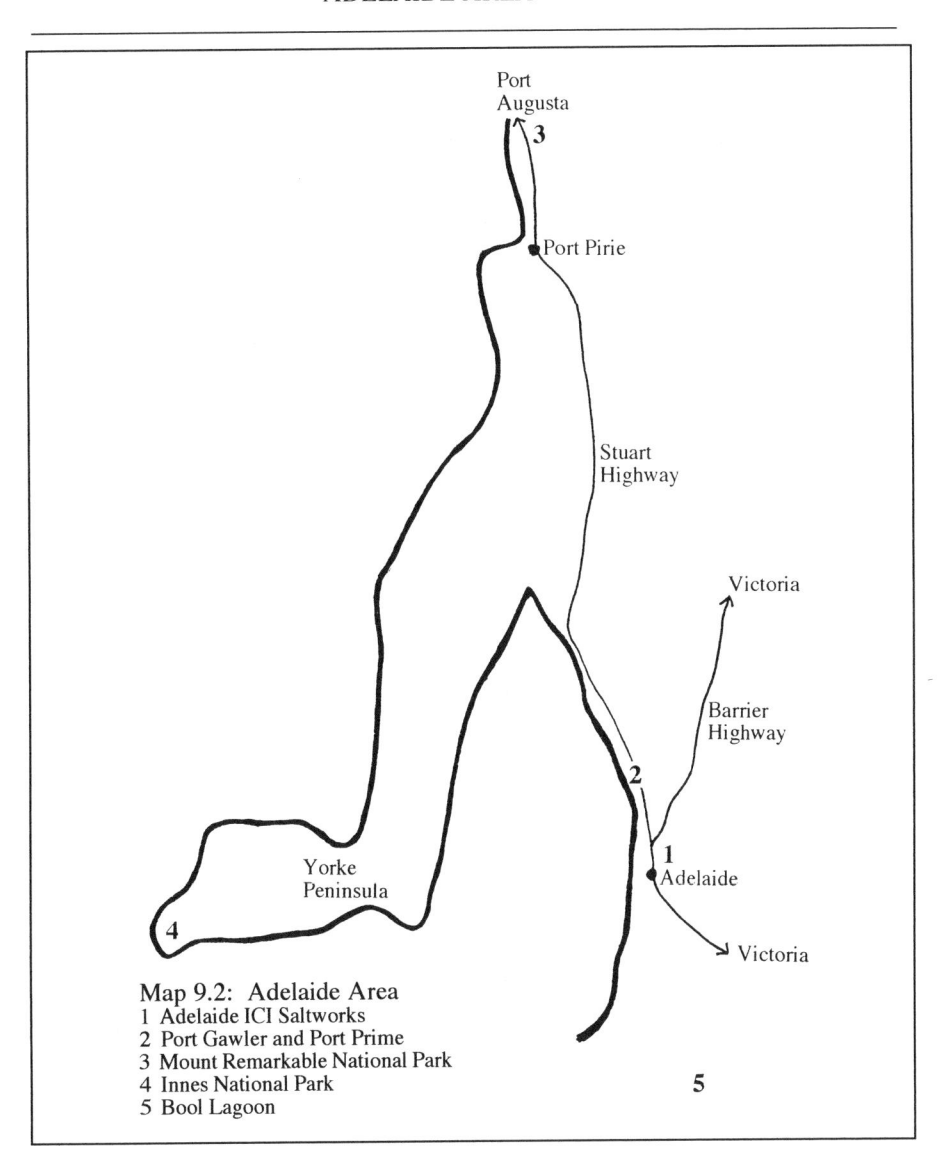

9.1 Adelaide ICI Saltworks

Key Species: **Banded Stilt**, waders
This is situated some 19 km north-west of Adelaide and is world famous for waders. Clearly the Austral summer is the best time of year for the northern hemisphere waders. The saltworks are private and to obtain admission you *must* be accompanied by a local birder who possesses a key to the St. Kilda Road

entrance gate. If you plan to visit, try contacting the South Australian Ornithological Association, c/o South Australian Museum, North Terrace, Adelaide SA 5000. Vagrant waders are usually reported each year, mostly North American species.

9.2 Port Gawler and Port Prime

Key Species: **Rock Parrot, Elegant Parrot, Slender-billed Thornbill**
To get to these places, drive north from Adelaide on the Princes Highway towards Port Wakefield. Port Gawler is a left turn 5 km north of Virginia. Drive down the road but stop and explore the samphire flats before reaching the mangroves and coast. The most interesting species regularly found are **Rock** and **Elegant Parrots** (mainly summer), also **Slender-billed Thornbill**. The same species occur at Port Prime which is reached by continuing north along the Princes Highway then turning left between Lower Light and Dublin. Drive right down to the coast and explore the samphire flats and coastal dunes.

9.3 Mount Remarkable National Park

Key Species: **Elegant Parrot**
Situated south-east of Port Augusta, this national park is reached from Melrose, which is 23 km south of Wilmington. Elegant Parrots are supposed to be common in the park, but there are no facilities to camp at this access point.

9.4 Innes National Park (Map 9.3)

Key Species: **Brush Bronzewing, Purple-gaped Honeyeater, Western Whipbird**
Situated on the tip of Yorke Peninsula, this national park is yet another **Western Whipbird** locality. I have no idea if they sing like the Western Australian or Eyre Peninsula birds, but suspect they will sound like the latter. There are quite a few territories within the park. To reach the park, drive down the peninsula to Marion Bay, carry on through Stenhouse Bay and round the park. For the best whipbird locality, take the track to West Cape. Park after 300 m, climb the dunes to the left and look down onto a hollow that has a big bush in it. Whipbirds have been seen by several people here when they use it as a song bush in the early morning. Another good area for them is some 2.5 km south of Brown Lake on the west side of the road. **Brush Bronzewing** and **Purple-gaped Honeyeaters** are also common. **Malleefowl** are also fairly common in this area. There is a good campsite just before the turning to West Cape. The bushes around the back of the campsite are good for whipbirds.

Map 9.3: Innes National Park

Brown Lake

Marion Bay

West Cape

Stenhouse Bay

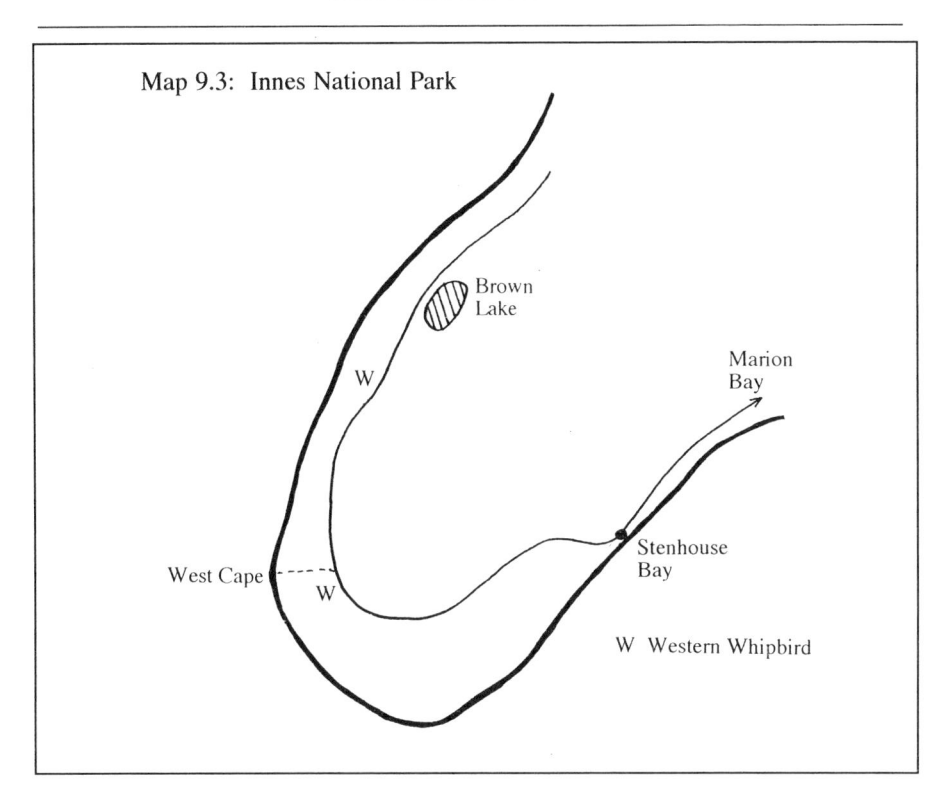

W Western Whipbird

9.5 Bool Lagoon

Key Species: Ducks, crakes, **Australasian Bittern**
Situated in the south-east of the state, Bool Lagoon is renowned as the best site in South Australia for waterbirds. From Naracoorte drive south for 17 km towards Mount Gambier then turn right in Struan towards Bool Lagoon. The main entrance is well signposted on the right hand side after a further 7 km. There are two good campsites here. This is a huge wetland area with many breeding waterbirds. The best areas for birds vary according to how dry the lagoons are and it is best to check with the rangers on the current situation. **Australasian Bitterns** are reasonably common in the reedbeds and there is a chance of **Black-backed Bittern**. You should also see **Brolga**, **Musk Duck**,and **Blue-billed Duck** along with many commoner species. **Freckled Duck** and **Plumed Whistling Duck** are frequently present, depending on how dry it is and what conditions are like elsewhere in the state.

B The Eyre Peninsula (Map 9.4)

This peninsula is largely ignored by the touring birder since there are no absolutely essential sites to visit. We went down here principally to look for

Western Whipbird, but also went to some other really good sites. This is also a place to get a couple of Western Australia birds (Blue-breasted Fairywren and Western Yellow Robin) for anyone who hasn't got the time to drive over to Perth. Other good birds include a Rock Parrot stake-out as well as a superb waterbird area north of Port Lincoln which held both Cape Barren Geese and Freckled Duck.

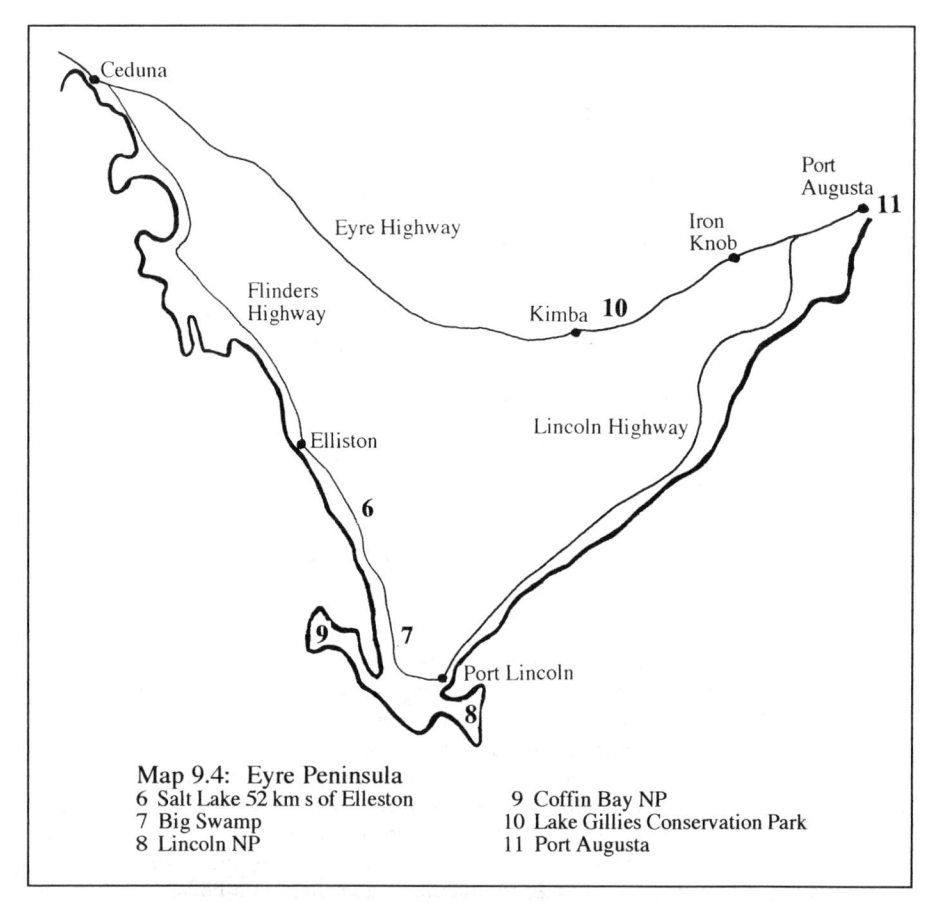

Map 9.4: Eyre Peninsula
6 Salt Lake 52 km s of Elleston
7 Big Swamp
8 Lincoln NP
9 Coffin Bay NP
10 Lake Gillies Conservation Park
11 Port Augusta

9.6 Salt Lake 52 km South of Elliston

This lake is partly visible from the Flinders Highway. Park by the 'South Eyre Peninsula Sign' and pick your way through the bushes to the lake shore. Some of the birds seen here were one (injured) **Banded Stilt** and **Musk Duck**. There were also a couple more salt lakes a bit further south next to the Highway which also looked good for **Banded Stilt**, although we didn't explore them.

9.7 Big Swamp

Key Species: **Cape Barren Goose**
This is located either side of the Elliston to Port Lincoln road, 21 km north-west of Port Lincoln. Hundreds of ducks plus a few waders could be seen from the roadside. Of these the best birds were **Cape Barren Goose** (8), **Freckled Duck** (30), **Musk Duck** and **Red-necked Avocet** (7). Another regular site for the goose is either side of the road between the Lincoln Highway and Louth Bay 20 km north of Port Lincoln.

9.8 Lincoln National Park (Map 9.5)

Key Species: **Western Whipbird**

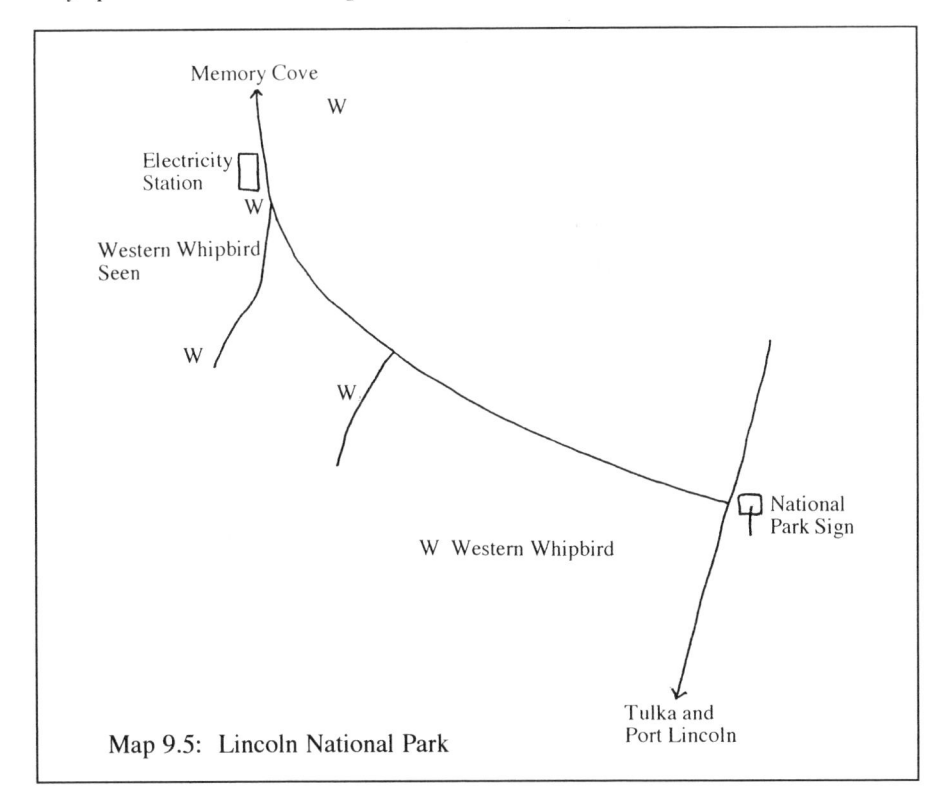

Map 9.5: Lincoln National Park

To get to Lincoln National Park, take the road from Port Lincoln to Tulka (best to ask) but continue past Tulka and turn left at the national park sign. Follow the road for 8.3 km (after bearing right towards Memory Cove after approximately 6 km) to where a track goes off to the left (just before an electricity station) where we bush camped. We heard at least three **Western Whipbirds** around this

166   CHAPTER 9: SOUTH AUSTRALIA

junction and eventually saw one. May is clearly not a good month to see this species here; the birds were only singing briefly at dawn and dusk and hardly at all during the day. The best months to be here are July to October. Note that this is later than in Western Australia where the birds at Two Peoples Bay seem to breed earlier i.e. May to July. The two populations (although of the same race) have a very different song, however, it is still recognisable as this species. The only bird we saw was as it crossed the track between song bushes during the early morning. Most of the other birds we saw at Lincoln National Park were seen around this junction or along the road between here and the 6 km junction. Other good birds recorded were **Southern Scrub-Robin** (common), **Diamond Firetail**, (3 by the entrance gate), **Western Yellow Robin** (1), **Chestnut Quail-Thrush**, **Blue-breasted Fairywren** (these were fairly common although in May very few males are in full plumage), **White-browed Scrubwren** (race *maculata*), **Shy Hylacola**, **Purple-gaped Honeyeater**, **Tawny-crowned Honeyeater** (both these Honeyeaters were around the flowering mallee, especially in the more open areas) and **Grey Currawong** (race *intermedia*).

9.9 Coffin Bay National Park (Map 9.6)

Key Species: **Rock Parrot, Hooded Plover**

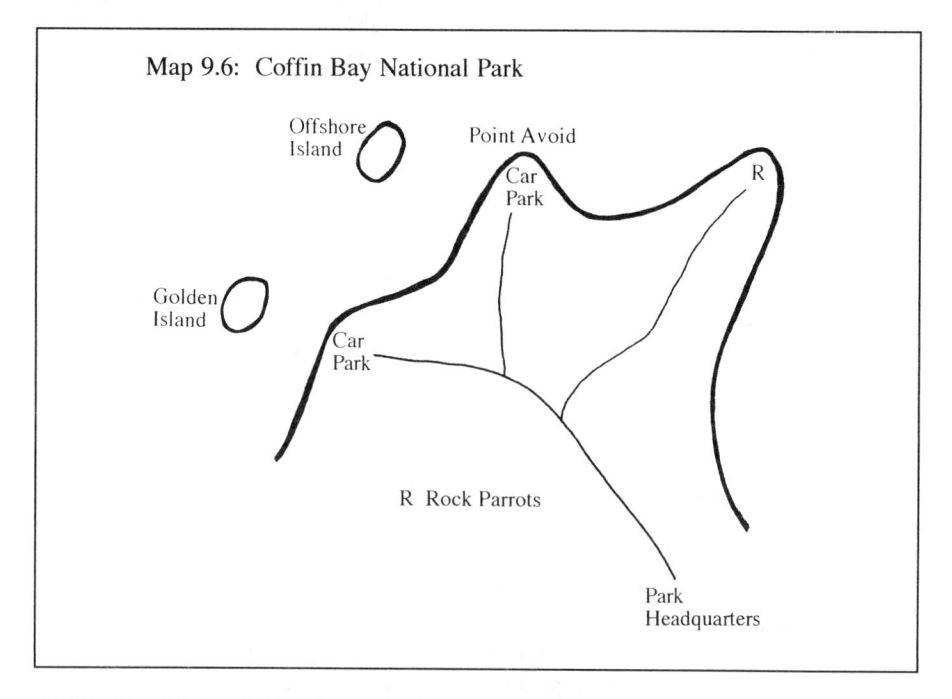

Map 9.6: Coffin Bay National Park

Offshore Island
Point Avoid
Car Park
R
Golden Island
Car Park
R Rock Parrots
Park Headquarters

Coffin Bay National Park is reached by turning right off the Flinders Highway, 32 km before Port Lincoln. It is a stake-out for **Rock Parrot**. After 15 km, you enter the park, follow the rough dirt track to Point Avoid where it is possible to bush camp. The parrots roost on Golden Island just offshore, but fly over to the mainland past Point Avoid in the early to mid-morning. Either tramp around the short heathy areas for them or wait until they fly over calling and see where they go down. We tracked them down to the next headland round to the west where they were feeding amongst the sand dunes. The birds seen here included **Rock Parrot** (20), **Osprey**, **Hooded Plover** (on the beach opposite Golden Island), **Pied** and **Sooty Oystercatchers**, **Brush Bronzewing**, **Southern Scrub-Robin**, **Blue-breasted Fairywren**, **White-browed Scrubwren**, **Purple-gaped** and **Tawny-crowned Honeyeaters**.

9.10 Lake Gilles Conservation Park

This is a mallee area close to the Eyre Highway between Kimba and Iron Knob. It is about the most easterly point for **Blue-breasted Fairywren** and **Western Yellow Robin**, although we didn't see the latter. Drive 17 km east of Kimba and turn north-west to Lake Gilles. Drive for about 4 km, park and search the mallee areas. The best birds here were **Australian Owlet-Nightjar, Blue-breasted Fairywren, Purple-crowned Lorikeet** and **Grey Currawong**.

9.11 Port Augusta

On salt pans opposite the BP service station in the middle of town we saw a **Banded Stilt** and **Red-necked Avocet** (5).

C North-east South Australia (Map 9.7)

This is a remote part of the continent so it is essential to make sure your vehicle is running well before entering this region and you will need to bush camp. The localities are described in the order in which we visited them after driving across from Bourke in New South Wales.

9.12 Cameron Corner to Merty-Merty Station

Key Species: **Eyrean Grasswren, Banded Whiteface**
Some 15 km west of Cameron Corner is Bollards Lagoon Homestead. From here to Merty-Merty Station the track crosses a series of clay capped sand dunes, thus they are passable to 2WD provided it is not wet. As you drive over these large sand dunes, look carefully for patches of healthy cane grass on the top of the dunes as this is the habitat favoured by **Eyrean Grasswrens** which are found in all suitable patches of habitat. In the valley areas between sand dunes at the following distances west of Bollards Lagoon Homestead 14.6, 21.3, 26.0, 28.6, and 46.1 km look for **Banded Whitefaces**. Other good birds found in the valley areas were **Red-browed Pardalote, Chestnut-crowned Babbler, Cinnamon Quail-Thrush** and **Little Button-Quail**.

168   CHAPTER 9: SOUTH AUSTRALIA

Map 9.7: North-eastern South Australia
12 Cameron Corner to Merty-Merty Station
13 The Strzelecki Track South
14 The Chestnut-breasted Whiteface Site
15 The Birdsville Track

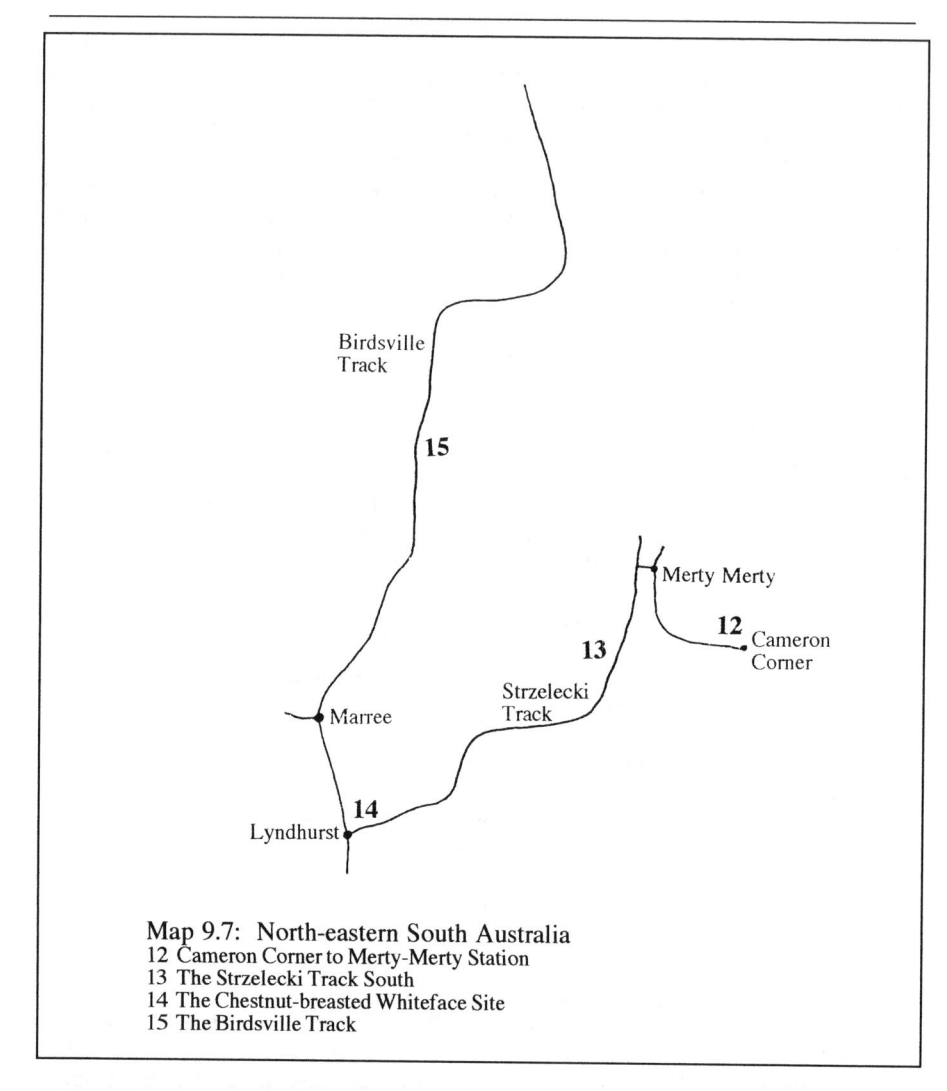

9.13 The Strzelecki Track South

Key Species: **Letter-winged Kite**, **Cinnamon Quail-Thrush**, **Banded Whiteface**, **Gibber Chat**
At 82 km west of Bollards Lagoon you reach a signpost 'Lyndhurst 372 km' and thus the Strzelecki track. 44 km down the track is the Strzelecki Crossing, search the area 9 km north of this in the barren saltbush for **Banded Whiteface**. About 5-6 km south of the Crossing is a stand of dead trees on the east side of the road. This is a regular day time roosting site for **Letter-winged Kites** in trees which

hold several pairs of nesting Black Kites. It is certainly worth searching any tall trees for roosting kites all the way along the Strzelecki track. As you drive along, look for flushed **Cinnamon Quail-Thrush**; we saw our first 25 km south of the crossing. Also look for **Gibber Chat** in the stony areas.

9.14 The Chestnut-breasted Whiteface Site (Map 9.8)

Key Species: **Rufous Calamanthus, Thick-billed Grasswren, Redthroat, Chestnut-breasted Whiteface**
This is the only regular site known for **Chestnut-breasted Whiteface**. The birds have been known here since about 1986. The key areas to search are 26 km and 27.2 km east of Lyndhurst on the Strzelecki Track.

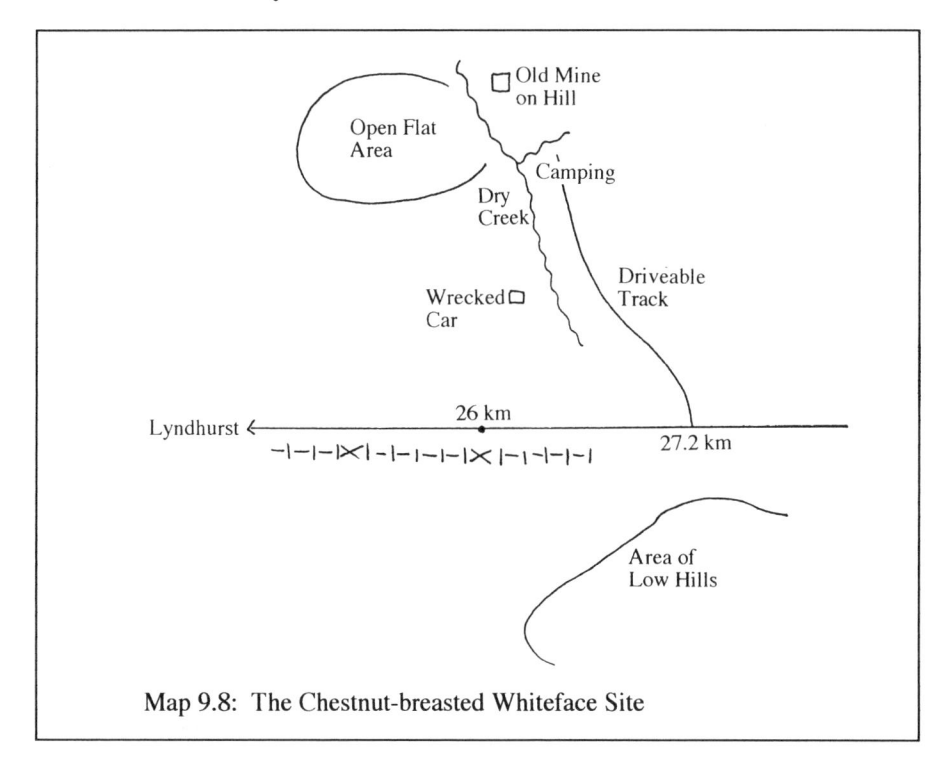

Map 9.8: The Chestnut-breasted Whiteface Site

Site at 27.2 km
Look for a faint track going north towards the old mine, you will pass an inconspicuous rusting car on your left as you go along it. Park before you get to the mine and cross the dry creek bed. The best area to search seems to be the flat plain directly opposite the old mine entrance. We saw two birds here in May 1993.

Site at 26 km
Coming from Lyndhurst, look carefully on your right for two gates in the fence close to the road which are approximately 100 m apart. Go through the second of these and search the low hills and plain up to 600 m from the road. We saw three birds here.

Although the habitat looks discouraging, it is definitely worth persevering. Although we had no real difficulty, the whitefaces can be very tricky to find, they feed inconspicuously on the ground so are easily overlooked. They have a soft trilling call. At the time of our visit they were not at all shy; some people have found them to be extremely wary and to flush from quite a distance.

Many other good birds are at both sites in this area, in particular are **Thick-billed Grasswrens**. These are common, particularly in the bigger saltbush along the dry creekbeds in the hills. Look for them as you come over a rise; they scurry back to cover. Sit down and wait patiently and they will come back out. Some individuals are not at all wary. **Cinnamon Quail-Thrushes** are found here in good numbers, listen for their high-pitched call as they run away ahead of you. **Redthroats** are fairly common in the larger saltbush. Listen for their loud scolding call or pretty song, note that they also mimic the **Rufous Calamanthus** which is another common bird in the area, look for these singing from the tops of bushes. We also found **Chirruping Wedgebills** to be common and flushed a **Spotted Nightjar** from a dry creek-bed. It is worth looking out for **Gibber Chats** which are regularly seen here although it is not optimal habitat for them.

9.15 The Birdsville Track (Map 9.9)

Key Species: **Eyrean Grasswren, Grey Grasswren, Yellow Chat, Flock Bronzewing**

The Birdsville Track can be approached from Windorah in the east, Mount Isa in the north or more easily from Marree in the south. The connecting roads are reputed to be much rougher than the track itself, so for 2WD, approach and return is recommended *via* Marree. All the usual warnings about outback travel apply here i.e. extra fuel, water, telling people when you'll be back. Note that it is dangerously hot here in summer, one British birdwatcher died of heat exhaustion here recently. The Track is much rockier than the Strzelecki Track so more than one spare tyre is recommended. The birds to be found here are basically the same as those on the Strzelecki Track and include **Grey Falcon, Eyrean** and **Grey Grasswrens, Letter-winged Kite, Flock Bronzewing** (water bores at dawn and dusk), **Cinnamon Quail-Thrush, Gibber, Orange** and **Crimson Chats**. The one bird which is not found on the Strzelecki is **Yellow Chat**. The best sand dune for both grasswrens is Koonchera Dune, the turning to which is signposted from the track 400 km north of Marree, 118 km south of Birdsville. Drive 20 km to the end of the dune where there is a waterhole. The cane grass on the dune tops is the best area for **Eyrean Grasswren**, whilst the lignum flats hold **Grey Grasswrens**. The waterhole is worth a look at dawn as **Red-necked Avocets, Australian Pratincoles** and **Flock Bronzewings** are all likely.

Map 9.9: The Birdsville Track

Birdsville 118 km

Kooncherie Dune

Kooncherie Waterhole

Pandie Burra Bore

Lake Surprise Dune

Birdsville Track

Mungeranie Roadhouse

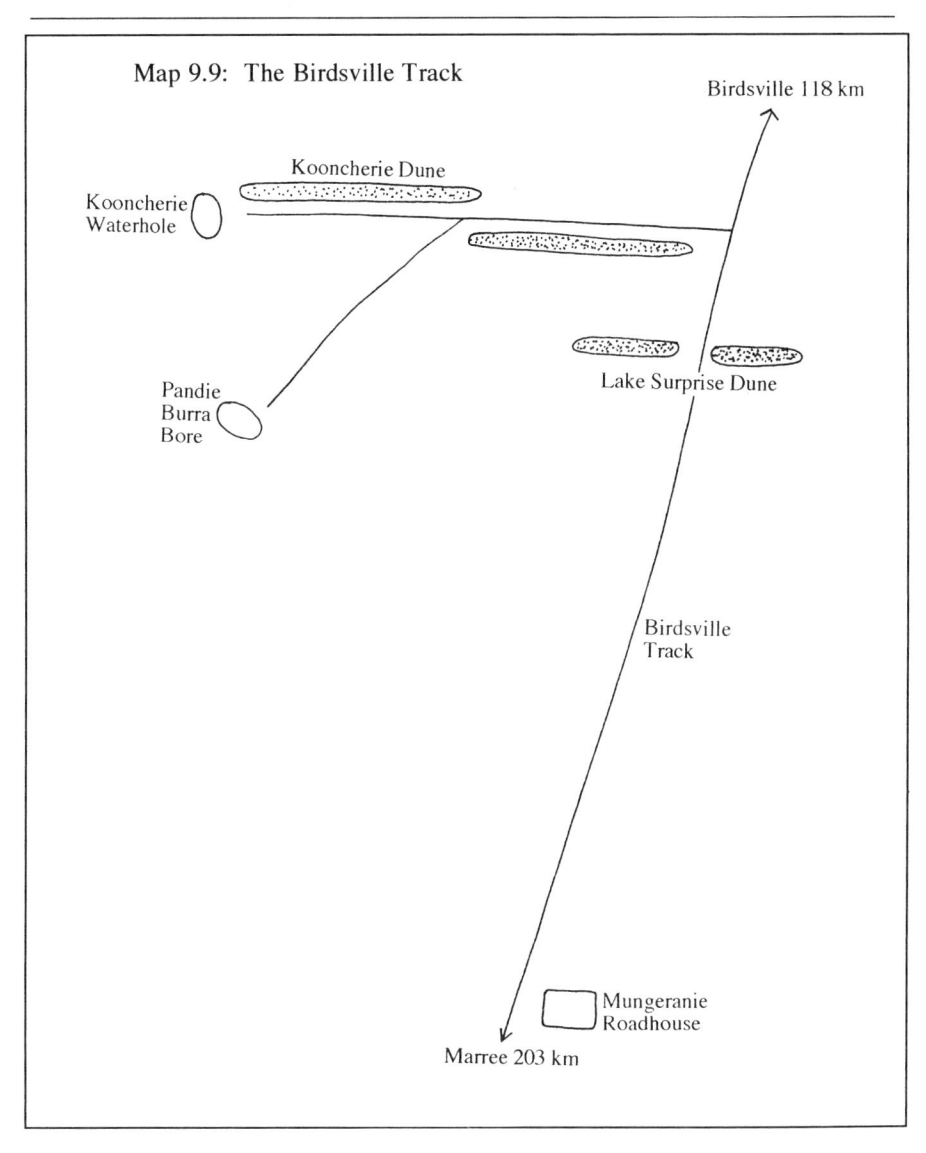

Marree 203 km

Halfway along the track to Koonchera Dune is a track which leads off to Pandie Burra Bore, this is where **Yellow Chats** occur, but only in the summer months from November onwards. For anyone who has seen **Grey**, but needs **Eyrean Grasswren**, they can be seen much further south at Mungeranie Roadhouse, only 203 km from Marree. They are found on the cane grass covered dunes that run parallel to the east side of the track behind the roadhouse. Also, Lake Surprise Dune, 20 km south of the turning to Koonchera Dune is a good place to find this species. **Gibber Chats**, **Cinnamon Quail-Thrushes** and **Inland Dotterels** occur anywhere along the track and have been seen as close as 20 km from Marree. For **Inland Dotterels**, it is best to drive around at night since they are largely nocturnal. **Orange** and **Crimson Chats** are dependent on recent rainfall in the area. **Grey Falcon** can occur anywhere, but like **Letter-winged Kite**, the best chance is to look in trees along dry creek beds.

D Great Victoria Desert Region (Map 9.10)

This area is remote even by Australian standards, but it is the only place where you can hope to see the incomparable Scarlet-chested Parrot. A reliable 4WD is essential to visit the region north of Cook as is full written permission from the relevant authorities and you will need to take all your own supplies with you and bush camp. The road between the Eyre Highway and Cook should present no problems unless it has just recently rained so there should be no difficulty in calling in to see Inland Dotterels.

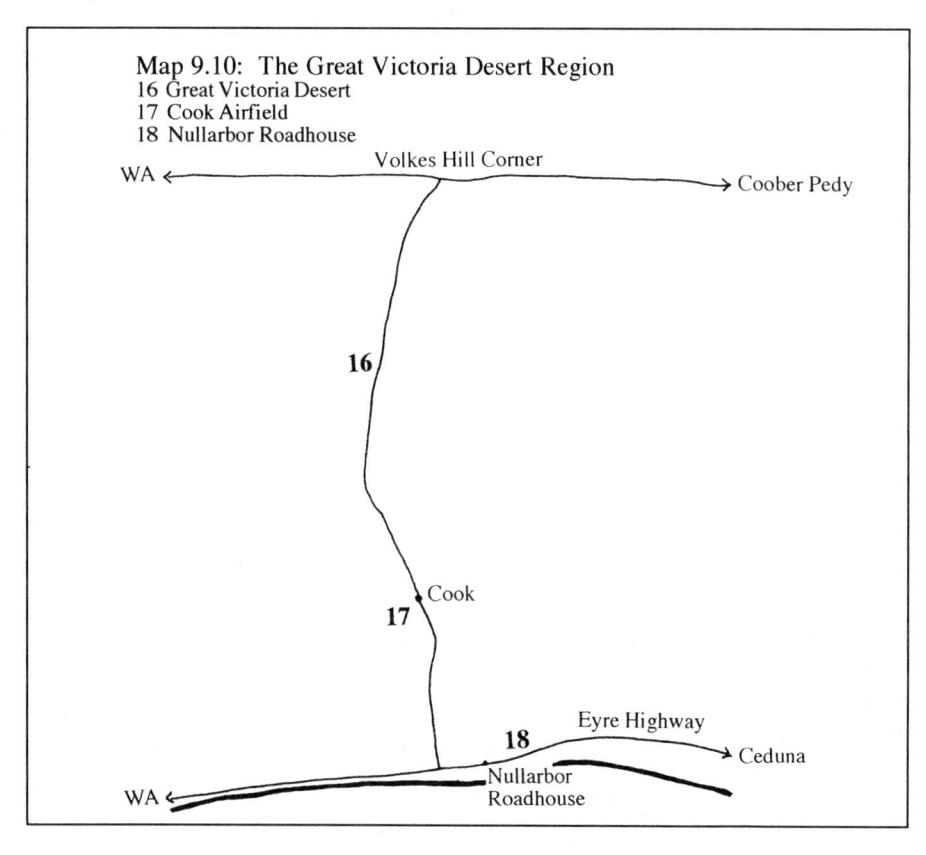

Map 9.10: The Great Victoria Desert Region
16 Great Victoria Desert
17 Cook Airfield
18 Nullarbor Roadhouse

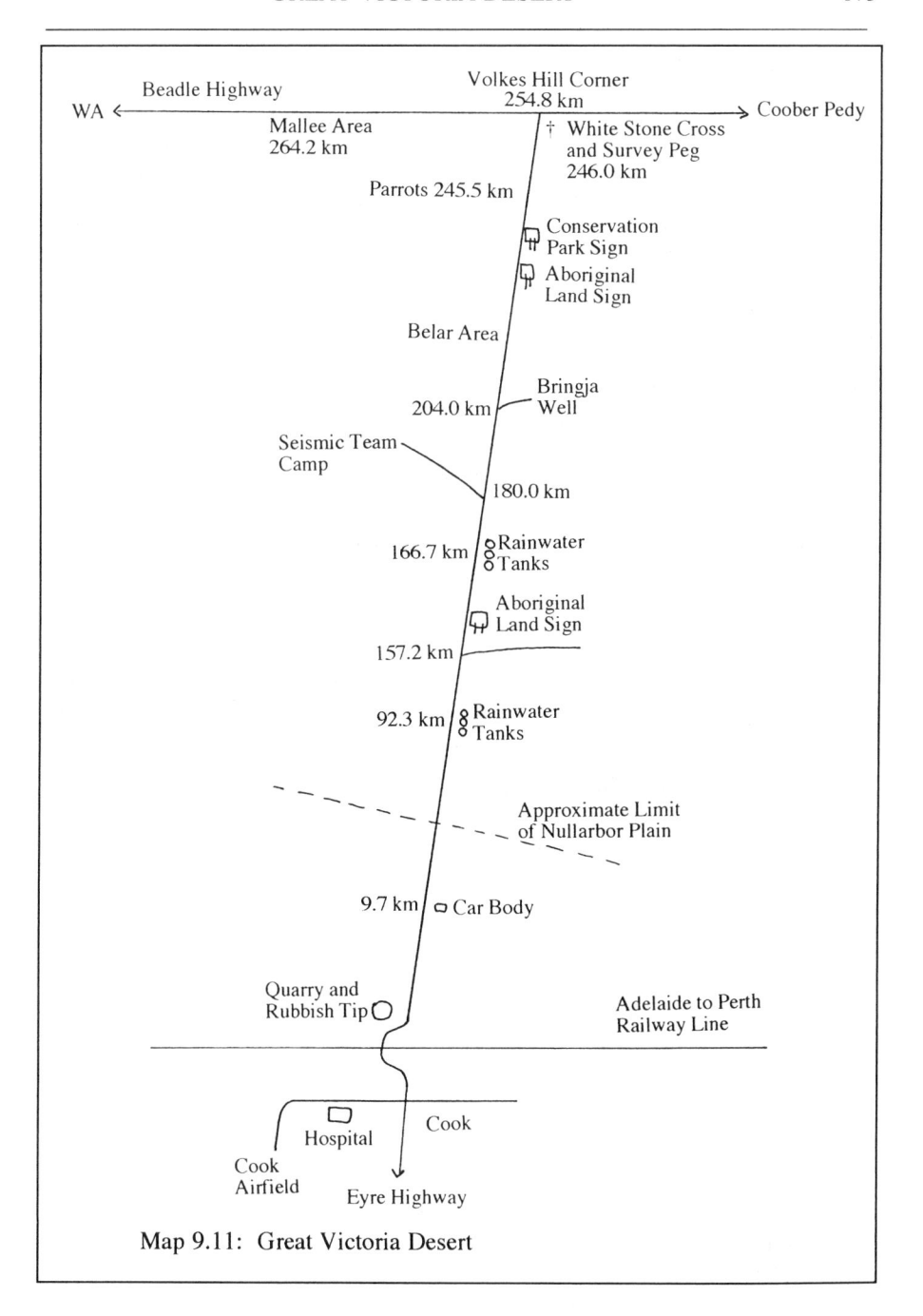

GREAT VICTORIA DESERT

Beadle Highway
WA ← ──────────── Volkes Hill Corner 254.8 km ──────────── → Coober Pedy

Mallee Area 264.2 km

† White Stone Cross and Survey Peg 246.0 km

Parrots 245.5 km

Conservation Park Sign
Aboriginal Land Sign

Belar Area

204.0 km — Bringja Well

Seismic Team Camp

180.0 km

166.7 km — Rainwater Tanks

Aboriginal Land Sign

157.2 km

92.3 km — Rainwater Tanks

— — — Approximate Limit of Nullarbor Plain

9.7 km — Car Body

Quarry and Rubbish Tip ○

Adelaide to Perth Railway Line

Hospital — Cook

Cook Airfield — Eyre Highway

Map 9.11: Great Victoria Desert

9.16 Great Victoria Desert (Map 9.11)

Key Species: Scarlet-chested Parrot, **White-browed Treecreeper**
In order to access the Great Victoria Desert, we cut through from the Stuart Highway *via* Kingoonya to Wirrulla on the Eyre Highway and camped and birded in a mallee area 104 km north of Wirrulla. The best birds seen here were **Jacky Winter, Port Lincoln Ringneck, Pink Cockatoo, Rufous Treecreeper, Grey-fronted Honeyeater, White-fronted Honeyeater** (common) and **Grey Currawong** (race *intermedia*.). Other birds seen on this journey were **Ground Cuckoo-Shrike** (6 at 'Skull Tanks') and a male **Spotted Harrier** between Ceduna and Nullarbor Roadhouse.

The track north of Cook to Volkes Hill Corner is very sandy and parts have very deep wheel ruts. It is necessary to be fully equipped for outback travel to go here. All the warnings about travel in remote areas applies i.e. carry extra fuel, food and water and tell reliable people when you expect to return and your intended route. A radio is almost essential. The danger with this place is the extreme remoteness. If you break down it could easily be another six weeks before another vehicle passes by, for this reason it is sensible to travel in with at least two vehicles. Spare parts must also be carried along with shovels, spare wheels and bull bags *etc*. Advice on outback travel can be obtained from one of the motoring organisations, such as the NRMA and a map of the desert area is also essential. It is also necessary to get permission to pass through the Maralinga Tjarutja Aboriginal land. This must be applied for in advance from Maralinga Tjarutja Inc., Ceduna, South Australia, (Tel (086) 252946). If you call in there, ask for Archie who should be able to give you the latest information about road conditions. It is not only polite to get permission, but remember, if you are caught on this land without it, the fine is $2000 per day. It is also essential to obtain a permit from the National Parks and Wildlife in Ceduna to enter the Unnamed Conservation Park in the Great Victoria Desert. Their office is opposite the main post office in Ceduna and permits are available over the counter for $3 per day per vehicle. Remember if you break down in the desert without permission and have to be rescued, you will certainly be charged for the cost of your rescue and vehicle recovery. This aside, the good news is that if you get in, you stand a very good chance of seeing the parrot. We struck it lucky and had a large flock of at least 250 birds 9.3 km south of Vokes Hill Corner. Most people seem to see the parrot west of Vokes Hill Corner along the Beadle Highway, they have been seen in the mallee areas 7, 30 and 50-52 km west of the corner. The birds we saw were not in mallee but in acacia scrub and belar. They were feeding on seeds on the ground and were quite tame and approachable. Adult males are quite simply stunning. To get to the site, drive west from Nullarbor Roadhouse for 42 km, and turn right onto a good dirt road to Cook. At Cook it is difficult to find the right track to Vokes Hill Corner - the road passes the old quarry/rubbish tip on the left then heads off almost due north. You should make sure you are on the right track by asking in town. It is also a good idea to let the matron at Cook hospital know you're going up the track and give her the expected date of return. To give an idea of driving times it took us about 10 hours each way between Cook and Volkes Hill Corner including meals and birding stops. Note, however, that we went through just after a seismic survey team had been through with a bulldozer as far as the 180 km turn-off. The track beyond here was very narrow with the bushes scratching along the side of the truck. This slowed progress from a comfortable 65 km per hour to around 40 km per hour. Incidentally, the vehicle we travelled in was a diesel Toyota Land Cruiser 'Troop Carrier', an excellent vehicle for this kind of work. Do remember to check underneath your vehicle for dry grass and spinifex which can get caught on the exhaust pipes of many models. Many vans have been burned out this way, although modern Land Cruisers are better designed than most to prevent this. The best bird seen was obviously **Scarlet-chested Parrot**, but other birds seen at the parrot site were **Grey-fronted Honeyeater, Inland Thornbill, Australian Owlet-Nightjar, Barn Owl** and **Crimson Chat**. Birds seen at the belar stands at 222.5 and 228.5 km included **White-browed Treecreeper** (9), **Slaty-backed Thornbill, Gilbert's Whistler** (2) and **Varied Sittella**. We also saw two **Ground Cuckoo-Shrikes** in the mallee at 264.2 km.

9.17 Cook Airfield

Key Species: **Inland Dotterel**
On the way out from the Great Victoria Desert we went to Cook Airfield which is a good place to see **Inland Dotterel**. Go to the west end of town, past the hospital and head out south to the airstrip. The dotterels gather on here in the late afternoon, we saw 20. It is well worth the 200 km detour to this site if driving across the Eyre Highway.

9.18 Nullarbor Roadhouse (Map 9.12)

Key Species: **Nullarbor Quail-Thrush**
Nullarbor Quail-Thrush is a small and brightly coloured race of the Cinnamon Quail-Thrush and has a solid black line across the chest. The song differs very slightly too. I would strongly suggest seeing both races (the two are currently lumped), particularly as the Nullarbor race is only a short diversion from the Eyre Highway. To get to the site, drive 1.3 km east from Nullarbor Roadhouse on the rough track then turn north and follow the fence for 6.7 km. We bush camped here for two nights. **Nullarbor Quail-Thrush** are common and not hard to see, we saw at least 10. The best techniques are either to wait until they come out onto the track (mornings and evenings are best) or walk about in the saltbush until you hear one. Walk fairly quickly towards it to catch up with it and you should see it on the ground. If you try to creep up on them they tend to just keep running away ahead of you. Note they regularly fly over the top of the fence. Other birds seen here included **Slender-billed Thornbill** (common), **Rufous Calamanthus** (fairly common), **Stubble Quail** and an immature male **Spotted Harrier**.

CHAPTER 9: SOUTH AUSTRALIA

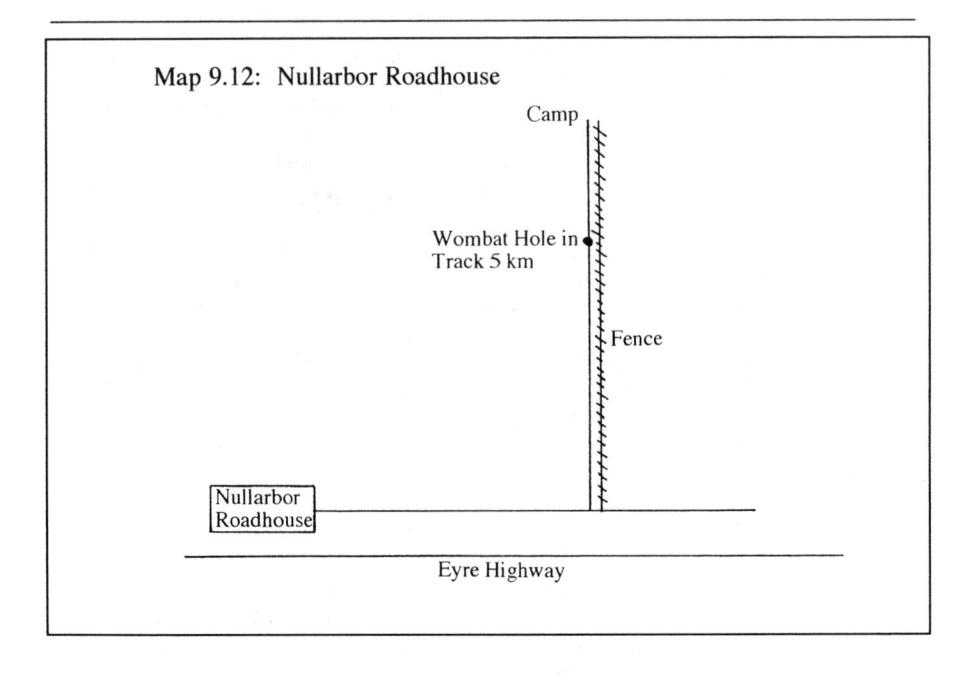

Map 9.12: Nullarbor Roadhouse

Camp

Wombat Hole in Track 5 km

Fence

Nullarbor Roadhouse

Eyre Highway

CHAPTER 10

PELAGIC TRIPS

Wandering Albatross, one of the most spectacular species regularly sighted on pelagics in Australian waters.

Introduction

Australia's offshore waters are feeding grounds for some of the worlds most exciting seabirds. An offshore pelagic trip at any time of year should produce some good birds, although the numbers and species composition are highly variable to say the least. My advice to the travelling birder is to go on as many offshore trips as possible although this will need considerable forward planning to ensure your visit to each area coincides with a pelagic. Whilst many of the inshore species can readily be seen from land based seawatches, to see the truly pelagic seabirds, such as the *Pterodroma* petrels, it is necessary to go out by boat beyond the continental shelf. In Australia this is approximately 20 km from shore. There is only one regular boat taking birders out this far and this goes out for one day each month from Wollongong and should be booked well in advance as it is often full. Apart from making sure you go on this, you will have to keep your ears open for news of any other offshore trips. During three years in Australia, I went on 35 pelagics, the vast majority from Wollongong. The following trips are recommended if they are running.

10.1 Wollongong

Key Species: **Solander's Petrel** (winter), **Gould's Petrel** (summer), **White-necked Petrel** (summer), **Black Petrel** (November), **Buller's Shearwater** (summer), **Fluttering** and **Hutton's Shearwaters**, **Wilson's** and **White-faced Storm-Petrels** (both autumn), **Skuas** (summer) and rarities (all months)

Arguably the best pelagic birding trips in the world, Wollongong has certainly produced an exceptional number of good seabirds. Trips are regularly organised, departing Wollongong Harbour at 6.00 or 7.00 a.m. and returning around 4.00 p.m. on the fourth Sunday of every month, weather permitting. There are several hotels and caravan parks in Wollongong although we regularly slept on the harbour quayside without any problem. The trips cost around A$45 each, take your own food, although tea is provided. The current organiser of the pelagics is Phil Hansbro and since he frequently changes his address, it is best to write to him c/o Research School of Biological Sciences, Australian National University, Canberra 0200, Australia, Tel (06) 249 3091, Fax (06) 249 4891, email hansbro@rsbs-central.anu.edu.au. His current home address is 56 David St, Turner Canberra ACT 2601, Tel (06) 249 8234. The species recorded vary greatly with the time of year and whilst for northern hemisphere birders keen to see albatrosses, the winter months are probably best, these months produce fewest rarities. The months most likely to produce a good variety of seabirds are September to November when both winter and summer species may overlap.

During three years, I went on 30 or so trips and below is a list of the seabirds I recorded, together with an approximate indication of abundance and time of year they are most likely to be seen. **Little Blue Penguin** (regular in calm weather, just offshore from the harbour), **Wandering Albatross** (regular May-September, although a drastic reduction in numbers in recent years because of Japanese long line fishing boats), **Royal Albatross** (1, May 1993), **Black-browed**, **Yellow-nosed** and **Shy Albatrosses** (all regular May-September), **Northern** and **Southern Giant Petrels** (few, May-September), **Cape Petrel** (May-September), **Great-winged Petrel** (common October-February), **White-headed Petrel** (small numbers May-September), **Solander's Petrel** (common May-September), **Mottled Petrel** (1, January 1992, the first Wollongong record), **Gould's Petrel** (formerly regularly seen January-March, but for some reason, none since February 1992). **Cook's Petrel** (1, December 1991), **White-necked Petrel** (4, all January-March), **Antarctic Prion** (several birds in May 1992), **Fairy Prion** (common May-September), **Black Petrel** (November 1992 to January 1993), **White-chinned Petrel** (1, November 1992), **Flesh-footed Shearwater** (small numbers October-March), **Wedge-tailed** and **Short-tailed Shearwaters** (common November-March), **Buller's**, **Sooty** and **Streaked Shearwaters** (small numbers November-March), **Fluttering** and **Hutton's Shearwaters** (October-March), **Wilson's** and **White-faced Storm-Petrels** (small numbers, mainly March and April), **Common Diving-Petrel** (1), **Red-tailed Tropicbird** (1, January 1991), **White-tailed Tropicbird** (1, April 1993), **Southern Skua** (small numbers), **Arctic** and **Pomarine Skuas** (regular November-March), **Long-tailed Skua** (regular January and February), **Silver**, **Kelp** and **Pacific** (1) **Gulls** and **White-fronted Tern** (regular May-September). Many other species have been recorded in the past and the range of possibilities is enormous. However, you need to go on numerous trips in order to see a really good selection of birds.

10.2 Portland

Key Species: **Grey-headed** (best July and August), **Royal**, **Buller's**, and **Sooty Albatrosses**, **Southern Fulmar** (annual), **Soft-plumaged** (regular in February), **Blue**, and **Grey Petrels**, **Grey-backed Storm-Petrel**, **Common Diving-Petrel** and rarities

Situated in the extreme south-west of Victoria, pelagics occasionally leave this small port in any month to go into the Great Australian Bight. They are very irregular to say the least, being highly weather dependant. The best way of finding out if any trips are planned is to contact the RAOU in Melbourne, their address is given in the useful information section. The birds recorded regularly include more sub-Antarctic species than off Wollongong and there have been some truly outstanding trips including one in July 1992 which recorded nine species of Albatross! Any time of year can be brilliant, but the spring months tend to be best. The first of my trips from here, in October 1991, was my most exciting pelagic of all time. We saw the following outstanding birds; **Royal** and **Sooty** (1) **Albatrosses**, **Southern Fulmar** (1), **White-headed Petrel** (1), **Blue Petrel** (1) and **White-chinned Petrel** (2). My second trip, in September 1992 was also brilliant with the highlights being **Royal** and **Light-mantled Sooty** (1) **Albatrosses**, **Antarctic** and **Thin-billed Prions** and **Grey-backed Storm-Petrel** (3). Recently there has been a move to run trips from Warrnambool, just to the east of Portland. So far this has failed to live up to the expectations of Portland, although that is surely a matter of time.

10.3 Tasmania

Key Species: **Buller's Albatross** and **White-chinned Petrel**
Very occasional pelagic trips are organised by Sydney birders from Eaglehawk Neck in Eastern Tasmania. Whilst the first of these in January 1992 was a real success, recording **Mottled** (5), **Cook's** (1) and **Gould's Petrels**, subsequent trips in July and October of that year were a dismal failure. My advice when visiting Tasmania is to ask around local fishermen to see if you can go out on one of their boats with them. Port Arthur is a good place to try, although you may find they are unable to take you because of insurance legalities.

10.4 Eden

Key Species: None, but an excellent chance of seeing whales in October/November
Regular commercial whale watching excursions are run from Eden which is situated in the extreme south-east corner of New South Wales. These take place during October and November each year and the main species of whale observed is the Humpback Whale. Whilst these trips do not really go far enough offshore for true pelagic seabirds, on the one trip we went on in October 1992 we did record a few interesting birds. These were **Wandering Albatross** (1), **Cape Petrel** (1), **Flesh-footed Shearwater** (1), **Wilson's** (2) and **White-faced Storm-Petrels** and **Southern Skua** (2). It is essential to book the whale watching trips, contact either Rosalind and Gordon Butt (064) 962027 or O'Brian's Boat Charter (064) 961824.

A number of full scale birding pelagics have been organised recently, mostly during the winter months to observe the large numbers of albatrosses visiting the Eden area. These do go all the way out to the continental shelf, but for some reason have so far failed to produce any real rarities. For further details, contact Alan Robertson (Gypsy Point Lodge) (051) 588205. I went on only one of these trips, in May 1991 and recorded only the commoner winter seabirds such as **Wandering** (1), **Black-browed, Yellow-nosed** and **Shy Albatrosses, Southern Giant Petrel, Fairy Prion, White-fronted Tern** and **Black-faced Cormorant**.

10.5 Brisbane

Key Species: **Tahiti Petrel, Streaked Shearwater** and rarities
Although infrequently run, and with the reputation of being exceedingly boring because of the four hours or so it takes to reach the continental shelf, pelagic trips do go out from Brisbane. They usually run in the summer months when there is a good chance of seeing the more tropical seabirds. Try contacting Paul Walbridge at 135 Walter Avenue, East Brisbane for the latest information on any planned trips.

See **Appendix 4** for further information on Sydney and Perth pelagics and contact names

CHAPTER 11

BIRD FINDER GUIDE

White-throated Grasswren, a bird confined to rocky spinifex covered escarpments in Arnhem Land

Introduction

This guide contains hints on finding every species other than those vagrants listed in Appendix 2 or introduced species listed in Appendix 3. These notes include, where appropriate, a guide to the habitat requirements and the behaviour of each species, together with suggested likely places to find it. The order of species follows that in 'Birds of the World, a Check List' by J. F. Clements. Some of the English names have been changed to bring them in line with those commonly used in Australia. There are also a few alterations to his taxonomy; see Appendix 1 for details of these changes.

Abbreviations: Australian Capital Territory (ACT), New South Wales (NSW), Northern Territory (NT), Queensland (QLD), South Australia (SA), Tasmania (TAS), Victoria (VIC), Western Australia (WA), National Park (NP).

Non-Passerines

Emu *Dromaius novaehollandiae* (Continental Australia; endemic): This species is a nomadic wanderer, found throughout the arid interior of Australia, usually on the open plains. It is a classic example of a bird that will undoubtedly be seen just by driving and touring the vast distances along inland roads. We encountered them in every state/territory except TAS, although even here there is a population of introduced birds easily seen at Maria Island NP (3.4). The most reliable place to see this bird is at Wyperfield NP (2.13) in VIC where numerous birds are found around the campground.

Southern Cassowary *Casuarius casuarius* (New Guinea and Aru Islands; north-east QLD): In Australia this species is confined to the rainforests of north-east QLD. The birds are rather shy although they do make their presence known with a loud coughing call, somewhat akin to a car engine being turned over. Despite their large size the birds are extremely hard to see in dense rainforest and the best chance of encountering one is along forest tracks and roads in the early morning. The best time of year to see cassowaries is October/November when the males are leading young chicks around. By far the best area to see them is around Mission Beach (6.23). Try asking local people for any recent sightings. Unfortunately the feeding station at Laceys Creek had to be closed because birds were becoming too tame and getting killed by road traffic. Other good places to try are Wallaman Falls NP near Ingham, (around the campsite), Mount Whitfield Environmental Park (6.27) in Cairns, and for those going to Iron Range NP (6.45) on Cape York, the area around the small concrete causeway is best.

Australasian Grebe *Tachybaptus novaehollandiae* (Pacific and New Guinea; throughout Australia and TAS): This common species is generally found on small ponds with some waterside vegetation, even on tiny farm dams.

Hoary-headed Grebe *Poliocephalus poliocephalus* (New Zealand; throughout Australia and TAS): Common on patches of open water, this species is highly nomadic and will turn up anywhere conditions are suitable. It is especially numerous in the south-east and there is a large breeding colony at Lake Bathurst (4.3b) in NSW.

Great Crested Grebe *Podiceps cristatus* (Eurasia and Australasia; eastern and south-western Australia and TAS): Rather patchily distributed in eastern Australia, this species favours large open areas of water. Regular sites are Lakes George and Bathurst (4.3) in NSW, and the lake adjacent to the campsite at Hattah-Kulkyne NP (2.14) in VIC.

Fiordland Crested Penguin *Eudyptes pachyrhynchus* (New Zealand, sub-Antarctic Islands; rare visitor): A few Fiordland Crested Penguins are always found on the shoreline moulting each year in Australia. The best time of year is March and the birds are generally along the south-western beaches of TAS or along the Victorian coast. Clearly encountering one of these penguins is just a matter of chance, but keep your eyes open, particularly in TAS. Fiordland Crested is by far the most regularly encountered species although eight other species have been recorded (see Appendix 2).

Little Blue Penguin *Eudyptula minor* (New Zealand; breeds south coast of Australia and TAS): This is a common bird all along the south coast of Australia, from Perth to Sydney, including TAS. They are easiest to see when coming ashore during the breeding season. The best place to go is the 'Penguin Parade' on Phillip Island (2.3) in VIC where birds can be seen year round, although numbers will be low from April to June.

Wandering Albatross *Diomedea exulans* (Sub-Antarctic Islands; offshore migrant): Most easily seen from pelagic trips during the winter months, this species has seen a drastic drop in numbers in recent years so can no longer be guaranteed. The best bet is a Wollongong (10.1) or Portland (10.2) pelagic in any month from May to September. There is also the possibility of seeing birds during seawatches from coastal headlands during strong onshore winds, such as Green Cape near Eden (4.6), NSW.

Buller's and **Royal Albatrosses** *D. epomophora* and *D. bulleri* (New Zealand Islands; offshore visitors): Both are much rarer than the above species, the only real chance of seeing either in Australia is to go on a Portland pelagic (10.2) during the winter months. However, both can easily be seen in New Zealand.

Black-browed Albatross *D. melanophris* (Southern Oceans; offshore migrant): The commonest albatross; easily seen on any southern pelagic or from land based seawatches during the winter months. Good numbers of albatrosses often collect just offshore from Eden in NSW. The New Zealand breeding race *impavida* is frequently seen off Wollongong (10.1).

Shy Albatross *D. cauta* (New Zealand; breeds islands in Bass Strait Australia): Fairly common on winter pelagics from Wollongong (10.1) and Portland (10.2). Easily seen from land in TAS, or from Green Cape (4.6) in NSW. The only albatross likely to be seen during the summer months.

Grey-headed Albatross *D. chrysostoma* (Sub-Antarctic Islands; offshore visitor): Regularly recorded in July/August from Portland (10.2). Reputedly regular off WA in the winter, but there are no regular pelagics in that part of Australia although you could try getting on a fishing boat from Albany.

Yellow-nosed Albatross *D. chlororhynchos* (Southern Oceans; offshore migrant): Common in the winter months off Wollongong (10.1). Easily seen from land off south-eastern Australia *e.g.* Green Cape (4.6), Jervis Bay (4.4).

Sooty and **Light-mantled Sooty Albatrosses** *Phoebetria fusca* and *P. palpebrata* (Sub-Antarctic Islands; offshore visitors): Very rare in Australian waters, the best chance is July to October on a Portland pelagic (10.2).

Southern and **Northern Giant Petrels** *Macronectes giganteus* and *M. halli* (Southern Oceans; offshore migrants): Regular in small numbers during winter pelagics. Readily seen from land based winter seawatches from headlands in VIC or TAS but specific identification rarely possible.

Southern Fulmar *Fulmarus glacialoides* (Southern Oceans; offshore visitor): Rare but annual visitor usually in the winter months. Best chance is on a Portland pelagic (10.2).

Cape Petrel *Daption capense* (Southern Oceans; offshore migrant): Fairly common winter and spring pelagics off Wollongong (10.1) and Portland (10.2). Very tame and approaches boats closely giving excellent views. Readily seen from land because of the easy identification at long range.

Kerguelen Petrel *Lugensa brevirostris* (Sub-Antarctic Islands; offshore visitor): Very rarely seen off south-eastern Australia during the winter months, however, this species is prone to spectacular wrecks some years when they can be seen in large numbers from the coast. Reputedly occurs regularly off WA.

Tahiti Petrel *Pseudobulweria rostrata* (Pacific Islands; offshore visitor): Regularly seen from Brisbane (10.5) pelagics, otherwise rarely seen in the summer off Wollongong (10.1).

Black-winged Petrel *Pterodroma nigripennis* (New Zealand Islands; breeds Lord Howe Island): Summer pelagics from Wollongong (10.1) are the best chance of seeing this bird, apart from visiting Lord Howe Island. It is also readily seen on mainland New Zealand.

White-necked Petrel *P. cervicalis* (Kermadec Islands; offshore visitor): This spectacular species is regularly seen on Wollongong summer pelagics (10.1) and seems more likely than most *Pterodromas* to come inshore where it is regularly sighted from Point Lookout on North Stradbroke Island (6.6), QLD.

Gould's Petrel *P. leucoptera* (Pacific Islands; breeds Cabbagetree Island NSW. Note that the Pacific Islands subspecies is often split as Collared Petrel *P. brevipes*, this would make Gould's Petrel an endemic breeding species): Wollongong pelagics (10.1) during the summer months used to be very reliable for seeing this species. In recent years, however, very few have been seen. The only other way to see them is to volunteer to help with ringing studies on Cabbagetree Island for the NSW National Parks and Wildlife Service.

Herald Petrel *P. heraldica* (Pacific Islands; breeds Raine Island off north-east QLD): Very rarely seen from east coast pelagics, otherwise an expensive boat charter to Raine Island off Cape York would be needed. Can be seen more easily in the Cook Islands.

Kermadec Petrel *P. neglecta* (Kermadecs ; breeds Lord Howe Island): Rarely seen off Wollongong (10.1), usually in April; apart from a boat trip from Lord Howe Island to Pyramid Rock, this is really the only place to see this petrel in Australia.

Solander's Petrel *P. solandri* (Breeds Lord Howe Island only; endemic): The commonest *Pterodroma* off Wollongong (10.1) during the winter months being recorded every trip. Very easy to see at Lord Howe Island, but otherwise doesn't come close to shore.

Great-winged Petrel *P. macroptera* (Sub-Antarctic Islands and New Zealand; breeds islands off WA): The commonest *Pterodroma* off Wollongong (10.1) on summer pelagics, sometimes in flocks of hundreds. Also fairly common off Portland (10.2). Very rarely comes close enough to shore to be seen from the land.

White-headed Petrel *P. lessonii* (Sub-Antarctic Islands; offshore migrant): Fairly common off Portland (10.2) and in small numbers off Wollongong (10.1) during the winter months although it never comes close to shore.

Soft-plumaged Petrel *P. mollis* (Sub-Antarctic Islands; offshore visitor): Rare, but seen fairly regularly offshore from Portland (10.2) in March. A dark morph has been found nesting on small islands off TAS.

Blue Petrel *Halobaena caerulea* (Sub-Antarctic Islands; offshore visitor): Rare but annually seen from Portland pelagics (10.2). Usually in the spring or winter months.

Antarctic and **Thin-billed Prions** *Pachyptila desolata* and *P. belcheri* (Southern Oceans; offshore visitors): Rare but regularly seen from Portland (10.2), also occasionally from Wollongong pelagics (10.1) during the winter months.

Fairy Prion *P. turtur* (New Zealand; breeds Bass Strait Islands): Very common offshore from south-east Australia during the winter months, and also readily seen from land based seawatches.

White-chinned Petrel *Procellaria aequinoctialis* (Sub-Antarctic Islands; offshore visitor): Rare off Wollongong (10.1) but regular in winter and spring off Portland (10.2).

Black Petrel *P. parkinsoni* (New Zealand Islands; offshore visitor): Rare but regularly seen in November on the Wollongong pelagics (10.1).

Streaked Shearwater *Calonectris leucomelas* (Japanese Islands; offshore visitor): This species is regularly seen on summer pelagics off Wollongong (10.1) and particularly Brisbane (10.5). It can often be seen from Point Lookout on North Stradbroke Island (6.6), QLD, during summer seawatches.

Wedge-tailed Shearwater *Puffinus pacificus* (Tropical and sub-tropical Islands; breeds in Australia on islands off WA, NSW and QLD): Abundant off Wollongong (10.1) during the summer months when large numbers follow the boat after food scraps, and also easily seen from land.

Buller's Shearwater *P. bulleri* (New Zealand Islands; offshore visitor): Regularly seen off Wollongong (10.1) on summer pelagics, in very small numbers, this species is however very common and easy to see in New Zealand.

Flesh-footed Shearwater *P. carneipes* (Pacific Ocean; breeds Lord Howe Island and off WA): Common during the summer months on pelagics off south-eastern Australia.

Sooty Shearwater *P. griseus* (Pacific Ocean; breeds on islands off NSW and TAS): Fairly common off Wollongong (10.1) in the spring when on passage with smaller numbers during the summer months.

Short-tailed Shearwater *P. tenuirostris* (Pacific Ocean; breeds islands off TAS and NSW): Very common offshore from Wollongong (10.1) in the spring when on passage, smaller numbers during the summer months. Can be seen at the nesting colony on Bruny Island (3.1) from October to April and abundant offshore from TAS at these times.

Fluttering and **Hutton's Shearwaters** *P. gavia* and *P. huttoni* (New Zealand Islands; offshore migrant): 'Fluttons' Shearwaters are common off Wollongong (10.1) during the summer months and I saw large flocks from the boat to Lady Musgrave Island (6.16) off QLD. Fluttering types predominate but a few Hutton's can usually be picked out.

Little Shearwater *P. assimilis* (Cosmopolitan including New Zealand; breeds Lord Howe Island and off WA): Rarely seen from Wollongong (10.1) during the summer, this species is more easily seen elsewhere in the world.

Wilson's Storm-Petrel *Oceanites oceanicus* (Southern Oceans; offshore migrant): The most abundant seabird in the world and readily seen from Wollongong (10.1), usually in March and April. It is less commonly seen off Portland (10.2) and we also saw it whilst out whale watching off Eden (10.4) in October.

Grey-backed Storm-Petrel *Garrodia nereis* (New Zealand Islands, Indian Ocean; offshore visitor): This species is very much a Portland (10.2) speciality, being very rare off

Wollongong (10.1). Any trip from Portland is likely to produce this bird, and I also saw them off TAS (10.3) on a winter pelagic.

White-faced Storm-Petrel *Pelagodroma marina* (Cosmopolitan; breeds on many islands off Australia): Regularly seen off both Portland (10.2) and Wollongong (10.1), except during the winter months. This is the most commonly seen storm-petrel in Australian waters and it breeds on many offshore islands. We also recorded it off Eden (10.4).

Black-bellied Storm-Petrel *Fregetta tropica* (Sub-Antarctic Islands; offshore migrant): Although reputedly very common well offshore from TAS in winter, this species rarely seems to come close to shore.

White-bellied Storm-Petrel *F. grallaria* (South Atlantic, Kermadec; breeds Lord Howe Islands): This species is rarely seen on Brisbane (10.5) and Wollongong (10.1) summer pelagics. No doubt these are wandering individuals from the Lord Howe breeding population where this species can readily be seen by taking a fishing trip to Pyramid Rock.

Common Diving-Petrel *Pelecanoides urinatrix* (Sub-Antarctic Islands; Bass Strait Islands): This is very much a Portland pelagic (10.2) speciality, although they are rarely seen off Wollongong (10.1) and I observed a remarkable passage off Green Cape (10.4) in NSW following severe southerly storms.

Red-tailed Tropicbird *Phaethon rubricauda* (Tropical Oceans; coastal Australia except south coast): This species can readily be seen during the summer breeding season at Sugarloaf Island (8.24), WA and Lady Elliot Island (6.16), QLD. It also breeds on Lord Howe island and can sometimes be seen on summer pelagics from Brisbane (10.5) or Wollongong (10.1).

White-tailed Tropicbird *P. lepturus* (Tropical Oceans; tropical northern Australia): Occasionally seen on summer pelagics from Brisbane (10.5) and Wollongong (10.1), there is also a chance of seeing this species whilst sailing to the Barrier Reef off Cairns. It is however much easier to see elsewhere in the world, for example Fiji or Western Samoa.

Great Frigatebird *Fregata minor* (Tropical oceans; tropical northern Australia): Much less common than the following species, Great Frigatebirds occur in small numbers on the outer Barrier Reef islands. A trip to Michaelmas Cay (6.25) off Cairns or Lady Elliot Island (6.16) off Bundaberg should produce sightings of this bird amongst much greater numbers of Lesser Frigatebirds. If visiting Iron Range NP (6.45) on Cape York, both Frigatebird species can be seen from the coast at Portland Roads.

Lesser Frigatebird *F. ariel* (Tropical oceans; tropical northern Australia): Common on any of the Barrier Reef Islands or on trips to them, this species can also be readily seen from Portland Roads (6.45) on Cape York Peninsula south to about North Stradbroke Island (6.6) near Brisbane QLD.

Australian Gannet *Morus serrator* (New Zealand; south coasts of Australia): A common species, easily seen from shore anywhere from southern QLD to southern WA. The majority of the population breeds in New Zealand, but some nest off VIC and TAS. Seen on every Wollongong (10.1) or Portland pelagic (10.2) or from the southern NSW coast, especially in winter.

Masked Booby *Sula dactylatra* (Tropical oceans; tropical northern Australia): Rather a hard species to see in Australia, it does breed on several Great Barrier Islands, off northwest Australia and on Lord Howe and Norfolk Islands. Apart from a visit to one of these islands, the best chance of seeing this bird is to find one roosting amongst the Brown Boobies on Michaelmas Cay (6.25) off Cairns. The race breeding on Lord Howe and Norfolk Islands has been split by the RAOU as the Tasman Booby *S. tasmani*.

Red-footed Booby *S. sula* (Tropical oceans; tropical north-eastern Australia): Again, a rather difficult species to see in Australia, since it only breeds on Raine Island, in the Coral Sea and off north-west Australia. Birds are rarely seen roosting on Michaelmas Cay (6.25), but this species is best seen elsewhere in the world.

Brown Booby *S. leucogaster* (Tropical oceans; tropical northern Australia): This species breeds on many tropical islands off northern Australia and can easily be seen on boat trips to the Great Barrier Reef, for example Michaelmas Cay (6.25) or Lady Elliot Island (6.16). This booby seems to fish closer inshore than other boobies and can often be seen from the mainland, for example off Bundaberg.

Little Pied Cormorant *Phalacrocorax melanoleucos* (South-east Asia, New Guinea and New Zealand; throughout Australia): The commonest cormorant in Australia, this species is found on almost any patch of water, even small farm dams and marine habitats.

Black-faced Cormorant *P. fuscescens* (South Australian coast, especially Bass Strait and TAS; endemic): An exclusively marine cormorant which favours rocky coastlines, this species is most readily seen in TAS where it is common. We had excellent views of several birds fishing close to the Bruny Island ferry terminal at Kettering, also several sightings offshore from Bruny Island (3.1) including Cape Bruny, Cloudy Bay, and the isthmus. In VIC both Point Lonsdale and Swan Island (2.8) near Queenscliffe or the rocky coastline of Wilson's Promontory are good places to see this bird, whilst in WA, try a boat trip from Esperance to Woody Island. This species is normally seen on Portland pelagics (10.2) and large breeding colonies are found in Spencer Gulf, SA, for example at Dangerous Reef.

Pied Cormorant *P. varius* (New Zealand; coastal and inland Australia, except TAS): Although this species does occur inland in eastern Australia, it is mainly a common coastal bird. It is particularly numerous off western WA, for example off the Peron Peninsula (8.16).

Little Black Cormorant *P. sulcirostris* (Indonesia, New Guinea and New Zealand; throughout Australia): This is a common cormorant, found both inland on large lakes and rivers and also in marine habitats, although it favours the former.

Great Cormorant *P. carbo* (Cosmopolitan; eastern and south-western Australia and TAS): This common cormorant in Australia is found mainly on fresh water in the southern half of the continent, being rarer in the north.

Australian Darter *Anhinga novaehollandiae* (New Guinea and Lesser Sundas; throughout Australia except TAS): This bird prefers large areas of open water, both fresh and in estuaries, but not the open sea. It is widespread but nowhere really numerous being commonest in the tropical northern wetlands such as Kakadu NP (7C).

Australian Pelican *Pelecanus conspicillatus* (New Guinea, throughout Australia): This very common pelican frequents fresh and salt water habitats throughout Australia.

Magpie Goose *Anseranas semipalmata* (New Guinea; tropical northern Australia): A characteristic bird of the Top End, this species becomes concentrated into huge flocks during the dry season. It can be found at almost any tropical wetland in the north for example Fogg Dam (7.11) or Kakadu NP (7C).

Plumed Whistling-Duck *Dendrocygna eytoni* (Tropical northern Australia, rarely as far south as VIC; endemic although has occurred as a vagrant in New Guinea and New Zealand): This species is commonest in the tropical north, look for it by any sizeable dam in the inland region. The Yellow Waters cruise (7.16), NT is probably the best guaranteed site for this species. Other good sites include Townsville Common Environmental Park (6.20) and Hasties Swamp (6.33) in QLD. In the southern part of its range, Bool Lagoon (9.5) in SA is a reliable site.

Wandering Whistling-Duck *D. arcuata* (New Guinea, Indonesia and Philippines; tropical northern Australia): This species favours tropical freshwater wetlands of northern Australia such as Kakadu NP (7C) or Lake Barrine (6.34). It is seen more frequently than the above species and generally in larger flocks.

Blue-billed Duck *Oxyura australis* (South-east and south-west Australia, also northern TAS; endemic): This is rather a secretive species, favouring freshwater lakes with plenty of cover. It is therefore often overlooked but fortunately there are several excellent sites to look for this bird, and we saw it regularly at Lake Bathurst (4.3b) in NSW, although access to here may be difficult. Lake Bindegolly (6.13) in south-west QLD is a good site as is Leeton Swamp (4.17) in inland NSW, also Werribee Sewage Works (2.5) in VIC, the ICI Saltworks (9.1) and Bool Lagoon (9.5) in SA. In WA, try Lakes Monger (8.18) or Herdsman near Perth.

Musk Duck *Biziura lobata* (South-east and south-west Australia, including TAS; endemic): Commoner than the preceding species, but favouring similar habitats and therefore it is found in the same places.

Freckled Duck *Stictonetta naevosa* (South-east and south-west Australia, not TAS; endemic): This strange primitive duck is highly nomadic and regarded as endangered. Nevertheless we saw this bird frequently and there are several excellent sites where it is nearly guaranteed. These are Leeton Swamp (4.17) (best in the summer months), Lake George (4.3a) (birds are present almost year round, mostly in the south-western corner with parties of up to 600 often present in the winter months), Lake Bathurst (4.3b) (very regular during the summer months, but access difficult. They tend to loaf about on the rocks at the western side) all in NSW. Phil Maher can normally show you this species near Deniliquin (4.18). Lake Bindegolly (6.13) in south-west QLD is an excellent site, although they can be hard to find; they seem to favour the area around the road bridge. Other good places include Bool Lagoon (9.5), the ICI Saltworks (9.1) and Big Swamp (9.7) in SA and Werribee Sewage Works (2.5) in VIC.

Black Swan *Cygnus atratus* (Southern Australia including TAS; endemic): An abundant waterbird in the better watered southern parts of Australia, although becoming rarer further inland and northwards.

Cape Barren Goose *Cereopsis novaehollandiae* (Coastal southern Australia including Bass Strait Islands and TAS; endemic): This rare bird breeds on islands in the Bass Strait but winters on the mainland preferring pasture and short grassy areas on which to graze. It is not an easy species to see; we saw two birds in flight whilst driving between Ocean Grove and Barwon Heads near Queenscliffe in VIC in July 1991 and also a party of eight birds at Big Swamp (9.7) near Port Lincoln on the Eyre Peninsula, SA; a reliable site for this species in the winter months. Near to here, explore the road between the Lincoln Highway and Louth Bay on the east side of the Eyre Peninsula. Other sites to try include Wilson's Promontory in VIC, particularly in the vicinity of Yanakie Isthmus, although try asking the park rangers for up to date information. In WA, a trip to Woody Island off Esperance should be successful. Introduced populations abound on Kangaroo Island in SA and Maria Island NP (3.4) in TAS.

Australian Shelduck *Tadorna tadornoides* (Southern Australia, commonest in the south-east and TAS; endemic): This species prefers large shallow areas of open water, fresh or saline and is easy to see at most wetland sites in southern Australia.

Radjah Shelduck *T. radjah* (New Guinea and Indonesia; tropical northern Australia): Thinly spread across the northern sub-coastal parts of Australia, this species tends to occur in pairs rather than large flocks. It is rather uncommon in eastern QLD, but can easily be found in the tropical wetlands of WA or the NT.

Green Pygmy-Goose *Nettapus pulchellus* (New Guinea and Indonesia; coastal northern Australia): Much commoner in the western part of its Australian range, this beautiful species prefers shallow lakes with plenty of aquatic vegetation. It is very numerous in Kakadu NP (7C).

Cotton Pygmy-Goose *N. coromandelianus* (Asia and New Guinea; north-east QLD): Rather an uncommon duck in Australia with a restricted range, being found mostly in the Townsville region. The only place we saw this species was on Horseshoe Lagoon (6.19), but it is virtually guaranteed at Townsville Common Environmental Park (6.20), try the Borrow Pits and at Nardellos Lagoon (6.36).

Maned Duck *Chenonetta jubata* (Eastern and western Australia; endemic although a vagrant to New Zealand): Abundant in the south-east or south-west of Australia, and sometimes seen well away from water.

Grey Teal *Anas gracilis* (New Guinea and New Zealand; throughout Australia): This species is very common and can be seen on almost any patch of water. It is a highly nomadic species and occurs wherever conditions are suitable.

Chestnut Teal *A. castanea* (Southern Australia, especially TAS; endemic): This common bird has TAS as its stronghold and it can be found on any lake there; elsewhere it is commonest near coastal regions.

Pacific Black Duck *A. superciliosa* (Pacific; throughout Australia): This species is extremely common and found throughout Australia even on small farm dams.

Garganey *A. querquedula* (Eurasia; uncommon visitor to Australia): This is a rare but annual visitor to northern Australia, chiefly in the Top End. Indeed it is almost annual at Knuckey's Lagoon (7.8) in Darwin which seems to be ideal habitat. There are records as far south as VIC however.

Australian Shoveler *A. rhynchotis* (New Zealand; south-western and south-eastern Australia including TAS): A widespread, but not particularly numerous bird, which prefers well vegetated lakes and can be found at all the expected waterbird sites in the southern half of the continent.

Pink-eared Duck *Malacorhynchus membranaceus* (Throughout Australia, including northern TAS; endemic): One of the most bizarre ducks in the world, this bird is well adapted to the arid interior of Australia, being highly nomadic and able to breed whenever conditions are suitable. Being a filter feeder, it is mainly found on shallow flood waters, and should be looked for whenever these are encountered in the outback. They are usually present at Bool Lagoon (9.5) in SA except during times of drought there when the pools have dried up.

Hardhead *Aythya australis* (Indonesia, New Guinea and Pacific; throughout Australia and TAS): This common species is mainly found on deep water lakes.

White-faced Heron *Egretta novaehollandiae* (New Zealand, New Guinea, Indonesia and Pacific; throughout Australia): The commonest heron in Australia, being found in all types of wetland habitats and also even in grasslands.

Little Egret *E. garzetta* (Africa and Eurasia; mainly coastal Australia in the west, inland in the east, also TAS): This is a reasonably common species and will be encountered when visiting the wetland sites.

Pacific Reef Heron *E. sacra* (Coastal south-east Asia and Pacific islands; coastal Australia except southern VIC and TAS): A common bird of all coastal areas around Australia with the dark morph tending to predominate in the southern half of the continent. A few birds are normally present along Cairns Esplanade (6.24).

Intermediate Egret *E. intermedia* (Africa, Asia and New Guinea; eastern and northern Australia including TAS): A fairly common species although probably often overlooked amongst the commoner Great Egrets.

Pacific Heron *Ardea pacifica* (Throughout continental Australia, rare in TAS; endemic but has occurred as a vagrant in New Guinea and New Zealand): This species is well adapted to the fluctuating water levels within the arid interior and is an inland nomad, appearing on the coast during periods of drought. You will certainly encounter this species whenever you come across inland flood areas.

Great-billed Heron *A. sumatrana* (Coastal south-east Asia; tropical northern Australia): Australia is as easy a place as anywhere to see this enormous heron which is mainly found in coastal mangroves, but does occur inland. They can be almost guaranteed on the Daintree River cruises (6.31) in northern QLD during the winter months but are hard to see them in the summer. At that time of year, try asking John Crowhurst in Cairns about trips out with local fishermen to look for them. The best site in the NT is Middle Arm (7.5) near Darwin, but be prepared to wait.

Pied Heron *A. picata* (New Guinea and Indonesia; tropical northern Australia): This is one of the characteristic birds of the Top End and whilst it does occur in coastal QLD, it is much easier to see further west. They are especially numerous and tame around the campsite at the Yellow Waters camping area in Kakadu NP (7.16).

Great Egret *Casmerodius albus* (Cosmopolitan; throughout Australia and TAS): This is a very common species in Australia being found in all the usual wetland areas.

Cattle Egret *Bubulcus ibis* (Cosmopolitan; coastal Australia and TAS): Although introduced to Australia early this century, the species really took hold when it began a massive world-wide range expansion in the 1930s. It is now common throughout Australia except for the driest parts of the interior and will be seen in all the usual wetland areas.

Striated Heron *Butorides striatus* (Cosmopolitan; coastal northern and eastern Australia): This is mainly a mangrove species in Australia so it is not found in the colder southern half of the continent. It is reasonably common though somewhat secretive.

Rufous Night-Heron *Nycticorax caledonicus* (Indonesia, Pacific, New Guinea; throughout wetter parts of Australia): This smart bird is nomadic and nocturnal so it is probably often overlooked. Fortunately however, it is reasonably common and can often be seen flying out from roost in the tropical north, and excellent places to find it include Townsville Common Environmental Park (6.20) and Lake Bindegolly (6.13) (in bushes by the road bridge) in QLD, the Yellow Waters cruise (7.16), NT and Lake Kununurra (8.2) in WA.

Black-backed Bittern *Ixobrychus novaezelandiae* (Probably a small population in New Guinea, New Zealand race probably extinct; south-west and south-east Australia): This shy, secretive species has recently been split from the old world Little Bittern *I. minutus* and is effectively an Australian endemic. Unfortunately it is not an easy species to see; by far the best area to find it is around Deniliquin (4.18) in NSW where you should ask Phil Maher at the same time as booking your Plains-wanderer trip. We saw a male at the swamp on Avalon Road (4.18d) and Phil usually has other local sites. The only other place we saw this species was at Sherwood Forest Park in the western Brisbane suburb of Sherwood, QLD and this is a reasonably regular summer site for this species, although you should seek local information on it. Apart from the Deniliquin area, you will just have to be lucky when visiting a reedbed site; they breed at Bool Lagoon (9.5) in SA, try asking the rangers there. Also worth a look is Herdsman Lake in Perth, WA.

Black Bittern *I. flavicollis* (Southern Asia, New Guinea; coastal Australia, except the south coast or TAS): A species that is much easier to find in the tropical north, although it does occur well south of Sydney. Good sites include Tinaroo Creek Road (6.37) in QLD, Fergusson River (7.20) in NT and the walk to Mitchell Falls (8.5b) in the Kimberleys, WA. It is also easy to find at Manning Gorge in the Kimberleys. Generally this species flushes up from stream sides into nearby trees where it freezes allowing good views.

Australasian Bittern *Botaurus poiciloptilus* (New Zealand, New Caledonia; south-west and south-east Australia including TAS): This is not an easy species to see because of its secretive nature and it is possibly easier to find in New Zealand. The one reliable area is around Deniliquin (4.18) where Phil Maher always knows of rice paddies where bitterns can be seen; again ask him about this species when booking your Plains-wanderer trip. We also saw one at the swamp on Avalon Road (4.18d). Other regular but by no means easy sites are Bool Lagoon (9.5) in SA (ask the rangers) and the reed bed at the north end of Lake George (4.3a) NSW where the stream flows into the lake. You will need to wade out there and be very wary of tiger snakes and semi-wild cattle both of which are common, this site is only good in the summer months. The reedbed adjacent to Cronulla Swamp (4.8) in Sydney is also good in summer, however, you will need to crash through the reeds in order to see a bittern here so the views will be poor at best.

Glossy Ibis *Plegadis falcinellus* (Cosmopolitan; mainly north Australia): This species is common in Australia, mainly in the tropical north, although strangely not in northern QLD.

Australian Ibis *Threskiornis molucca* (New Guinea, vagrant New Zealand; continental Australia, rare TAS): A very common bird found in city parks and indeed a nuisance in suburban Sydney. Common and tame in many areas including all wetland pastures *etc.*

Straw-necked Ibis *T. spinicollis* (New Guinea; throughout Australia, uncommon TAS): A very common bird of wet pastures and swamps *etc.* This bird will be seen at all the usual wetland sites.

Royal Spoonbill *Platalea regia* (New Guinea, Indonesia, New Zealand; mainly eastern and northern Australia, rare TAS): A common spoonbill of both marine and fresh shallow waters. This species will be encountered at all the usual wetland sites.

Yellow-billed Spoonbill *P. flavipes* (Wetter areas of continental Australia, vagrant TAS; endemic but a vagrant to New Zealand): A fairly common species that is nomadic in the interior and is less common on the coast than the former species. Nevertheless it should not be hard to find on freshwater lakes and even small farm dams.

Black-necked Stork *Ephippiorhynchus asiaticus* (Asia, New Guinea; northern and eastern Australia as far south as Sydney): A characteristic bird of the Top End wetlands where it is usually called the Jabiru. It is conspicuous on the Yellow Waters cruise (7.16) and at other tropical wetlands.

Osprey *Pandion haliaetus* (Cosmopolitan; coastal Australia except VIC and TAS): Thinly distributed, but commoner in the north and mostly seen in coastal regions although sometimes along larger rivers.

Pacific Baza *Aviceda subcristata* (Lesser Sundas, New Guinea, Solomons; tropical north and eastern Australia): This species is a summer visitor to the southern part of its range, from about Brisbane to Sydney. It is most easily seen in the early spring when pairs are displaying; at other times they are rather quiet and unobtrusive. A pair nest each October/November in the botanical gardens at Coffs Harbour (4.14), NSW. Otherwise the best areas to see this species are around Brisbane (Mount Glorious (6.5)) and Cairns (Julatten (6.40), Lake Barrine (6.34)). We also saw a pair at Waterfall Creek (7.18).

Australian Kite *Elanus axillaris* (Throughout Australia, uncommon in TAS; endemic): Recently given full species status, this bird is common in the better watered parts of continental Australia, but is less common in the drier north. It is often found along roadsides and open areas in the south-east.

Letter-winged Kite *E. scriptus* (Core range is in the Channel country of south-west QLD, but may occur anywhere in continental Australia; endemic): One of the strangest and most enigmatic of Australian birds, this species can never be guaranteed since it occurs at very low density in remote outback country. It is prone to periodic population explosions following good breeding seasons of its' main prey, the long-haired rat. Following these boom years there is an equally dramatic population crash when starving birds move towards the coast and occur anywhere in continental Australia. That said, a fairly regular place to find them is along the Strzelecki Track (9.13) in SA, in the stand of dead trees about 20 km south of the Strzelecki Crossing, on the east side of the road. Another place is the Tablelands Highway north of Barkly Homestead (7.1) in the NT; we saw birds just north of Alroy Downs. Any isolated stand of trees along dry watercourses on the Birdsville (9.15) or Strzelecki Tracks is worth checking; remember that the adults are nocturnal hunters but usually appear just before dusk, juveniles tend to fly about more just before dark. In late 1993 a small breeding population was found near Deniliquin (4.18) NSW, with sightings of parties in Brisbane and Fogg Dam (7.11), NT. In 1995 birds were seen near Townsville.

Square-tailed Kite *Lophoictinia isura* (Continental Australia, except desert regions and rare in the south-east; endemic): This species is very thinly scattered and not easy to see, although this is partly because of their hunting technique, cruising the tree tops looking for honeyeater nests to raid. The only place we saw this species was 8 km west of Charleville on the road to Quilpie in inland QLD. The best place to look for them however is in the tropical north in the dry season *i.e.* Kakadu NP (7C), NT, and along the Gibb River Road (8.5) in WA, especially the western end. There is also a reasonable chance in Dryandra State Forest (8.19) and the Stirling Ranges NP (8.22) in south-west WA.

Black-breasted Buzzard *Hamirostra melanosternon* (Northern interior of Australia; endemic): Much commoner than the previous species, this bird will mainly be seen in forested areas of the tropical north.

Black Kite *Milvus migrans* (Eurasia, Africa; continental Australia): Abundant in the tropical north, rarer further south.

NON-PASSERINES

Whistling Kite *Haliastur sphenurus* (New Guinea and New Caledonia; throughout Australia, rarer in TAS): Almost as numerous as the previous species, and usually associated with water.

Brahminy Kite *H. indus* (Asia; coastal northern Australia): A common bird, especially in the northern mangrove areas.

White-bellied Sea-eagle *Haliaetus leucogaster* (Asia, New Guinea; throughout coastal Australia): A common bird of all coastal habitats in Australia, it is also found inland along larger rivers and lakes.

Swamp Harrier *Circus approximans* (New Zealand, New Guinea and Pacific Islands; mainly eastern and south-western Australia): A common bird of reed beds and marshes.

Spotted Harrier *C. assimilis* (Sulawesi, Lesser Sundas; throughout inland and sub-coastal Australia): This species replaces the swamp harrier in the areas of dry, open grassland of inland Australia. It is nowhere numerous but will certainly be encountered on the long drives through inland areas, for example along the Barkly Highway (7.1) or across the Nullarbor Plain.

Variable Goshawk *Accipiter novaehollandiae* (New Guinea, Indonesia; eastern and northern Australia including TAS): In Australia, this bird occurs in either a white or grey phase. It is reasonably common but not frequently seen because it is mainly a forest species. Take care not to overlook the white phase for a cockatoo. Barren Grounds (4.1) and Fitzroy Falls (4.2a) in NSW and Lamington NP (6.7) in QLD are all excellent places to find this bird. Interestingly, we spotlighted three white phase birds roosting in trees right over the Mount Lewis road (6.40).

Brown Goshawk *A. fasciatus* (New Guinea, Lesser Sundas; throughout Australia and TAS): The commonest *Accipiter* in Australia, this species is readily seen in all woodland areas. The NT race, *didimus*, has been suggested as a possible split.

Collared Sparrowhawk *A. cirrocephalus* (New Guinea; throughout continental Australia and TAS): Less common than the above species but found in all woodlands and open forests, it seems to be particularly associated with inland gorges and pools in northern Australia.

Red Goshawk *Erythrotriorchis radiatus* (Tropical northern Australia; endemic): One of the hardest of Australian birds to find; we failed and it is extremely hard to get information on nest sites *etc.* Undoubtedly their stronghold is in Kakadu NP and the best time of year to look for them is in July/August when the birds display and are more conspicuous. They nest along the largest rivers and are regularly seen from the Arnhem Highway (7.13). Other areas they have been seen include Mitchell Falls (8.5b) and Manning Gorge (patrolling up and down the gorge) in the Kimberleys, Iron Range NP (6.45) and Big Mitchell Creek (6.39) in QLD.

Wedge-tailed Eagle *Aquila audax* (New Guinea; throughout continental Australia and TAS): A very common raptor seen on all drives through the outback, often feeding on roadside kills. It is also common in TAS.

Little Eagle *Hieraaetus morphnoides* (New Guinea, Indonesia; continental Australia): A fairly common raptor of wooded areas that frequently soars so is not hard to find.

Brown Falcon *Falco berigora* (New Guinea; throughout continental Australia and TAS): Easily the commonest large falcon in Australia, it is frequently seen perched on posts along roadsides in all open areas. Note that some individuals can appear very dark and others very pale, but all forms are readily identified by the fact that they always glide with their wings in a sharp V.

Australian Kestrel *F. cenchroides* (New Guinea, Indonesia; Australia): A common bird of open woodland and fields and like its European counterpart, it is often seen hovering over roadside verges. It is most numerous in the southern half of the continent.

Australian Hobby *F. longipennis* (New Guinea, Indonesia; throughout Australia): This is a fairly common species that is mainly a summer visitor in the south of the continent. Like other hobbies it is an insect and bird predator and on summer evenings this species can usually be seen at Kelly's Swamp (5.2) in the ACT.

Grey Falcon *F. hypoleucos* (Arid continental Australia; endemic although has occurred as a vagrant in New Guinea): A rare bird and one of the hardest to see in Australia. This species is associated with lightly timbered plains and the traditional areas to find it include Sturt NP (4.24) in north-west NSW, dry watercourses along the Birdsville (9.15) and Strzelecki tracks (9.13) in SA, along the Stuart Highway between Katherine and Alice Springs, and Simpson's Gap (7.29) in the NT. The only individual we saw was over the campsite at Victoria River (7.24) in the NT, early one morning. In WA, the Great Northern Highway between Kununurra and Derby is good and recently there have been regular sightings at Broome Bird Observatory (8.9). Try also asking Sydney birders for any recent stake-outs in NSW.

Black Falcon *F. subniger* (Arid continental Australia; endemic): Fortunately much easier to see than the preceding species, although still rather rare. Phil Maher is often able to show you this species near Deniliquin (4.18) and indeed you are very likely to see this bird whilst visiting the sites in this region. Another good area is the Barkly Highway between Mount Isa and Barkly Homestead (7.1) in the NT.

Peregrine Falcon *F. peregrinus* (Cosmopolitan; throughout Australia): Widely but thinly distributed and like elsewhere in its huge world-wide range, often found on coastal and inland cliffs (*e.g.* Simpson's Gap (7.29), NT) or even on city skyscrapers (*e.g.* in Melbourne).

Orange-footed Scrubfowl *Megapodius reinwardt* (New Guinea, Indonesia; monsoon rainforests of northern Australia): Despite the rather restricted range in Australia, there should be little difficulty finding this species since it is common and reasonably tame at several sites, for example at Kingfisher Park (6.40), Mount Whitfield Environmental Park (6.27), Cairns Botanic Gardens (6.26), and Iron Range NP (6.45) in QLD and Howard Springs (7.6) in the NT.

Malleefowl *Leipoa ocellata* (Mallee of southern Australia; endemic): Confined to mallee areas, by far the best place to find this species is Wyperfield NP (2.13) in VIC where a hide has been built in front of a mound. However, the birds do not tend their mounds in April so they will be harder to find at this time of year. Other places you can find this bird are Hattah-Kulkyne NP (2.14), also in VIC; try the Nowingi Track. Innes NP (9.4) in SA is also good, and they also occur rarely at Round Hill Nature Reserve (4.20), NSW.

Australian Brush-Turkey *Alectura lathami* (North-east QLD and eastern NSW; endemic): A very common and tame species in nearly all coastal NPs in QLD. Indeed they are a campground nuisance at Lamington NP (6.7). At Iron Range NP (6.45) the purple-collared race is found, although it is relatively uncommon.

Stubble Quail *Coturnix pectoralis* (Continental Australia except the tropical north and desert areas; endemic): The most widespread and commonest quail in Australia, but difficult to get good views of. The most reliable site is when out spotlighting with Phil

Maher at Deniliquin (4.18). We regularly flushed birds when walking through grassy areas, particularly on the walk from the road to the shoreline at Lake Bathurst (4.3b).

Brown Quail *C. ypsilophora* (Lesser Sundas, New Guinea; coastal and sub-coastal Australia and TAS): Although less widespread than the preceding species, it is often easier to get good views of this species, for example when searching for Chestnut-backed Button-Quails in Kakadu NP (7.17) or at Holmes Jungle Swamp (7.7). Further south, they are regularly found along the Glen Davis road (4.12) in NSW.

Blue-breasted Quail *C. chinensis* (South-east Asia; coastal northern and eastern Australia): The occurrence of this bird is heavily confused by the numbers of releases of the Japanese race. The most regular sites are Holmes Jungle Swamp (7.7) near Darwin, Cooloola NP (6.15), and Lake Samsonvale (6.4) near Brisbane. Further south, most birds are probably releases or escapes.

Red-backed Button-Quail *Turnix maculosa* (Lesser Sundas, New Guinea; coastal northern and eastern Australia): A bird of tall grasses and marshes. Although nomadic, there are two regular sites; Holmes Jungle Swamp (7.7) and Lake Samsonvale (6.4). It is very difficult to obtain adequate views of this species. Most people only obtain flight views of flushed birds.

Black-breasted Button-Quail *T. melanogaster* (Rainforests near Brisbane; endemic): As with other woodland button-quails, the key to finding this species and seeing it on the ground is to first find the platelets they have made. These are the circular cleared areas made by the birds as they scuff up leaves with their feet. They are small, circular, roughly six or eight inches across and are quite easy to recognise once you have your eye in. Once you have found fresh platelets (often with recent droppings in them), the birds are sure to be close by. With care they can be picked out before they see you; listen carefully for any leaves being turned over. Although very restricted in range, there are two excellent sites to find this bird. The first is along Duck Creek Road at Lamington NP (6.7), the second is Neumgna State Forest (6.9) close to Yarraman, north-west of Brisbane.

Painted Button-Quail *T. varia* (Formerly? New Caledonia; eastern and south-western Australia and TAS): The most frequently encountered button-quail in woodland areas. Probably the best site is Chiltern State Forest (2C) in VIC, but along the Glen Davis road (4.12) in NSW and the eucalyptus forest along the Mount Glorious road (6.5) from Brisbane are both excellent for this species. They even sometimes feed along the roadsides at dawn. They also occur at the Buff-breasted Button-Quail site near Mount Molloy (6.43), QLD.

Chestnut-backed Button-Quail *T. castanota* (Tropical northern Australia; endemic): Found throughout the eucalyptus woodland of Kakadu NP and the Kimberley region. Easily the best place to look for this bird is the Old Darwin Road turn off in Kakadu NP (7.17). If the area has been very recently burned out, just find the closest piece of identical looking forest, usually across the road. It is definitely worth persevering here as the birds seem to be somewhat local in their occurrence in apparently suitable looking habitat. It is also worth a try at Edith River (7.21), just north of Katherine. For those going to Mitchell Falls (8.5b) in the Kimberleys, there is a good chance of seeing this species on the walk from the car-park to the falls.

Buff-breasted Button-Quail *T. olivii* (Eastern Cape York peninsula; endemic to QLD): Until recently one of the least observed of all Australian birds. Several have now been found in woodland near Mount Molloy (6.43) in northern QLD. Ask for the most up to date information from Geoff at Kingfisher Park or Lloyd Nielson in Mount Molloy. The only other chance of seeing this species is in the thick rainforest edge scrub along the roadsides at Iron Range NP (6.45) where this bird is a dry season visitor.

Red-chested Button-Quail *T. pyrrhothorax* (Eastern Australia; endemic): A highly nomadic species, particularly in the southern part of its range where it is found in grassland following recent heavy rains. Probably the best chance of seeing this bird is when out spotlighting with Phil Maher around Deniliquin (4.18), although they will not occur there every year. They also occur at Round Hill Nature Reserve (4.20) in NSW when the conditions are suitable. The other regular place to look for them is in the grasslands along the Tableland Highway (7.1) in the NT.

Little Button-Quail *T. velox* (Grasslands of continental Australia, except tropical north; endemic): Again another highly nomadic grassland species, but easily the most regularly encountered button-quail. This species should be seen when out with Phil Maher at Deniliquin (4.18) and is regular every spring at Round Hill Nature Reserve (4.20). This species was particularly numerous at all the sites around Alice Springs in November 1993 following rains there in September and it is extremely easy to walk around and spotlight them with a powerful torch since they roost in shallow depressions on the ground.

Red-necked Rail *Rallina tricolor* (Eastern Indonesia, New Guinea; north-east QLD): A rail of wet forests and although rather restricted in range in Australia, not too difficult to see. The best site is probably Kingfisher Park (6.40), around the pool at night. Other good places are along the boardwalk in Cairns Botanical Gardens (6.26) at dusk and along the creeks at Iron Range NP (6.45). We also saw one crossing the road at Mount Spec NP (6.21) following a heavy rainstorm.

Buff-banded Rail *Gallirallus philippensis* (Eastern Indonesia, New Guinea, Pacific Islands; coastal Australia and TAS): Much commoner in the northern part of its Australian range, the best places to see this species include the Atherton Tablelands (6E) where birds are very easy to see along roadside verges in the early morning and wooded Great Barrier Reef islands such as Lady Elliot or Musgrave Islands (6.16). Birds are hand tame on the former. Further south, Werribee (2.5) in VIC is also good, but you should concentrate your efforts for this bird on north-east QLD.

Lewin's Rail *Rallus pectoralis* (Lesser Sundas and New Guinea; coastal eastern Australia and TAS): A difficult bird to get to grips with because of its secretive nature. Probably the most reliable site is Dharug NP (4.10) near Sydney. Cronulla Swamp (4.8) in NSW and Kelly's Swamp (5.2) in the ACT are also good but only if the water levels are suitable. Birds are also sometimes seen at Werribee (2.5) in VIC. Perhaps surprisingly, this species is also found in rainforest *Lantana* thickets. Ask Wollongong birders about the site at Mount Keira just west of Wollongong. From the Mount Keira Lookout car-park, take the track leading downhill to the east and look for this bird in any large *Lantana* patches. This species will sometimes also respond to two stones being hit together.

Bush-Hen *Amaurornis moluccanus* (Eastern Indonesia, New Guinea; north-eastern Australia): Again a difficult species to observe because of its secretive habits. The best places to look for it are along roadside verges in the Atherton Tablelands (6E) in the early morning or at Hasties Swamp (6.33). We sat and watched from the car here and two birds came out onto the road one morning. Otherwise, there is a reasonable chance at Kingfisher Park (6.40); ask about any recent sightings.

Baillon's Crake *Porzana pusilla* (Eurasia, Australasia; coastal and sub-coastal Australia and TAS): Mainly seen in southern Australia and generally in smaller numbers than Australian Crake, this species should be seen at the usual crake sites (Werribee (2.5), Cronulla Swamp (4.8), Sherwood Forest Park near Brisbane *etc.*). Sometimes occurs in big numbers inland, for example we observed over 40 at midday at Lake Bindegolly (6.13) in south-west QLD.

Australian Crake *P. fluminea* (Swamps of south-western and eastern Australia and TAS; endemic): Usually the commonest crake seen. During the summer months, Kelly's Swamp (5.2) is a good place to observe them if water levels are low. Also good are the superb Leeton (4.17) and Avalon (4.18d) Swamps, both in inland NSW and Werribee (2.5) in VIC.

Spotless Crake *P. tabuensis* (New Guinea, Pacific Islands; south-west and south-east Australia and TAS): Generally in the same places but at lower density than the previous species. Recommended are Leeton (4.17), Avalon (4.18d) and Kelly's (5.2) Swamps, all best in the summer months and Werribee Sewage Works (2.5).

White-browed Crake *P. cinerea* (South-east Asia, New Guinea, Pacific Islands; tropical northern Australia): A bird of tropical wetland swamps, probably the best site in Australia is along the causeway at Fogg Dam (7.11). Also good is Abattoir Swamp (6.41) near Kingfisher Park and the board walk in Cairns Botanic Gardens (6.26).

Chestnut Rail *Eulabeornis castaneoventris* (Aru Islands; mangroves in WA and NT): An inhabitant of mangroves, but fortunately not too hard to see. The best place is undoubtedly Middle Arm (7.5) near Darwin, although we also saw a pair at Buffalo Creek (7.9). A former excellent site in Darwin itself has now unfortunately been 'developed'.

Purple Swamphen *Porphyrio porphyrio* (Cosmopolitan except the Americas; all wetland areas of Australia and TAS): A common bird of all wetland sites.

Dusky Moorhen *Gallinula tenebrosa* (Indonesia and New Guinea; wetter eastern and south-western Australia): A common bird of wetlands in south-eastern Australia.

Black-tailed Native-Hen *G. ventralis* (Continental Australia; endemic): A highly nomadic bird of inland areas and said to appear in numbers shortly before or after heavy rains. This species is regularly found at Avalon (4.18d) and Leeton (4.17) Swamps during the summer months, Lake Bindegolly (6.13) in QLD or Kunoth Well (7.28), near Alice Springs. Keep a look out as you drive through inland areas, for example we saw literally hundreds between Bourke and Tibooburra (4.22).

Tasmanian Native-Hen *G. mortierii* (Wetlands in TAS; endemic to TAS): Common throughout TAS in wet pastures and near ponds.

Eurasian Coot *Fulica atra* (Palearctic, Asia and Australasia; throughout Australia and TAS): Common in wetland areas.

Sarus Crane *Grus antigone* (Asia; tropical northern Australia): A rather restricted range in Australia, the best places to find this bird are Hasties Swamp (6.33) in the Atherton Tablelands or along the Matilda Highway between Normanton and Karumba (6.47) in QLD.

Brolga *G. rubicunda* (New Guinea; generally northern Australia): A frequently seen bird of the northern tropical wetlands (Fogg Dam (7.11) *etc.*), and plains (Matilda Highway (6.47)), but rare in the south of its range although up to 150 are usually present at Bool Lagoon (9.5) in SA.

Australian Bustard *Ardeotis australis* (New Guinea; arid northern Australia): Still reasonably common in the tropical north, this bird will be seen whilst driving through the outback. Regular places to see it include the Bruce Highway near Rockhampton, the

Peninsula Developmental Road between Mount Molloy and Mount Carbine (6.42) in QLD and the Gibb River Road (8.5) and Great Northern Highway in WA.

Comb-crested Jacana *Irediparra gallinacea* (Indonesia and New Guinea; tropical northern Australia): A common bird of the tropical northern wetlands (Yellow Waters (7.16), Fogg Dam (7.11) etc..

Painted Snipe *Rostratula benghalensis* (Africa and Asia; eastern Australia): A difficult bird to catch up with in Australia as it seems to be rare everywhere although it is reasonably regular in the Deniliquin area, *i.e.* Avalon Swamp (4.18d) in the summer months and at Abattoir Swamp (6.41) in north-east QLD. Check with birders in VIC for any recent sightings as this also seems to be a good state for the species, but this is a bird found more easily elsewhere in the world.

Latham's Snipe *Gallinago hardwickii* (Breeds Japan, winters in Australia and New Zealand; eastern Australia and TAS): The commonest snipe in Australia but only found during the Austral summer months. It is readily seen at many wetland sites, for example Kelly's Swamp (5.2), Lake Samsonvale (6.4), Werribee (2.5), Knuckey's Lagoon (7.8), Cairns Botanic Gardens (6.26).

Swinhoe's Snipe *G. megala* (Breeds Siberia, winters south-east Asia, Australia; Top End wetlands): Recorded annually in the Darwin Area from November onwards, *e.g.* at Knuckey's Lagoon (7.8) and also from Broome Bird Observatory (8.9). This species is extremely difficult to identify with certainty in the field. There is some controversy regarding the identification of snipe seen along the rainforest creeks at Iron Range NP (6.45) and in wetlands in the Cairns area. Almost certainly some are this species and tape recordings by Dave Stewart support this claim.

Black-tailed Godwit *Limosa limosa* (Palearctic, winters Africa, Asia and Australasia; mainly coastal eastern Australia): Commonest in the north of its Australian range, large numbers occur at Broome Bird Observatory (8.9), Cairns *etc*.

Bar-tailed Godwit *L. lapponica* (Palearctic, winters Africa, Australasia; throughout coastal Australia): A very common coastal wader in the Australian summer months.

Little Curlew *Numenius minutus* (Breeds Siberia, winters Indonesia, Australasia; tropical northern Australia): Huge numbers of this species pour into the Top End from late October when they can be found on any park or even roadsides in the Darwin area, from there they disperse to short grasslands throughout that region, for example Mamukala (7.14). They are also found in north-eastern QLD, for example the turf farms near Cairns (6.29) and a few birds always penetrate to southern Australia.

Whimbrel *N. phaeopus* (Cosmopolitan; throughout coastal Australia): A common coastal wader of the north and east, being especially found on the Barrier Reef Islands.

Eastern Curlew *N. madagascariensis* (Breeds Asia, winters Indonesia, Australasia; throughout coastal Australia): A common coastal wader, readily seen at Cairns Esplanade (6.24) for example.

Marsh Sandpiper *Tringa stagnatilis* (Palearctic, winters Africa, Asia, Australasia; mainly eastern Australia): Commonest in the tropical north and frequently found inland (Kakadu NP (7C), Lake Argyle (8.1), Fogg Dam (7.11) *etc.*), but occurs throughout the eastern half of the continent.

Greenshank *T. nebularia* (Palearctic, winters Africa, Asia, Australasia; throughout Australia and TAS): Common both on the coast and suitable inland wetlands.

NON-PASSERINES

Wood Sandpiper *T. glareola* (Palearctic, winters Africa, Asia, Australasia; wetter areas of continental Australia): Small numbers are found on wet inland marshes throughout the continent, although this species is commonest in the tropical north.

Terek Sandpiper *T. cinerea* (Palearctic, winters Africa, Asia, Australasia; coastal continental Australia): Commonest in the north, and easily seen at coastal wader sites.

Common Sandpiper *T. hypoleucos* (Palearctic, winters Africa, Asia, Australasia; coastal Australia): Commonest in the north and east, both on the coast and inland. A regular site is Portland Harbour in VIC.

Grey-tailed Tattler *T. brevipes* (Breeds Siberia, winters Australasia; coastal Australia): Much the commonest tattler in Australia, this is the only one found in the south and west of the country. Easily seen at many coastal wader sites (Botany Bay, Manly Yacht Club (6.1), Cairns Esplanade (6.24) *etc.*).

Wandering Tattler *T. incana* (Breeds Siberia, winters in the Pacific; coastal northeastern Australia): Not a common species in Australia; the best places to see it include the Barrier Reef Islands or the sites near Brisbane *i.e.* Redcliffe (6.3), North Stradbroke Island (6.6), Caloundra.

Ruddy Turnstone *Arenaria interpres* (Cosmopolitan; coastal Australia): Fairly common in suitable habitat.

Asiatic Dowitcher *Limnodromus semipalmatus* (Breeds Siberia, winters Asia, Australasia; north-west Australia): Every year several hundred spend the Austral summer in the extreme north-west *i.e.* Port Hedland Salt Works and amongst the huge Bar-tailed Godwit flocks at Broome Bird Observatory (8.9). Apart from visiting these areas at this time of year, the best chance of seeing this species in Australia is by checking the godwit flocks around Brisbane, *i.e.* Manly (6.1) and Thornside since one or two are recorded here most summers.

Great Knot *Calidris tenuirostris* (Breeds Siberia, winters Australasia; coastal Australia): A common wader of northern Australia, but scarce further south. Cairns Esplanade (6.24) is a good place for obtaining close views.

Red Knot *C. canutus* (Cosmopolitan; coastal Australia): A common coastal wader.

Sanderling *C. alba* (Cosmopolitan; coastal Australia): Rather a scarce wader in Australia, which could occur on sandy beaches anywhere.

Red-necked Stint *C. ruficollis* (Breeds Siberia, winters Asia and Australasia; throughout wet areas of Australia): A very common wader on all coasts and often inland throughout Australia and TAS. Rarely seen in full breeding plumage.

Long-toed Stint *C. subminuta* (Palearctic, winters Asia; annual migrant in very small numbers to Australia): There are no really regular places to see this bird in Australia. Any suitable inland marsh should be checked out. Perhaps the most regular sites are Leeton Swamp (4.17) in NSW, and Adelaide ICI Saltworks (9.1).

Pectoral Sandpiper *C. melanotos* (Breeds Arctic regions, winters South America; mainly southern Australia): A regular migrant in small numbers that should be searched for amongst Sharp-tailed Sandpiper flocks. Annual at Lake Bathurst (4.3b) and in the Sydney region.

Sharp-tailed Sandpiper *C. acuminata* (Breeds Siberia, winters Australasia; throughout Australia and TAS): An abundant wader of both coastal and inland sites throughout the continent.

Curlew Sandpiper *C. ferruginea* (Breeds Siberia, winters Africa, Asia and Australasia; throughout coastal Australia and TAS): A common wader in Australia, found mainly in coastal localities.

Broad-billed Sandpiper *Limicola falcinellus* (Palearctic, winters Asia and Australasia; coastal northern Australia): Rather a scarce wader, easily the best place to see it is Cairns Esplanade (6.24) where several birds are always present in summer although birds can also be found at Broome Bird Observatory (8.9) at this time of year.

Ruff *Philomachus pugnax* (Palearctic, winters Africa and Asia; mainly south-eastern Australia): A rare but annual migrant to Australia. The most regular site is probably Adelaide ICI Saltworks (9.1), but they are also frequently recorded at the Victorian wader sites.

Red-necked Phalarope *Phalaropus lobatus* (Holarctic, winters southern hemisphere; ponds and lakes in continental Australia): Easily the most regularly recorded phalarope in Australia, mostly in the south-east, but there are no regular sites.

Plains-wanderer *Pedionomus torquatus* (South-east Australia; endemic): The only realistic chance of seeing this endemic family bird is by hiring Phil Maher to take you out spotlighting around Deniliquin (4.18) when a number of other good birds should also be seen.

Bush Thick-knee *Burhinus grallarius* (New Guinea; continental Australia): Widespread but not easy to see because of its nocturnal habits. Commonest in the north of its range. Fortunately there are several excellent places to see this species. These include Kingfisher Park (6.40) and Cairns cemetery in QLD and Waterfall Creek campsite (7.18). We also recorded it at Iron Range NP (6.45) and Mount Molloy (6.43) in QLD.

Beach Thick-knee *B. giganteus* (South-east Asia and Australasia; coastal northern Australia): Several good sites exist for this species, the best of which is Yule Point (6.30) near Cairns, but East Point Recreational Reserve (7.10) in Darwin, Red Rock Caravan Park (4.15) in NSW and Cape Hillsborough NP (6.18) in QLD are also all reliable places to find it.

Pied Oystercatcher *Haematopus longirostris* (Australasia; coastal Australia and TAS): Common on coastal wader sites in the south of the continent and particularly in TAS but rarely on rocky shores.

Sooty Oystercatcher *H. fuliginosus* (Coastal Australia and TAS; endemic): Much less common than the preceding species and usually found in small parties on rocky shores in the south of the country. Small numbers are usually on the rocks below Wollongong lighthouse (10.1) and the rocky coastline south of here is excellent for this species, for example around Kiama Blowhole. TAS is also a good place for this species, try looking around Cloudy Bay on Bruny Island (3.1). The rare northern race, *ophthalmicus*, has even been proposed as a separate species.

Black-winged Stilt *Himantopus himantopus* (Cosmopolitan; throughout continental Australia): Found in all wader habitats throughout Australia, although rare in TAS, this species seems commonest in the north.

NON-PASSERINES

Banded Stilt *Cladorhynchus leucocephalus* (Southern Australia; endemic): This strange bird of inland salt lakes congregates in large coastal flocks at commercial salt fields. The best site is probably Adelaide ICI Saltworks (9.1), but birds also occur in numbers in VIC, for example at Laverton Saltworks (2.4). In WA, you should see this species on Rottnest Island, and we recorded several in Oyster Bay, between Albany and Two Peoples Bay.

Red-necked Avocet *Recurvirostra novaehollandiae* (Continental Australia; endemic although has occurred as a vagrant in New Zealand): Found mainly on brackish swamps and estuaries, this wader is widely but thinly scattered and often found in the same places as Banded Stilts. Probably the most reliable site is Adelaide ICI Saltworks (9.1) where if permission is denied to enter the works, try searching the salt pans on either side of the road between Adelaide and St Kilda. Other good places include Avalon (4.18d) and Leeton (4.17) Swamps and the south end of Lake George (4.3a), all in NSW and Laverton Saltworks (2.4) in VIC. We also saw several on the estuary adjacent to the BP petrol station as you drive through Port Augusta in SA.

Oriental Pratincole *Glareola maldivarum* (Asia and Australasia; tropical northern Australia): Huge flocks of this pratincole pour into the north-west every October where they disperse widely across the grassy plains of the tropical north and sometimes occur as vagrants in the south of the continent. They can be encountered in any suitable habitat in the north during the wet season, however the only place we saw any was at Yarrabah Turf Farm (6.29) near Cairns.

Australian Pratincole *Stiltia isabella* (Winters New Guinea and Asia; endemic breeder in northern Australia): A characteristic bird of the dry open plains of the tropical north, being much less common further south. A bird that will be seen during the long outback drives, for example along the Matilda Highway between Normanton and Karumba, or crossing the Barkly Tablelands (7.1). Other good sites include Knuckey's Lagoon (7.8) in Darwin, Mamukala (7.14) and the turf farms south of Cairns (6.29).

Pacific Golden Plover *Pluvialis fulva* (Breeds Siberia, winters Asia and Australasia; coastal Australia and TAS): A common Austral summer visitor, mostly on the coast but also found inland in suitable habitat.

Grey Plover *P. squatarola* (Cosmopolitan; coastal Australia and TAS): Rather local in occurrence, but can be found in suitable habitat on the coast. Cairns Esplanade (6.24) in the summer months is a reliable place to see it.

Red-capped Plover *Charadrius ruficapillus* (Throughout Australia and TAS; endemic but has occurred as a vagrant in New Zealand): Common on the coast, *e.g.* Botany Bay, but rarer inland, although good numbers are regularly at Lake Bathurst (4.3b).

Double-banded Plover *C. bicinctus* (Breeds New Zealand; winters coastal southern Australia and TAS): One of the very few birds to cross the Tasman for the winter months, this species arrives in Australia around March, departing in August. A common coastal wader particularly in the south-east, for example in Botany Bay and Port Phillip Bay and dispersing as far north as Cairns. Excellent numbers are found in TAS; try the mud flats around the Isthmus on Bruny Island (3.1), and some even penetrate as far as the south coast of WA, around Albany. Uncommon inland, although flocks of juveniles are found at Lake Bathurst (4.3b) each winter.

Lesser Sandplover *C. mongolus* (Breeds Asia, winters Africa, Asia and Australasia; throughout coastal Australia and TAS): Much the commonest sandplover in the east of Australia and common at all wader sites around the north and east coasts as far as Sydney where it becomes scarcer. Small numbers in VIC, *e.g.* Swan Island (2.8), and TAS.

Greater Sandplover *C. leschenaultii* (Breeds Asia, winters Africa, Asia and Australasia; throughout coastal Australia and TAS): Common in WA, for example at Monkey Mia (8.16) and along the north coast. Much scarcer in the east than the above species although fairly regular on Cairns Esplanade (6.24).

Oriental Plover *C. veredus* (Breeds Siberia, winters Indonesia and Australasia; mainly tropical northern Australia): Like the Little Curlew, large numbers of this species pour into the Top End from October onwards from where they disperse widely over the dry open plains of the tropical north. They often occur with flocks of Little Curlew and a traditional site to see them near Darwin is the RAAF station along Lee Point (7.9). Places we saw them include Yarrabah Turf Farm (6.29) near Cairns, Mamukala (7.14) and in suburban Darwin. Birds are occasionally recorded in the southern half of the country.

Hooded Plover *C. rubricollis* (Sandy coastal southern Australia and TAS; endemic): An uncommon and apparently declining species of the southern coasts of Australia. There are several regular places to find this species. In NSW, the beach next to the campground at Nadgee NP (4.6) has them, whilst in VIC, try any of the following places; the sandy beach at Barwon Heads some 15 km west of Queenscliffe, any sandy beach on Wilson's Promontory or the beach between Lakes Entrance and Lake Tyers, around Wingan Inlet in Croajingolong NP (turn south off the Princes Highway onto West Wingan road and follow to the end). In TAS, the most reliable site is probably Darlington Beach where the ferry lands at Maria Island NP (3.4), but the east side of the Isthmus and Cloudy Bay on Bruny Island (3.1) are also worth checking. In SA, we saw birds on the beach opposite Golden Island in Coffin Bay NP (9.9). In WA a large party is often found in the northeast corner of Lake Gore; turn south off the South Coast Highway 36 km west of Esperance into McCalls Road. Follow to the end and explore the lake shore to your left.

Red-kneed Dotterel *Erythrogonys cinctus* (Continental Australia; endemic, although occurs rarely and may breed in New Guinea): A wader mainly of inland swamps, moving towards the coast in summer. It is fairly common but patchy in occurrence and mainly in the south-east of the continent. Reliable places to see it include Avalon (4.18d) and Leeton (4.17) Swamps in NSW, and Kelly's Swamp (5.2) in the ACT often has them. Wader sites around Port Phillip Bay also hold this species whilst in QLD, try Lake Bindegolly (6.13) and Townsville Common Environmental Park (6.20).

Inland Dotterel *Peltohyas australis* (Arid central Australia; endemic): A spectacular, but somewhat elusive wader of the arid interior of Australia. It is mainly nocturnal in habits. This species should be seen along the Birdsville Track (9.15), particularly if you drive at night (extreme care!). Phil Maher can sometimes show you this species near Deniliquin (4.18), but a more reliable site is Cook airfield (9.17) in SA. We recorded it at Kunoth Well (7.28) near Alice Springs, whilst crossing the Tanami Desert, and in the Channel Country on the bare open plains to the west of Windorah, before the turn to Birdsville.

Black-fronted Dotterel *Elseyornis melanops* (New Zealand and Australia; throughout continental Australia and TAS): A wader mainly found in the interior, rarely on the coast. It is found in similar places to the Red-kneed Dotterel, but also along rivers and is decidedly commoner than that species.

Banded Lapwing *Vanellus tricolor* (Continental Australia, except tropical north and TAS; endemic): A bird of dry open plains and short grassy areas and rather uncommon and nomadic. It is not easy to give a totally reliable site for this species, but try the following; the north side of Lake Bathurst (4.3b), Hobart Airfield in TAS and Rottnest Island Airfield off Perth. We also recorded this species at Kunoth Well (7.28) near Alice Springs and whilst crossing the Tanami Desert. If really struggling, Phil Maher can probably show you this species near Deniliquin (4.18), but it is a bird you should see on those long outback drives.

Masked Lapwing *V. miles* (New Guinea and New Zealand; throughout continental eastern Australia and TAS, except desert areas): A common bird of grasslands and wetlands.

Pacific Gull *Larus pacificus* (Southern coasts of Australia and TAS; endemic): The stronghold for this species is the Bass Strait Islands. It is common in all coastal localities in TAS, and along the south Victorian coast. A population also exists along the south coast of WA.

Kelp Gull *L. dominicanus* (Southern oceans; southern coasts of Australia and TAS): This species has a similar distribution in Australia to the Pacific Gull, however it is rather patchy and this species seems to be a fairly recent colonist of the country. It is common around Bruny Island (3.1) in TAS, and around Wollongong (10.1) in NSW where several are seen every pelagic trip.

Silver Gull *L. novaehollandiae* (New Caledonia and New Zealand; throughout Australia and TAS): Abundant in the southern part of the country, even inland, but rarer in the north; this is the commonest gull in Australia. The New Zealand population has sometimes been split as *L. scopulinus*, the Red-billed Gull.

Whiskered Tern *Chlidonias hybridus* (Africa, Asia and Australasia; throughout continental Australia): A common marsh tern in Australia and found on inland freshwater wetlands as well as on brackish lagoons and saltwater lakes *etc*.

White-winged Tern *C. leucopterus* (Africa, Asia and Australasia; coastal and sub-coastal Australia, rare in the south and TAS): Mainly a coastal estuary bird in Australia, this species is a regular Austral summer migrant in fluctuating numbers mainly to the north and east. Parties are regularly seen at Werribee (2.5) in VIC, whilst in the north, places like Townsville Common Environmental Park (6.20) are good. The only group we saw was from the boat from Cairns to Michaelmas Cay (6.25).

Gull-billed Tern *Sterna nilotica* (Cosmopolitan; throughout continental Australia): Widespread and fairly common throughout the continent, large numbers will sometimes congregate and breed on inland lakes when conditions are suitable. It is most regularly found in coastal areas, from Cairns Esplanade (6.24) to Carnarvon (8.14) in WA, but is a vagrant to TAS.

Caspian Tern *S. caspia* (Cosmopolitan; throughout continental Australia and TAS): Widespread but not numerous in all coastal situations; rather rare inland.

Crested Tern *S. bergii* (Africa, Asia and Australasia; coastal Australia and TAS): The commonest tern in Australia, especially in the south.

Lesser Crested Tern *S. bengalensis* (Africa, Asia and Australasia; coastal northern Australia): Found only in tropical and sub-tropical seas and generally in much smaller numbers than the preceding species. Occurs on the Barrier Reef Islands (Lady Elliot and Musgrave Islands (6.16)) right round to WA where they can easily be seen at Carnarvon harbour (8.14).

Roseate Tern *S. dougallii* (Cosmopolitan; tropical northern Australia): Generally rare in Australia, this is a tern that breeds on offshore islands. Breeding colonies are found on the Abrolhos Islands off WA where access is difficult, however a few can usually be found in Carnarvon harbour (8.14). Off the eastern seaboard, a breeding colony is easily viewable on Lady Elliot Island (6.16).

White-fronted Tern *S. striata* (Breeds New Zealand and Bass Strait; winter visitor to south-east Australia and TAS): Another species that crosses the Tasman for the winter months, this species is thinly scattered, but not uncommon in the south-east. It is very probable you will see one on a winter Wollongong pelagic (10.1), but failing this the NSW coast south of here has birds all along it. Try the Shoalhaven River mouth, or any of the coastline between there and Eden.

Black-naped Tern *S. sumatrana* (Tropical Indian and Pacific Oceans; tropical north-eastern Australia): Mainly a bird of offshore islands, it can readily be seen on any trip to the Great Barrier Reef.

Common Tern *S. hirundo* (Cosmopolitan; coastal, mainly eastern Australia): A rather uncommon and local migrant during the Austral summer, this species can usually be found at the birding sites around Port Phillip Bay and Botany Bay. They are also found in WA, for example at Carnarvon harbour (8.14).

Arctic Tern *S. paradisaea* (Cosmopolitan; mainly south coasts of Australia and TAS): A rare migrant during the Austral summer and apparently keeping well offshore. There is no regular location to see this species in Australia, and indeed the only ones I saw were on a pelagic trip from Portland (10.2) in VIC.

Bridled Tern *S. anaethetus* (Tropical oceans; tropical northern Australia): Easiest to see in Australia on a trip to the Great Barrier Reef where this species breeds in large numbers on the southern islands (Lady Elliot and Musgrave Islands (6.16)). Does not breed on Michaelmas Cay (6.25) off Cairns, but a few should be seen on the boat trip out there.

Sooty Tern *S. fuscata* (Tropical oceans; tropical eastern and western Australia): Again easiest to see on a trip to Michaelmas Cay (6.25) where they breed in large numbers. This species does not breed on the southern Barrier Reef Islands so a visit further north is required. Also found off WA breeding on the Abrolhos Islands.

Little Tern *S. albifrons* (Cosmopolitan except the Americas; eastern Australia and TAS): A fairly common bird in the east of the country and likely to be seen at many coastal sites around Port Phillip Bay and Botany Bay as far north as Townsville and Cairns Esplanade (6.24).

Fairy Tern *S. nereis* (New Zealand and New Caledonia; coastal southern and western Australia and TAS): This species occurs around the remainder of the coastline that Little Terns do not occupy with an area of overlap in SA, VIC and TAS (hybridisation does occur). This species is probably easiest to find in WA, as they are common along the Peron Peninsula (8.16) and several can usually be seen in Carnarvon harbour (8.14). In VIC, try areas around Port Phillip Bay such as Werribee (2.5) and the salt marsh between Ocean Grove and Barwon Heads. This species is also reasonably common in SA, around the ICI Saltworks (9.1) and Port Gawler (9.2).

Brown Noddy *Anous stolidus* (Tropical oceans; tropical northern Australia): This species is most easily seen by visiting the Great Barrier Reef, they breed in large numbers on Lady Elliot and Lady Musgrave Islands (6.16) and at Michaelmas Cay (6.25).

Black Noddy *A. minutus* (Tropical Atlantic and Pacific Oceans; tropical north-eastern Australia): Again, most easily seen by visiting the Barrier Reef, but note that although this species breeds in reasonable numbers on Lady Elliot and Musgrave Islands (6.16), there are only a few breeding pairs on Michaelmas Cay (6.25) so be prepared to spend a lot of time scrutinising the Brown Noddy flocks.

Lesser Noddy *A. tenuirostris* (Tropical Indian Ocean; western Australia): This species only breeds on the Abrolhos Islands off WA. Your only chance of seeing it in Australia is to arrange an expensive boat charter from Geraldton or to try and talk your way onto a fishing boat going out there.

Southern Skua *Catharacta antarctica* (Southern oceans; southern coastal Australia and TAS in winter): This species occurs in small numbers during the winter months and can usually be seen on any winter pelagic trip off NSW or VIC. Seawatching from shore may also prove successful.

Pomarine Skua *Stercorarius pomarinus* (Cosmopolitan; southern offshore waters of Australia): The commonest skua on offshore pelagic trips from Wollongong (10.1), but rarely seen from land.

Arctic Skua *S. parasiticus* (Cosmopolitan; southern coastal waters of Australia and TAS): The commonest skua of inshore waters in the summer months and readily seen on offshore pelagics at this time of year.

Long-tailed Skua *S. longicaudus* (Cosmopolitan; southern offshore waters of Australia): Uncommon but regular on most summer Wollongong pelagics (10.1) and always seen well out to sea.

White-headed Pigeon *Columba leucomela* (Forests of eastern Australia; endemic): Although fairly common in east coast rainforests, the key to seeing this pigeon is to learn the call and find fruiting trees. Probably the easiest site is Lamington NP (6.7) where birds regularly fly over the campsite and entrance road. Mount Glorious (6.5) and the Bunya Mountains NP (6.10) to the north-west of Brisbane are also good and further north rainforest areas in the Atherton Tablelands (6E), Cairns Botanical Gardens (6.26) and Mount Spec NP (6.21) all hold this species.

Brown Cuckoo-Dove *Macropygia phasianella* (Rainforests of eastern Australia; endemic): Although it occurs in the same areas mentioned for the previous species, this species seems particularly numerous along the rainforest walks around O'Reilly's in Lamington NP (6.7). The Blue Pool trail is especially good.

Common Bronzewing *Phaps chalcoptera* (Throughout Australia and TAS; endemic): Fairly common in most habitats except waterless deserts, this species can be found at many sites in this guide. They are always present in Canberra Botanical Gardens (5.1) for example and many can be seen feeding on roadsides in scrub areas, such as the road from Lake Cargelligo to Round Hill Nature Reserve (4.20). Other good areas for this species include Hattah-Kulkyne NP (2.14), the Brisbane Ranges NP (2.7), both in VIC, and TAS.

Brush Bronzewing *P. elegans* (Southern coastal Australia and TAS; endemic): Rather a scarce species and mostly found in coastal areas. Easy to see in Nadgee NP (4.6) where birds feed on the roadside that leads to the car-park. Also fairly common in the coastal scrub of Coffin Bay NP (9.9) and Innes NP (9.4), both in SA. This species is also reasonably plentiful in TAS, Maria Island NP (3.4) being an especially good place for them whilst in VIC, you are likely to find this species whilst searching for Rufous Bristlebirds along the Great Ocean Road (2.9). Other sites include Dryandra State Forest (8.19) in WA and Cooloola NP (6.15) in QLD.

Flock Bronzewing *P. histrionica* (Arid interior Australia; endemic): Although this species forms huge flocks in the arid plains of inland Australia, it can nevertheless be hard to find. It is a highly nomadic species and the most accessible area to search for it is when crossing the Barkly Tablelands (7.1). Birds regularly come in to drink at the water holes across this plain and the best bet is to camp next to different waterholes until you find them. They fly in to drink shortly after dawn and sometimes just before dusk. The other regular place to find this bird is at Pandie Burra Bore on the Birdsville Track (9.15). We also recorded a lone male whilst on a Yellow Waters cruise (7.16), another single male on the drive between Tibooburra and the Strzelecki Track in western NSW and several flocks in the Channel Country.

Crested Pigeon *Geophaps lophotes* (Throughout arid central Australia; endemic): An abundant bird in all arid areas, particularly in the north.

Spinifex Pigeon *G. plumifera* (Arid northern Australia; endemic): A delightful pigeon that is fortunately not uncommon or difficult to see. Perhaps the best place to see them is Ormiston Gorge NP (7.31) west of Alice Springs where birds in the campground can be hand fed. Birds are similarly tame at Wyndham Caravan Park (8.4), other good areas are the Gibb River Road (8.5), Boroloola (7.3) and Cape Crawford (7.2). The western race *ferruginea* is found at Cape Range NP (8.13) in north-west WA.

Squatter Pigeon *G. scripta* (North-east Australia; endemic): Although its range does just extend into NSW, it is rare that far south so this is essentially a QLD endemic. There are several very good places to find it. These are Tinaroo Creek Road (6.37), the roadside verges between Mount Molloy and Mount Carbine (6.42) and Cumberland Dam (6.46), which is an early morning drinking site.

Partridge Pigeon *G. smithii* (Top End and Kimberley region; endemic): Fairly common and easy to find in Kakadu NP (7C). Try driving the roads in the early morning or evening, they often feed on the lawns of the visitor centre. Other areas where we recorded them include the campground at Waterfall Creek (7.18) and the area around the gate that leads to the CSIRO Research Station at Kapalga (no access). Away from Kakadu NP, we saw them along the dirt road leading to Middle Arm (7.5) in the early morning. The yellow-eyed Kimberley race is fairly common on the track from Mitchell Falls (8.5b) car-park to the Falls.

White-quilled Rock-Pigeon *Petrophassa albipennis* (North-west Australia; endemic): This species is common at Mitchell Falls (8.5b) in the Kimberleys, however if you are not visiting this remote site, the best place to find this bird is the escarpment just west of Victoria River Roadhouse (7.24) or Keep River NP in the NT.

Chestnut-quilled Rock-Pigeon *P. rufipennis* (Arnhem Land; endemic to NT): This species should definitely be seen whilst searching for White-throated Grasswrens above Waterfall Creek (7.18). Recently they have been sighted around Nourlangie Rock carpark and walks to the escarpments above it (7.15).

Diamond Dove *Geopelia cuneata* (Arid northern Australia; endemic): Common in all the arid areas of the north, but rarer in the south of its range. You should find this bird at any inland site in QLD and the NT *etc.*, although it is nomadic to some extent.

Peaceful Dove *G. placida* (New Guinea; northern and eastern Australia): Common in open scrublands, grassy woodlands, roadsides, parks and gardens *etc.* in the north and east of Australia. Common in the mangroves at Bundaberg (6.16),QLD.

Bar-shouldered Dove *G. humeralis* (New Guinea; tropical northern and eastern Australia): Abundant in the tropical north, usually in the vicinity of water, in scrubs, eucalyptus woodlands and even mangroves. Common and easily seen in the mangroves at Bundaberg (6.16).

Wonga Pigeon *Leucosarcia melanoleuca* (Temperate forests of eastern Australia; endemic): This delightful pigeon is fairly common in the wet eucalyptus forests of the east. Probably the easiest site to see them is Lamington NP (6.7) where birds walk around the campsite at O'Reilly's. They are also relatively common at Tidbinbilla (5.4) in the ACT; try the Camelback Firetrail and Lyrebird Trail.

Black-banded Fruit-Dove *Ptilinopus alligator* (Arnhem Land; endemic to NT): A Kakadu NP speciality which is easily found in Stag Creek (7.19). Make sure that you don't walk too far up the creek past the fig tree. Has also been seen on the escarpment up the side of Waterfall Creek (7.18) and on the escarpment above Nourlangie Rock (7.15).

Wompoo Fruit-Dove *P. magnificus* (New Guinea; rainforests of eastern Australia): Fairly common in sub-tropical and tropical rainforest sites from Brisbane to Cape York. Its presence at any site is highly dependant on whether fruiting trees are present. Listen for its very distinctive call. Usually present at Lamington NP (6.7), and Mount Glorious (6.5) in southern QLD, and it was abundant at Iron Range NP (6.45) at the time of our visit.

Superb Fruit-Dove *P. superbus* (Australasia; north-east Australia): Breeds in the tropical north-eastern rainforests but disperses south to Sydney in the non-breeding season. This species is not easy to find except at Iron Range NP (6.45) where it is common. Further south, Cape Tribulation NP and the Atherton Tablelands (6E) are the best places to look.

Rose-crowned Fruit-Dove *P. regina* (Lesser Sundas; tropical northern and eastern Australia): The easiest places to find this rainforest pigeon are Fogg Dam (7.11) (around the car-park), Darwin Botanical Gardens, and East Point Recreational Reserve (7.10) in the NT, and Mount Glorious (6.5) in southern QLD. Whilst it does occur at rainforest sites in between these areas, this species seems strangely uncommon in many of them.

Torresian Imperial-Pigeon *Ducula spilorrhoa* (New Guinea; tropical northern and eastern Australia): A pigeon of coastal areas that is a breeding migrant to Australia, arriving in September and departing around March. Very common in tropical coastal areas at this time of year, for example flocks will be seen from Cairns on their daily flights to and from their offshore roosting islands and even flying past the boat to Michaelmas Cay (6.25). Common at Iron Range NP (6.45) and further west around the Darwin area.

Topknot Pigeon *Lopholaimus antarcticus* (Coastal eastern Australia; endemic): This rainforest species is highly nomadic in response to food availability and ranges from northern QLD to VIC. However, it is fairly common in the central part of its range, around Brisbane where birds can regularly be seen flying over the campsite at O'Reilly's. Another excellent place to look for them is by scanning from Illawarra Lookout at Barren Grounds (4.1), NSW where birds can regularly be seen flying along the escarpment.

Double-eyed Fig-Parrot *Opopsitta diopthalma* (New Guinea; eastern Australia): Three distinct and well separated races are found in Australia; the southern race, *coxeni* is nearly or now extinct, the northern QLD race *macleayana* is reasonably common in the Cairns area. Probably the best site is the fig trees along the Esplanade (6.24), but it is also found at the rainforest sites on the Atherton Tablelands (6E). The final race, *marshalli*, is fairly common at Iron Range NP (6.45), particularly in the roadside bushes along Portland Road around the Coen turn off.

Red-cheeked Parrot *Geoffroyus geoffroyi* (Australasia; confined to Cape York Peninsula): Common at Iron Range NP (6.45), but it is difficult to get good views of this noisy parrot. Birds are frequently seen in flight over the Portland Road, especially in the evening.

Eclectus Parrot *Eclectus roratus* (Australasia; confined to Cape York Peninsula): Common at Iron Range NP (6.45) and nests along the Coen Road. Frequently seen flying over the Portland Road.

Australian King-Parrot *Alisterus scapularis* (Eastern Australia; endemic): Common in rainforest and eucalyptus woodlands all down the eastern edge of the continent, this species is easy to see. Birds at O'Reilly's are hand tame and highly photogenic!

Red-winged Parrot *Aprosmictus erythropterus* (New Guinea; northern and eastern Australia): Common and easy to see throughout the drier (but not desert) regions of inland NT, QLD and northern NSW.

Superb Parrot *Polytelis swainsonii* (Inland south-east Australia; endemic): Locally common within its restricted range which is mostly in western NSW. The Deniliquin area (4.18) is the stronghold for this species and they are usually to be found at Gulpa State Forest (4.18b). Phil Maher can always show you them if struggling. It is also worth driving roads to the north-west of Yass (4.16) any time from late October to February in search of this species.

Regent Parrot *P. anthopeplus* (Southern Australia; endemic): This species has a curious disjunct range with a population in south-west WA and another in western VIC and SA. In WA the most reliable site is Dryandra State Forest (8.19), however this species is much easier to see in the eastern part of its' range. Birds can be seen coming in to drink daily at Hattah-Kulkyne NP (2.14) in VIC and are common at nearby Wyperfield NP (2.13).

Princess Parrot *P. alexandrae* (Deserts of central Australia; endemic): There is a remote possibility of seeing this parrot when travelling through the centre of Australia, however the only real chance is to organise an expedition along the Canning Stock Route (8.7) in July when you can almost guarantee to see this species provided you can get there!

Red-capped Parrot *Purpureicephalus spurius* (South-west Australia; endemic to WA): A spectacular species and fortunately common in its restricted range in all wooded habitats.

Mallee Ringneck *Barnardius* (*barnardi*) *barnardi* (Inland eastern Australia; endemic): Common in all mallee and mulga areas in inland eastern Australia and easily seen as it frequently feeds along roadsides. Usually lumped with the following two races as 'Ringneck Parrot'.

Port Lincoln Ringneck *B.* (*barnardi*) *zonarius* (Inland western Australia; endemic): Common in all mallee and mulga areas of the western half of the continent. The 'Twenty-eight' race is common at Dryandra State Forest (8.19) in WA.

Cloncurry Ringneck *B.* (*barnardi*) *macgillvrayi*. (The Gulf Country; endemic): Rather an uncommon bird that is isolated from other populations of 'Ringneck' Parrots and as its name suggests it occurs around the Cloncurry area of north-western QLD. It is not hard to find at the Carpentarian Grasswren site near Mount Isa (6.50).

Green Rosella *Platycercus caledonicus* (Bass Strait Islands and TAS; endemic to TAS): Common in all woodland areas of TAS.

Crimson Rosella *P. elegans* (Eastern Australia; endemic): Abundant in the south-east of the country. Birds are hand tame at many picnic sites and NPs, for example at Lamington NP (6.7). Sometimes lumped with the following race as 'Blue-cheeked Rosella'.

Yellow Rosella *P.* (*elegans*) *flaveolus* (Southern NSW and Victorian mallee sites; endemic): A yellow rosella found in mallee regions and particularly associated with river red gum trees. A good place to see them is the campsite at Lake Hattah in Hattah-Kulkyne NP (2.14).

Eastern Rosella *P. eximius* (Eastern and northern Australia and TAS; endemic): The nominate race is common in woodland areas throughout the south-east, but less so in TAS where it can be found at Pittwater Road (3.3). Often lumped with the following two races as the 'White-cheeked Rosella'.

Pale-headed Rosella *P. (eximius) adscitus* (Northern NSW and eastern QLD; endemic): This rosella is common in eucalyptus woodland in the north-east of Australia and it is easily found around the town of Canungra on the way up to Lamington NP (6.7). We saw them as far north as Musgrave Station (6.44) on Cape York Peninsula.

Northern Rosella *P. (eximius) venustus* (The Top End; endemic): This rosella is thinly scattered in dry woodlands across the Top End. Good places to find it include Caranbirini Springs (7.3), Waterfall Creek (7.18), Katherine Gorge NP (7.22) and the Gibb River Road (8.5).

Western Rosella *P. icterotis* (South-west Australia; endemic to WA): Fairly common in open woodlands of the extreme south-west of WA, you should have little difficulty finding this species at Dryandra State Forest (8.19) or Porongurup NP (8.21).

Bluebonnet *Northiella haematogaster* (Arid south-eastern Australia; endemic): Common in the arid southern interior in mulga, mallee and often along roadsides. Good places to find this bird include the road from Hopetoun to Wyperfield NP (2.13) or the road from Lake Cargelligo to Round Hill Nature Reserve (4.20), and even the Stuart Highway north of Port Augusta. You should have little difficulty finding this bird on your travels.

Naretha Bluebonnet *N. (haematogaster) narethae* (Inland south western Australia; endemic): This isolated western population has sometimes been split. It is rare, found only north of the Nullarbor Plain and almost entirely within WA but it does just occur in SA. Perhaps the best chance of seeing it is at Eyre Bird Observatory in eastern WA or when on an expedition to look for Scarlet-chested Parrots in the Great Victoria Desert (9.16).

Red-rumped Parrot *Psephotus haematonotus* (South-east Australia; endemic): This is a common bird of open woodlands, grasslands *etc.* in the south-east of Australia, usually not far from water.

Mulga Parrot *P. varius* (Southern Australia; endemic): A common and spectacular parrot of mallee, mulga and other inland scrubs. This species will be encountered in all the mallee sites suggested and also mulga areas such as Eulo Bore (6.14) in QLD, Round Hill Nature Reserve (4.20) in NSW, Mount Magnet area (8.17) in WA and Kunoth Well (7.28) in NT.

Hooded Parrot *P. dissimilis* (Arnhem Land; endemic to the NT): Several excellent dry season waterholes exist where you can easily see this breathtaking parrot. Best known are Chinaman Creek (7.23) near Katherine and the Fergusson River (7.20). Keep a look out for this species whilst driving through the dry woodlands of Kakadu NP (7C).

Golden-shouldered Parrot *P. chrysopterygius* (Cape York Peninsula; endemic to QLD): The only real possibility for seeing this species is a visit during the dry season to the Musgrave Station (6.44) area of Cape York.

Paradise Parrot *P. pulcherrimus* (Areas north-west of Brisbane; endemic): Presumed extinct, last reliably reported in the 1920s, but a claim of three birds was made in March 1990 west of Brisbane and others claim to know of birds seen in the 1980s.

Bourke's Parrot *Neophema bourkii* (Widespread through central Australia; endemic): Widespread, although nowhere common. This species favours mulga and there are several good areas to look for it. Perhaps best are Eulo Bore (6.14) and the road between Quilpie and Windorah (6.12) in QLD, Kunoth Well (7.28) in NT and the area around Mount Magnet (8.17) in WA.

Blue-winged Parrot *N. chrysostoma* (Southern Australia and TAS; endemic): Although mainly associated with coastal heaths, this parrot does occur well inland, even into QLD. The best area for this species, however, is the coastal heaths of southern VIC along the Great Ocean Road (2.9). Another reliable site is Werribee Sewage Works (2.5).

Elegant Parrot *N. elegans* (Southern Australia; endemic): This species has two widely separated populations. In the south-west of WA, we saw them *en route* to Stirling Ranges NP (8.22) and they also occur regularly at Dryandra State Forest (8.19). However, it is easier to find them in SA, try the ICI Saltworks (9.1), Port Gawler and Port Prime (9.2), and especially Mount Remarkable NP (9.3).

Rock Parrot *N. petrophila* (Coastal southern Australia; endemic): A parrot found almost exclusively in coastal sand dunes and heaths, there are several excellent sites to find it. These are Rottnest Island and Two Peoples Bay (8.20) in WA, Coffin Bay NP (9.9), Port Gawler and Port Prime (9.2) in SA.

Orange-bellied Parrot *N. chrysogaster* (Breeds TAS, winters coastal VIC; endemic): During the summer months, the only option for seeing this bird is a trip to Mount Melaleuca (3.10) in remote south-west TAS. During the winter they can be found in coastal VIC, notably at Werribee (2.5) and Swan Island (2.8), but contact the RAOU in Melbourne for latest sightings.

Turquoise Parrot *N. pulchella* (Inland south-eastern Australia; endemic): Patchily distributed in open woodlands in inland VIC, NSW and QLD this is rather a scarce parrot. Fortunately there are several excellent sites where it should be found. These are Chiltern State Forest (2C) in VIC, Glen Davis (4.12) and Back Yamma State Forest (4.19) in NSW and Girraween NP (6.8) in QLD. Another place worth trying is the Weddin Mountains NP in NSW.

Scarlet-chested Parrot *N. splendida* (Inland southern Australia; endemic): The parrot apparently occurs at very low density over a huge area. The only realistic chance of seeing it is an expedition into the Great Victoria Desert (9.16) in SA. However, there is a very slim chance of encountering it elsewhere, birds are seen almost annually at Hattah-Kulkyne NP (2.14) in the Victorian mallee and there are sightings from around Ayers Rock and the Olgas, but you would have to be very lucky indeed to see them.

Swift Parrot *Lathamus discolor* (Breeds TAS, winters south-east Australia; endemic): Easiest to see on TAS during the summer months (November to March) at Forest Glen Tea Gardens (3.6), this species winters widely in the south-east of Australia. The most reliable wintering sites are You Yangs Forest Park (2.6) and Chiltern State Forest (2C) in VIC, however they are sometimes found in NSW and in winter 1995 many were seen at Glen Davis (4.12).

Budgerigar *Melopsittacus undulatus* (Throughout continental Australia; endemic): A characteristic bird of the arid outback, this species forms huge flocks that are nomadic throughout the interior. Particularly numerous in areas where it has recently rained.

Ground Parrot *Pezoporus wallicus* (Coastal south-east Australia and TAS; endemic): A very localised parrot of coastal heaths, it is now very rare in WA and should be looked for in the east. The stronghold for this species is in remote south-west TAS but fortunately they are common in the accessible heathland around Strahan (3.8). In NSW, the classic place to find them is Barren Grounds (4.1), however access on to the heathland there is not allowed. They are also reasonably plentiful on the southern heaths of Nadgee NP (4.6) and are found on Green Cape (4.6). In QLD, the best area is Cooloola NP (6.15).

Night Parrot *Geopsittacus occidentalis* (Arid interior of Australia; endemic): Probably the hardest bird to see in Australia, the first official confirmation of its continued existence came in 1990 when a dried corpse was found near Boulia in QLD. There were reliable reports in the 1960s along the Canning Stock Route (8.7) in WA. In October 1993, however, two birds were seen at night near Cloncurry (6.48) and there are rumours of recent sightings in SA. No doubt one day they will be properly tracked down, but this species seems to be not only exceedingly rare but also nomadic over a huge area and very secretive to boot. Perhaps you will be lucky.

Palm Cockatoo *Probosciger aterrimus* (New Guinea; confined to Cape York Peninsula): Fairly common at Iron Range NP (6.45) and frequently heard and seen flying over the Portland Road.

White-tailed Black-Cockatoo *Calyptorhynchus latirostris* (South-west Australia; endemic to WA): Much the commoner of the two black-cockatoos in south-west WA, this species is reasonably common and forms large flocks that roam mallee and drier eucalyptus woodlands. It is reasonably common in and around Perth itself. You will certainly see flocks as you drive around this part of Australia, but good areas include Porongurup NP (8.21), Stirling Ranges NP (8.22) and Two Peoples Bay (8.20). Yalgoo NP just to the north of Perth is also supposed to be good.

Long-billed Black-Cockatoo *C. baudinii* (South-west Australia; endemic to WA): Rather less common than the above species, this one tends to occur in much smaller flocks and to sit quietly in the canopy making very little noise. Only really safely identified when you can see the long pointed upper mandible being used to spike a marri seed whilst the lower mandible turns the seed as it is opened. To search for this species it is probably best to drive around looking for flying cockatoos. Places they have been seen are; Cape Naturaliste (8.24), the road from Two Peoples Bay to Porongurup NP, between Porongurup and Stirling Ranges NP, the Muirs Highway east of Manjimup (8.23) and near Margaret River and Mundaring Weir (part of Kalamunda NP) to the east of Perth. Just off the Great Eastern Highway about 15 km east of Perth, John Forrest NP is also worth trying.

Yellow-tailed Black-Cockatoo *C. funereus* (South-east Australia and TAS; endemic): A cockatoo of temperate and coastal forests, this species is relatively common in TAS, for example on Bruny Island (3.1) around Adventure Bay, on Mount Wellington (3.2) and at Maria Island NP (3.4). It is quite common along the southern NSW coastline for example in Royal NP (4.7) but one of the best places to see them is Tidbinbilla (5.4) in the ACT.

Red-tailed Black-Cockatoo *C. banksii* (North-eastern and south-western Australia; endemic): Widespread and abundant forming large loose flocks in open areas of the tropical north *e.g.* around Kakadu NP (7C). Less common in the south-west where we only encountered them near Mount Magnet (8.17) and between Geraldton and Perth.

Glossy Black-Cockatoo *C. lathami* (Eastern Australia and Kangaroo Island; endemic): Rather an uncommon cockatoo that seems to be somewhat nomadic in south-eastern near-coastal districts. They feed almost exclusively on *Casuarina* seeds, siting quietly in the trees which makes the birds very hard to find. There are no absolutely guaranteed sites for finding this species but fortunately the following areas regularly hold small parties. Most reliable is probably Dharug NP (4.10), however, this park was extensively damaged by fires in 1994, so check with Sydney birders for the latest information. The next best site is probably Lamington NP (6.7) where birds regularly visit the *Casuarinas* along Duck Creek Road. I saw birds around the turn off to the Black-breasted Button-Quail site. For the past few years, small groups have been almost resident on Mount Majura and Mount Ainslie, just north of Campbell Park (5.3) in the east of Canberra. Check with local birders or phone the Canberra hotline on (06) 2475530 for the latest information. Another place they are regularly seen is Gypsy Point Lodge in eastern VIC.

Gang-gang Cockatoo *Callocephalon lathami* (South-east Australia; endemic): A delightful cockatoo that is somewhat of a Canberra speciality. Birds nest on the Australian National University campus and in the adjacent Botanic Gardens (5.1). Tidbinbilla (5.4) is also a good place to find them and they are common generally throughout the Brindabellas Ranges (5.7). In NSW, Barren Grounds (4.1) is a good place to see this species.

Galah *Eolophus roseicapillus* (Throughout continental Australia; endemic): Abundant throughout the continent except wet eastern forests. Huge flocks are often seen in the outback.

Pink Cockatoo *Cacatua leadbeateri* (Inland southern Australia; endemic): A beautiful cockatoo, widespread in the arid and semi-arid interior, being generally found in small numbers. There are many good sites where you will find this species, such as Hattah-Kulkyne (2.14) and Wyperfield (2.13) NPs in VIC, Eulo Bore (6.14) and all roads around the Cunnamulla area in QLD, Round Hill Nature Reserve (4.20) in NSW and the Stuart Highway in SA as far north as Erldunda in southern NT.

Sulphur-crested Cockatoo *C. galerita* (New Guinea; northern and eastern Australia and TAS): Abundant throughout the eastern and north-eastern states.

Little Corella *C. sanguinea* (Some winter in New Guinea; inland eastern, northern and north-western Australia): Abundant in the arid interior, forming large flocks. Feral populations exist in most eastern cities.

Western Corella *C. pastinator* (Around Perth; endemic to WA): Recently split and a rather uncommon cockatoo of the Perth region and areas to the north. The best places to look for it are the southern end of Monger Lake (8.18) (where possibly introduced), and the agricultural region between Moora and Dongara along the Midlands Road. Also try Perup Nature Reserve, 40 km north-east of Manjimup.

Long-billed Corella *C. tenuirostris* (South-eastern Australia; endemic): This species is common within its very restricted range. They are abundant at Hall's Gap in VIC, or along the Western Highway (2.11) between Ararat and Horsham. Also reasonably common around Deniliquin (4.18) in NSW.

Cockatiel *Nymphicus hollandicus* (Throughout inland Australia; endemic): Abundant, although highly nomadic in the interior, this species often occurs in numbers with flocks of Budgerigars.

Rainbow Lorikeet *Trichoglossus haematodus* (Australasia; coastal eastern Australia): Abundant throughout eastern coastal districts in all wooded areas, even suburban parks and gardens.

Red-collared Lorikeet *T. (haematodus) rubritorquis* (The Top End; endemic): This common, noisy lorikeet is found from Caranbirini Springs near Boroloola (7.3) right across to the Kimberleys.

Scaly-breasted Lorikeet *T. chlorolepidotus* (Eastern Australia; endemic): Abundant in mostly coastal eucalyptus woodlands in eastern QLD and northern NSW, less common south of Sydney.

Varied Lorikeet *Psitteuteles versicolor* (Tropical northern Australia; endemic): Common in the Top End, for example in Kakadu NP (7C) and the Kimberleys, but less common in western QLD.

Musk Lorikeet *Glossopsitta concinna* (South-eastern Australia and TAS; endemic): The stronghold for this species is TAS where it is common in flowering eucalyptus woodlands. Mainly coastal in NSW where it can be very common in flowering stands of eucalyptus from Wollongong southwards, mainly in the winter months. In VIC, two good areas are the You Yangs (2.6) and Chiltern State Forest (2C), particularly in the spring when the eucalypts are flowering. Also regularly found in city parks around Adelaide.

Little Lorikeet *G. pusilla* (Coastal and sub-coastal south-eastern Australia; endemic): Rather uncommon and highly nomadic, being found on flowering eucalypts almost anywhere from VIC to Cairns. Probably the best place to find this species is Chiltern State Forest (2C) in the spring when the ironbarks are flowering, but you should check any flowering trees in the south-east as this is invariably how we were able to locate them. We recorded them at the following places; the 'Dog on the Tinderbox' rest area off the Hume Highway near Gundagai NSW, Campbell Park (5.3) in the ACT, and in QLD between Esk and Toogoolawah and at Bundaberg Airport.

Purple-crowned Lorikeet *G. porphyrocephala* (Coastal southern Australia; endemic): Like the previous two species, highly nomadic and favouring flowering eucalyptus trees. One very regular site is the car-park at Tullamarine, Melbourne Airport (2.1). Otherwise check flowering trees across the whole of southern Australia, even in mallee areas. This species seems to be fairly common in southern WA, we saw a large party at Porongurup NP (8.21) for example.

Oriental Cuckoo *Cuculus saturatus* (Eurasia, winters in Australasia; tropical northern and eastern Australia): An uncommon wet season migrant to tropical areas, although occasionally seen as far south as Sydney. Found in mangroves and dense forests, arriving in November and departing in April.

Pallid Cuckoo *C. pallidus* (Australasia; breeding migrant throughout Australia and TAS): A common cuckoo, the majority arriving in the south of the continent around September, departing in February. A bird of open forests and cleared areas, the key to finding it is to learn the very distinctive call.

Brush Cuckoo *Cacomantis variolosus* (Australasia; northern and eastern Australia): A breeding migrant to the south-east, arriving in September and leaving in March, this is a common cuckoo mainly of rainforests and woodlands, especially once you have learned the call. Particularly common at Dharug NP (4.10) and readily seen in spring at Campbell Park (5.3) in the ACT although any coastal rainforest will hold good numbers.

Chestnut-breasted Cuckoo *C. castaneiventris* (New Guinea; Cape York Peninsula): Fairly common during the summer months in the rainforest at Iron Range NP (6.45); the call is similar to that of Fan-tailed Cuckoo. It does occur further south but is rare, for example it has been seen on Mount Lewis (6.40) in the Atherton Tablelands.

Fan-tailed Cuckoo *C. flabelliformis* (New Guinea, Pacific Islands; eastern and south-western Australia and TAS): A common cuckoo in Australia, being mainly a breeding summer visitor in the south although many over winter. Found in wooded areas, again the key is to learn the call. Common in the Brindabella Ranges in the ACT in spring.

Little Bronze-Cuckoo *Chrysococcyx minutillus* (Asia; tropical northern and eastern Australia): Rather rare in the east but common in mangroves of the north of Australia, *e.g.* Karumba (6.47), Adelaide River (7.12), Middle Arm (7.5).

Gould's Bronze-Cuckoo *C. russatus* (Indonesia; north-eastern QLD): Found in open woodlands, mangroves and scrubs from Cape York to Bowen. The key to seeing this bird is to learn the call. Common at Iron Range NP (6.45) in the open eucalyptus woodland along Portland Road, beyond the rainforest. Reasonably plentiful in the Atherton Tablelands, for example at Julatten (6.40) and even around Cairns along the Esplanade (6.24) and in the Botanic Gardens (6.26).

Shining Bronze-Cuckoo *C. lucidus* (New Guinea, New Zealand and Pacific Islands; coastal and sub-coastal eastern and southern Australia and TAS): A breeding migrant to the south, arriving around September and leaving by January. Fairly common in forested areas once you have learned the call, even in rainforest such as Lamington NP (6.7) or coastal eucalypts such as Royal NP (4.7).

Horsfield's Bronze-Cuckoo *C. basalis* (Australasia; throughout Australia and TAS): The most widespread and common small cuckoo occurring mainly as a breeding migrant in the summer months to southern Australia. Fairly common in all open habitats, even in scrub in inland Australia and coastal islands; for example we saw a pair on Swan Island (2.8) in VIC in July. Fairly common around Alice Springs. Easily seen at Campbell Park (5.3) in the ACT during the spring months when calling.

Black-eared Cuckoo *C. osculans* (Winters New Guinea, Indonesia; continental Australia): A very uncommon, local cuckoo found throughout the arid interior of Australia. This species is best located in the spring months when calling and probably the best areas to see them are the old field at Round Hill Nat Park (4.20), Eulo Bore (6.14), Kunoth Well (7.28) and in the north-west of Australia where birds are frequently seen on the Peron Peninsula (8.16), Cape Range NP (8.13) and even at Wyndham Caravan Park (8.4).

Australian Koel *Eudynamys cyanocephala* (Australasia; coastal northern and eastern Australia): A breeding migrant, mainly to the coastal lowlands, arriving in August and departing in April. Common in suburban areas in Brisbane south to Sydney and like other koels, a secretive but noisy species.

Channel-billed Cuckoo *Scythrops novaehollandiae* (Australasia; northern and eastern Australia): A fairly common breeding migrant to wetter areas of QLD and northern NSW, rarer elsewhere. Arrives August, leaves in March and common on the Atherton Tablelands (6E) and forests around Cairns and Brisbane with a preference for fruiting fig trees. Easily found by its loud raucous call.

Pheasant Coucal *Centropus phasianinus* (New Guinea; coastal northern Australia): Common in wet vegetation and swamps mainly near the coast from northern NSW to WA. Good places to find it are Lake Kununurra (8.2), Fogg Dam (7.11) and Yellow Waters (7.16) in the NT whilst any sugar cane fields around Cairns or Bundaberg hold this species.

Lesser Sooty Owl *Tyto multipunctata* (North-east Australia; endemic to QLD): Fairly common in the Atherton Tablelands where the best place to look for it is Kingfisher Park

NON-PASSERINES

(6.40) (it has bred in the park) and the road up Mount Lewis (6.40). Has also been spotlighted along the entrance road to The Crater NP (6.32) and the campsite at Wallaman Falls NP near Ingham.

Sooty Owl *T. tenebricosa* (New Guinea; coastal south-east Australia): Widespread in wet coastal forests from southern QLD to VIC. The best place to see this species is Bunya Mountains NP (6.10) in the usual roosting tree, otherwise expect to spend hours at night spotlighting for them and whistling an imitation of a falling bomb which sometimes attracts birds in. Other good places to try are Mount Glorious (6.5) where a begging juvenile often seems to be present in December, Lamington NP (6.7) (ask about recent sightings), but try the Wishing Well Track or the Duck Creek Road turn-off, Royal NP (4.7) (along Lady Carrington Drive), and Nullica State Forest. A pair certainly nest in one of the caves at Jenolan in the Blue Mountains near Sydney, try asking the rangers there, although you are unlikely to be told which one it is. If you are feeling adventurous, try spotlighting in any of the forested parks in the Dandenong Ranges east of Melbourne. It seems that you are more likely to get a response from birds that are not already accustomed to hearing falling bomb imitations.

Masked Owl *T. novaehollandiae* (Coastal Australia and TAS; endemic): This species is probably easiest to see at Pittwater Road (3.3) in TAS, however it is widely but very thinly scattered around Australia. There are no consistent differences between the birds on TAS and those on the adjacent mainland of Australia. In QLD, birds are seen regularly on spotlighting trips run from Kingfisher Park (6.40) and on roads around Ingham (6.22), sometimes in recently cut sugar cane fields (you can always hire John Young in Ingham to show you all the owls in this part of Australia). It is also worth investigating our site at Kioloa Rest area (4.5) or Nullica State Forest if you happen to be in coastal southern NSW.

Barn Owl *T. alba* (Cosmopolitan; throughout Australia and TAS): Widespread and prone to periodic irruptions following rodent plagues. Spotlighting around Julatten (6.40) and Ingham (6.22) on cut sugar cane fields is the best way to find this species in Australia.

(Australasian) Grass Owl *T. longimembris* (Asia and Australasia; north-eastern Australia): Rare and not easy to see in Australia. The best places to look are Cooloola NP (6.15) and cut sugar cane fields around Ingham (6.22) and Julatten (6.40). Often found wherever long-haired rats are in plague, such as when we visited the Channel Country.

Rufous Owl *Ninox rufa* (New Guinea; tropical northern and eastern Australia): Widespread but not easy to see in tropical rainforests. Birds are often staked out in Cairns or sometimes near Kingfisher Park (6.40). The best places to try spotlighting are Mission Beach (6.23), Iron Range NP (6.45), Waterfall Creek (7.18) and Daly River (7.4).

Powerful Owl *N. strenua* (Coastal south-eastern Australia; endemic): Although quite widely distributed in coastal and sub-coastal eucalyptus forests, this is not an easy species to see. The easiest place is at the day time roost at North Epping (4.9), however, if this is no longer in use, birds are sometimes found roosting near Audley in Royal NP (4.7a). Good places to try spotlighting for this species include J C Slaughter Falls near Brisbane (6.2), Lady Carrington Drive in Royal NP (4.7b), Ferntree Gully NP (2.2) and Brisbane Ranges NP (2.7). It is also worth trying at Jervis Bay (4.4). Try to pick a dark, moonless night when birds seem to be more active and try to be at your chosen spotlighting site at dusk as this is when the birds often call. This advice applies to all *Ninox* owls, but particularly this species.

BIRD FINDING GUIDE

Barking Owl *N. connivens* (New Guinea; continental Australia except desert areas): Although this species has a wide distribution in Australia, it is much easier to see in the tropical north than elsewhere. Readily spotlighted in wooded areas, even parks and gardens, in the north, and the best places to see it are Kingfisher Park (6.40), where roosting sites are often known, and the regularly fed birds at Victoria River Roadhouse (7.24). We also saw it in Karumba (6.47) and around Waterfall Creek campsite (7.18).

Southern Boobook *N. boobook* (Throughout Australia and TAS; endemic): Easily the commonest owl throughout Australia and often found in suburban locations, you should have no trouble hearing and spotlighting this species. We regularly saw them in the Brindabellas (5.7) west of Canberra, even flushing them during the day. On TAS, Maria Island NP (3.4) seems a particularly good place for this species. The birds in the Atherton Tablelands (6E), race *lurida*, may be a good split. They can be seen fairly readily along the Mount Lewis road (6.40) at night.

Tawny Frogmouth *Podargus strigoides* (Throughout Australia and TAS; endemic): Common throughout wooded areas, even parks and gardens. Difficult to locate when calling, but common enough that you should encounter birds during the day.

Papuan Frogmouth *P. papuensis* (New Guinea; Cape York Peninsula): A nest of this species is normally staked out in Cairns; ask John Crowhurst for details. Relatively easy to spotlight as they sine sit on exposed branches, we saw birds at Iron Range NP (6.45) and Kingfisher Park (6.40), and also a bird roosting in mangroves when cruising on the Daintree River (6.31).

Marbled Frogmouth *P. ocellatus* (New Guinea; southern QLD and Cape York Peninsula): The northern race *ocellatus* is common at Iron Range NP (6.45), try spotlighting along Portland Road in the rainforest patches listening for them calling. The southern race *plumiferus* is more localised. They are quite numerous at Mount Glorious (6.5), we heard up to eight at night, but access through the heavily vine strewn rainforest is difficult. The pair on the Lamington NP (6.7) access road have been easy recently.

Australian Owlet-Nightjar *Aegotheles cristatus* (New Guinea; throughout Australia and TAS): Widespread and fairly common and frequently heard calling, although difficult to spotlight since they seem to be shy of lights and do not possess highly reflective eyes. In remote areas, such as the mulga area between Quilpie and Windorah (6.12), birds will sometimes appear to investigate observers during the day. It is worth tapping the roosting tree at Lamington NP (6.7) as you pass by and indeed this technique can be very successful at locating birds during the daytime. Tap any tree with a suitable looking hollow, particularly in mallee areas such as Hattah-Kulkyne NP (2.14).

Spotted Nightjar *Eurostopodus argus* (Aru Islands; throughout arid areas of continental Australia): Fairly common in mallee and mulga scrubs, even dry open eucalyptus woods. Frequently heard calling in the spring in mallee areas; Round Hill Nature Reserve (4.20) seems particularly good. Also seen by us at the Chestnut-breasted Whiteface site (9.14) when flushed during the day roosting along one of the dry watercourses. Seems commoner in the north, for example birds frequently sit on the roads at night in Keep River NP near the NT border with WA.

White-throated Nightjar *E. mystacalis* (New Guinea; coastal eastern Australia): Mainly a breeding migrant to the eastern seaboard of Australia although rare as far south as VIC. Easy to find in the spring in Morton NP (4.2), NSW, and at J C Slaughter Falls (6.2) in Brisbane although this is a common species in all coastal spotted gum forests.

Large-tailed Nightjar *Caprimulgus macrurus* (Asia and Australasia; tropical north-eastern Australia): Very common at Iron Range NP (6.45) where birds often sit on the road at dusk. It can also be seen in the Atherton Tablelands, for example at Kingfisher Park (6.40), and in the Top End where this species is common at Middle Arm (7.5) and around Darwin.

Australian Swiftlet *Collocalia terraereginae* (North-east Australia; endemic to QLD): Very common throughout the Cairns area in all lowland habitats.

White-throated Needletail *Hirundapus caudacautus* (Breeds Asia, winters in Australia; eastern Australia and TAS): The commonest swift in eastern Australia, this species is a non-breeding migrant, arriving in October and leaving by April. Flocks are regular in the south-east during the summer months, often over suburban Sydney but more frequently over hilltops. Groups are often seen gathering around black thunderstorm clouds.

Pacific Swift *Apus pacificus* (Breeds in Asia, winters in Australasia; throughout Australia and TAS): The commonest swift in western Australia, this is also a non-breeding migrant arriving in October, leaving in April. Uncommon in the east although surprisingly one flock was seen 20 km offshore from Wollongong on one occasion.

Azure Kingfisher *Alcedo azurea* (Australasia; coastal and sub-coastal northern and eastern Australia and TAS): Rather uncommon generally but found along rivers, swamps and mangrove areas. The easiest place to see this species is on a Daintree River cruise (6.31) north of Cairns, but it is also easy at Yellow Waters (7.16) and Middle Arm (7.5) in the NT and at Royal NP (4.7) near Sydney.

Little Kingfisher *A. pusilla* (Australasia; coastal tropical northern Australia): Found along creeks and especially in mangrove areas, this is not a common species, but fortunately there are several excellent places to look for it. These are as follows; a Daintree River cruise (6.31) where you are virtually guaranteed to find it; Cairns Botanic Gardens (6.26), on the saltwater pool; Thomsons Road (6.28); creeks in the rainforest at Iron Range NP (6.45); Yellow Waters cruise (7.16) and finally Middle Arm (7.5) in the NT.

Laughing Kookaburra *Dacelo novaeguineae* (Eastern continental Australia introduced to WA and TAS; endemic): Common in all open woodland and forests, even mallee areas throughout the south and east.

Blue-winged Kookaburra *D. leachii* (New Guinea; tropical northern Australia): Fairly common in woodlands in the Top End and northern QLD, and easily found because of its loud awful calls. Plentiful throughout Kakadu NP (7C).

Forest Kingfisher *Todirhamphus macleayii* (New Guinea; northern and eastern Australia): A fairly common bird of open woodlands and coastal areas, resident in the tropical north but a breeding migrant to the southern parts of its range. Commonly seen perched on roadside telegraph wires but if struggling, try the Yellow Waters cruise (7.16) or Howard Springs (7.6) in the NT, Cairns Botanic Gardens (6.26) or Brisbane area in QLD.

Red-backed Kingfisher *T. pyrrhopygia* (Arid inland Australia; endemic): Widespread throughout the dry interior but nomadic and generally uncommon and not found in the extreme south. Generally found in arid areas that have had recent rains. We mostly found this species perched on telegraph wires during long outback drives. Best areas seem to be the parks west of Alice Springs, along the Stuart Highway in the NT, the Dusky Grasswren site near Mount Isa (6.49) and around Carnarvon (8.14) in WA. Also seen at Hattah-Kulkyne NP (2.14).

Collared Kingfisher *T. chloris* (Asia and Australasia; mangroves in coastal Australia): Common in all mangrove areas in the tropics and sub-tropics, for example at Bundaberg (6.16), the Daintree River cruise (6.31), Middle Arm (7.5).

Sacred Kingfisher *T. sanctus* (Australasia and Pacific; throughout Australia and TAS): Resident in the northern half of the continent but a breeding summer migrant to the south of the country. The commonest kingfisher, being found both in woodlands and near water, but not in the arid interior. Always breeds in Campbell Park (5.3) in the ACT.

Yellow-billed Kingfisher *Syma torotoro* (New Guinea; north-east QLD): Fairly common at Iron Range NP (6.45), the key to finding this rainforest kingfisher is to learn the trilling call. It is often found in the forest edge along Portland Road. Very rare south of Cape York but has been seen at Mission Beach (6.23).

Buff-breasted Paradise-Kingfisher *Tanysiptera sylvia* (New Guinea; north-east QLD): A fairly common breeding migrant to north-east QLD, arriving in October, departing in March. This spectacular species is common at Iron Range NP (6.45) but can also be found in the Cairns area, for example at Kingfisher Park (6.40) and Mount Whitfield Environmental Park (6.27). The key to finding it is to learn the call.

Rainbow Bee-eater *Merops ornatus* (Australasia; throughout continental Australia): A common breeding migrant to the south of the continent, from September to March, but resident in the north. This is a common bird of open habitats. Always breeds at Uriarra Crossing on the Murrumbidgee in the ACT.

Dollarbird *Eurystomus orientalis* (Asia and Australasia; northern and eastern Australia): A breeding migrant to Australia arriving in September and leaving in March, this is a common bird mainly of coastal wooded regions. Often seen whilst driving the Pacific and Princes Highways, and always nests in Campbell Park (5.3) in the ACT.

Passerines

Red-bellied Pitta *Pitta erythrogaster* (Australasia; Cape York Peninsula): Common at Iron Range NP (6.45) during the summer months in all rainforest areas. A few individuals probably over winter in this area. Birds call throughout the day and night, very often perched high up in the trees.

Rainbow Pitta *P. iris* (The Top End and Kimberleys; endemic): This species is very easy to see at Howard Springs (7.6) where birds are both tame and confined to the narrow rainforest patches around the main pool. Relatively easy to see at Fogg Dam (7.11) and East Point (7.10), and in Kakadu, this species is found in the rainforest along Stag Creek (7.19).

Noisy Pitta *P. versicolor* (New Guinea; eastern Australia): This species is common in rainforest areas from northern NSW to Cape York. Probably easiest to find at Lamington NP (6.7) in the south, but also easy around Cairns, *e.g.* at Kingfisher Park (6.40) and Mount Spec NP (6.21). Not as numerous as Red-bellied Pitta at Iron Range NP (6.45), but still fairly easy to see there.

White-throated Treecreeper *Cormobates leucophaeus* (Eastern and southern Australia; endemic): The commonest treecreeper of eastern sub-tropical and temperate forests and easily found at any of the coastal south-eastern sites, *e.g.* Royal NP (4.7). Abundant at Tidbinbilla (5.4) in the ACT. The northern race, *minor*, is sometimes split as Little Treecreeper. It can be seen at Eungella NP (6.17) or Mount Spec NP (6.21) fairly easily.

White-browed Treecreeper *Climacteris affinis* (Inland southern Australia; endemic): Generally rather an uncommon, local species of the arid interior with a strong preference for areas of thick mulga and stands of belar (native pine). You should concentrate on finding this species at the Halls Babbler site between Quilpie and Windorah (6.12). Other places to look are the north end of Wyperfield NP (2.13) and the mulga around Kunoth Well (7.28). Common in the belar areas along the track north of Cook for anyone lucky enough to be going into the Great Victoria Desert (9.16) in search of Scarlet-chested Parrot.

Red-browed Treecreeper *C. erythrops* (Coastal south-eastern Australia; endemic): Again a rather uncommon, local species that favours wet eucalyptus forests, particularly in hilly areas. A highly recommended site for this species is the Fishing Gap Trail at Tidbinbilla (5.4d) in the ACT, another good place is the area of eucalyptus forest along Duck Creek Road in Lamington NP (6.7), after you pass out of the rainforest.

Brown Treecreeper *C. picumnus* (Eastern Australia; endemic): Common in drier forests, mainly of the sub-coastal regions. Numerous at several of the other good treecreeper sites, such as between Quilpie and Windorah (6.12), Kunoth Well (7.28) and very common at Campbell Park (5.3) in the ACT.

Black-tailed Treecreeper *C. melanura* (The Top End and north-western Australia; endemic): Common in dry woodlands of the Top End, *e.g.* the Chestnut-backed Button-Quail site in Kakadu NP (7.17).

Rufous Treecreeper *C. rufa* (South-west Australia; endemic): Common in most woodland areas of the south-west of WA, this species also occurs in mallee areas in SA. The easiest place to find it is Porongurup NP (8.21) where birds are tame all around the picnic table and car-park. Another good site in WA is Dryandra State Forest (8.19) where birds should be seen whilst birding the forest tracks. In SA we saw this species in a mallee area between Kingoonya and Wirrulla, 104 km north of the latter.

Albert's Lyrebird *Menura alberti* (Sub-tropical rainforest in eastern Australia; endemic): This species has a very restricted range, centred around Lamington NP (6.7), which is certainly the area to concentrate on to see it, along walking tracks around O'Reilly's. Reputedly fairly easy to see at nearby Mount Tambourine along the walking tracks in Palm Grove NP which is situated 3 km east of Doughty Park along Curtis Road.

Superb Lyrebird *M. novaehollandiae* (South-eastern Australia; endemic): Common in the wetter coastal forests of NSW and VIC. Easy to see and tame along the riverside vegetation at Royal NP (4.7), straightforward along the Lyrebird Trail at Tidbinbilla (5.4c) or along the roadside verges of the Illawarra Highway at dawn. Frequently heard singing in the winter months at Fitzroy Falls (4.2a), Dharug NP (4.10) *etc.* There is an introduced population on TAS.

Rufous Scrub-bird *Atrichornis rufescens* (Antarctic Beech forests in eastern Australia; endemic): A highly localised, secretive species. Best found when singing in the spring following rain and often responds well to loud pishing. The best places to look for this bird are Lamington NP (6.7) or Barrington Tops (4.13) in NSW where the birds have the reputation of being easier to see because of the more open habitat at the latter.

Noisy Scrub-bird *A. clamosus* (South-western Australia; endemic to WA): Two Peoples Bay (8.20) is the only place to see this bird. Like Rufous Scrub-bird they often react well to loud pishing and they scurry about on the ground like a rodent. The best months to hear them are June to October and they are probably easiest to see as they cross over tracks or respond to pishing; persevere!

Spotted Catbird *Ailuroedus melanotis* (New Guinea; north-eastern QLD): Common in rainforest on the Atherton Tablelands, *e.g.* The Crater NP (6.32) and Mount Lewis (6.40). There is an isolated population on Cape York which is fairly common at Iron Range NP (6.45). Like all catbirds this is mainly a noisy canopy species that favours fruiting trees.

Green Catbird *A. crassirostris* (Coastal eastern Australia; endemic): Very common in rainforest areas around Brisbane *e.g.* Lamington NP (6.7), and Mount Glorious (6.5). Rarer further south around Sydney. Easily located by their extraordinary cat-like calls.

Tooth-billed Catbird *A. dentirostris* (North-eastern Australia; endemic to north-east QLD): Common in highland rainforest sites of the Atherton Tablelands; The Crater NP (6.32), Mount Lewis (6.40), Lake Barrine (6.34) *etc*. Also common at Mount Spec NP (6.21) near Townsville. Usually found by voice but search any fruiting trees.

Golden Bowerbird *Prionodura newtoniana* (North-eastern Australia; endemic to north-east QLD): Fairly common but not easy to find away from its bower. If visiting the Atherton Tablelands in the summer months, there should be no problem finding out the location of a currently attended bower if the traditional one at The Crater NP (6.32) is not in use. The location of a bower at Mount Spec NP (6.21) is usually known. Birds do attend their bower outside of the wet season, but it may be a very long wait at one for a bird to come in. During the dry season, the way to locate this species is to find a fruiting tree and watch it. The entrance road leading to the car-park at The Crater NP (6.32) is often a good place to try.

Regent Bowerbird *Sericulus chrysocephalus* (Coastal eastern Australia; endemic): Fairly common in east coast rainforests, easily the best place to see this species is Lamington NP (6.7) where males are often hand tame around O'Reilly's, although they only visit when fruiting trees are scarce in the forest and then only in the early morning. Female plumaged birds are always to be found around the buildings and campsite however. Fairly common along Dalrymple Road at Eungella NP (6.17) and found as far south as Barrington Tops (4.13).

Satin Bowerbird *Ptilonorhynchus violaceus* (Eastern Australia; endemic): Common and reasonably tame in many rainforest areas and wet eucalyptus forests in the east. An isolated population in the Atherton Tablelands (6E), but this species is really a bird of the south-east. Common all around O'Reilly's in Lamington NP (6.7) and at Tidbinbilla (5.4c) in the ACT where birds regularly attend the winter bird feeding station, also common at Barren Grounds (4.1).

Western Bowerbird *Chlamydera guttata* (Arid central interior; endemic): Locally common, this species is found mostly in areas where native figs occur in the arid interior. Probably the best place to find them is around the campsite at Ormiston Gorge NP (7.31), west of Alice Springs. The golf course at Mount Magnet (8.17), Cape Range NP (8.13) in WA and the area of scrub 6 km north of the SA border (7.34) along the Stuart Highway in the NT are other places we saw them.

Spotted Bowerbird *C. maculata* (Inland eastern Australia; endemic): Fairly common in inland scrub of the east of the continent although apparently declining in the southern parts of its range. The best place to see this species is Eulo Bore (6.14) in QLD where birds come in to drink. They are also frequently seen flying across roads in the outback, such as the Mitchell Highway between Nyngan and Bourke (4.21), the mulga scrub between Lake Cargelligo and Round Hill Nature Reserve (4.20).

Great Bowerbird *C. nuchalis* (Tropical northern Australia; endemic): Very common at virtually any picnic stop and pull-in in drier woodlands of the NT, but much less numerous in QLD. An excellent place to see them is Katherine Gorge NP (7.22) where many tame birds attend their bowers around the car-park.

Fawn-breasted Bowerbird *C. cerviniventris* (New Guinea; Cape York Peninsula): Only found on Cape York Peninsula, this species is fairly common at Iron Range NP (6.45) in the dry scrubby areas along the Portland Road after you have left the rainforest walking towards the coast.

Red-backed Fairywren *Malurus melanocephalus* (Tropical northern and eastern Australia; endemic): Common in grasslands and drier tropical woodlands in the NT such as Kakadu NP (7C), and eastern QLD *e.g.* Bundaberg (6.16). Like all fairywrens, this species can usually be attracted by squeaking.

White-winged Fairywren *M. leucopterus* (Throughout arid interior of Australia; endemic): Common in open bushes of generally treeless arid areas throughout the whole interior of Australia. This species will frequently be seen whilst searching for other species such as at the Chestnut-breasted Whiteface site (9.14) in SA. Often the adult males are rather shy.

Superb Fairywren *M. cyaneus* (South-eastern Australia and TAS; endemic): Common in wooded areas of the south-east, this is the only fairywren found in much of its range. Abundant in Canberra Botanic Gardens (5.1) where the population has been studied for many years and at Tidbinbilla (5.4) in the ACT.

Splendid Fairywren *M. splendens* (Mostly inland southern Australia; endemic): A bird of arid areas, mainly mallee and mulga habitats, it is very widespread but rather patchy in occurrence. Places you should see it include Kunoth Well (7.28) in NT and Round Hill Nature Reserve (4.20) in NSW, although you will no doubt encounter them elsewhere as well.

Variegated Fairywren *M. lamberti* (Throughout all except southern parts of continental Australia; endemic): Usually found in shrubby arid areas of mallee, mulga *etc.*, this species is very widespread and often encountered whilst searching for other specialities at many sites, for example the saltbush area for Thick-billed Grasswrens on the Peron Peninsula (8.16), the mallee at Round Hill Nature Reserve (4.20) and the mulga at Kunoth Well (7.28). The northern races are sometimes split. These can be seen as follows; *rogersi* is common at Mitchell Falls (8.5b) in the Kimberleys; *dulcis*, the 'Lavender-flanked Fairywren' is commonly seen whilst searching for White-throated Grasswrens at Waterfall Creek (7.18).

Lovely Fairywren *M. (lamberti) amabilis* (Cape York Peninsula; endemic to QLD): This distinctive fairywren is common along the rainforest roadsides and small clearings at Iron Range NP (6.45). It is also fairly common at Mount Whitfield Environmental Park (6.27) in Cairns or Cape Tribulation NP, north of Cairns. Often now regarded as a race of Variegated Fairywren.

Red-winged Fairywren *M. elegans* (South-western Australia; endemic to WA): Common in areas of thick scrub and vegetation in coastal south-western WA, the best place to find this bird is Two Peoples Bay where parties are frequently encountered around Lake Gardener whilst searching for the other specialities of the reserve.

Blue-breasted Fairywren *M. pulcherrimus* (Southern western Australia; endemic): Although mainly found in woodlands of south-western WA, there is an isolated population in SA that is common at Lincoln NP (9.8) on the Eyre Peninsula. In WA, this species is common along the walking tracks at Porongurup NP (8.21), and in the undergrowth at Dryandra State Forest (8.19).

Lilac-crowned Fairywren *M. coronatus* (Tropical northern Australia; endemic): Two isolated populations of this bird are found, one in the Gulf Country, the other around the Kimberleys. Both populations are much reduced by destruction of their habitat by cattle. They are invariably found close to water, usually where *Pandanus* palms are present. The best place to see them is undoubtedly Victoria River Roadhouse (7.24) where birds are numerous between the campsite and the river. They often climb up to the top of the tall grass stems here to preen and sing in the early morning and are readily attracted by pishing. The population at Caranbirini Springs (7.3) has apparently been wiped out, but the eastern race can still be seen in the campsite at Lawn Hill NP in western QLD.

Rufous-crowned Emuwren *Stipiturus ruficeps* (Arid western and central Australia; endemic): Despite the huge range of this species it is very local in occurrence and secretive and hard to find in large spinifex clumps. Listen for the high pitched, barely audible calls which are fairywren like, but even weaker. The best areas are west of Alice Springs, especially Ormiston Gorge NP (7.31) where birds occur in the spinifex along the Ormiston Pound circuit. Also good is Ellery Creek Big Hole (7.30) where birds occur in the spinifex clumps on the plain east of the road off the sharp left hand bend and also along the ridges running west from the Hole itself. Also reported from Cape Range NP (8.13) in WA and Tennant Creek (7.26) in the NT.

Southern Emuwren *S. malachurus* (Coastal southern Australia and TAS): Not as secretive as the other emuwrens, this is a bird of coastal heaths and swamps. It is not hard to find when birding this kind of habitat, for example at Barren Grounds (4.1) in NSW, Strahan (3.8) in TAS, or Two Peoples Bay (8.20) in WA.

Mallee Emuwren *S. mallee* (Mallee in southern Australia; endemic): Equally as secretive and hard to find as Rufous-crowned Emuwren, this is again a bird associated with spinifex clumps in the mallee areas of western VIC and SA. The most reliable locality is Hattah-Kulkyne NP (2.14) where birds occur in the spinifex by the track to the Gypsum Mines, at Beesite 8 and along the Nowingi Track. Again, the key to finding them is to listen for the whispy high-pitched calls and they occur in even small spinifex clumps.

Thick-billed Grasswren *Amytornis textilis* (Saltbush of central western Australia; endemic): The grasswrens are amongst the most highly rated of Australian birds because they are secretive, difficult to observe, and are found in some of the most remote areas of the continent. There is a definite knack to finding them. The secret is to listen intently for the high-pitched calls. These often appear to be coming from only a few feet away, but often the birds making them are 50 yards or more away so keep looking further ahead than you expect the birds to be. Follow up any calls like this you hear immediately, since the birds move quickly away. Inevitably most will turn out to be fairywren parties, although grasswrens often associate with them. The usual first sighting of a grasswren is of it bounding away with the tail held cocked as it crosses from one patch of cover to another. Often if you wait quietly, the birds will peer out around this cover to observe the intruder; they seem to be very curious birds and indeed pishing is often a successful technique to bring them in. Finally, perseverance will usually lead to excellent views. This particular species is widely distributed and not too hard to find near Monkey Mia on the Peron Peninsula (8.16). It is also a common bird at the Chestnut-breasted Whiteface site (9.14) near Lyndhurst.

Dusky Grasswren *A. purnelli* (Spinifex of central northern Australia; endemic): This is the easiest grasswren to observe since the birds at Simpson's Gap (7.29) near Alice Springs are so accustomed to people that they have become tame. They are also common on the Ormiston Gorge Pound walk (7.31). The isolated race in north-west QLD is common at Micra Creek near Mount Isa (6.49).

Black Grasswren *A. housei* (Kimberley; endemic to WA): This rock inhabiting grasswren is only found in the remote Kimberley region of north-western Australia. The best option for seeing this grasswren is to get to Mount Elizabeth Station (8.5a) and hire the owners to drop you at their site for a couple of days. Grasswrens are reasonably common here but easier to find at Mitchell Falls or Surveyor's Pool on the Mitchell Plateau (8.5b) although these sites can only be reached by 4WD. There is a remote possibility of finding them at Manning Gorge. All these places require a long drive along the notorious Gibb River Road however you are unlikely to dip if you are able to reach the site since this is not an especially shy grasswren.

Striated Grasswren *A. striatus* (Spinifex of central Australia; endemic): There are several sites to find the different races of this grasswren. The mallee race is quite easy to find along the Nowingi Track at Hattah-Kulkyne NP (2.14) in VIC, whilst the area behind the Sunset viewing car-park at Ayers Rock (7.33) is an excellent place to see one of the (more attractive) inland races.

White-throated Grasswren *A. woodwardi* (Spinifex of Arnhem Land; endemic to NT): The only easily accessible place to see this rock loving grasswren is at Waterfall Creek (7.18). Take plenty of water and persevere as this is probably the most spectacular looking grasswren, but it can be very elusive. The pair we found were tracked down by hearing them singing. Watch carefully for birds bounding over the rocks well ahead of you and follow up any sightings quickly.

Carpentarian Grasswren *A. dorotheae* (Spinifex areas in the Gulf Country; endemic): There are two accessible places to find this highly elusive grasswren. The first, near Boroloola (7.3), is the traditional site and is a rocky plateau with spinifex clumps across it. The birds here seem particularly shy and have even been known to dive into holes in the rock in order to hide so that they could only be seen with the aid of a torch! The technique for finding them is very much the same as for White-throated Grasswrens. Recently a new population was found near Mount Isa inhabiting the flat spinifex plains there. Although this population is quite widespread in this area, the easiest place to find them is along the Lady Loretta Mine Road (6.50). Despite the very different habitat, the birds are thought to be of the same species as those at Boroloola (7.3) and apparently each responds to tapes of the others song. The birds tend to be found in the largest spinifex clumps along the dry creek beds.

Grey Grasswren *A. barbatus* (Lignum swamps of inland Australia; endemic): Fairly common within its very restricted specialised habitat, there are two fairly accessible places to see this grasswren. The best is probably Pyampa Station (4.23) in QLD where large groups are found in the tall lignum patches across the (usually dry) swamp there. This species is also straightforward at Koonchera Dune on the Birdsville Track (9.15) in SA.

Eyrean Grasswren *A. goyderi* (Cane grass covered dunes in central Australia; endemic): A bird with a very restricted and localised range, this species almost exclusively inhabits cane grass growing on top of sand dunes. The best place to find this bird is Koonchera Dune on the Birdsville Track (9.15), but also try the sand dunes behind Mungeranie Roadhouse which is further south on the Birdsville. The other area to try is any cane grass covered dune between Cameron Corner and Merty-Merty Station (9.12) on the Strzelecki Track.

Spotted Pardalote *Pardalotus punctatus* (Sub-coastal southern Australia; endemic): Wooded areas, especially in areas of higher rainfall. A very common treetop bird of the south-east of the country, particularly once the call has been learned. Abundant in the ACT, for example in the Botanic Gardens (5.1) or at Tidbinbilla (5.4).

Yellow-rumped Pardalote *P. (punctatus) xanthopygus* (Mallee areas of southern Australia; endemic): Usually regarded as a race of the previous species, this pardalote is plentiful in all mallee areas, for example Round Hill Nature Reserve (4.20), Hattah-Kulkyne NP (2.14).

Forty-spotted Pardalote *P. quadragintus* (South-eastern TAS; endemic to TAS): Rare and local, this species often occurs with, and apparently loses out to, the other pardalote species. Its stronghold is Maria Island NP (3.4), however, the best place to see this bird is on Bruny Island (3.1) south of Dennes Point. Colonies on the main island (Tinderbox peninsula) are now rather sparse.

Red-browed Pardalote *P. rubricatus* (Central northern Australia; endemic): A widespread species of the arid interior that is very easy to overlook until the distinctive call has been learned. It is found in all large eucalyptus trees along watercourses on the Birdsville Track (9.15). Places we observed it include right at the end of the sealed part of the road west of Windorah, between Cameron Corner and Merty-Merty Station (9.12), Alice Springs airport, and at China Wall near Halls Creek (8.6) in northern WA.

Striated Pardalote *P. striatus* (Throughout Australia and TAS; endemic): A very widespread bird that has several distinct races which between them occur in all wooded habitats in Australia. The most numerous pardalote in the northern half of the country. Although there is regional variation in the calls, they are all distinctive enough to be recognised as this species.

Western Bristlebird *Dasyornis longirostris* (Albany region; endemic to WA): Rare and confined to a small area of coastal heath near Albany, the only place to concentrate on seeing this species is at Two Peoples Bay (8.20). The area around Little Beach car-park is the best with birds frequently being seen around the toilet block and on the firebreaks on the hill behind. Also seen on the tracks across the coastal heath above here. If struggling, try asking the warden. Like other bristlebirds they are secretive ground dwellers, however this species seems more prone than the other bristlebirds to perch in the open on top of a bush when singing.

Eastern Bristlebird *D. brachypterus* (Coastal south-eastern Australia; endemic): Mainly a bird of coastal heaths, there are several good places to find this species. Probably the best is Barren Grounds (4.1) where birds can often be seen feeding out in the open along the tracks, especially in the spring when they also call more. Jervis Bay (4.4) is also an excellent place to find this species, around the Cape St George Lighthouse car-park. Perhaps surprisingly this species is also fairly common along Duck Creek Road in Lamington NP (6.7), although it is generally very hard to see them here.

Rufous Bristlebird *D. broadbenti* (Coastal heaths of southern Australia; endemic): Probably now extinct in WA, the best area to look for this bird is in coastal VIC where birds can be found relatively easily at many picnic and tourist sites along the Great Ocean Road (2.9).

Pilotbird *Pycnoptilus floccosus* (Wet forests of south-east Australia; endemic): A ground feeding bird of wet gullies that is secretive but not too hard to find once you know the call. Good places to find it are the nature trail at Barren Grounds (4.1), Pierces Pass (4.11) and Fitzroy Falls (4.2a) all in NSW, the Lyrebird Trail at Tidbinbilla (5.4c) and Corin Dam (5.5) in the ACT.

Origma *Origma solitaria* (Sandstone outcrops in Hawkesbury region; endemic to NSW): Also known as Rock Warbler, this species is invariably found close to sandstone outcrops feeding unobtrusively and with a liking for foraging along streambeds. There are several good places to find it, the best of which is Morton NP (4.2), but also try Royal NP (4.7),

Pierces Pass (4.11) and Dharug NP (4.10). Reputed to be common around Jenolan Caves in the Blue Mountains although we tried there without success.

Fernwren *Oreoscopus gutturalis* (Atherton Tablelands; endemic to QLD): An undergrowth feeder in rainforests of the Atherton Tableland. Fairly common along the Mount Lewis road (6.40); try anywhere you can get under the canopy of the rainforest, also gullies in The Crater NP (6.32) and the Cloud Creek walking track at Mount Spec NP (6.21).

Yellow-throated Scrubwren *Sericornis citreogularis* (Forests of eastern Australia; endemic): A ground feeder in tropical and sub-tropical rainforests. In northern QLD only found in the Atherton Tablelands (6E) where it is common in rainforest areas. A southern population occurs from the Brisbane area, where it is abundant at Lamington NP (6.7), to around Royal NP (4.7) near Sydney where it is uncommon.

White-browed Scrubwren *S. frontalis* (Coastal and sub-coastal eastern and southern Australia; endemic): A common, inquisitive and noisy bird of the undergrowth in both coastal and inland forests and even in mountainous areas. The distinctive western race, *maculatus*, is common from the Eyre peninsula, (Lincoln NP (9.8)) to south-western WA, (Dryandra State Forest (8.19)).

Brown Scrubwren *S. humilis* (Bass Strait Islands; endemic to TAS): Recently split, although perhaps rather dubiously, this scrubwren is common in thick undergrowth of Tasmanian forests. Very common at Mount Wellington (3.2) along the Fern Glade Track.

Atherton Scrubwren *S. keri* (Atherton Tablelands; endemic to QLD): This species is found in the under storey of all the rainforest sites on the Atherton Tablelands. Not terribly common and outnumbered by Large-billed Scrubwren, we found this species to be most numerous at Mount Lewis (6.40) and at The Crater NP (6.32).

Tropical Scrubwren *S. beccarii* (New Guinea; Cape York Peninsula): Fairly common at Iron Range NP (6.45), mostly being found in small openings in the rainforest where tree falls have taken place, always close to the ground.

Large-billed Scrubwren *S. magnirostris* (Eastern Australia; endemic): Common in all types of rainforest from the Atherton Tablelands to VIC. Unlike other scrubwrens, this species tends to forage high up in trees, often picking its way along branches in a thornbill-like manner. It is very common at places like Dharug NP (4.10), Lamington NP (6.7) right up to Mount Lewis (6.40).

Scrubtit *Acanthornis magnus* (Throughout TAS; endemic to TAS): Fairly common but rather a secretive inhabitant of dense undergrowth. The best site is the Fern Glade Track on Mount Wellington (3.2), however you may have to put some time in here. It can also be seen on Bruny Island (3.1) and even in the Alpine scrub at Cradle Mountain NP (3.7). Usually responds well to pishing.

Redthroat *Pyrrholaemus brunneus* (Central southern Australia; endemic): Despite the wide range of this species, it is nowhere common, favouring inland scrubby areas. Most numerous in WA, we saw several in roadside scrub 1 km west of Yalgoo and also several along the road from north of Carnarvon to Rocky Pool (8.14). A good reliable area is the saltbush at the Chestnut-breasted Whiteface site (9.14) where you should come across this species whilst searching for the whiteface.

Speckled Warbler *Chthonicola sagittatus* (South-eastern Australia; endemic): A bird of open woodlands, this species is a ground feeder amongst leaf and stick debris. It is rather local in its distribution but can usually be found in the eucalyptus forest along the Glen

Davis road (4.12). This species is also relatively common in the ACT, for example they are always present in Campbell Park (5.3) or along the walking tracks on Black Mountain, behind the Botanic Gardens.

Rufous Calamanthus *Calamanthus campestris* (Southern central Australia; endemic): The most widely distributed calamanthus but nowhere very numerous. They are rather secretive although they usually sing from the top of a small bush. An excellent site is the saltbush plain at the Chestnut-breasted Whiteface site (9.14), but other areas you should see this species are the Nullarbor Quail-Thrush site (9.18), New Beach (8.15) and the coastal heath at Two Peoples Bay (8.20) in WA.

Striated Calamanthus *C. fuliginosus* (Southern Australia and TAS; endemic): Very much a bird of coastal heathlands on the Australian mainland, this species also occurs quite commonly in the Alpine scrub at Cradle Mountain NP (3.7) in TAS. It is also fairly common on the west coast of TAS in heathland near Strahan (3.8). On the mainland this species can be found fairly easily in coastal heath at Nadgee NP (4.6) in NSW, but the main population is on the south Victorian coastline; try the heathland between Point Wilson and the Princes Highway east of Geelong in Port Phillip Bay.

Chestnut-rumped Hylacola *Hylacola pyrrhopygius* (South-eastern Australia; endemic): This is rather an uncommon, shy species, mainly found in coastal heaths but also found in open woodland areas and always feeding on or near the ground. Good places to find it are Barren Grounds (4.1) (especially around the edges of any small bare patches), Nadgee NP (4.6), both in the coastal heath and along the road leading to the car-park, and perhaps surprisingly Chiltern State Forest (2C) where birds inhabit the undergrowth along the tracks leading off Cyanide Road.

Shy Hylacola *H. cautus* (Throughout mallee areas of southern Australia; endemic): An uncommon species found in all the better mallee sites although apparently much commoner at some than others. It seems to be especially numerous in the roadside mallee along the road to Big Billy Bore (2.12) in VIC, and also occurs at nearby Wyperfield NP (2.13) (the walking track to Lake Brambruk seems best) and Hattah-Kulkyne NP (2.14). Fairly common around the campsite at Round Hill Nature Reserve (4.20).

Buff-rumped Thornbill *Acanthiza reguloides* (Eastern Australia; endemic): A common bird of open eucalyptus forests in sub-coastal eastern Australia. This species is very common in the ACT, for example at Campbell Park (5.3).

Western Thornbill *A. inornata* (South-western Australia; endemic to WA): Common in tall forests and open woodlands of the south-west corner, this species will be found easily at Stirling Ranges NP (8.22) (try the Gold Holes area, 5 km south of the Information Centre on the east side of the road, north of the creek), Dryandra State Forest (8.19), and woodland along the Muirs Highway 50 km east of Manjimup (8.23).

Slender-billed Thornbill *A. iredalei* (Southern central Australia; endemic): Rather an uncommon species found mostly in saltbush and samphire plains. There are several sites where it is reasonably common, these are; New Beach (8.15) in WA, the Nullarbor Quail-Thrush site (9.18), Port Gawler and Port Prime (9.2) and Adelaide ICI Saltworks (9.1).

Mountain Thornbill *A. katherina* (Atherton Region; endemic to QLD): A common bird of the mountain rainforests of the Atherton Tableland, this species should be found foraging through the canopy in small parties at any of the following places without too much difficulty; Mount Spec NP (6.21), Mount Lewis (6.40) and The Crater NP (6.32).

Brown Thornbill *A. pusilla* (South-eastern Australia and TAS; endemic): Common in woodlands, rainforests and scrubs of coastal and sub-coastal districts.

Inland Thornbill *A. (pusilla) apicalis* (Throughout interior southern Australia; endemic): Usually regarded as conspecific with the Brown Thornbill, this species is common in all wooded habitats, even dry mulga, throughout the southern half of the continent, except in the south-east where *pusilla* is found.

Tasmanian Thornbill *A. ewingii* (Bass Strait Islands; endemic to TAS): Found throughout the woodlands and forested areas of TAS, this species tends to favour wetter habitats than the Brown Thornbill. It is common along the Fern Glade Track on Mount Wellington (3.2) and on Bruny Island (3.1).

Yellow-rumped Thornbill *A. chrysorrhoa* (Throughout Australia and TAS except tropical north; endemic): Very common in open woodlands and parks *etc.*, but not rainforest areas, this thornbill often feeds on the ground.

Chestnut-rumped Thornbill *A. uropygialis* (Throughout interior southern Australia; endemic): The commonest thornbill in most of the arid interior, found in mallee areas such as Round Hill Nature Reserve (4.20) and in thick mulga areas such as Kunoth Well (7.28).

Slaty-backed Thornbill *A. robustirostris* (Interior of central Australia; endemic): Rather an uncommon thornbill that is usually found in ones and twos rather than small parties, this species is associated with areas of thick mulga. The best places to look for it are; Mount Magnet and Yalgoo areas (8.17) in WA and Kunoth Well (7.28) in the NT. In both areas, check carefully through any thornbill parties, particularly groups of Brown Thornbills for this species.

Yellow Thornbill *A. nana* (Eastern Australia; endemic): A not uncommon thornbill that is especially found in woodland along rivers and with a preference for areas of acacias. A good place to find this species is Uriarra Crossing in the ACT or the You Yangs (2.6) in VIC. Birds on the NSW coast are much yellower than those around Canberra.

Striated Thornbill *A. lineata* (Coastal and sub-coastal south-eastern Australia; endemic): Common in woodlands of the south-east, even in temperate rainforests, this species is found in noisy small parties. Very common in the Brindabella ranges west of Canberra.

Weebill *Smicrornis brevirostris* (Throughout continental Australia; endemic): Generally found in drier forests, this is a very common widespread bird. Often forages in the company of thornbills, the distinctive loud call quickly gives this species away. Common in the ACT, for example at Campbell Park (5.3). The small, yellow, northern race, *flavescens*, is common in Kakadu, for example along Stag Creek (7.19).

Green-backed Gerygone *Gerygone chloronotus* (New Guinea; the Top End): Fairly common in the canopy of monsoon rainforest around Darwin, this species has a rather strange un-gerygone like reeling song. Common at East Point Recreational Reserve (7.10) and Buffalo Creek (7.9) near Darwin, also found at Mitchell Falls (8.5b) in the Kimberleys.

Fairy Gerygone *G. palpebrosa* (New Guinea; north-east QLD): Found in lowland rainforests usually near water, even in mangroves in north-eastern QLD, this is a common species. The northern race is common in rainforest roadside edges at Iron Range NP (6.45), whilst further south this species can be easily found around the Cairns area, for example in the Botanic Gardens (6.26) or in mangroves at Thomsons Road (6.28).

White-throated Gerygone *G. olivacea* (New Guinea; coastal and sub-coastal northern and eastern Australia): A fairly common bird of open woodlands, this species is resident in the north but is a breeding migrant to the south-east, arriving in September and leaving in April. Almost invariably found by hearing the distinctive typical gerygone descending whistle, this species is common during the spring and summer around Canberra, for example in Campbell Park (5.3) or on Black Mountain. Found in similar habitats in the north, for example Mamukala (7.14) or Townsville Common Environmental Park (6.20).

Large-billed Gerygone *G. magnirostris* (New Guinea; coastal northern Australia): Found in swamps, mangroves and woods along streams, this species is most easily found in mangroves around Cairns *i.e.* on a Daintree River cruise (6.31) or at Thomsons Road (6.28) but can also be seen at Middle Arm (7.5) near Darwin.

Dusky Gerygone *G. tenebrosa* (North-western Australia; endemic to WA): This is a common mangrove species in the north-west of WA. It responds well to pishing and can be easily seen in the mangroves at New Beach (8.15), Carnarvon Fishing Harbour (8.14), and Point Samson (8.11).

Brown Gerygone *G. mouki* (Eastern Australia; endemic): A common gerygone of east coast rainforests behaving and sounding rather like a thornbill. Easily seen at Lamington NP (6.7), and around Sydney.

Mangrove Gerygone *G. levigaster* (New Guinea; coastal northern and eastern Australia except Cape York Peninsula): A common mangrove species, readily attracted to pishing. This species can be found easily at many mangrove sites, for example; Bundaberg (6.16), Karumba (6.47), Derby (8.8).

Western Gerygone *G. fusca* (Interior continental Australia; endemic): Despite its name, this species is found throughout the arid interior mainly in open woodlands. The only region in which it is common, however, is the south-west of WA. It can be found in all the parks around Perth; Monger Lake (8.18), Mundaring Weir *etc.* and even suburban gardens. In the east, this bird is rather more local in occurrence but an excellent place to find it in the summer months is Campbell Park (5.3) in the ACT where it occurs alongside the White-throated Gerygone. Fairly common at Round Hill Nature Reserve (4.20); try around the campsite in the spring months and at Kunoth Well (7.28).

Southern Whiteface *Aphelocephala leucopsis* (Throughout central southern Australia; endemic): A generally common species of the arid interior favouring open forests, scrubs and mulga. Easily the commonest whiteface and readily found at many sites such as Gulpa State Forest (4.18b) in VIC, Erldunda Banded Whiteface site (7.32), Mount Magnet area (8.17).

Chestnut-breasted Whiteface *A. pectoralis* (Lyndhurst area; endemic to SA): A very rare species, the only place to find it is the site on the Strzelecki Track east of Lyndhurst (9.14). Persevere here, they are present year round but can be very elusive and shy. Often they will flush from some distance away and then fly several hundred metres. Concentrate on the area in front of the old mine.

Banded Whiteface *A. nigricincta* (Arid central Australia; endemic): Despite its' large range this is a very thinly scattered species of mainly open plains of the interior. The Ayers Rock (7.33) region is the most reliable place to find this species; either in recently burned areas of the park or north of Erldunda (7.32). Apart from here, the best chance is along the Strzelecki Track (9.13).

Green-backed Honeyeater *Glycichaera fallax* (New Guinea; Cape York Peninsula): Rather uncommon at Iron Range NP (6.45); most people find this species in trees along the roadsides. The best area is definitely around the back of the toilet building.

Brown Honeyeater *Lichmera indistincta* (New Guinea; continental Australia except south-east): A common species in most wooded habitats especially in the south-west; for example this species is common at Perth airport car-park!

White-streaked Honeyeater *Trichodere cockerelli* (Cape York Peninsula; endemic to QLD): Fairly common, noisy and conspicuous, but in very variable numbers in the dry country along the Portland or Coen Roads in Iron Range NP (6.45) depending upon where the paperbark (*Melaleuca*) trees are flowering. Occasionally seen along the roadside in the rainforest areas. Not found on Cape York as far south as Musgrave Station (6.44).

Dusky Honeyeater *Myzomela obscura* (Australasia; tropical northern Australia): Common from Cairns to Darwin, in coastal woodlands and mangroves *etc*. Rather uncommon south to about Brisbane. A good place to find this species is Cairns Botanic Gardens (6.26).

Red-headed Honeyeater *M. erythrocephala* (New Guinea; tropical northern Australia): A mangrove species of the far north that does not occur around Cairns but is reputedly common at Portland Roads on Cape York Peninsula. Easily found at Karumba (6.47), Middle Arm (7.5), Buffalo Creek (7.9) *etc*. Readily attracted by pishing.

Scarlet Honeyeater *M. sanguinolenta* (Eastern Australia; endemic, however birds in some Pacific islands sometimes treated as races of this species): Common in rainforests, eucalyptus woodlands, parks *etc*., wherever there are flowering trees. Apparently a summer visitor to areas south of Sydney where uncommon but common in the north. Good places to find it are Royal NP (4.7), Mount Glorious (6.5), Lamington NP (6.7), and the Atherton Tablelands (6E). This is a canopy species and the key to finding it is to learn its distinctive song.

Banded Honeyeater *Certhionyx pectoralis* (Tropical northern Australia; endemic): Common throughout the tropical north wherever there are flowering eucalyptus or paperbark trees; this is a fairly nomadic species but should not be hard to find. Places we recorded it include Musgrave Station (6.44), Cape Crawford (7.2), Caranbirini Springs (7.3), Victoria River (7.24), and Waterfall Creek (7.18).

Black Honeyeater *C. niger* (Arid central Australia; endemic): A highly nomadic honeyeater of the arid interior that occurs in regions where there have been recent rains. This species has a particular liking for flowering *Eremophila* bushes. For this reason it is difficult to give a reliable site, however, the Macdonnell Ranges west of Alice Springs *i.e.* Ormiston Gorge NP (7.31) is fairly reliable, as is the Nyngan to Bourke road (4.21) in spring and the scrub around Ayers Rock (7.33). You should learn the call. Often seen around Deniliquin (4.18) in the spring following wet winters; ask Phil Maher, and fairly regular at Round Hill Nature Reserve (4.20). This species seems to have a more eastern distribution than Pied Honeyeater.

Pied Honeyeater *C. variegatus* (Arid central Australia; endemic): Again a highly nomadic honeyeater that may appear in numbers to feed on flowering *Eremophila* bushes, following heavy rainfall about six weeks previously, almost anywhere in the arid outback. It is a very difficult bird to pin down. The Peron Peninsula (8.16) in WA is a fairly regular spot as is Alice Springs where this species was common along the Stuart Highway north of Alice in November 1993 and especially common at Kunoth Well (7.28). At other times, seems to be fairly regular in the Macdonnell Ranges, but this is a species you should hope to find in north-western WA either on the Peron Peninsula (8.16) or around Mount Magnet (8.17) or Cape Range NP (8.13). Occasionally found as far east as Round Hill Nature Reserve (4.20).

Graceful Honeyeater *Meliphaga gracilis* (New Guinea; north-east QLD): Fairly common in lowland rainforest areas and woodland around Cairns and on Cape York; good places to find this species are Cairns Botanic Gardens (6.26), Thomsons Road (6.28) and the rainforest edges at Iron Range NP (6.45). It is essential to learn the calls of this species to separate it from Yellow-spotted Honeyeater.

Yellow-spotted Honeyeater *M. notata* (Cape York Peninsula; endemic to QLD): Common and found in the same places as Graceful Honeyeater, it is essential to learn their respective calls in order to separate them.

Lewin's Honeyeater *M. lewinii* (Coastal eastern Australia; endemic): Common, noisy and conspicuous in rainforests from Royal NP (4.7) to Cairns area. Birds are hand tame at O'Reilly's in Lamington NP (6.7).

White-lined Honeyeater *M. albilineata* (Arnhem Land and the Kimberleys; endemic): Fairly common and not hard to find in Kakadu NP. Nourlangie Rock (7.15) or Stag Creek (7.19) are both good sites, although this species occurs near any sandstone gorges in this area. Birds are also found around Mitchell Falls (8.5b) if you manage to get into the Kimberleys.

Bridled Honeyeater *Lichenostomus frenatus* (North-eastern Australia; endemic to QLD): Common in all highland rainforest of the Atherton Tablelands. This species is hand tame at the Ivy Cottage Tea Garden at Mount Spec NP (6.21) and at picnic tables in the car-park at The Crater NP (6.32).

Eungella Honeyeater *L. hindwoodi* (Eungella area; endemic to QLD): This species is not particularly common around Eungella NP (6.17) near Mackay. Most of the population is found outside the Park itself and the key area to find this species is Dalrymple Road. In January/February, this species is often seen in the flowering Umbrella Tree next to Range Road View Point, a short walk from Sky View Lookout which is on the left, before Broken River Campsite. They respond very well to pishing.

Yellow-faced Honeyeater *L. chrysops* (Eastern Australia; endemic): A common honeyeater of most woodland habitats of the south-east. Abundant in the summer months in the Brindabellas (5.7) west of Canberra. Large numbers can be observed on autumn migration throughout the ACT but especially at Point Hut Crossing on the Murrumbidgee River.

Varied Honeyeater *L. versicolor* (New Guinea; north-eastern QLD): Found mainly in mangroves all the way around Cape York Peninsula, this is a noisy inquisitive bird readily attracted by pishing. Good places to see it include Thomsons Road (6.28), Cairns Esplanade (6.24), Daintree River cruises (6.31) and Portland Roads.

Mangrove Honeyeater *L. fasciogularis* (Coastal eastern Australia; endemic): Very similar in habits and habitat to the previous species and possibly conspecific. This bird is rather rare in the southern part of its range but can be seen easily in the mangroves at Thornside in Brisbane or at Bundaberg (6.16).

Singing Honeyeater *L. virescens* (Throughout continental Australia except eastern parts; endemic): A very widespread honeyeater that is found in all arid areas of the continent and in almost any isolated bush in the outback.

Yellow Honeyeater *L. flavus* (North-eastern Australia; endemic to QLD): Fairly common in most wooded habitats, especially near water in northern QLD. Good places to find this species are Townsville Common Environmental Park (6.20), Cairns Botanic Gardens (6.26) and Tinaroo Creek Road (6.37).

White-gaped Honeyeater *L. unicolor* (Tropical northern Australia; endemic): A large, noisy conspicuous honeyeater most numerous in coastal regions of the Top End. This species is common at Victoria River (7.24), the Darwin region, Caranbirini Springs (7.3) etc.

White-eared Honeyeater *L. leucotis* (Southern Australia; endemic): A fairly common bird in the south-east of wet forests and woodland, but also occurring in mallee areas, particularly in the western part of its range. Good places to find it include Barren Grounds (4.1), Tidbinbilla (5.4) in the summer months (best along the Lyrebird Trail), and the Victorian mallee sites (2.12, 2.13, 2.14).

Yellow-throated Honeyeater *L. flavicollis* (Bass Strait Islands; endemic to TAS): Common in all woodland habitats of TAS, mostly at lower altitudes.

Yellow-tufted Honeyeater *L. melanops* (South-eastern Australia; endemic): This is a locally very common honeyeater but it is extremely patchy in its distribution depending on the occurrence of ironbark trees. It will be seen at many sites but is abundant along the Glen Davis road (4.12) and at Chiltern State Forest (2C) for example. The Victorian race, *cassidix* is sometimes split as the Helmeted Honeyeater. This is a highly endangered taxon, numbering only about two hundred individuals found mainly around the Yellingbo State Wildlife Reserve about 50 km east of Melbourne.

Purple-gaped Honeyeater *L. cratitius* (Southern Australia; endemic): This is a rather uncommon honeyeater that is nomadic in response to flowering in the mallee regions of both the south-eastern and western mallee areas. In VIC it is regularly found, particularly in the spring months, along the road to Big Billy Bore (2.12) but the most reliable sites are Innes NP (9.4) and Lincoln NP (9.8) in SA. In WA, probably the best locality to look for this species is Stirling Ranges NP (8.22), around Bluff Knoll car-park.

Grey-headed Honeyeater *L. keartlandi* (Inland north-western Australia; endemic): A widespread, fairly common honeyeater of the interior that is mainly found in trees near watercourses. Common at Mica Creek near Mount Isa (6.49), Simpson's Gap (7.29) and Ormiston Gorge NP (7.31) etc.

Yellow-tinted Honeyeater *L. flavescens* (New Guinea; tropical northern Australia): Common in vegetation near water in the tropical north and readily found at many sites, for example Cumberland Dam (6.46) near Georgetown, Cape Crawford (7.2), Caranbirini Springs (7.3), Wyndham Caravan Park (8.4) etc.

Fuscous Honeyeater *L. fuscus* (Eastern Australia; endemic): A fairly common honeyeater in the south-east favouring drier open forests but apparently partly nomadic. They are easy to find along the Glen Davis road (4.12) in NSW and in the summer months at Namadgi NP (5.6) in the southern ACT, especially around the Ororral camping area, also regular at Chiltern State Forest (2C) in VIC.

Grey-fronted Honeyeater *L. plumulus* (Throughout arid continental Australia; endemic): Despite the huge range of this species it is not terribly common. It is found only in arid areas including regenerating mallee such as in the old field at Round Hill Nature Reserve (4.20), but it is not common even there. Readily accessible and easy places to find it are; China Walls near Hall's Creek (8.6) and the area north of Tennant Creek (7.26), whilst for those travelling further afield, this species is fairly common in the Bredon Hills along the Canning Stock Route (8.7) and along the track north of Cook into the Great Victoria Desert (9.16).

Yellow-plumed Honeyeater *L. ornatus* (Southern Australia; endemic): Very common in mallee areas such as Round Hill Nature Reserve (4.20), Hattah-Kulkyne NP (2.14), Wyperfield NP (2.13) etc.

White-plumed Honeyeater *L. penicillatus* (Throughout continental Australia except far north and south-west; endemic): A common, noisy honeyeater of virtually all Australia and found in open forests and trees along watercourses in the interior.

Tawny-breasted Honeyeater *Xanthotis flaviventer* (New Guinea; Cape York Peninsula): Common in the rainforest at Iron Range NP (6.45).

Macleay's Honeyeater *X. macleayana* (North-east Australia; endemic to QLD): Common in rainforests of the Atherton Tablelands. This species is very easy to find at Kingfisher Park (6.40) and hand tame birds will land on your table at the Ivy Cottage Tea Garden at Mount Spec NP (6.21).

White-naped Honeyeater *Melithreptus lunatus* (South-east and south-west Australia; endemic): A common honeyeater in the south of Australia, found in woodlands and parks during the summer months, but huge migrations northwards occur in the autumn. Abundant in the Brindabellas, e.g. Tidbinbilla (5.4), in the ACT during the breeding season and a few over winter there and readily found in Royal NP (4.7) and Dharug NP (4.10) near Sydney. In WA this species is fairly common at both Dryandra State Forest (8.19) and Porongurup NP (8.21).

Black-headed Honeyeater *M. affinis* (Bass Strait Islands; endemic to TAS): Common in forests and woodlands throughout northern and eastern TAS.

White-throated Honeyeater *M. albogularis* (New Guinea; tropical northern and eastern Australia): A common honeyeater in forests and woodland in the north. Good places to find it include the dry woodland beyond the rainforest on Duck Creek Road in Lamington NP (6.7), the dry country along Portland Road at Iron Range NP (6.45), Townsville Common Environmental Park (6.20), the campsite at Waterfall Creek (7.18) and Howard Springs (7.6).

Golden-backed Honeyeater *M. laetior* (Tropical northern Australia; endemic): Recently split from the following species, this is a really smart honeyeater of open woodlands of the tropical north. It is not a common species but is much easier to find if you learn the call which sounds identical to a Black-chinned Honeyeater, i.e. a deep, far-carrying 'chree chree chree', often given in flight. Reliable localities for this species are; the Carpentarian Grasswren site near Mount Isa (6.50); Cape Crawford (7.2) and China Walls near Halls Creek (8.6).

Black-chinned Honeyeater *M. gularis* (Eastern Australia; endemic): Like Yellow-tufted Honeyeater, this is a locally very common species but it is extremely patchy in its distribution depending on the occurrence of ironbark trees. It is common along the Glen Davis road (4.12) and at Chiltern State Forest (2C) for example.

Strong-billed Honeyeater *M. validirostris* (Bass Strait Islands; endemic to TAS): Common throughout wooded areas of TAS, this species has the habit of searching around strips of bark whilst foraging, rather in the manner of a treecreeper.

Brown-headed Honeyeater *M. brevirostris* (Southern Australia; endemic): Widespread in woodlands of the southern interior except for the arid regions. This species is not especially common. Good places to find it are; Campbell Park (5.3) and the Camelback Firetrail at Tidbinbilla (5.4b), both in the ACT; Hattah-Kulkyne NP (2.14) (around Hattah Lake campground), Wyperfield NP (2.13) and the You Yangs (2.6), all in VIC.

PASSERINES

Little Friarbird *Philemon citreogularis* (New Guinea; northern and eastern Australia): This is a bird of open woodlands throughout the north and east of the continent although it is only a breeding migrant to the southern part of its range. It is common across the tropical north, being easy to see in suburban Cairns, Cape Crawford (7.2), Caranbirini Springs (7.3), Kakadu NP (7C) *etc.* In the south, this species is regular at Hattah-Kulkyne NP (2.14) and Gulpa State Forest (4.18b) for example.

Helmeted Friarbird *P. buceroides* (Lesser Sundas and New Guinea; coastal northern and eastern Australia): A friarbird of vegetation in sandstone gorges and nearby woodlands when in flower as well as suburban gardens. This is a fairly common species in QLD, but much less common in the NT. Cairns area is good; try trees and gardens along the Esplanade (6.24) as well as the Botanic Gardens (6.26). Quite plentiful in the dry country along Portland Road in Iron Range NP (6.45) and in Kakadu NP, try the rocky escarpments around Waterfall Creek (7.18) and Nourlangie Rock (7.15). Note that the QLD race is sometimes included with *P. novaeguineae*, the New Guinea Friarbird.

Silver-crowned Friarbird *P. argenticeps* (Tropical northern Australia; endemic): Rather more widespread than the previous species, there should be little difficulty finding this in tropical open forests and woods. Good areas are Tinaroo Creek Road (6.37), Cape Crawford (7.2), the escarpment walk near Victoria River (7.24), and Mitchell Falls (8.5b).

Noisy Friarbird *P. corniculatus* (New Guinea; eastern Australia): A very common bird of open woodlands and parks *etc.* In the east of the continent, this species is a breeding migrant to the southern part of its range where it is noisy and conspicuous. Reliable sites include Campbell Park (5.3) and the Botanic Gardens (5.1) in Canberra, from September to April.

Crescent Honeyeater *Phylidonyris pyrrhoptera* (South-eastern Australia and TAS; endemic): A honeyeater of wetter woodlands and dense coastal scrubs, the stronghold of this species is TAS where it is common and found even in suburban gardens. On the mainland, the best sites to find it are Barren Grounds (4.1), Fitzroy Falls (4.2a) and in the ACT, the flowering *Grevillea* bushes in the Botanic Gardens (5.1) during the winter months. This species is easily located by its loud distinctive 'egypt' call.

New Holland Honeyeater *P. novaehollandiae* (Southern Australia and TAS; endemic): A common honeyeater in the south-east and TAS, being found particularly in coastal areas with *Banksias* and *Grevilleas*. Abundant in Canberra Botanic Gardens (5.1), Jervis Bay (4.4), the Great Ocean Road (2.9) and throughout TAS.

White-cheeked Honeyeater *P. nigra* (Coastal eastern and western Australia; endemic): An isolated population is found on the Atherton Tablelands (6E), but this is mainly a bird of wetter coastal scrubs and forests in the extreme west and east of the continent. It is a common, noisy, conspicuous honeyeater and in WA it is found at Dryandra State Forest (8.19) and the heathland at Stirling Ranges NP (8.22), whilst in the east try the heathlands of Cooloola NP (6.15) or the Mill Creek circuit in Dharug NP (4.10).

White-fronted Honeyeater *P. albifrons* (Throughout arid central Australia; endemic): Despite the vast range of this species it is nowhere very numerous and like the Black and Pied Honeyeaters it is highly nomadic, sometimes being locally very common in regions where bushes are flowering following recent rains. Fortunately it is not as elusive as those two species and can usually be found in small numbers at the following places; Hattah-Kulkyne NP (2.14) (spring is best around beesite 8), Round Hill Nature Reserve (4.20) (around the campsite), Ellery Creek Big Hole (7.30), and the Peron Peninsula (8.16). Other places we recorded it include the mallee area 104 km north of Wirrulla on the road to Kingoonya in SA, and the Stuart Highway north of Alice.

Tawny-crowned Honeyeater *P. melanops* (Coastal southern Australia and TAS; endemic): A honeyeater of mainly coastal heathlands, this species is readily found at Barren Grounds (4.1) (along the Griffith Trail), Nadgee NP (4.6) (south of the car-park), Green Cape (4.6), Strahan (3.8) in TAS, Lincoln NP (9.8) in SA, and in WA this species is common on heathland areas at Stirling Ranges NP (8.22) (try the roadside heath along South Road between Chester Pass Road and the Mount Trio turn-off).

Brown-backed Honeyeater *Ramsayornis modestus* (New Guinea; coastal northern Australia): Common in coastal northern QLD, for example at Cairns Botanic Gardens (6.26) and Townsville Common Environmental Park (6.20).

Bar-breasted Honeyeater *R. fasciatus* (Tropical northern Australia; endemic): This is a common species in vegetation near water but mainly in the Top End. Easy places to find it are Chinaman Creek (7.23) and Fergusson River (7.20) near Katherine, Victoria River (7.24), Jim-Jim Creek in Kakadu NP (7C), and Katherine Gorge NP (7.22).

Striped Honeyeater *Plectorhyncha lanceolata* (Eastern Australia; endemic): Fairly common in dry woodland and scrubs including mallee areas of the inland eastern continent, this species is much easier to find once you know the call which is somewhat similar to an Olive-backed Oriole. This species sometimes indulges in conspicuous song flights. Good areas to find it are; the Painted Honeyeater Wildlife Refuge site south of Hay (4.18c), the Bourke to Tibooburra road (4.22), Round Hill Nature Reserve (4.20), all in NSW, and the Victorian mallee sites (2.12, 2.13, 2.14).

Rufous-banded Honeyeater *Conopophila albogularis* (New Guinea; coastal northern Australia): A common honeyeater within its restricted Australian range that is always found in vegetation near water. Easy to find in the Top End *e.g.* Adelaide River (7.12), Howard Springs (7.6), Fogg Dam (7.11) and East Point Recreational Reserve (7.10).

Rufous-throated Honeyeater *C. rufogularis* (Tropical northern Australia; endemic): A very common honeyeater in vegetation near water across the tropical north. Easily found at many sites such as; Cumberland Dam (6.46), Cape Crawford (7.2), Jim-Jim Creek in Kakadu NP (7C) and Wyndham Caravan Park (8.4).

Grey Honeyeater *C. whitei* (Central western Australia; endemic): A rare honeyeater of inland mulga in the western half of the continent, this is one of the hardest Australian birds to see and is probably nomadic within this large area. It is very inconspicuous, not least because of its small size and drab coloration. The call is rather weak, sounding like a distant Black-faced Cuckoo-Shrike. There is one reliable site, Kunoth Well (7.28) near Alice Springs but be prepared to put in a lot of time looking for them. Fortunately this is also an excellent site for many other good birds. One other place where this species is often seen is the area of mulga 1 km west of Yalgoo in WA, on the north side of the highway.

Painted Honeyeater *Grantiella picta* (Inland eastern Australia; endemic): A rather scarce honeyeater that is easiest to find in spring and summer in the south of its range. It is found in dry open eucalypt areas where the trees are heavily infected with mistletoe and is quite easy to locate when breeding because the males display almost constantly by flying up into the air and singing 'Gee-or-dee. The best places to find it are Clunes State Forest (2.10) and Kingower, both in VIC during October/November and the Wildlife Refuge south of Hay (4.18c) in NSW from around January. This is one of the species Phil Maher can usually show you in the summer around Deniliquin (4.18).

Regent Honeyeater *Xanthomyza phrygia* (South-east Australia; endemic): A rare honeyeater of the south-east that is declining alarmingly in numbers, currently there are an estimated 1000 individuals, and it is nomadic over quite a large range. Sadly there are now no totally reliable sites to find this species and it is always worth asking Sydney birders if any are currently known about since this is one of the most searched for birds in Australia. That said, birds are still regularly seen along the Glen Davis road (4.12) when the eucalypts are flowering, which can be at almost any time of year although spring is best. Another fairly regular site is Chiltern State Forest (2C) in the spring. Birds are still seen annually in the ACT and occasionally breed so it is worth enquiring about any recent sightings there too.

Eastern Spinebill *Acanthorhynchus tenuirostris* (South and eastern Australia and TAS; endemic): A common noisy honeyeater of the south-east, mostly in the coastal fringe in all well vegetated areas. Very common throughout the year in Canberra Botanic Gardens (5.1).

Western Spinebill *A. superciliosus* (South-western Australia; endemic to WA): A very common honeyeater of the south-west corner and found at all the birding sites; Dryandra State Forest (8.19), Two Peoples Bay (8.20) *etc.*

Blue-faced Honeyeater *Entomyzon cyanotis* (New Guinea; northern and eastern Australia): A common honeyeater in open woods and forests of the tropical north, but much rarer further south. This species is abundant around Cairns whilst in the NT, birds can be hand fed around the car-park at Katherine Gorge NP (7.22).

Bell Miner *Manorina melanophrys* (South-eastern Australia; endemic): A common miner of the coastal south-east that lives in discrete colonies that may persist in one area for years. They utter a metallic bell-like 'ping' almost constantly and this is the best way to locate a colony whilst driving along. They are abundant in the eastern suburbs of Melbourne and in south QLD a large colony can be found along the Cunningham Highway, just below the summit on the east side of Cunninghams Gap and at Mount Nebo (6.5). In NSW colonies can be heard whilst driving along the Princes Highway between Nowra and Eden.

Noisy Miner *M. melanocephala* (Eastern Australia and TAS; endemic): A common aggressive honeyeater in open forests of the eastern half of the continent. Numerous at the campground at Hattah-Kulkyne NP (2.14) and in the ACT in suburban Canberra and other areas, such as Campbell Park (5.3).

Yellow-throated Miner *M. flavigula* (Throughout arid continental Australia; endemic): A very common bird found in all wooded habitats except the wet east coast forests and often in large noisy parties.

Black-eared Miner *M. (flavigula) melanotis* (Formerly in mallee regions of north-west VIC and SA; endemic): Usually regarded as a race of Yellow-throated Miner, this species is now on the verge of extinction through interbreeding with *flavigula* since the latter has been able to gain access to the mallee because of habitat clearance and road building. Hybrids between the two are still found at Hattah-Kulkyne (2.14) and Wyperfield (2.13) NPs and we were able to observe a party of miners on the Dattuck Track in April 1991 that contained two pure bred *melanotis*. These have now since disappeared but some pure bred birds are still found in SA; ask birders for current information.

Spiny-cheeked Honeyeater *Acanthagenys rufogularis* (Throughout arid continental Australia; endemic): A common honeyeater of the arid outback, found in all wooded areas for example at Kunoth Well (7.28) and even saltbush areas such as the Chestnut-breasted Whiteface site (9.14).

Brush Wattlebird *Anthochaera chrysoptera* (Coastal south-eastern Australia and TAS; endemic): A common honeyeater of coastal heaths, scrubs, and *Banksia* woodlands.

Common in coastal TAS, VIC (Great Ocean Road (2.9)), NSW (Nadgee NP, Green Cape (4.6)) and SA (Lincoln NP (9.8)).

Little Wattlebird *A. (chrysoptera) lunulata* (Coastal south-western Australia; endemic to WA): Probably best regarded as a race of Brush Wattlebird, this taxon has been split in the past although supposed racial differences are not consistent. Common at Two Peoples Bay (8.20).

Red Wattlebird *A. carunculata* (Southern continental Australia; endemic): A common, noisy honeyeater of southern forests, not usually in arid areas. Abundant in the Brindabellas (5.7) in the ACT during the summer months but most leave the high mountains for the winter. Found year-round in Canberra Botanic Gardens (5.1).

Yellow Wattlebird *A. paradoxa* (Bass Strait Islands; endemic to TAS): Commonest in all the wooded areas of south and east TAS, easily found because of its loud retching calls.

Crimson Chat *Epthianura tricolor* (Throughout arid continental Australia; endemic): A highly nomadic chat of the arid interior which, like Pied and Black Honeyeaters, will sometimes appear in very large numbers in areas where it has recently rained. Unlike them, however, it seems much more widely distributed as small numbers are seen on most long outback drives. Indeed this species often feeds by roadsides and if you find a party it usually indicates that it has rained there relatively recently so it is worth stopping and checking for other desert nomads. Areas we recorded it include Kunoth Well (7.28), the Stuart Highway north of Alice Springs (7.27), Round Hill Nature Reserve (4.20), the Strzelecki Track (9.13) the road between Windorah and the Birdsville turn-off and Rocky Pool near Carnarvon (8.14) WA. This species is rare as far south as VIC.

Orange Chat *E. aurifrons* (Arid central southern Australia; endemic): Like the Crimson Chat, this species is another nomadic chat of the arid zone. However, it is very much scarcer and has a preference for open habitats. There are no guaranteed places to find it although this species is regularly recorded at New Beach (8.15) in WA, along the Birdsville Track (9.15), around the edge of Lake Bindegolly (6.13) in QLD, and around Deniliquin (4.18) where Phil Maher can probably show you it. Other places we saw it include Pyampa Station (4.23) in south-west QLD, the Chestnut-breasted Whiteface site (9.14) in SA, and the Banded Whiteface site north of Erldunda (7.32) in NT.

Yellow Chat *E. crocea* (Swamps in northern Australia; endemic): This chat has a very patchy local distribution being found in swamps and rushes around bore drains mainly in the north of the continent. This is one of the hardest Australian birds to see. The only guaranteed site is Pandie Burra Bore on the Birdsville Track (9.15) during the hot summer months when it is very unpleasant and potentially dangerous to visit. The next best bet is the Barkly Tablelands (7.1) where you should check any of the water bores visible from the Barkly Highway that have rushes around them. Recently, the northern shore of Lake Argyle (8.1) in WA has been found to be a breeding site; the birds being found on the bare open shore. Birds are occasionally seen at Derby Sewage works and during the wet season in Kakadu NP (7C). We also saw birds at a private water bore in the Channel Country.

White-fronted Chat *E. albifrons* (Southern Australia and TAS; endemic): Easily the commonest chat and one that is found in damp areas, especially around ponds and lakes. The best sites to find it include; the saltbush areas of Port Gawler (9.2) and the Adelaide ICI Saltworks (9.1) area in SA, the west side of Lake Bathurst (4.3b) where this species is always found on rocky boulders, although access may be difficult, the Victorian mallee sites (2.12, 2.13, 2.14), especially after rain, and the Victorian coastal zone.

Gibber Chat *Ashbyia lovensis* (Central eastern Australia; endemic): An uncommon chat that is mainly found on bare open gibber plains of SA. Easily the best area to find it is whilst driving across the gibber plains of the Birdsville Track (9.15) where this species is reasonably common, even the southern part up to 20 km from Marree holds them. Apart from driving the Birdsville Track, your only other chances of finding this bird are along the Strzelecki Track, although there is very little really suitable gibber habitat. Birds are sometimes seen at the Chestnut-breasted Whiteface site (9.14) however. We recorded this species in the Channel Country west of Windorah and the track between Windorah and Birdsville is another good site for them.

Jacky Winter *Microeca fascinans* (New Guinea; throughout continental Australia): A fairly common and widespread bird of open forests throughout the mainland but usually not found near habitation. Usually present in small numbers and most easily tracked down by its song, it is often seen perched prominently low down. We recorded them in many areas particularly in the south-east, for example You Yangs (2.6), Chiltern State Forest (2C), Victorian mallee sites (2.12, 2.13, 2.14), Campbell Park (5.3), and Glen Davis (4.12).

Lemon-bellied Flycatcher *M. flavigaster* (New Guinea; tropical northern Australia): Fairly common in open woodlands of the tropical north, this species seems to be most numerous in northern QLD. Common at Iron Range NP (6.45) in roadside rainforest and on the Atherton Tablelands at Kingfisher Park (6.40). In the Top End, good places include Mamukala (7.14), the forest at Fogg Dam (7.11), and Adelaide River (7.12).

Brown-tailed Flycatcher *M. (flavigaster) tormenti* (Coastal Kimberley region; endemic to WA): Generally regarded as a race of Lemon-bellied Flycatcher, this flycatcher is found mostly in mangroves of the Kimberley region of north-western Australia. It is rather uncommon, however, the most accessible sites where it can be seen are; Barred Creek 44 km north of Broome, ask local people for directions, or Derby boat ramp (8.8); try the mangroves opposite the new boat ramp. There seems little doubt that this form does not warrant full species status.

Yellow-legged Flycatcher *M. griseoceps* (New Guinea; Cape York Peninsula): This is rather an uncommon bird at Iron Range NP (6.45); it is mainly a canopy feeding species so easy to overlook. The best area is the roadside forest along Portland Road between the Coen turn off and the concrete causeway.

Scarlet Robin *Petroica multicolor* (Australasia and Pacific Islands; southern Australia and TAS): A common bird of open woodland in the south-east and TAS that breeds in the mountains but disperses to more open habitat in winter. It can be readily found in the ACT at Campbell Park (5.3) or at Tidbinbilla (5.4) and at many sites in TAS and NSW.

Red-capped Robin *P. goodenovii* (Arid continental Australia except tropical north; endemic): A very common bird of arid woodlands of the interior, especially mallee and mulga areas. This species is easy to find at numerous sites; for example Round Hill Nature Reserve (4.20), Victorian mallee sites (2.12, 2.13, 2.14), and Kunoth Well (7.28).

Flame Robin *P. phoenicea* (South-eastern Australia and TAS; endemic): Found in similar areas and habitats as the Scarlet Robin, this species is particularly common in TAS, for example on Bruny Island (3.1). Good places to find it on the mainland include places like Glen Davis (4.12) and the Brindabella ranges (5.7) in the ACT during the summer months; try the car-park at Piccadilly Circus.

Rose Robin *P. rosea* (Eastern Australia; endemic): A bird of wet temperate and sub-tropical forests, this species is an altitudinal migrant, breeding at higher altitudes and dispersing to lower altitude during the winter. It is not very common although it is often overlooked since it usually feeds in the canopy. Learning the distinctive trilling song is the easiest way to find this species. The best place we found for it was the Scenic Circuit at Bunya Mountains NP (6.10), however it is also fairly common at Lamington NP (6.7) (the canopy walk is good), also Barrington Tops (4.13), and in the ACT a few pairs always breed during the summer along the Lyrebird Trail (5.4c), especially along the wet gully section.

Pink Robin *P. rodinogaster* (Southern Australia and TAS; endemic): This is an uncommon bird on the Australian mainland, breeding almost entirely in VIC. Wet forest areas are best, such as Ferntree Gully NP (2.2), Point Addis, East Gippsland NP. Fortunately this species is reasonably common in TAS where it can be found easily around the church and along Fern Tree Bower on Mount Wellington (3.2). Other excellent places to find Pink Robins are around the rubbish tip at Maria Island NP (3.4), the Russell Falls Nature Walk (best around the Falls) at Mount Field NP and the southern section of the Overland Track at Lake St Clair (3.9) where it skirts the lake shore.

Hooded Robin *Melanodryas cucullata* (Throughout continental Australia except Cape York; endemic): A widespread but rather thinly scattered species of drier open woodlands and scrub, this bird will be readily found in small numbers at many sites. Good places include Kunoth Well (7.28), all mallee sites *etc*. Regularly seen at Campbell Park (5.3) in the ACT.

Dusky Robin *M. vittata* (Bass Strait Islands; endemic to TAS): A common bird of forest edge and open areas in TAS, this species is readily found on Bruny (3.1) and Maria (3.4) Islands, often seen perched on fence posts.

Pale-yellow Robin *Tregellasia capito* (Coastal eastern Australia; endemic): A robin of the under storey of tropical and sub-tropical forests, this species seems to have a preference for small creek sides. It is common at Mount Glorious (6.5), but strangely rather rare at Lamington NP (6.7), whilst the isolated northern population is common on the Atherton Tablelands (6E).

White-faced Robin *T. leucops* (New Guinea; Cape York Peninsula): Common and tame in all areas of rainforest at Iron Range NP (6.45), this species is often found clinging to the side of tree trunks.

Eastern Yellow Robin *Eopsaltria australis* (Eastern Australia; endemic): A common, often tame, robin of coastal and sub-coastal forests, this species is particularly vocal at dawn and dusk. Numerous at Lamington NP (6.7), Glen Davis (4.12), Tidbinbilla (5.4) *etc.*, usually feeding on or near the ground.

Western Yellow Robin *E. griseogularis* (South-western Australia; endemic): A fairly common robin of the south-west that occurs in open woodland there. It is *not* found at Two Peoples Bay but should be straightforward to find at Stirling Ranges NP (8.22); the cleared area opposite the rangers house is a stake out, also the Western Thornbill site nearby. Along the Muirs Highway east of Manjimup (8.23) is another good area. In SA we found this species at Lincoln NP (9.8).

White-breasted Robin *E. georgiana* (South-western Australia; endemic to WA): Common in rather wet, dense under storey in the extreme south-west, this species is common around the car-park at Two Peoples Bay (8.20) and along the track edges at Porongurup NP (8.21).

Mangrove Robin *E. pulverulenta* (New Guinea; coastal northern Australia): Found in mangroves throughout the tropical north, this species seems rather local in occurrence and is definitely easiest to see in north-east QLD. The birds feed out on the open mud at low tide and can be readily attracted by whistling an imitation of their song. Probably the best site is Thomsons Road (6.28) this species is very easy to see on a Daintree River cruise (6.31); just pish loudly at the mangroves. Recently there has been a pair in residence in Cairns Botanic Gardens (6.26), around the Saltwater Pool. In the west, Point Samson (8.11) is a good site.

White-browed Robin *Poecilodryas superciliosa* (Tropical northern Australia; endemic): Rather an uncommon, local species, that favours vegetation along watercourses and is rather skulking in nature. A stake out in QLD is Big Mitchell Creek (6.39) and we also saw this species at Iron Range NP (6.45), in a roadside thicket about 200 m before the Coen turn-off. There are several good places to find the western race, best is probably Dunham River near Kununurra (8.3) in WA, but also good are Stag Creek (7.19) and near Waterfall Creek campsite (7.18), both in Kakadu NP.

Grey-headed Robin *Heteromyias cinereifrons* (Atherton area; endemic to QLD): A very common rainforest species in the Atherton Tablelands (6E). The birds at The Crater NP (6.32) car-park are almost hand tame. This species is sometimes lumped with the Ashy Robin *H. albispecularis* of New Guinea.

Northern Scrub-Robin *Drymodes superciliaris* (New Guinea; Cape York Peninsula): A bird commonly heard calling at Iron Range NP (6.45) and easily whistled out although somewhat shy. A pair regularly found around the toilet block.

Southern Scrub-Robin *D. brunneopygia* (Southern Australia; endemic): A reasonably common bird mainly of mallee habitats and one that is readily whistled out into view. Good places to find this species are; around the campsite at Round Hill Nature Reserve (4.20), the Lowan Track at Wyperfield NP (2.13) (they often feed out on the track itself), the road to Big Billy Bore (2.12), and Hattah-Kulkyne NP (2.14). In SA this species is fairly common in coastal heathland at Lincoln NP (9.8) and Coffin Bay NP (9.9).

Varied Sittella *Daphoenositta chrystoptera* (New Guinea; throughout continental Australia): Several well marked races of this widespread, though not especially numerous, species are found around Australia with intergrades found at the zones of contact between them. It is found in all wooded habitats in the continent from dry outback trees to rainforests and occurs in small noisy parties that bound over a woodland before landing on a tree and working their way over the bark in nuthatch fashion. Campbell Park (5.3) in the ACT is a regular place to find them.

Crested Shrike-Tit *Falcunculus frontatus* (South-eastern and western Australia and the tropical north; endemic): A bird of dry eucalyptus forests, this species is usually found by hearing it tearing at strips of bark. It is nowhere very common, however the eastern race is much more numerous than the western and especially northern races. Probably the most reliable site is Glen Davis (4.12), although Back Yamma (4.19) and Gulpa (4.18b) State Forests are both also good and we also recorded them in the rainforest at Lamington NP (6.7). In the ACT, this species regularly nests in trees close to the horse gate in Campbell Park (5.3). The best place to look for the western race, *leucogaster*, is Dryandra State Forest (8.19) although it is very uncommon, but not nearly as rare as the northern race, *whitei*, for which I have heard of no good sites.

Crested Bellbird *Oreoica gutturalis* (Throughout arid continental Australia; endemic): A common bird of dry woodlands and scrubs of the interior, this species can be heard calling all day, although singing birds are usually hard to track down because they are highly ventriloquial. Often encountered feeding on the ground, with thornbill or whiteface flocks. All mallee and mulga areas are good for this species.

Olive Whistler *Pachycephala olivacea* (South-eastern Australia and TAS; endemic): This is a skulking whistler of dense under storey habitats, especially in coastal habitats and mountains. An isolated population occurs in the Antarctic Beech forest at Lamington NP (6.7) and should be seen whilst searching the Rufous Scrub-bird areas there. The easiest State to find this bird is TAS where it is fairly common; the Adventure Bay to Lunawanna road (3.1f) and Fern Glade on Mount Wellington (3.2) both have excellent habitat for this species. On the mainland, it can be found fairly easily in coastal heath along the Great Ocean Road (2.9); try the heath around Sherbrooke picnic site. In the ACT, this species is apparently an altitudinal migrant but is fairly easy to find at Corin Dam (5.5) in the winter months and in the higher Brindabellas (5.7) at other times of the year, especially Mount Ginini.

Red-lored Whistler *P. rufogularis* (Mallee of south-eastern Australia; endemic): This is a rare bird and one of the hardest to see in Australia. There is only one realistic site; Round Hill Nature Reserve (4.20) and then only in the spring months (late August until October) when the birds are singing. At other times of the year they apparently either leave this area or possibly the males loose their red face so that they become indistinguishable from Gilbert's Whistlers which are also fairly common at Round Hill. The usual song is very similar to that of Gilbert's Whistler, *i.e.* a loud 'chew chew chew chew chew', about twenty notes that rise and fall in volume somewhat. Birds occur in the mallee both around the edge of the old fields and along the back road to Lake Cargelligo. They tend to be rather shy unless singing. The best way to see them is to wait until you hear a singing bird than move in quickly to locate it before it stops singing. There may be long periods between song bursts so be patient and take care not to get lost. The only other chance you have of finding this species is along the Big Billy Bore road (2.12) in VIC; try the pull-in 15.5 km south of the Bore itself.

Gilbert's Whistler *P. inornata* (Arid southern Australia; endemic): A whistler found in dry scrubs across the southern inland, it is rather an uncommon species but fortunately there are some very good sites to find it. Best is probably Round Hill Nature Reserve (4.20) in spring when you are looking for Red-lored Whistler; also good are Gulpa (4.18b) and Back Yamma (4.19) State Forests where this species favours *Callitris* trees and the Victorian mallee sites (2.12, 2.13, 2.14); particularly along the Nowingi Track at Hattah-Kulkyne NP (2.14).

Grey Whistler *P. griseiceps* (New Guinea; coastal north-eastern QLD): A fairly common whistler in rainforests and mangroves of north-eastern QLD. This species is reasonably numerous at Iron Range NP (6.45) and further south it is found in the Yule Point mangroves (6.30) and at Kingfisher Park (6.40).

Brown Whistler *P. simplex* (Coastal Top End; endemic to NT): A bird of swamp woodlands, monsoon forest, and mangroves; this is a fairly common species in the tropical north. It is fairly easy to find at Buffalo Creek (7.9) where it occurs in bushes around the car-park and other good sites are Middle Arm (7.5), Fogg Dam (7.11) and Howard Springs (7.6). Note that this species is sometimes lumped with Grey Whistler.

Golden Whistler *P. pectoralis* (Australasia, Wallacea and the Pacific; southern and eastern Australia and TAS): A common species of all closed woodlands, *e.g.* Lamington NP (6.7), the Brindabellas (5.7) in the south and east.

Mangrove Golden Whistler *P. melanura* (New Guinea; coastal northern Australia): Rather a local whistler in mangroves of the tropical north. It seems to have a preference for taller mangroves than the White-breasted Whistler where the two co-exist. There are several good sites for finding this species; best are Point Samson mangroves (8.11) in WA and Adelaide River (7.12) in NT. Also worth trying are the mangroves at Broome Bird Observatory (8.9) and Karumba (6.47).

Rufous Whistler *P. rufiventris* (New Caledonia; throughout continental Australia): A widespread common whistler of open forests and even arid woods throughout the continent although it is only a breeding summer migrant to the south-east of Australia, including the ACT, where it is very common during the spring and summer months.

White-breasted Whistler *P. lanioides* (Coastal northern and western Australia; endemic): A whistler of mangroves in the north and west, this species has apparently declined markedly in the Darwin region in recent years where it is rare but is still seen occasionally at Middle Arm (7.5). Fortunately this species is common at Karumba (6.47), Point Samson (8.11) and Derby (8.8) and also occurs at Broome Bird Observatory (8.9). Like nearly all mangrove species it reacts well to pishing and is found mostly in small, scrubby mangrove bushes.

Rufous Shrike-Thrush *Colluricincla megarhyncha* (Australasia; northern and eastern Australia): The commonest shrike-thrush in rainforests of north-eastern QLD, this species is abundant at Iron Range NP (6.45) and in the Atherton Tablelands (6E) where it overlaps with Bower's Shrike-Thrush. Further south it is fairly common at Mount Glorious (6.5) but rare at Lamington NP (6.7). The north-western race is fairly common in coastal rainforest; Howard Springs (7.6) is a good site for example. This species is usually found picking through dry leaves in the mid to upper canopy.

Bower's Shrike-Thrush *C. boweri* (Atherton area; endemic to QLD): A fairly common shrike-thrush in the higher rainforests of the Atherton Tablelands. It is fairly common at Mount Lewis (6.40) (but is not found at Kingfisher Park), around the Cathedral and Curtain Fig Trees (6.35) and at Mount Spec NP (6.21).

Sandstone Shrike-Thrush *C. woodwardi* (Top End and Kimberleys; endemic): A fairly uncommon shrike-thrush that is found only on sandstone escarpments and gorges. It should be seen whilst looking for grasswrens either at Boroloola (7.3), Waterfall Creek (7.18) or at Mitchell Falls (8.5b). Alternatively, the White-quilled Rock-Pigeon site just west of Victoria River (7.24) is excellent for this species.

Grey Shrike-Thrush *C. harmonica* (New Guinea; throughout Australia and TAS): A widespread common species in wooded areas throughout the continent. There are several well marked races and this is always one of the richest most beautiful songs heard in the bush.

Logrunner *Orthonyx temminckii* (New Guinea; eastern Australia): A bird that rummages noisily through leaf litter on the forest floor. This species is abundant at Lamington NP (6.7) and also found at Mount Glorious (6.5) and the Bunya Mountains NP (6.10). Further south it is much less common but can be found at Mount Keira behind Wollongong for example.

Chowchilla *O. spaldingii* (Atherton area; endemic to QLD): A common rainforest ground dweller in the Atherton Tablelands, behaving in much the same fashion as Logrunners. Birds are very noisy at dawn and this species is easily found at The Crater NP (6.32), Mount Lewis (6.40), and Mount Spec NP (6.21).

Grey-crowned Babbler *Pomatostomus temporalis* (New Guinea; northern and eastern Australia): A fairly common bird of open woodlands and dry scrubby areas that is frequently seen along roadsides. Like other members of this family it associates in noisy, inquisitive flocks that are readily attracted by pishing. Apparently declining in heavily settled parts of its range, however, there should be no difficulty finding this species, and the road between Lake Cargelligo and Round Hill Nature Reserve (4.20) is as good as anywhere.

White-browed Babbler *P. superciliosus* (Arid southern Australia; endemic): Widespread in scrubby areas of the southern half of the continent, and found in noisy inquisitive parties, often along roadsides. This species will be encountered at many sites especially in all mallee areas.

Hall's Babbler *P. halli* (Inland eastern Australia; endemic): A very local bird of mulga areas that tends to occur in smaller, less noisy parties than the other babblers. It seems to favour the dense mulga along watercourses and is rather shy and skulking in nature. The best place to find it is the mulga between Quilpie and Windorah (6.12), but it is also possible around Eulo Bore (6.14) although it is heavily outnumbered by other babbler species there. Reputedly fairly common at Mungo NP near Mildura in southern NSW.

Chestnut-crowned Babbler *P. ruficeps* (Inland south-eastern Australia; endemic): A locally common babbler of mallee and mulga areas of the inland that behaves much like Grey-crowned and White-browed Babblers but is probably even more inquisitive. Good places to find this species are between Quilpie and Windorah (6.12), Eulo Bore (6.14), the rest area between Bourke and Nyngan (4.21), and Hattah-Kulkyne NP (2.14) (the Lake Mournpoul Track).

Eastern Whipbird *Psophodes olivaceus* (Eastern Australia; endemic): A common species in dense undergrowth in wetter east coast forests; the distinctive whiplash call is often heard. Usually quite shy but tame around Lamington NP (6.7). Common further south too at Barren Grounds (4.1) *etc.* An isolated population is found in the Atherton Tablelands (6E).

Western Whipbird *P. nigrogularis* (Coastal southern Australia; endemic): A rare, secretive and shy species that is one of the hardest Australian species to see although it can be heard singing fairly easily. It is found in dense coastal heath; the populations found formerly in the Victorian mallee are now apparently extinct although this species is supposed to still occur in mallee at Billiat Conservation Park in SA. Undoubtedly the best place to see and hear this bird is Two Peoples Bay (8.20) in the heathland around Little Beach car-park. They sing regularly here in calm weather and can sometimes be seen perched on top of a bush whilst doing so. This is probably the best way of seeing one as they are almost impossible to sneak up on. Alternatively, many people just bump into one whilst they are birding along the heathland tracks, but be prepared to put plenty of time in looking for them. In WA they also occur inland at Stirling Ranges NP (8.22) where they have been seen at Bluff Knoll (although this was largely burned out when we visited in 1991) and at Mount Trio (about 150 m to the west of the car-park). We failed to hear them at either place. The song is very distinctive, rather an unpleasant grating noise that is difficult to pin down. Each population seems to have quite a different song repertoire but all are readily identified as Western Whipbird. In SA, Innes NP (9.4) and Lincoln NP (9.8) are good and the latter is where we finally saw this species; one bird which was singing in the late evening and strongly again next morning. We saw it as it paused on the side of a track when it was moving between song posts.

Chiming Wedgebill *P. occidentalis* (Inland western Australia; endemic): A locally common bird of dense scrubs in the western half of the country. Easily the best area to find this species is north-western WA; the Peron Peninsula Thick-billed Grasswren site (8.16) is excellent and also Cape Range NP (8.13). It can be seen much further west however in NT where we recorded it at the Erldunda Banded Whiteface site (7.32) and also the ridge 6 km north of the SA border (7.34).

Chirruping Wedgebill *P. cristatus* (Inland eastern Australia; endemic): This species likes similar habitats to the one above but tends to form larger flocks in the eastern inland. One excellent place to find it is the Chestnut-breasted Whiteface site (9.14) on the Strzelecki Track and also the roadside scrub 7 km south of Lyndhurst. Other areas you could find it include Pyampa Station (4.23), the Tibooburra region, and the area of scrub around the Cariewerloo Homestead turn-off 8 km north of Port Augusta on the Woomera Road. In addition, we saw a large flock between Quilpie and Windorah (6.12).

Spotted Quail-Thrush *Cinclosoma punctatum* (South-eastern Australia and TAS; endemic): A rather local species that unlike the other quail-thrushes is found in coastal and highland forests. It favours drier forests that have plenty of fallen leaf litter and like the other quail-thrushes, it often flushes up into trees when disturbed but otherwise feeds on the ground. The key to finding it is to listen carefully for the high pitched almost inaudible 'seep'. The best area to visit for this species is Namadgi NP (5.6), especially the trail to Nursery Swamp and also around Orroral campground. Also in the ACT, this species is fairly common along the Camelback Fire Trail at Tidbinbilla (5.4b), in the dry forest about 90 minutes walk from the car-park. Dharug NP (4.10) is another good locality; try the dry woodland along the Old North Road. In TAS, probably the best locality is the walk between Wineglass Bay and Hazards Lagoon in Freycinet NP (3.5). Bellbird Grove near Mount Glorious (6.5) in QLD is also a good site.

Chestnut Quail-Thrush *C. castanotus* (Southern Australia; endemic): A bird mainly found in mallee habitats where it is quite common and again it is best located by listening for the high pitched calls. Found at all the Victorian mallee sites, the best area is probably along the start of the Lowan Track at Wyperfield NP (2.13). Also good is Round Hill Nature Reserve (4.20) and we saw this species in coastal heathland at Lincoln NP (9.8).

Chestnut-breasted Quail-Thrush *C. castaneothorax* (Inland eastern and western Australia; endemic): A bird of open mulga scrubs that has two widely separated races. The western race, *marginatum*, is most easily found at Mount Magnet golf course (8.17) or the surrounding area, whilst the best area for the eastern race, *castaneothorax*, is around Quilpie and Eulo Bore (6.14). Look for them as they fly across the road in front of the car.

Cinnamon Quail-Thrush *C. cinnamomeum* (Inland central Australia; endemic): A fairly common bird of dry open areas of the central continent. Easily found whilst driving along the southern Strzelecki Track (9.13) and the Birdsville Track (9.15), this species is also numerous at the Chestnut-breasted Whiteface site (9.14). In NT, this species nests at the Banded Whiteface site north of Erldunda (7.32).

Nullarbor Quail-Thrush *C. (cinnamomeum) alisteri* (Nullarbor Plain; endemic): This quail-thrush is generally uncommon on the Nullarbor Plain although it is quite numerous around the Nullarbor Roadhouse (9.18). The key to finding them is to listen for the high pitched calls and walk quickly towards them, scanning the ground well ahead of you. You should see birds moving between clumps of vegetation. Alternatively, find a place where you can easily watch a section of track and wait for the birds to cross it or feed along it.

White-winged Chough *Corcorax melanorhamphos* (South-eastern Australia; endemic): A common bird of drier forests and woodlands in the south-east, often in parties feeding along roadsides, for example it is regular along the Glen Davis road (4.12). This species is common in the ACT at Campbell Park (5.3) or around the koala enclosure car-park at Tidbinbilla (5.4a). They always nest on ANU campus behind the John Curtin School of Medical Research.

Apostlebird *Struthidea cinerea* (Arid eastern Australia; endemic): A common bird of the arid interior that occurs in small inquisitive parties and is readily seen on outback drives. Groups regularly come to drink at Eulo Bore (6.14).

Willie-wagtail *Rhipidura leucophrys* (New Guinea; throughout continental Australia): A very common widespread species in all except dense forests. Often tame and apparently fearless, often mobbing raptors and even snakes.

Northern Fantail *R. rufiventris* (Australasia; tropical northern Australia): Usually found quietly sitting in the mid-canopy of rainforest or monsoon forest, this is an easy species to overlook but is in fact quite common. Fairly common along Portland Road at Iron Range NP (6.45), other places we recorded it include Mitchell Falls (8.5b), Dunham River Bridge near Kununurra (8.3), Stag Creek (7.19), and Howard Springs (7.6).

Mangrove Fantail *R. phasiana* (New Guinea; northern and western Australia): A fairly common bird of mangroves in the north-west of WA, this species is rare in the Top End and Gulf regions. The best places to find it are the Lagoon at Denham on the Peron Peninsula (8.16), New Beach (8.15), Point Samson (8.11), and Derby (8.8) mangroves. It is a very easy species to attract by pishing. Further east, this species occurs in the mangroves along Cambridge Gulf west of Wyndham.

Grey Fantail *R. fuliginosa* (Australasia and New Caledonia; throughout Australia and TAS): A very common widespread species in almost any habitat and one of the most responsive to pishing. The inland race, *albicauda*, has an attractive white tail and is rather rare although it is found at Kunoth Well (7.28).

Rufous Fantail *R. rufifrons* (New Guinea, Indonesia and Pacific; northern and eastern Australia): A delightful bird of dense undergrowth in wet woodland, this species is readily attracted by pishing but remains rather shy. It is a breeding migrant in the south-east, arriving in November and leaving in March. During this period it is fairly common in coastal temperate rainforests (*e.g.* Kioloa Rest area (4.5) and surrounds) and in wet gullies in the mountains (*e.g.* Lyrebird and Camelback Fire Trails at Tidbinbilla (5.4)). Further north it is fairly common at Lamington NP (6.7), around Cairns, and on the Atherton Tablelands (6E).

Black-winged Monarch *Monarcha frater* (New Guinea; Cape York Peninsula): A rather uncommon breeding migrant to the north-east of QLD, this species can be found fairly easily along the roadside rainforest edges at Iron Range NP (6.45) during the summer months.

Black-faced Monarch *M. melanopsis* (New Guinea; coastal eastern Australia): This species is resident in north-east QLD but is a breeding migrant from September to March in coastal areas of the south-east. It can be found quite easily in coastal forests of the southern NSW coast at this time of year; Kioloa Rest area (4.5), Nadgee NP (4.6), Barren Grounds (4.1); Royal NP (4.7) *etc.* Further north, this species is fairly common at Lamington NP (6.7).

White-eared Monarch *M. leucotis* (Coastal north-east Australia; endemic): Rather an uncommon bird of coastal rainforests that is most easily found by learning its call since it is mainly a canopy species. It is a summer migrant to the south of its range. The best places to find it are Kingfisher Park (6.40), at the Blue-faced Parrot-Finch Gully (6.40), and along Portland Road in Iron Range NP (6.45). Further south the only place where we saw this species was at Lamington NP (6.7), at the button-quail site along Duck Creek Road. It also regular at Cape Tribulation NP.

PASSERINES

Spectacled Monarch *M. trivirgatus* (New Guinea and Indonesia; northern and eastern Australia): Common in thick foliage of rainforests, usually in the mid canopy. This species is a migrant in the southern part of its range where it is common from October to April in places like Lamington NP (6.7) (the Duck Creek Road button-quail site), and Mount Glorious (6.5). In the north it is common in rainforest sites around Cairns, the Atherton Tablelands (6E), and at Iron Range NP (6.45).

Frilled Monarch *Arses telescopthalmus* (New Guinea; Cape York Peninsula): This species is fairly common at Iron Range NP (6.45) where it is most easily found if you learn the call. It tends to creep nuthatch like around tree trunks in the mid canopy. The favoured areas are where the dry forest meets the rainforest.

Pied Monarch *A. kaupi* (Atherton area; endemic to QLD): A fairly common monarch of rainforests in the Atherton region, often being found near water and behaving much like the Frilled Monarch. Good places to find it are Kingfisher Park (6.40) itself, the Blue-faced Parrot-Finch site on Mount Lewis (6.40), the Cathedral Fig Tree (6.35), and Mount Spec NP (6.21).

Leaden Flycatcher *Myiagra rubecula* (New Guinea; northern and eastern Australia): Generally the commonest *Myiagra* flycatcher in Australia and like others of the genus easily tracked down once the characteristic 'schreep' call is learned. This species is found in open forests and woodlands near water in the north. It is a common breeding migrant in the south-east arriving in September and leaving in March. It can be easily found, for example in Campbell Park (5.3) or Royal NP (4.7). Further north, this species is a common resident around Cairns and Kakadu NP (7C).

Broad-billed Flycatcher *M. ruficollis* (Wallacea; tropical northern Australia): A fairly common bird in the tropical north that is mainly found in mangroves but also monsoon forest. We found it to be fairly common in the rainforest at Iron Range NP (6.45) and at Fogg Dam (7.11). This species can be found most easily in mangroves such as at Karumba (6.47), Adelaide River (7.12), Middle Arm (7.5), Barred Creek north of Broome, and Derby boat ramp (8.8).

Satin Flycatcher *M. cyanoleuca* (New Guinea; eastern Australia and TAS): A breeding migrant from September to March from New Guinea to the south-east of Australia and TAS with a few birds over wintering in northern Australia. This is rather a scarce species and much less common than Leaden Flycatcher. The exception however is TAS, the breeding stronghold for Satin Flycatchers, where it is fairly common but Leaden Flycatchers are rare. Good places to find it on TAS during the summer months are Mount Wellington (3.2), Bruny Island (3.1) (the Adventure Bay to Lunawanna Road), and Maria Island (3.4). On the mainland it is found in tall wet sclerophyll forests in the ranges of eastern Australia and good places to find it are Barrington Tops (4.13), Brisbane Ranges (2.7), Ferntree Gully NP (2.2), and especially the Brindabella Ranges in the ACT where this species nests in the koala enclosure at Tidbinbilla (5.4a).

Restless Flycatcher *M. inquieta* (New Guinea; northern, eastern and southern Australia): This is a common flycatcher of open forests and woodlands, very often near water, is especially common in the Top End. There should be little difficulty finding this species at many sites because of its habit of calling loudly with a rasping 'schezzp.' The northern race, *nana*, has sometimes been split in the past as the Paperbark Flycatcher.

Shining Flycatcher *M. alecto* (New Guinea and Indonesia; tropical northern Australia): A fairly common flycatcher in the Top End that is much less common in QLD. This species is always found close to water, usually low down in riverside vegetation or mangroves. Readily found along the Claudie River tributaries at Iron Range NP (6.45) and in the Top End at places like Jim Jim Creek and the Yellow Waters cruise (7.16), Adelaide River (7.12), Howard Springs (7.6), and Middle Arm (7.5).

Yellow-breasted Boatbill *Machaerirhynchus flaviventer* (New Guinea; north-east QLD): A rather uncommon flycatcher of the Cairns region and Cape York Peninsula. Usually found in the canopy of rainforest, the key to locating this species is to learn the distinctive song. It is fairly common at Iron Range NP (6.45) and further south probably the best places to try are Kingfisher Park (6.40), the Mount Lewis Blue-faced Parrot-Finch gully (6.40), and the Licuala State Forest walking track at Mission Beach (6.23).

Spangled Drongo *Dicrurus bracteatus* (New Guinea and Indonesia; northern and eastern Australia): Mainly a breeding migrant to Australia, arriving in September and leaving in April, this is a fairly common bird of rainforest edges from coastal northern NSW to the Kimberleys. Regularly found along Duck Creek road and the road leading to O'Reilly's at Lamington NP (6.7), along the Mount Glorious road (6.5), and around Cairns and Darwin in the north.

Torresian Crow *Corvus orru* (New Guinea and Indonesia; mostly northern and western Australia): The Australian corvids are not a very inspiring group of birds and the safest way to identify them is to see each one in a zone where it does not overlap with any of the other corvids. In zones of overlap, calls are definitely the best means of identification, although behaviour can help, as in this species, which repeatedly shuffles its wings but does not raise them whilst calling. In addition this species has a bluish cast to the plumage. All the Australian corvids are common and this is the only one found in coastal eastern QLD, the Kimberley region and the Top End.

Little Crow *C. bennetti* (Arid central and western Australia; endemic): The common corvid of the arid outback that often scavenges around human habitation along the Birdsville (9.15) and Strzelecki Tracks (9.13). In these areas it overlaps only with Australian Raven, however Little Crow is much smaller with a very different call.

Australian Raven *C. coronoides* (Eastern and south-western Australia; endemic): Common over a huge area, this is the largest Australian corvid with an amazing call, resembling a baby bawling its eyes out. It is the only corvid found in the extreme south-west and also around suburban Canberra.

Little Raven *C. mellori* (South-eastern Australia; endemic): Found only in the southern parts of SA and NSW, and throughout VIC, this species overlaps everywhere with Australian Raven except in the high mountains of the south-east. It is the only corvid in the alpine woodlands of Mount Kosciusko NP south of the ACT, and in the Brindabellas (5.7) it is found in flocks in all except the summer months. This species is also common in the farmland around Lake Bathurst (4.3b).

Forest Raven *C. tasmanicus* (Coastal VIC and TAS; endemic): This corvid is the only one found on TAS where it is common throughout. It is scarce along the southern Victorian coast but can be found around Portland Harbour and on Wilson's Promontory.

Relict Raven *C. (tasmanicus) boreus* (New England Tablelands; endemic to NSW): Often regarded as an isolated race of Forest Raven, this bird is found in forested areas around Armidale, particularly near Ebor. It is best identified by call as both Australian Raven and Torresian Crow also occur there and it is usually found feeding under the forest canopy. Drive slowly from Armidale eastwards on highway 78 carefully checking any corvids you find between here and Ebor. Reputedly this is also the commonest corvid around Coffs Harbour (4.14).

Trumpet Manucode *Manucodia keraudrenii* (New Guinea; Cape York Peninsula): This species is fairly common inside the rainforest at Iron Range NP (6.45) where it is usually found at fruiting trees, sometimes in groups. It is most readily tracked down by hearing the remarkable loud trumpeting call.

Magnificent Riflebird *Ptiloris magnificus* (New Guinea; Cape York Peninsula): A common species at Iron Range NP (6.45). Adult males are elusive, although the loud wolf whistle call is frequently heard, and the loud rustling noise of their wings in flight often draws attention to them.

Victoria's Riflebird *P. victoriae* (Atherton area; endemic to QLD): This species is fairly common in rainforests on the Atherton Tablelands. Like the other riflebirds this species can often be located by hearing the birds ripping through dead foliage, especially dry staghorn ferns, high in the trees. Readily found at The Crater NP (6.32) although by far the easiest place to see this species is at the Ivy Cottage Tea Gardens at Mount Spec NP (6.21) where tame birds will come to your table.

Paradise Riflebird *P. paradiseus* (Eastern Australia; endemic): The best place to find this species is certainly Lamington NP (6.7) where birds can be seen on all the trails from O'Reilly's especially the Python Rock Trail and also at the button-quail site on Duck Creek Road. Other good places to find this bird are Mount Glorious (6.5), the Scenic Circuit at Bunya Mountains NP (6.10) and in northern NSW, at Barrington Tops (4.13).

White-breasted Woodswallow *Artamus leucorynchus* (Asia, Australasia and Pacific; northern and eastern Australia): Fairly common in the coastal north and northern QLD, this species is usually found near water. It is a breeding migrant to the south of its range. As with all the woodswallows, the easiest way to locate them is to see birds perched on roadside wires whilst driving between sites.

Masked Woodswallow *A. personatus* (Throughout continental Australia; endemic but has occurred as a vagrant in New Zealand): A very widespread woodswallow that is highly nomadic, tending to occur in the north during the winter and the south in summer. It is found in arid open forests and woodlands in all except the extreme south-west and Cape York Peninsula. Good places to regularly find this species include the Victorian mallee sites (2.12, 2.13, 2.14), Round Hill Nature Reserve (4.20), and around Alice Springs.

White-browed Woodswallow *A. superciliosus* (Throughout Australia; endemic but has occurred as a vagrant in New Zealand): A generally fairly common or locally abundant woodswallow of open forests and woodlands. It is most frequently encountered in the south-east of Australia where large numbers breed in the spring months. Good places to find it include Chiltern State Forest (2C), the Victorian mallee sites (2.12, 2.13, 2.14), and Round Hill Nature Reserve (4.20).

Black-faced Woodswallow *A. cinereus* (Lesser Sundas; throughout continental Australia): This is probably the commonest woodswallow of the open outback areas in Australia. It is usually seen perched along roadside telegraph wires.

Dusky Woodswallow *A. cyanopterus* (South-western and eastern Australia and TAS; endemic): This is the commonest woodswallow in the wetter areas of the south-east of Australia and in TAS during the summer months where it is a breeding migrant. It will be found in all the open forests and woodlands in this region at this time, for example at Campbell Park (5.3) in the ACT and throughout VIC. During the winter months this species largely retreats to eastern QLD.

Little Woodswallow *A. minor* (Northern Australia; endemic): This is probably the least common of the woodswallows. Found mainly in the north of the continent it can be found in association with rocky gorges in many areas. For example, Mica Creek near Mount Isa (6.49), Boroloola (7.3), Waterfall Creek (7.18), Mitchell Falls (8.5b), and Simpson's Gap (7.29). It does also occur in more open areas however, for example we saw it at Eulo Bore (6.14).

Black-backed Butcherbird *Cracticus mentalis* (New Guinea; Cape York Peninsula): Confined to the dry areas of the southern Peninsula, the only readily accessible place to see this species is along the Peninsula Developmental Road north of Laura. They are reasonably common along this road; we saw three plus a pair at Windmill Creek (6.44) itself. Note that Pied Butcherbirds are equally numerous in this region too.

Grey Butcherbird *C. torquatus* (Southern Australia, the Kimberleys and TAS; endemic): This is a very widespread species found in all open forests from wet sclerophyll forests and rainforest margins to dry mallee regions. It is nowhere very numerous but can be seen in many localities such as Dennes Point on Bruny Island (3.1) in TAS, the Victorian mallee sites (2.12, 2.13, 2.14), the Kimberleys where an isolated race, *argentus*, is found. The birds on the Ormiston Gorge Pound walk (7.31) in the Macdonnell Ranges west of Alice are distinctly small and pale.

Pied Butcherbird *C. nigrogularis* (Throughout continental Australia except south-east and south-west; endemic): This is the commonest butcherbird in Australia being found especially in open arid areas of the northern outback but much less common in the south-east. Tame birds are found around some tourist sites, such as Ayers Rock (7.33) and this species is common along the Stuart Highway and as noted above it occurs alongside Black-backed Butcherbird on Cape York Peninsula.

Black Butcherbird *C. quoyi* (New Guinea; tropical northern Australia): This is quite a shy bird most easily located from its loud calls and found in rainforests and vegetation near watercourses, even mangroves in the tropical north. It is reasonably plentiful in north-eastern QLD; Cairns Botanic Gardens (6.26) is a good site as is Iron Range NP (6.45). In NT this species can be found at Middle Arm (7.5), Buffalo Creek (7.9) and East Point Recreational Reserve (7.10).

Australian Magpie *Gymnorhina tibicen* (New Guinea; throughout Australia and TAS): Very common and widespread in all areas with trees. Several well marked races are found around the country, although all intergrade in zones of overlap. Tame birds are often found around picnic sites and in the south-east this species is often a nuisance in the spring, dive bombing people and even drawing blood on anyone in the vicinity of their nests.

Pied Currawong *Strepera graculina* (Eastern Australia; endemic): A common bird of woodlands in the eastern counties, also in mountain forests. The calls of this species vary with locality and it is also an altitudinal migrant. Common in the Brindabellas during the summer and found in suburban Canberra during the winter.

Black Currawong *S. fuliginosa* (Bass Strait Islands; endemic to TAS): Abundant at Cradle Mountain NP (3.7) and Lake St Clair (3.9) but much less common in the south-east of TAS, although it does occur on Mount Wellington (3.2).

Grey Currawong *S. versicolor* (Southern Australia and TAS; endemic): Found in forests, coastal heathlands and mallee areas this is a locally distributed currawong with several well marked races. The TAS race, *arguta*, is fairly common at Maria Island NP (3.4) whilst the mallee race, *melanoptera*, is found at the Victorian mallee sites (2.12, 2.13, 2.14) and Lincoln NP (9.8) in SA. Both races are sometimes split as Clinking Currawong and Brown Currawong respectively. In the south-east, Mount Majura in the ACT is an excellent place to find this species whilst in WA Dryandra State Forest (8.19) is a good site.

Magpie-Lark *Grallina cyanoleuca* (New Guinea and Lesser Sundas; throughout continental Australia): Very common and widespread in all wooded areas except dense forests; especially common near habitation, even in the centre of big cities.

Olive-backed Oriole *Oriolus sagittatus* (New Guinea and Lesser Sundas; northern and eastern Australia): A fairly common bird of wooded areas, even rainforests and mallee. This species is a breeding migrant to the southern part of its range arriving in August and leaving in April. Common at this time of year at Campbell Park (5.3) in the ACT, Chiltern State Forest (2C) *etc*. Further north this species is fairly common in rainforest around Brisbane, the Atherton Tablelands (6E), Waterfall Creek (7.18), and Howards Springs (7.6).

Yellow Oriole *O. flavocinctus* (New Guinea and Lesser Sundas; tropical northern Australia): Fairly common in rainforests of the tropical north, this species is most easily found by call as it is a canopy dweller. Best places to find it include Mount Whitfield Environmental Park (6.27), the Botanic Gardens (6.26) at Cairns, Iron Range NP (6.45), Howard Springs (7.6), Katherine Gorge NP (7.22), and Mitchell Falls (8.5b).

Figbird *Sphecotheres viridis* (New Guinea; northern and eastern Australia): A common species in the east and tropical north which is common in suburban habitats in many towns and cities in trees and small parks.

Ground Cuckoo-Shrike *Coracina maxima* (Arid continental Australia; endemic): An uncommon bird of open arid areas usually with scattered trees. The best way to find this bird is from the car on long outback drives. It is readily identifiable by its gleaming white rump as it flies away. Roads we recorded it on include; between Charleville and Windorah, between Eulo Bore (6.14) and Lake Bindegolly (6.13) in QLD, between Coober Pedy and Kingoonya in SA, between Barkly Homestead and Cape Crawford (7.1), between Katherine and Victoria River Roadhouse (7.24), and around Kunoth Well (7.28) in the NT.

Black-faced Cuckoo-Shrike *C. novaehollandiae* (New Guinea and Wallacea; throughout Australia and TAS): A very common widespread bird in woodlands, even suburban parks.

Barred Cuckoo-Shrike *C. lineata* (New Guinea; eastern Australia): This is rather an uncommon cuckoo-shrike of eastern forests from northern NSW to Cape York. It is a nomadic species, moving to areas with good fruiting trees. It is easily overlooked because it feeds almost exclusively in the canopy and is probably most easily located by watching a fruiting tree. Areas it is reasonably regular include; the Mount Glorious road (6.5), Eungella NP (6.17) (especially around the campground), Mount Spec NP (6.21), the entrance road at The Crater NP (6.32), and Kingfisher Park (6.40). It is rare in the southern part of its range.

White-bellied Cuckoo-Shrike *C. papuensis* (New Guinea and Indonesia; northern and eastern Australia): A very common bird in the tropical north in woodland areas but much rarer in the southern part of its range.

Cicadabird *C. tenuirostris* (New Guinea, Wallacea and the Pacific; northern and eastern Australia): A canopy forest species that is best located by voice which varies regionally but is always rather an insect-like buzz. It is generally rather an uncommon bird and occurs as a breeding summer migrant to the south-east where it is reasonably common at Glen Davis (4.12), the Fishing Gap Trail at Tidbinbilla (5.4d), and other areas of wet sclerophyll forest in the Brindabellas (5.7). In the north, this species is quite common at Kingfisher Park (6.40) and Tinaroo Creek Road (6.37) in the Atherton Tablelands and in the NT try Buffalo Creek (7.9) car-park and Howard Springs (7.6). The northern and eastern races may be split in the near future.

White-winged Triller *Lalage tricolor* (New Guinea; throughout continental Australia): A common species in Australia, usually found near water in the tropical north but breeds in open woodlands in the south-eastern states where it is a breeding summer migrant. Rather nomadic and not always found in the same localities each year, this species is nevertheless not difficult to find; it breeds at Glen Davis (4.12) and at Campbell Park (5.3) for example.

Varied Triller *L. leucomela* (New Guinea; northern and eastern Australia): Common in the tropical north in woodland along watercourses and mangroves, but rather uncommon in the south of its range where it is a breeding migrant although it is regular at Lamington NP (6.7) during the spring and summer around O'Reilly's and Duck Creek Road. In the north good places to find it include the Cairns and Atherton (6E) areas, Adelaide River (7.12), Howard Springs (7.6), and Holmes Jungle Swamp (7.7).

Bassian Ground-Thrush *Zoothera lunulata* (New Guinea; eastern Australia): A reasonably common bird of the leaf litter in wet forest and rainforests. Tends to be tamer than most *Zoothera* and easily found by listening for its high pitched 'seep' calls. Mount Wellington (3.2) in TAS, the Lyrebird Trail at Tidbinbilla (5.4c), and Lamington NP (6.7) are all excellent places to find this bird. The race found in the Atherton Tablelands, *cuneata*, is fairly common at Mount Spec NP (6.21) along the rainforest walking trails.

Russet-tailed Ground-Thrush *Z. heinei* (Eastern Australia; endemic): Found in the mountainous sub-tropical rainforests around Brisbane, this species overlaps in range with the previous one but tends to occur at slightly lower altitudes although there is much overlap. It is most safely identified by hearing it sing; a distinctive two note whistle. Both species are found around O'Reilly's in Lamington NP (6.7), especially along the entrance roadsides in the rainforest patches in the early morning and at dusk. Bassian is the commoner species here but this one may be found in the rainforest along Duck Creek Road and on the Blue Pool Trail. The best site is probably the rainforest trail at Mount Glorious (6.5) where both species are found easily, this one being the commoner of the two.

Metallic Starling *Aplonis metallica* (New Guinea and Indonesia; north-eastern QLD): This is a breeding migrant to Australia, arriving in August, departing in March. It is common only in north QLD in the coastal lowlands; Cairns Botanic Gardens (6.26) is a good site or even along the Esplanade (6.24). Abundant at Iron Range NP (6.45) where there is a large breeding colony a short way along the Coen Road. Be careful not to stand underneath a colony as you can become infested with extremely painful burrowing mites.

White-backed Swallow *Cheramoeca leucosternus* (Arid central Australia; endemic): A widespread but not uncommon swallow of the arid interior and drier coastal regions of Australia. This species will be seen on long outback drives, in mallee areas, and other arid birding localities. A particularly good area to find this species is the road between Erldunda and Ayers Rock where it is common and nests in all the sandy roadside cuttings.

Welcome Swallow *Hirundo neoxena* (Southern Australia and TAS; endemic): Very common in the southern half of the country and the east in all except the arid inland.

Appropriately, this is probably the first Australian bird you will see if you land at Sydney airport.

Barn Swallow *H. rustica* (Cosmopolitan; tropical northern Australia): A regular migrant to the tropical north during the Austral summer and sometimes recorded in large flocks. The most regular areas are Broome Bird Observatory (8.9), Derby (8.8), Darwin, and Innisfail in north-east QLD.

Tree Martin *H. nigricans* (New Guinea and Lesser Sundas; throughout Australia and TAS): A common breeding migrant to the whole of southern Australia and TAS with a permanent presence in the north although many birds leave Australia for the winter months. Generally found nesting near water where birds usually nest in tall gum trees, feeding birds are often seen flying low over the canopy of eucalyptus woodlands.

Fairy Martin *H. ariel* (New Guinea and Lesser Sundas; throughout continental Australia): This is a common bird throughout Australia except on the Cape York Peninsula. It is a summer breeding migrant only to the south-eastern states where it is very common. This species is often found nesting under bridges over rivers. Often forms large autumn flocks with the previous species.

Yellow White-eye *Zosterops luteus* (Coastal northern Australia; endemic): A common mangrove inhabitant of the tropical north except in north-east QLD. Easily found and pished out at many sites including Karumba (6.47), Derby boat ramp (8.8), Point Samson (8.11), Carnarvon fishing harbour (8.14), New Beach (8.15), and Denham (8.16). Strangely, it does not seem to be very common around Darwin.

Pale White-eye *Z. citrinellus* (Lesser Sundas; islands off Cape York): A common species on wooded islands in Torres Strait and off eastern Cape York. Probably the best chance of seeing this species in Australia is a boat charter to the northern Barrier Reef islands (such as a trip to Raine Island to see Herald Petrel). Some people maintain that the white-eyes on Green Island off Cairns are this species.

Silver-eye *Z. lateralis* (Australasia and Pacific; southern, eastern and western Australia and TAS): An abundant white-eye with several well marked races. This species is especially common in the south-east in all coastal and sub-coastal localities during the winter months when a very large proportion of the Tasmanian population migrates to the mainland. This species is very common on the southern Barrier Reef Islands.

Zitting Cisticola *Cisticola juncidis* (Eurasia; north-eastern Australia): This is a very patchily distributed species in northern Australia, found in grasslands of coastal plains and nearby sedge areas. The easiest areas to find this bird are the tall grassland just as you enter Karumba (6.47) on the Matilda Highway and Knuckey's Lagoon (7.8) in Darwin. We also recorded it in the tall sedgeland behind the mangroves at the western end of Karumba.

Golden-headed Cisticola *C. exilis* (Asia; sub-coastal northern and eastern Australia): A common bird of grasslands, swamps and even roadside verges throughout coastal regions except the south-western region. Readily found at many sites, for example Jerrabomberra Wetlands (5.2) in the ACT.

Australian Reed Warbler *Acrocephalus australis* (Throughout Australia and TAS; endemic): This is a very common bird of reedbeds throughout the country although it is only a breeding migrant to the southern half of the country. Readily found at many sites during the spring when it is singing, including Avalon Swamp (4.18d), Cronulla Swamp (4.8), Jerrabomberra Wetlands (5.2), and ANU Campus.

Tawny Grassbird *Megalurus timoriensis* (Australasia and Philippines; northern and eastern Australia): A rather uncommon bird of wet grasslands and cumbungi swamps of the north and east. This is a very inquisitive species that will frequently perch on top of reeds to observe an intruder but is otherwise highly skulking in nature. Readily found in the Top End, for example at Knuckey's Lagoon (7.8), Holmes Jungle Swamp (7.7), Ludmilla Creek in East Point Recreational Reserve (7.10), and Fogg Dam (7.11). Around Brisbane, Lake Samsonvale (6.4) is an excellent site.

Little Grassbird *M. gramineus* (New Guinea; eastern and south-western Australia and TAS): A fairly common bird of reedbeds and dense swamps of the southern half of the continent. It is generally rather skulking but can be readily attracted by imitating its rather mournful downward whistles. Good places to find it include Lake Bindegolly (6.13); Sherwood Forest Park in Brisbane; Cronulla Swamp (4.8), Jerrabomberra Wetlands (5.2) (especially during the summer when they feed on the dry muddy edges), Leeton Swamp (4.17), Avalon Swamp (4.18d), and Herdsman Lake in WA.

Brown Songlark *Cincloramphus cruralis* (Continental Australia except tropical north; endemic): A local and uncommon bird of the whole of the southern half of the continent that is nomadic, but usually found in the southern part of its range from July to March. It is found in open grasslands and farmlands and good areas to find it include the pastures around Deniliquin (4.18) (ask Phil Maher), the plains west of Windorah, Lake Bathurst (4.3b), the Nullarbor Quail-Thrush site (9.18), and even the southern section of the Birdsville Track (9.15). Fortunately this species often perches prominently on roadside fence posts making it easy to locate.

Rufous Songlark *C. mathewsi* (Throughout continental Australia; endemic): Found in grassy woodlands throughout the continent, this is commoner than the previous species. It is a breeding summer visitor to the south-east of the continent where it is readily found during the spring months when singing loudly from prominent perches. At other times this species tends to feed inconspicuously on the forest floor. Excellent sites to find this bird in spring are Chiltern State Forest (2C), Campbell Park (5.3), and Gulpa State Forest (4.18b). It is even found in dry inland areas following heavy rainfalls, for example this species was common around Alice Springs in November 1993.

Spinifexbird *Eremiornis carteri* (Arid central Australia; endemic): A fairly common bird throughout the central part of Australia, this can be an infuriatingly skulking bird of spinifex grass but can usually be enticed into view to scold someone who is pishing loudly. It is found in all types of spinifex, even small scattered clumps and will be seen at several sites whilst searching for other spinifex specialities. It is not difficult to find at Lady Loretta Mine (6.50), Ellery Creek Big Hole (7.30), Ormiston Gorge Pound walk (7.31), and Tennant Creek (7.26).

Australasian Bushlark *Mirafra javanica* (Asia and Australasia; northern and eastern Australia): Apparently nomadic in Australia, this species is locally common in open grassland areas. It is usually reasonably common in the Deniliquin area (4.18) during the summer and it is very common at Townsville Common Environmental Park (6.20). Other areas we found this species to be plentiful included Sturt NP in north-west NSW and around the edge of Knuckey's Lagoon (7.8) in Darwin.

Painted Firetail *Emblema pictum* (Arid central Australia; endemic): This species is found on rocky spinifex covered ridges of the arid interior. It is most easily seen drinking at pools usually mid-morning and excellent places to find it include Mica Creek near Mount Isa (6.49), Tennant Creek (7.26), Simpson's Gap (7.29) (early morning around the pool before the tourists arrive), Ormiston Gorge Pound walk (7.31), Cape Range NP (8.13),

China Wall near Halls Creek (8.6), and if driving the Canning Stock Route (8.7) then this species is abundant at the Bredon Hills.

Beautiful Firetail *Stagonopleura bella* (South-eastern Australia and TAS; endemic): The stronghold for this species is undoubtedly TAS where this is a reasonably common species in dense vegetation of heaths and even woodlands. It is a shy bird, easily overlooked as it skulks inside thick bushes and views are best obtained by following up flying birds quickly. Good places to find it include the heathland at Strahan (3.8) and the Adventure Bay to Lunawanna Road on Bruny Island (3.1). On the mainland the best site is the heathland at Barren Grounds (4.1), particularly along the Griffith Trail. This species is also frequently seen by walking upstream along the creek at Triabunna Falls (4.2b) in Morton NP.

Red-eared Firetail *S. oculata* (South-west Australia; endemic to WA): Essentially the western counterpart of the above species being found in similar coastal heathlands. It should be seen whilst searching the heathland for the specialities at Two Peoples Bay (8.20), particularly above Little Beach car-park. We also found this species around the car-park at Porongurup NP (8.21) and it has been recorded in the woodland 5 km west of Boxwood Hill on the north side of the South Coast Highway and in the heathland along Cape Naturaliste (8.24).

Diamond Firetail *S. guttata* (Eastern Australia; endemic): A rather uncommon but patchily distributed bird of open eucalyptus forests, there are fortunately several superb places to find this bird. It is always to be found along the Glen Davis road (4.12), Campbell Park (5.3), Back Yamma State Forest (4.19), You Yangs (2.6), and Girraween NP (6.8). The furthest west we recorded this species was Lincoln NP (9.8) in SA.

Red-browed Firetail *Neochmia temporalis* (Eastern Australia; endemic): The commonest grass-finch in eastern Australia, this species is found in woodland edges, around campsites, picnic areas, even gardens *etc*. The race at Iron Range NP (6.45) is distinctly brighter than the one further south.

Crimson Finch *N. phaeton* (New Guinea; tropical northern Australia): This is a very common finch in the Top End and Kimberleys and is found in waterside vegetation. Easily found at many sites for example, Fergusson River (7.20), Adelaide River (7.12), Fogg Dam (7.11), and Kununurra (8.2). In QLD, the Cape York race, *evangeliae* is occasionally seen at Musgrave Station (6.44) whilst the east coast race *iredalei* nests along Swallow Road just past Cairns airport (ask John Crowhurst) and is reasonably common in the cane fields around Horseshoe Lagoon (6.19).

Star Finch *N. ruficauda* (Northern and western Australia; endemic): Fairly common in the Top End, the eastern Australian nominate race is now either very rare or extinct. This species favours vegetation near water. Excellent places to find it are Ivanhoe Road irrigation area and the caravan park at Kununurra (8.2), and Wyndham Caravan Park (8.4). We also recorded it at Victoria River (7.24), opposite the escarpment track.

Plum-headed Finch *N. modesta* (Eastern Australia; endemic): An uncommon grass-finch of grasslands and reedbeds of sub-inland Australia. It is apparently a highly nomadic species; the only reliable place to find it is the Glen Davis road (4.12) where it is usually to be found around the road bridge creek crossings in waterside vegetation. Other sites we recorded this species were Eulo Bore (6.14) and Cumberland Dam (6.46). Girraween NP (6.8) is another good site.

Zebra Finch *Taeniopygia guttata* (Lesser Sundas; arid continental Australia): An abundant bird of the arid outback, always found in the vicinity of water *i.e.* around water bores. Roadside flocks are very often seen from the car.

Double-barred Finch *T. bichenovii* (Northern and eastern Australia; endemic): The northern race, *annulosa*, is very common in the tropical north and may be found at many dry season drinking pools such as Caranbirini Springs (7.3), Cape Crawford (7.2), Fergusson River (7.20), Victoria River (7.24), Kununurra (8.2), Wyndham Caravan Park (8.4), and Howard Springs (7.6). The white rumped race is found throughout the eastern half of the country from about Cumberland Dam (6.46) to VIC. It is generally less common than in the north but can usually be found at Glen Davis (4.12) or in the ACT on Mount Taylor.

Masked Finch *Poephila personata* (Tropical northern Australia; endemic): A fairly common finch in the Top End, readily found at dry season drinking holes such as Wyndham Caravan Park (8.4), Dingo Creek (7.25), Waterfall Creek (7.18), and Chinaman Creek (7.23) near Katherine. The Cape York race, *leucotis*, is easily seen drinking at Windmill Creek near Musgrave Station (6.44).

Long-tailed Finch *P. acuticauda* (Tropical northern Australia; endemic): Generally more common than the above species and found at all the same sites as those mentioned above, except Cape York. Additional sites for this species include Cape Crawford (7.2), Caranbirini Springs (7.3), Fergusson River (7.20), and the Gibb River Road (8.5).

Black-throated Finch *P. cincta* (North-eastern Australia; endemic): This species is rather uncommon and local. It is now very rare in the southern part of its range so you should concentrate on finding this species in north-eastern QLD. The most reliable site is the drinking pool at Pickford Road (6.38) on the Atherton Tablelands. If the pool has dried up, check this area thoroughly as the birds have been seen nearby drinking from a horse trough in an adjacent paddock. The roadside vegetation along the Mount Molloy to Mount Carbine Road (6.42) is also an excellent area to look for this bird and we also found birds nesting in termite mounds at Tinaroo Creek Road (6.37). This species is common at Cumberland Dam (6.46), drinking in the early morning.

Blue-faced Parrot-Finch *Erythrura trichroa* (Wallacea, New Guinea and the Pacific; north-eastern Australia): This is a very local uncommon species in Australia. The best place to find it is Mount Lewis (6.40), either in the gully (late morning best) or around the clearing (dawn best, often with Red-browed Firetails). Birds are present and seen year round although there is sometimes a gap of several months between sightings. This is probably largely related to the skill and patience of the observers looking. Birds tend to fly quickly by calling with a faint 'tsit' and you just have to be lucky to see exactly where they land.

Gouldian Finch *Chloebia gouldiae* (Tropical northern Australia; endemic): A rather scarce, local species that is best found at regular dry season drinking pools. Probably the most reliable of these is Wyndham Caravan Park (8.4), but other good sites include Chinaman Creek (7.23), Fergusson River (7.20), and Dingo Creek (7.25) near Kununurra. Birds are also regularly seen at Cumberland Dam (6.46) in the autumn and sometimes at Caranbirini Springs (7.3). If really struggling, ask the rangers at Katherine Gorge NP about possible access to the private area around Mount Todd where this species is intensively studied.

Yellow-rumped Mannikin *Lonchura flaviprymna* (North-western Australia; endemic): This is generally a scarce bird of tall grasslands and reedbeds in the tropical north-west. Easily the best site is the Ivanhoe irrigation area at Kununurra (8.2). It has also been seen in the reedbeds at the eastern end of Diversion Dam, just west of Kununurra.

Chestnut-breasted Mannikin *L. castaneothorax* (New Guinea; northern and eastern Australia): A fairly common bird in areas of grasslands and wastelands, usually near water. This bird is very common in the Kununurra (8.2) irrigation fields and in northeastern QLD.

Pictorella Mannikin *Heteromunia pectoralis* (Tropical northern Australia; endemic): A generally uncommon grass-finch of the tropical north, found in tall grassland usually near water. Easily the best location to see this bird is Golden Gate Drive at Lake Argyle (8.1) where this species is abundant during the dry season in the tall grass along this track. This bird is also found in small parties along the eastern end of the Gibb River Road (8.5) and is sometimes recorded at the Kununurra irrigation area (8.2), Caranbirini Springs (7.3), and Cumberland Dam (6.46) (best in autumn).

Yellow Wagtail *Motacilla flava* (Palearctic, Asia and Africa; tropical northern Australia): A regular migrant in small numbers to the tropical north during the wet season. This species is recorded annually at Knuckey's Lagoon (7.8) and grassy areas around Darwin, Broome Bird Observatory (8.9), and the turf farms near Cairns (6.29). It could be encountered on short grassland anywhere in the north at this time of year. Three other wagtail species occur as vagrants.

Australasian Pipit *Anthus novaeseelandiae* (Australasia; throughout Australia and TAS): This is a very common bird of grasslands, open plains, coastal dunes and agricultural areas everywhere. It is sometimes regarded as a race of Richard's Pipit *A. richardi*.

Mistletoebird *Dicaeum hirundinaceum* (Indonesian Islands; throughout continental Australia): This is a common, although nomadic, bird throughout Australia. It is found in any type of vegetation that can support mistletoe bushes. Any eucalyptus woodland in the south-east will have this species, although it is a breeding summer migrant to some areas, such as the Uriarra Crossing (5.7) in the ACT where this species is common from November.

Olive-backed Sunbird *Nectarinia jugularis* (Asia; mainly coastal north-eastern Australia): A common bird of vegetation near water, including mangroves, in northern QLD. Always nests near Kingfisher Park (6.40) but readily seen at many sites such as Cairns Botanic Gardens (6.26) and Thomsons Road (6.28).

Appendix 1: Taxonomy of Australian Birds

For various political and scientific reasons the taxonomy of Australia's birds has not yet been fully decided upon. There are a number of controversial splits and lumps and no doubt the application of DNA-DNA hybridisation will further complicate the whole taxonomy issue. Below is a list of those controversial species/subspecies that I prefer to adopt, not all of them are recognised by all the current field guides but they are the ones mostly used by Australian birders. Those changes which differ from the reference works 'Birds of the World, a Check List' by J. F. Clements are marked with an asterisk (*) and from the RAOU's 'The Taxonomy and Species of Australia and its Territories' by L. Christidis and W. Boles (1994) with a dagger (†). Full details of how to see these well marked races are given in the guide as no doubt some will be split in the future.

Royal Penguin *Eudyptes schlegeli* split from **Macaroni Penguin** *E. chrysolophus*†
Australian Darter *Anhinga novaehollandiae* split from **Darter** *A. melanogaster*†
Black-backed Bittern *Ixobrychus novaezelandiae* split from **Little Bittern** *I. minutus*†
Australian Ibis *Threskiornis molucca* split from **Black-headed Ibis** *T. melanocephalus*
Australian Kite *Elanus axillaris* split from **Black-shouldered Kite** *E. caeruleus*†
Buff-breasted Button-Quail *Turnix olivii* split from **Chestnut-backed Button-Quail** *T. castanota*
Australian Bustard *Ardeotis australis* split from **Kori Bustard** *A. kori*
Silver Gull *Larus novaehollandiae* lumped with **Red-billed Gull** *L. scopulinus**
Southern Skua *Catharacta antarctica* split from **Great Skua** *C. skua*†
White-quilled Rock-Pigeon *Petrophassa albipennis* split from **Chestnut-quilled Rock-Pigeon** *P. rufipennis*
Black-banded Fruit-Dove *Ptilinopus alligator* split from **Black-backed Fruit-Dove** *P. cinctus*†
Torresian Imperial-Pigeon *Ducula spilorrhoa* split from **Pied Imperial-Pigeon** *D. bicolor*†
Port Lincoln Ringneck *Barnardius zonarius*, **Mallee Ringneck** *B. barnardi* and **Cloncurry Ringneck** *B. macgillivrayi* all lumped as races of the **Ringneck Parrot** *B. barnardi**
Yellow Rosella *Platycercus flaveolus* lumped as a race of the **Crimson (or Blue-cheeked) Rosella** *P. elegans**
Northern Rosella *Platycercus venustus*, **Pale-headed Rosella** *P. adscitus* and **Eastern Rosella** *P. eximius* all lumped as races of the **Eastern (or White-cheeked) Rosella** *P. eximius*†*
Naretha Bluebonnet *Northiella narethae* lumped as a race of **Bluebonnet** *N. haematogaster*
Long-billed Black-Cockatoo *Calyptorhynchus baudinii* split from **White-tailed Black-Cockatoo** *C. latirostris*
Western Corella *Cacatua pastinator* split from **Little Corella** *C. sanguinea*
Red-collared Lorikeet *Trichoglossus rubritorquis* lumped as a race of **Rainbow Lorikeet** *T. haematodus**
Gould's Bronze-Cuckoo *Chrysococcyx russatus* split from **Little Bronze-Cuckoo** *C. minutillus*
Australian Koel *Eudynamys cyanocephala* split from **Asian Koel** *E. scolopacea*†
Lesser Sooty Owl *Tyto multipunctata* split from **Sooty Owl** *T. tenebricosa*
Tasmanian Masked Owl *Tyto castanops* lumped as a race of **Masked Owl** *T. novaehollandiae**
Australasian Grass Owl *Tyto longimembris* split from **Grass Owl** *T. capensis*†
Australasian Swiftlet *Collocalia terraereginae* split from **White-rumped Swiftlet** *C. spodiopygius*†
Spotted Catbird *Ailuroedus melanotis* split from **Green Catbird** *A. crassirostris*

Western Bowerbird *Chlamydera guttata* split from **Spotted Bowerbird** *C. maculata*
Lovely Fairywren *Malurus amabilis* lumped as a race of **Variegated Fairywren** *M. lamberti*†*
Mallee Emuwren *Stipiturus mallee* split from **Rufous-crowned Emuwren** *S. ruficeps*
Yellow-rumped Pardalote *Pardalotus xanthopygus* lumped as a race of **Spotted Pardalote** *P. punctatus*
Brown Scrubwren *Sericornis humilis* split from **White-browed Scrubwren** *S. frontalis*
Rufous Calamanthus *Calamanthus campestris* split from **Striated Calamanthus** *C. fuliginosus*
Inland Thornbill *Acanthiza apicalis* lumped as a race of **Brown Thornbill** *A. pusilla*†
Varied Honeyeater *Lichenostomus versicolor* split from **Mangrove Honeyeater** *L. fasciogularis*
Yellow-tinted Honeyeater *Lichenostomus flavescens* split from **Fuscous Honeyeater** *L. fuscus*
Golden-backed Honeyeater *Melithreptus laetior* split from **Black-chinned Honeyeater** *M. gularis*†
Helmeted Friarbird *Philemon buceroides* regarded as two races, *yorki* in Queensland and *melvillensis* in Northern Territory*
Black-eared Miner *Manorina melanotis* lumped as a race of **Yellow-throated (White-rumped) Miner** *M. flavigula*†
Little Wattlebird *Anthochaera lunulata* lumped as a race of **Brush Wattlebird** *A. chrysoptera**
Grey-headed Robin *Heteromyias cinereifrons* split from **Ashy Robin** *H. albispecularis*†
Brown-tailed Flycatcher *Microeca tormenti* lumped as a race of **Lemon-bellied Flycatcher** *M. flavigaster*
Brown Whistler *Pachycephala simplex* split from **Grey Whistler** *P. griseiceps*†
Chiming Wedgebill *Psophodes occidentalis* split from **Chirruping Wedgebill** *P. cristatus*
Chestnut-breasted Quail-Thrush *Cinclosoma castaneothorax* split from **Cinnamon Quail-Thrush** *C. cinnamomeum*
Nullarbor Quail-Thrush *Cinclosoma alisteri* lumped as a race of **Cinnamon Quail-Thrush** *C. cinnamomeum*
Mangrove Fantail *Rhipdura phasiana* split from **Grey Fantail** *R. fuliginosa*
Relict Raven *Corvus boreus* lumped as a race of **Forest Raven** *C. tasmanicus**
Paradise Riflebird *Ptiloris paradiseus* split from **Victoria's Riflebird** *P. victoriae*
White's Thrush *Zoothera dauma* split into **Bassian Ground-Thrush** *Z. lunulata* and **Russet-tailed Ground-Thrush** *Z. heinei*
Australian Reed Warbler *Acrocephalus australis* split from **Clamorous Reed Warbler** *A. stentorus*†
Australasian Pipit *Anthus novaeseelandiae* split from **Richard's Pipit** *A. richardi*†

Appendix 2: Vagrants Recorded in Australia

The majority of birds in this list have been recorded on only a few occasions in Australia and the travelling birder therefore has only a very small chance of seeing many of them. Most of the seabirds have been found as beach washed corpses or seen on pelagic trips, many of the waders have recorded in Victoria or South Australia and the majority of the passerines have been seen in the tropical north. Birds only recorded on offshore islands and Territories are not included.

King Penguin *Aptenodytes patagonicus* (Antarctic)
Gentoo Penguin *Pygoscelis papua* (Antarctic)
Adelie Penguin *P. adeliae* (Antarctic)

APPENDICES

Chinstrap Penguin *P. antarctica* (Antarctic)
Rockhopper Penguin *Eudyptes chrysocome* (Sub-Antarctic)
Snares Crested Penguin *E. robustus* (Snares Island)
Erect-crested Penguin *E. sclateri* (Sub-Antarctic New Zealand Islands)
Royal Penguin *E. schlegeli* (Macquarie Island)
Magellanic Penguin *Spheniscus magellanicus* (Southern South America)
Antarctic Petrel *Thalassoica antarctica* (Antarctic)
Snow Petrel *Pagodroma nivea* (Antarctic)
Mottled Petrel *Pterodroma inexpectata* (New Zealand Islands)
Cook's Petrel *P. cooki* (New Zealand Islands)
Juan Fernandez Petrel *P. externa* (Juan Fernandez Islands)
Barau's Petrel *P. baraui* (Mascarene Islands)
Broad-billed Prion *Pachyptila vittata* (New Zealand Islands)
Salvin's Prion *P. salvini* (Indian Ocean Islands)
Fulmar Prion *P. crassirostris* (New Zealand Islands)
Bulwer's Petrel *Bulweria bulwerii* (Tropical Oceans)
Grey Petrel *Procellaria cinerea* (Sub-Antarctic)
Westland Black Petrel *P. westlandica* (South Island of New Zealand)
Pink-footed Shearwater *Puffinus creatopus* (Juan Fernandez Islands)
Great Shearwater *Puffinus gravis* (Atlantic Oceans)
Manx Shearwater *P. puffinus* (Atlantic)
Audubon's Shearwater *P. lherminieri* (Coral Sea)
Leach's Petrel *Oceanodroma leucorhoa* (Atlantic and Pacific Oceans)
Matsudaira's Petrel *O. matsudairae* (Japan)
South Georgian Diving-Petrel *Pelecanoides georgicus* (Sub-Antarctic)
Christmas Island Frigatebird *Fregata andrewsi* (Christmas Island)
Cape Gannet *Sula capensis* (South Africa): One bird has been resident just off Queenscliffe in Victoria for about ten years. Check with the RAOU for any recent reports. Others seen on rocks just off Portland in Victoria.
Spotted Whistling-Duck *Dendrocygna guttata* (New Guinea)
Northern Shoveler *Anas clypeata* (Northern Hemisphere)
Northern Pintail *A. acuta* (Northern Hemisphere)
Yellow Bittern *Ixobrychus sinensis* (Asia)
Papuan Harrier *Circus spilonotus* (New Guinea, Asia)
Red-legged Crake *Rallina fasciata* (Asia)
Corncrake *Crex crex* (Palearctic)
Pheasant-tailed Jacana *Hydrophasianus chirurgus* (Asia)
Pin-tailed Snipe *Gallinago stenura* (Asia)
Hudsonian Godwit *Limosa haemastica* (Nearctic) One has been seen several Austral summers running near Sorell, Tasmania at Midway Point.
American Golden Plover *Pluvialis dominica* (N. America)
Ringed Plover *Charadrius hiaticula* (Palearctic)
Little Ringed Plover *C. dubius* (Palearctic): This species is recorded almost annually, mostly in the vicinity of Darwin.
Kentish Plover *C. alexandrinus* (Palearctic)
Caspian Plover *C. asiaticus* (Palearctic)
Upland Sandpiper *Bartramia longicauda* (N. America)
Common Redshank *Tringa totanus* (Palearctic): Recorded almost annually in the tropical north, especially at Broome Bird Observatory.
Spotted Redshank *T. erythropus* (Palearctic)
Lesser Yellowlegs *T. flavipes* (Nearctic)
Long-billed Dowitcher *Limnodromus griseus* (Nearctic)
Stilt Sandpiper *Micropalama himantopus* (Nearctic)
Baird's Sandpiper *Calidris bairdii* (Nearctic)

White-rumped Sandpiper *C. fuscicollis* (Nearctic)
Dunlin *C. alpina* (Holarctic)
Little Stint *C. minuta* (Palearctic)
Buff-breasted Sandpiper *Tryngites ruficollis* (Nearctic)
Wilson's Phalarope *Phalaropus tricolor* (Nearctic)
Grey Phalarope *P. fulicaria* (Holarctic)
South Polar Skua *Catharacta maccormicki* (Southern Oceans)
Black-tailed Gull *Larus crassirostris* (Eastern Palearctic)
Sabine's Gull *L. sabini* (Holarctic)
Black-headed Gull *L. ridibundus* (Palearctic)
Franklin's Gull *L. pipixcan* (Nearctic)
Laughing Gull *L. atricilla* (Nearctic)
Antarctic Tern *Sterna vittata* (Southern Oceans)
Black Tern *Chlidonias nigra* (Holarctic)
Grey Ternlet *Procelsterna albivitta* (Tropical Oceans, breeds Lord Howe)
White Tern *Gygis alba* (Tropical Oceans, breeds Lord Howe)
Elegant Imperial-Pigeon *Ducula concinna* (Indonesian Islands)
Brown Hawk-Owl *Ninox scutulata* (South east Asia)
White-bellied Swiftlet *Collocalia esculenta* (Asia)
Uniform Swiftlet *Aerodramus vanikorensis* (Asia)
House Swift *Apus affinis* (Palearctic)
Common Paradise-Kingfisher *Tanysiptera galatea* (New Guinea)
Blue-winged Pitta *Pitta moluccensis* (Asia)
Pacific Swallow *Hirundo tahitica* (Asia and Pacific)   Recently found breeding near Cairns.
Red-rumped Swallow *H. daurica* (Asia)
Red-throated Pipit *Anthus cervinus* (Palearctic)
Citrine Wagtail *Motacilla citreola* (Asia)
Grey Wagtail *M. cinerea* (Palearctic)   Apparently regular in Arnhem Land each wet season.
Pied Wagtail *M. alba* (Palearctic)
Black-backed Wagtail *M. lugens* (Asia)
Oriental Reed Warbler *Acrocephalus orientalis* (Asia)
Arctic Warbler *Phylloscopus borealis* (Palearctic)
House Crow *Corvus splendens* (Asia)

Appendix 3: Introduced Birds

This list contains those species that are still surviving as introductions to Australia. Many more attempted introductions took place but fortunately the majority failed. We wasted no time or effort whatsoever in trying to see any of these birds so only the briefest indication of where you may encounter them is given.

Ostrich *Struthio camelus* (Africa): North of Port Augusta, SA.
Mute Swan *Cygnus olor* (Palearctic): Avon River at Northam, WA.
Mallard *Anas platyrhynchos* (Palearctic): Town ponds in the south-east and TAS.
Peacock *Pavo cristatus* (Asia): Rottnest Island, WA.
Red Junglefowl *Gallus gallus* (Asia): Heron Island, QLD.
Ring-necked Pheasant *Phasianus colchicus* (China): Rottnest Island, WA.
Californian Quail *Callipepla californica* (N. America): King Island, TAS.
Domestic Pigeon *Columba livia* (Palearctic): Towns.
Spotted Dove *Streptopelia chinensis* (Asia): Sydney.
Laughing Dove *S. senegalensis* (Asia): Perth.
Eurasian Skylark *Alauda arvensis* (Palearctic): Grasslands, e.g. Lake Bathurst.

Red-whiskered Bulbul *Pycnonotus jocosus* (Asia): Sydney.
Blackbird *Turdus merula* (Palearctic): Canberra suburbs.
Song Thrush *T. philomelos* (Palearctic): Melbourne Botanic Gardens.
Goldfinch *Carduelis carduelis* (Palearctic): Canberra suburbs.
Greenfinch *C. chloris* (Palearctic): Victoria coast.
House Sparrow *Passer domesticus* (Palearctic): Eastern towns.
Tree Sparrow *P. montanus* (Palearctic): Melbourne area.
Nutmeg Mannikin *Lonchura punctulata* (Asia): Cairns.
Common Starling *Sturnus vulgaris* (Palearctic): South-eastern Australia.
Common Myna *Acridotheres tristis* (Asia): Eastern cities.

Appendix 4: Useful Addresses and Contacts

Some useful addresses of bird societies are given below together with the addresses of several national parks and individuals when it is necessary to contact them in advance in order to book accommodation or a trip out.

Bird Societies: The RAOU addresses, including the main office, have recently changed. The name of the organisation has also changed to 'Birds Australia'. The new addresses and those of other useful contacts are:

Birds Australia National Office, 415 Riversdale Road, Hawthorn East, Victoria 3123, Tel. (03) 9882 2622, Fax (03) 9882 2677, email: raou@raou.com.au

Birds Australia Sydney Office, GPO Box 3943, Sydney, New South Wales 2001, Tel. (02) 9290 1810, Fax (02) 9290 1812

Birds Australia Perth Office, Perry House, 71 Oceanic Drive, Floreat, Western Australia 6014, Tel. (09) 383 7749, Fax (09) 387 8412

Birders of North Queensland, c/o 22 Bishop St, Belgian Gardens, Queensland 4810, Tel. (077) 71 4707

Birds Australia Central Australian Group, c/o Gosse Street, Alice Springs, Northern Territory 0870, Tel. (08) 8952 8248

Bird Observers Association of Tasmania, GPO Box 68A, Hobart, Tasmania 7001

NSW Field Ornithologists Club, Box C436, PO Clarence Street, Sydney, NSW 2000

Queensland Ornithological Society, PO Box 97, St Lucia, Qld 4067

South Australian Ornithological Association, c/o South Australian Museum, North Terrace, Adelaide, SA 5000

Australian Birding Association, 24 Milkwood Circuit, Sanderson, NT 5793

Canberra Ornithologists Group, PO Box 301, Civic Square, ACT 2608

David Andrew, the editor of the magazine 'Australian Birding', can be contacted at PO Box 9, World Trade Centre, Melbourne Vic 3005. Tel. +61 3 9534 9909; Fax. +61 3 9535 8454; email: davida@lonelyplanet.com.au

Birdlines: New South Wales Birdline; (029) 290 1778: ACT Hotline; (06) 2475530

Queensland (07) 3283 4921

National Parks and Reserves:
Maria Island National Park, Tel. (002) 57 1420

The Warden, Barren Grounds Bird Observatory, PO Box 3, Jamberoo, NSW 2533

Lamington National Park, Tel. (075) 440634 (Campsite), Tel. (075) 440644 (O'Reilly's)

The Officer in Charge, Nadgee National Park, Armstrong and Evans Building, Inley St Eden, Eden PO Box 186, NSW 2551

The Warden, Broome Bird Observatory, Crab Creek Road, Broome WA 6725, Tel. (091) 935600

Special Bird Trips:
Phil Maher, who runs Plains Wanderer trips (p. 52) and inland birding tours can be contacted at; Australian Ornithological Services, P.O.Box 382, Balwyn Victoria 3103, Australia. Tel/Fax +61 03 98176555. email: mahert@patash.com.au

Daintree River Cruises: Denise Collins, Tel. (From Cairns) 986168

Black Grasswren: Peter Lacey, Mount Elizabeth Station, Tel. (091) 914644

Scarlet-chested Parrot: Maralinga Tjarutja Inc., Ceduna, South Australia, Tel. (086) 252946

Pelagic Trips:
For general information on all pelagic trips from Australia, check out Tony Palliser's Web Site if you have Internet access. http://www.zip.com.au/~palliser

Pelagic trips have just started running out from Perth. It is hoped to run four per year. For details contact: Frank O'Connor, 8C Hardy Road, Nedlands, WA 6009. Tel. (09) 386 5694. Fax (091) 671 438. email: foconnor@iinet.net.au

Brisbane and Gold Coast: Paul Walbridge, 135a Lytton Road, East Brisbane, Qld 4169. Tel. (07) 3391 8839.

Wollongong and Sydney pelagics: *Either:* Dr Peter Milburn, John Curtin School of Medical Research, Australian National University, Canberra, ACT 0200, email: peter.milburn@anu.edu.au *Or:* Tony Palliser, Tel. +61 299001678; Fax +61 29900 1669. email: tpallise@au.oracle.com *Or:* Alan McBride, P. O. Box 190, Newport Beach, NSW 2106 Tel. +61 29973 1536; Fax +61 29973 2306; email: mcbird@zip.com.au
Sydney Pelagics run every second month.

Eden: *Either:* Rosalind and Gordon Butt, Tel. (064) 962027 *Or:* Alan Robertson, (Gypsy Point Lodge), Tel. (051) 58820

Appendix 5: Glossary

The terms used to describe many of the habitat types in which certain bird species are found will, no doubt, be unfamiliar to many readers. This glossary is only a very rough guide as to what they appear like and you are strongly recommended to ask someone who really knows to point out the various vegetation types.

APPENDICES

Banksia; very common genus in coastal regions; ground covers (in WA), shrubs or small trees, with characteristic large yellow or orange 'flower cones', drying to resemble large pine cones when old. Much beloved by honeyeaters.
Belah; (also Belar) a species of Casuarina (qv), forming semi-arid woodlands inland of the mallee (qv) belt. Dark grey rough bark, stiff slender branchlets. Favoured by White-browed Treecreepers.
Billabong; semi-permanent pool in an often dry creekline in the outback.
Callitris; a genus of native cypress pine, closely resembling 'garden' cypresses. Usually greyish foliage. Common at Back Yamma and Gulpa State Forests. Favoured by Gilbert's Whistlers.
Cane Grass; a low shrubby grass which grows on top of red sand dunes along the Birdsville and Strzelecki Tracks and is the preferred habitat of Eyrean Grasswrens. It does not resemble grass but instead is rather pale yellow with intertwined thin stems that frequently divide. Usually under one metre high.
Casuarina; a genus of superficially pine-like shrubs or trees up to 20 metres high with long slender leafless branchlets, drooping or erect. Female plants have small woody cones up to 3 cm long. The main diet of Glossy Black-Cockatoos.
Cumbungi; the largest of several species of reeds in reedbeds throughout Australia; up to 2 m high.
Eremophila; also known as emu-bush, a large genus of shrubs found throughout inland Australia. Leaves vary greatly between species, broad or narrow, green or grey. Flowers are tubular with a curled back 'bottom lip' and conspicuous stamens; they may be red, pink, yellow, white or mauve. Excellent for nomadic honeyeaters when flowering.
Gibber; the rocky plains in the southern outback. The stones are frequently small and almost black and in some areas they form an almost continuous cover, giving the appearance of a thin crust of bitumin on the ground. Favoured by Gibber Chats.
Grevillea; a large genus of bushes with red, yellow or white spidery flowers, singly or in spikes. They attract many honeyeater species.
Ironbark; a group of eucalyptus trees with hard rough furrowed bark, commonly almost black, often grey. Like other eucalypts, much favoured by honeyeaters when flowering.
Lantana; an introduced species of South American shrub that forms dense undergrowth in rainforest areas and is often covered with small pink flowers. Thickets are well liked by Black-breasted Button-Quails.
Lignum; a tall rather spindly domed bush that grows to about 5 m with many intertwined thin branches. Grows around the edges of inland swamps; favoured by Grey Grasswrens.
Mallee; a shrub form, with several stems growing from ground level, adopted by many eucalyptus species in low nutrient soils right across drier southern Australia. Also refers to the habitat so created.
Marri; along with karri and jarrah, these tall eucalyptus trees are only found in the south-west of the continent where their woody fruits are much liked by black-cockatoos.
Melaleuca; the bottlebrushes; a genus of trees or shrubs with usually white fluffy flower spikes, followed by spikes of 'nuts'. The paperbark group, often growing in swamps, have flaking thin paper-like bark.
Mulga; a stunted acacia tree with fine grey foliage and a slender rough black trunk. Forms open woodlands throughout central Australia.
River Red Gum; massive eucalypts with smooth creamy bark, found along creeks - including dry creek lines - and rivers throughout inland Australia.
Sclerophyll; means 'hard-leaved', used to characterise most Australian forests (especially eucalypts), as opposed to soft-leaved rainforests.
Spinifex; also known as porcupine grass, this is a grass up to a metre high, usually growing in circular clumps or rings that is found in the arid interior. It is extremely sharp and painful, easily able to penetrate through clothes. It is the preferred habitat of many species including several grasswrens and emuwrens.

Scientific Name Index

Acanthagenys rufogularis, 235
Acanthiza apicalis, 257
  chrysorrhoa, 227
  ewingii, 227
  inornata, 226
  iredalei, 226
  katherina, 226
  lineata, 227
  nana, 227
  pusilla, 226, 257
  (pusilla) apicalis, 227
  reguloides, 226
  robustirostris, 227
  uropygialis, 227
Acanthorhynchus superciliosus, 235
  tenuirostris, 235
Acanthornis magnus, 225
Accipiter cirrocephalus, 193
  fasciatus, 193
Accipiter novaehollandiae, 193
Acridotheres tristis, 260
Acrocephalus australis, 251, 257
  orientalis, 259
  stentorus, 257
Aegotheles cristatus, 216
Aerodramus vanikorensis, 259
Ailuroedus crassirostris, 220, 256
  dentirostris, 220
  melanotis, 220, 256
Alauda arvensis, 259
Alcedo azurea, 217
  pusilla, 217
Alectura lathami, 194
Alisterus scapularis, 208
Amaurornis moluccanus, 196
Amytornis barbatus, 223
  dorotheae, 223
  goyderi, 223
  housei, 223
  purnelli, 222
  striatus, 223
  textilis, 222
  woodwardi, 223
Anas acuta, 258
  castanea, 189
  clypeata, 258
  gracilis, 189
  platyrhynchos, 259
  querquedula, 189
  rhynchotis, 189
  superciliosa, 189
Anhinga novaehollandiae, 189, 256
  melanogaster, 256
Anous minutus, 204
  stolidus, 204
  tenuirostris, 205
Anseranas semipalmata, 187
Anthochaera carunculata, 235
  chrysoptera, 257
  (chrysoptera) lunulata, 236
  lunulata, 257

paradoxa, 236
Anthus cervinus, 259
  novaeseelandiae, 255, 257
  richardi, 257
Aphelocephala leucopsis, 228
  nigricincta, 228
  pectoralis, 228
Aplonis metallica, 250
Aprosmictus erythropterus, 208
Aptenodytes patagonicus, 257
Apus affinis, 259
  pacificus, 217
Aquila audax, 193
Ardea pacifica, 190
  picata, 190
  sumatrana, 190
Ardeotis australis, 197, 256
  kori, 256
Arenaria interpres, 199
Arses kaupi, 245
  telescopthalmus, 245
Artamus cinereus, 247
  cyanopterus, 247
  leucorynchus, 247
  minor, 247
  personatus, 247
  superciliosus, 247
Ashbyia lovensis, 237
Atrichornis clamosus, 219
  rufescens, 219
Aviceda subcristata, 192
Aythya australis, 189
Barnardius barnardi, 256
  (barnardi) barnardi, 208
  (barnardi) macgillvrayi, 256
  (barnardi) zonarius, 208
  zonarius, 256
Bartramia longicauda, 258
Biziura lobata, 188
Botaurus poiciloptilus, 191
Bubulcus ibis, 190
Bulweria bulwerii, 258
Burhinus giganteus, 200
  grallarius, 200
Butorides striatus, 190
Cacatua galerita, 212
  leadbeateri, 212
  pastinator, 212, 256
  sanguinea, 212, 256
  tenuirostris, 212
Cacomantis castaneiventris, 213
  flabelliformis, 214
  variolosus, 213
Calamanthus campestris, 226, 257
  fuliginosus, 226, 257
Calidris acuminata, 200
  alba, 199
  alpina, 259
  bairdii, 258
  canutus, 199
  ferruginea, 200
  fuscicollis, 259
  melanotos, 199
  minuta, 259

INDEX

ruficollis, 199
subminuta, 199
tenuirostris, 199
Callipepla californica, 259
Callocephalon lathami, 212
Calonectris leucomelas, 185
Calyptorhynchus banksii, 211
　baudinii, 211, 256
　funereus, 211
　lathami, 211
　latirostris, 211, 256
Caprimulgus macrurus, 216
Carduelis carduelis, 260
　chloris, 260
Casmerodius albus, 190
Casuarius casuarius, 182
Catharacta antarctica, 205, 256
　maccormicki, 259
　skua, 256
Centropus phasianinus, 214
Cereopsis novaehollandiae, 188
Certhionyx niger, 229
　pectoralis, 229
　variegatus, 229
Charadrius alexandrinus, 258
　asiaticus, 258
　bicinctus, 201
　dubius, 258
　hiaticula, 258
　leschenaultii, 202
　mongolus, 201
　rubricollis, 202
　ruficapillus, 201
　veredus, 202
Chenonetta jubata, 189
Cheramoeca leucosternus, 250
Chlamydera cerviniventris, 221
　guttata, 220, 257
　maculata, 220, 257
　nuchalis, 220
Chlidonias hybridus, 203
　leucopterus, 203
　nigra, 259
Chloebia gouldiae, 254
Chrysococcyx basalis, 214
　lucidus, 214
　minutillus, 256
　osculans, 214
　russatus, 214
Chthonicola sagittatus, 225
Cincloramphus cruralis, 252
　mathewsi, 252
Cinclosoma alisteri, 257
　castaneothorax, 243, 257
　castanotus, 243
　cinnamomeum, 243, 257
　(cinnamomeum) alisteri, 243
　punctatum, 242
Circus approximans, 193
　assimilis, 193
　spilonotus, 258
Cisticola exilis, 251
　juncidis, 251
Cladorhynchus leucocephalus, 201

Climacteris affinis, 219
　erythrops, 219
　melanura, 219
　picumnus, 219
　rufa, 219
Collocalia esculenta, 259
　spodiopygius, 256
　terraereginae, 217, 256
Colluricincla boweri, 241
　harmonica, 241
　megarhyncha, 241
　woodwardi, 241
Columba leucomela, 205
　livia, 259
Conopophila albogularis, 234
　rufogularis, 234
　whitei, 234
Coracina lineata, 249
　maxima, 249
　novaehollandiae, 249
　papuensis, 249
　tenuirostris, 249
Corcorax melanorhamphos, 243
Cormobates leucophaeus, 218
Corvus bennetti, 246
　boreus, 257
　coronoides, 246
　mellori, 246
　orru, 246
　splendens, 259
　tasmanicus, 246, 257
　(tasmanicus) boreus, 246
Coturnix chinensis, 195
　pectoralis, 194
　ypsilophora, 195
Cracticus mentalis, 248
　nigrogularis, 248
　quoyi, 248
　torquatus, 248
Crex crex, 258
Cuculus pallidus, 213
　saturatus, 213
Cygnus atratus, 188
　olor, 259
Dacelo leachii, 217
　novaeguineae, 217
Daphoenositta chrysoptera, 239
Daption capense, 183
Dasyornis brachypterus, 224
　broadbenti, 224
　longirostris, 224
Dendrocygna arcuata, 188
　eytoni, 188
　guttata, 258
Dicaeum hirundinaceum, 255
Dicrurus bracteatus, 246
Diomedea bulleri, 183
　cauta, 183
　chlororhynchos, 183
　chrysostoma, 183
　epomophora, 183
　exulans, 183
　melanophris, 183
Dromaius novaehollandiae, 182

SCIENTIFIC NAME INDEX

Drymodes brunneopygia, 239
 superciliaris, 239
Ducula bicolr, 256
 concinna, 259
 spilorrhoa, 207, 256
Eclectus roratus, 208
Egretta garzetta, 190
 intermedia, 190
 novaehollandiae, 190
 sacra, 190
Elanus axillaris, 192, 256
 caeruleus, 256
 scriptus, 192
Elseyornis melanops, 202
Emblema pictum, 252
Entomyzon cyanotis, 235
Eolophus roseicapillus, 212
Eopsaltria australis, 238
 georgiana, 238
 griseogularis, 238
 pulverulenta, 238
Ephippiorhynchus asiaticus, 191
Epthianura albifrons, 236
 aurifrons, 236
 crocea, 236
 tricolor, 236
Eremiornis carteri, 252
Erythrogonys cinctus, 202
Erythrotriorchis radiatus, 193
Erythrura trichroa, 254
Eudynamys cyanocephala, 214, 256
 scolopacea, 256
Eudyptes chrysocome, 258
 chrysolophus, 256
 pachyrhynchus, 182
 robustus, 258
 schlegeli, 256, 258
 sclateri, 258
Eudyptula minor, 183
Eulabeornis castaneoventris, 197
Eurostopodus argus, 216
 mystacalis, 216
Eurystomus orientalis, 218
Falco berigora, 193
 cenchroides, 194
 hypoleucos, 194
 longipennis, 194
 peregrinus, 194
 subniger, 194
Falcunculus frontatus, 239
Fregata andrewsi, 258
 ariel, 186
 minor, 186
Fregetta grallaria, 186
 tropica, 186
Fulica atra, 197
Fulmarus glacialoides, 183
Gallinago hardwickii, 198
 megala, 198
 stenura, 258
Gallinula mortierii, 197
 tenebrosa, 197
 ventralis, 197
Gallirallus philippensis, 196

Gallus gallus, 259
Garrodia nereis, 185
Geoffroyus geoffroyi, 207
Geopelia cuneata, 206
 humeralis, 206
 placida, 206
Geophaps lophotes, 206
 plumifera, 206
 scripta, 206
 smithii, 206
Geopsittacus occidentalis, 211
Gerygone chloronotus, 227
 fusca, 228
 levigaster, 228
 magnirostris, 228
 mouki, 228
 olivacea, 227
 palpebrosa, 227
 tenebrosa, 228
Glareola maldivarum, 201
Glossopsitta concinna, 213
 porphyrocephala, 213
 pusilla, 213
Glycichaera fallax, 228
Grallina cyanoleuca, 249
Grantiella picta, 234
Grus antigone, 197
 rubicunda, 197
Gygis alba, 259
Gymnorhina tibicen, 248
Haematopus fuliginosus, 200
 longirostris, 200
Haliaeetus leucogaster, 193
Haliastur indus, 193
 sphenurus, 193
Halobaena caerulea, 184
Hamirostra melanosternon, 192
Heteromunia pectoralis, 255
Heteromyias albispecularis, 239, 257
 cinereifrons, 239, 257
Hieraaetus morphnoides, 193
Himantopus himantopus, 200
Hirundapus caudacutus, 217
Hirundo ariel, 251
 daurica, 259
 neoxena, 250
 nigricans, 251
 rustica, 251
 tahitica, 259
Hydrophasianus chirurgus, 258
Hylacola cautus, 226
 pyrrhopygius, 226
Irediparra gallinacea, 198
Ixobrychus flavicollis, 191
 minutus, 191, 256
 novaezelandiae, 191, 256
 sinensis, 258
Lalage leucomela, 250
 tricolor, 250
Larus atricilla, 259
 crassirostris, 259
 dominicanus, 203
 novaehollandiae, 203, 256
 pacificus, 203

pipixcan, 259
  ridibundus, 259
  sabini, 259
  scopulinus, 203, 256
Lathamus discolor, 210
Leipoa ocellata, 194
Leucosarcia melanoleuca, 207
Lichenostomus chrysops, 230
  cratitius, 231
  fasciogularis, 230, 257
  flavescens, 257
  flavicollis, 231
  flavus, 230
  frenatus, 230
  fuscus, 231, 257
  hindwoodi, 230
  keartlandi, 231
  leucotis, 231
  melanops, 231
  ornatus, 232
  penicillatus, 232
  plumulus, 231
  unicolor, 231
  versicolor, 230, 257
  virescens, 230
Lichmera indistincta, 229
Limicola falcinellus, 200
Limnodromus griseus, 258
  semipalmatus, 199
Limosa haemastica, 258
  lapponica, 198
  limosa, 198
Lonchura castaneothorax, 254
  flaviprymna, 254
  punctulata, 260
Lophoictinia isura, 192
Lopholaimus antarcticus, 207
Lugensa brevirostris, 184
Machaerirhynchus flaviventer, 246
Macronectes giganteus, 183
  halli, 183
Macropygia phasianella, 205
Malacorhynchus membranaceus, 189
Malurus amabilis, 257
  coronatus, 222
  cyaneus, 221
  elegans, 221
  lamberti, 221, 257
  (lamberti) amabilis, 221
  leucopterus, 221
  melanocephalus, 221
  pulcherrimus, 221
  splendens, 221
Manorina flavigula, 235, 257
  (flavigula) melanotis, 235
  melanocephala, 235
  melanophrys, 235
  melanotis, 257
Manucodia keraudrenii, 247
Megalurus gramineus, 252
  timoriensis, 252
Megapodius reinwardt, 194
Melanodryas cucullata, 238
  vittata, 238

Meliphaga albilineata, 230
  gracilis, 230
  lewinii, 230
  notata, 230
Melithreptus affinis, 232
  albogularis, 232
  brevirostris, 232
  gularis, 232, 257
  laetior, 232, 257
  lunatus, 232
  validirostris, 232
Melopsittacus undulatus, 210
Menura alberti, 219
  novaehollandiae, 219
Merops ornatus, 218
Microeca fascinans, 237
  flavigaster, 237, 257
  (flavigaster) tormenti, 237
  griseoceps, 237
  tormenti, 257
Micropalama himantopus, 258
Milvus migrans, 192
Mirafra javanica, 252
Monarcha frater, 244
  leucotis, 244
  melanopsis, 244
  trivirgatus, 245
Morus serrator, 186
Motacilla alba, 259
  cinerea, 259
  citreola, 259
  flava, 255
  lugens, 259
Myiagra alecto, 245
  cyanoleuca, 245
  inquieta, 245
  rubecula, 245
  ruficollis, 245
Myzomela erythrocephala, 229
  obscura, 229
  sanguinolenta, 229
Nectarinia jugularis, 255
Neochmia modesta, 253
  phaeton, 253
  ruficauda, 253
  temporalis, 253
Neophema bourkii, 210
  chrysogaster, 210
  chrysostoma, 210
  elegans, 210
  petrophila, 210
  pulchella, 210
  splendida, 210
Nettapus coromandelianus, 189
  pulchellus, 189
Ninox boobook, 216
  connivens, 216
  rufa, 215
  scutulata, 259
  strenua, 215
Northiella haematogaster, 209, 256
  (haematogaster) narethae, 209
  narethae, 256
Numenius madagascariensis, 198

SCIENTIFIC NAME INDEX

minutus, 198
phaeopus, 198
Nycticorax caledonicus, 190
Nymphicus hollandicus, 212
Oceanites oceanicus, 185
Oceanodroma leucorhoa, 258
  matsudairae, 258
Opopsitta diopthalma, 207
Oreoica gutturalis, 239
Oreoscopus gutturalis, 225
Origma solitaria, 224
Oriolus flavocinctus, 249
  sagittatus, 249
Orthonyx spaldingii, 241
  temminckii, 241
Oxyura australis, 188
Pachycephala griseiceps, 240, 257
  inornata, 240
  lanioides, 241
  melanura, 240
  olivacea, 240
  pectoralis, 240
  rufiventris, 241
  rufogularis, 240
  simplex, 240, 257
Pachyptila belcheri, 185
  crassirostris, 258
  desolata, 185
  salvini, 258
  turtur, 185
  vittata, 258
Pagodroma nivea, 258
Pandion haliaetus, 192
Pardalotus punctatus, 223, 257
  (*punctatus*) *xanthopygus*, 224
  quadragintus, 224
  rubricatus, 224
  striatus, 224
  xanthopygus, 257
Passer domesticus, 260
  montanus, 260
Pavo cristatus, 259
Pedionomus torquatus, 200
Pelagodroma marina, 186
Pelecanoides georgicus, 258
  urinatrix, 186
Pelecanus conspicillatus, 187
Peltohyas australis, 202
Petroica goodenovii, 237
  multicolor, 237
  phoenicea, 237
  rodinogaster, 238
  rosea, 237
Petrophassa albipennis, 206, 256
  rufipennis, 206, 256
Pezoporus wallicus, 211
Phaethon lepturus, 186
  rubricauda, 186
Phalacrocorax carbo, 187
  fuscescens, 187
  melanoleucos, 187
  sulcirostris, 187
  varius, 187
Phalaropus fulicaria, 259

lobatus, 200
tricolor, 259
Phaps chalcoptera, 205
  elegans, 205
  histrionica, 205
Phasianus colchicus, 259
Philemon argenticeps, 233
  buceroides, 233, 257
  citreogularis, 233
  corniculatus, 233
Philomachus pugnax, 200
Phoebetria fusca, 183
  palpebrata, 183
Phylidonyris albifrons, 233
  melanops, 234
  nigra, 233
  novaehollandiae, 233
  pyrrhoptera, 233
Phylloscopus borealis, 259
Pitta erythrogaster, 218
  iris, 218
  moluccensis, 259
  versicolor, 218
Platalea flavipes, 191
  regia, 191
Platycercus adscitus, 256
  caledonicus, 208
  elegans, 208, 256
  (*elegans*) *flaveolus*, 208
  eximius, 209, 256
  (*eximius*) *adscitus*, 209
  (*eximius*) *venustus*, 209
  flaveolus, 256
  icterotis, 209
  venustus, 256
Plectorhyncha lanceolata, 234
Plegadis falcinellus, 191
Pluvialis dominica, 258
  fulva, 201
  squatarola, 201
Podargus ocellatus, 216
  papuensis, 216
  strigoides, 216
Podiceps cristatus, 182
Poecilodryas superciliosa, 239
Poephila acuticauda, 254
  cincta, 254
  personata, 254
Poliocephalus poliocephalus, 182
Polytelis alexandrae, 208
  anthopeplus, 208
  swainsonii, 208
Pomatostomus halli, 242
  ruficeps, 242
  superciliosus, 242
  temporalis, 241
Porphyrio porphyrio, 197
Porzana cinerea, 197
  fluminea, 197
  pusilla, 197
  tabuensis, 197
Prionodura newtoniana, 220
Proboseiger aterrimus, 211
Procellaria aequinoctialis, 185

INDEX

cinerea, 258
  parkinsoni, 185
  westlandica, 258
Procelsterna albivitta, 259
Psephotus chrysopterygius, 209
  dissimilis, 209
  haematonotus, 209
  pulcherrimus, 210
  varius, 209
Pseudobulweria rostrata, 184
Psitteuteles versicolor, 213
Psophodes cristatus, 243, 257
  nigrogularis, 242
  occidentalis, 242, 257
  olivaceus, 242
Pterodroma baraui, 258
  cervicalis, 184
  cooki, 258
  externa, 258
  heraldica, 184
  inexpectata, 258
  lessonii, 184
  leucoptera, 184
  macroptera, 184
  mollis, 184
  neglecta, 184
  nigripennis, 184
  solandri, 184
Ptilinopus alligator, 207, 256
  cinctus, 256
  magnificus, 207
  regina, 207
  superbus, 207
Ptilonorhynchus violaceus, 220
Ptiloris magnificus, 247
  paradiseus, 247, 257
  victoriae, 247, 257
Puffinus assimilis, 185
  bulleri, 185
  carneipes, 185
  creatopus, 258
  gavia, 185
  gravis, 258
  griseus, 185
  huttoni, 185
  lherminieri, 258
  pacificus, 185
  puffinus, 258
  tenuirostris, 185
Purpureicephalus spurius, 208
Pycnonotus jocosus, 260
Pycnoptilus floccosus, 224
Pygoscelis adeliae, 257
  antarctica, 258
  papua, 257
Pyrrholaemus brunneus, 225
Rallina fasciata, 258
  tricolor, 196
Rallus pectoralis, 196
Ramsayornis fasciatus, 234
  modestus, 234
Recurvirostra novaehollandiae, 201
Rhipdura fuliginosa, 244, 257
  leucophrys, 244

phasiana, 244, 257
rufifrons, 244
rufiventris, 244
Rostratula benghalensis, 198
Scythrops novaehollandiae, 214
Sericornis beccarii, 225
  citreogularis, 225
  frontalis, 225, 257
  humilis, 225, 257
  keri, 225
  magnirostris, 225
Sericulus chrysocephalus, 220
Smicrornis brevirostris, 227
Sphecotheres viridis, 249
Spheniscus magellanicus, 258
Stagonopleura bella, 253
  guttata, 253
  oculata, 253
Stercorarius longicaudus, 205
  parasiticus, 205
  pomarinus, 205
Sterna albifrons, 204
  anaethetus, 204
  bengalensis, 203
  bergii, 203
  caspia, 203
  dougallii, 203
  fuscata, 204
  hirundo, 204
  nereis, 204
  nilotica, 203
  paradisaea, 204
  striata, 204
  sumatrana, 204
  vittata, 259
Stictonetta naevosa, 188
Stiltia isabella, 201
Stipiturus malachurus, 222
  mallee, 222, 257
  ruficeps, 222, 257
Strepera fuliginosa, 248
  graculina, 248
  versicolor, 248
Streptopelia chinensis, 259
  senegalensis, 259
Struthidea cinerea, 244
Struthio camelus, 259
Sturnus vulgaris, 260
Sula capensis, 258
  dactylatra, 186
  leucogaster, 187
  sula, 187
  tasmani, 187
Syma torotoro, 218
Tachybaptus novaehollandiae, 182
Tadorna radjah, 189
  tadornoides, 189
Taeniopygia bichenovii, 254
  guttata, 253
Tanysiptera galatea, 259
  sylvia, 218
Thalassoica antarctica, 258
Threskiornis melanocephalus, 256
  molucca, 191, 256

SCIENTIFIC NAME INDEX

spinicollis, 191
Todirhamphus chloris, 218
  macleayii, 217
  pyrrhopygia, 217
  sanctus, 218
Tregellasia capito, 238
  leucops, 238
Trichodere cockerelli, 229
Trichoglossus chlorolepidotus, 213
  haematodus, 212, 256
  (haematodus) rubritorquis, 213
  rubritorquis, 256
Tringa brevipes, 199
  cinerea, 199
  erythropus, 258
  flavipes, 258
  glareola, 199
  hypoleucos, 199
  incana, 199
  nebularia, 198
  stagnatilis, 198
  totanus, 258
Tryngites ruficollis, 259
Turdus merula, 260
  philomelos, 260
Turnix castanota, 195, 256

maculosa, 195
melanogaster, 195
olivii, 195, 256
pyrrhothorax, 196
varia, 195
velox, 196
Tyto alba, 215
  capensis, 256
  castanops, 256
  longimembris, 215, 256
  multipunctata, 214, 256
  novaehollandiae, 215, 256
  tenebricosa, 215, 256
Vanellus miles, 203
  tricolor, 202,
Xanthomyza phrygia, 234
Xanthotis flaviventer, 232
  macleayana, 232
Zoothera dauma, 257
  heinei, 250, 257
  lunulata, 250, 257
Zosterops citrinellus, 251
  lateralis, 251
  luteus, 251

Bird Index

Albatross; Black-browed, 178, 180, 183
  Buller's, 179, 180, 183
  Grey-headed, 179, 183
  Light-mantled Sooty, 179, 183
  Shy, 27, 30, 179, 180, 183
  Sooty, 179, 183
  Wandering, 178, 180, 183
  Yellow-nosed, 178, 180, 183
  Royal, 41, 178, 179, 183
Apostlebird, 244
Avocet; Red-necked, 38, 52, 103, 165, 167, 170, 201
Babbler; Chestnut-crowned, 19, 57, 58, 79, 167, 242
  Grey-crowned, 56, 131, 241
  Hall's, 77, 78, 79, 242
  White-browed, 19, 22, 56, 131, 137, 242
Baza; Pacific, 50, 71, 83, 87, 92, 94, 123, 192
Bee-eater; Rainbow, 22, 65, 82, 218
Bellbird; Crested, 239
Bittern; Australasian, 46, 52, 54, 163, 191
  Black, 92, 115, 125, 144, 148, 191
  Black-backed, 52, 54, 163, 191, 256
  Little, 256
  Yellow, 258
Blackbird, 260
Bluebonnet, 17, 57, 209, 256
  Naretha, 209, 256
Boobook; Southern, 29, 95, 216
Booby; Brown, 81, 86, 187
  Masked, 86, 186
  Red-footed, 187
  Tasman, 187
Bowerbird; Fawn-breasted, 99, 102, 221
  Golden, 83, 91, 94, 95, 220
  Great, 99, 102, 110, 112, 123, 220

Regent, 73, 77, 82, 220
Satin, 73, 220
Spotted, 56, 57, 79, 220, 257
Western, 134, 137, 150, 152, 220, 257
Bristlebird; Eastern, 34, 36, 39, 40, 41, 71, 74, 224
  Rufous, 14, 224
  Western, 155, 156, 224
Boatbill; Yellow-breasted, 84, 94, 95, 246
Brolga, 57, 102, 103, 112, 141, 163, 197
Bronzewing; Brush, 41, 162, 167, 205
  Common, 61, 62, 112, 205
  Flock, 57, 58, 110, 121, 170, 205
Brush-Turkey; Australian, 194
Budgerigar, 58, 102, 110, 130, 134, 210
Bulbul; Red-whiskered, 260
Bush-Hen, 89, 92, 196
Bushlark; Australasian, 58, 116, 252
Bustard; Australian, 95, 102, 104, 144, 148, 152, 197, 256
  Kori, 256
Butcherbird; Black, 114, 248
  Black-backed, 97, 99, 248
  Grey, 247
  Pied, 99, 248
Button-Quail; Black-breasted, 71, 74, 76, 195
  Buff-breasted, 96, 102, 195, 256
  Chestnut-backed, 122, 125, 145, 195, 256
  Little, 52, 53, 58, 111, 131, 133, 167, 196
  Painted, 21, 22, 48, 96, 155, 195
  Red-backed, 70, 115, 116, 118, 195
  Red-chested, 52, 55, 110, 141, 196
Buzzard; Black-breasted, 58, 120, 122, 130, 141, 192
Calamanthus; Rufous, 156, 169, 170, 175, 226, 257
  Striated, 30, 31, 226, 257

Cassowary; Southern, 84, 88, 102, 182
Catbird; Green, 44, 74, 220, 256
  Spotted, 83, 94, 95, 220, 256
  Tooth-billed, 83, 84, 91, 92, 94, 95, 220
Chat; Crimson, 130, 132, 136, 137, 150, 170, 172, 175, 236
  Gibber, 77, 168, 169, 170, 172, 237
  Orange, 53, 57, 58, 79, 136, 150, 170, 172, 236
  White-fronted, 39, 54, 236
  Yellow, 110, 141, 170, 236
Chough; White-winged, 243
Chowchilla, 83, 91, 94, 95, 241
Cicadabird, 48, 65, 82, 249
Cisticola; Golden-headed, 118, 251
  Zitting, 103, 104, 116, 251
Cockatiel, 57, 102, 212
Cockatoo; Gang-gang, 36, 40, 48, 61, 64, 65, 212
  Glossy Black-47, 48, 74, 211
  Long-Billed Black-156, 158, 211, 256
  Palm, 99, 101, 211
  Pink, 17, 19, 56, 57, 77, 131, 136, 174, 212
  Red-tailed Black-128, 152, 211
  Sulphur-crested, 16, 19, 212
  White-tailed Black-155, 157, 211, 256
  Yellow-tailed Black-211
Coot; Eurasian, 197
Corella; Little, 16, 128, 150, 212, 256
  Long-billed, 16, 52, 54, 212
  Western, 154, 212, 256
Cormorant; Black-faced, 180, 187
  Great, 121, 187
  Little Black, 187
  Little Pied, 121, 187
  Pied, 187
Corncrake, 258
Coucal; Pheasant, 92, 121, 214
Crake; Australian, 11, 12, 54, 61, 79, 197
  Baillon's, 16, 78, 79, 196
  Red-legged, 258
  Spotless, 52, 54, 61, 79, 197
  White-browed, 86, 87, 89, 95, 118, 119, 197
Crane; Sarus, 92, 103, 197
Crow; House, 259
  Little, 246
  Torresian, 246
Cuckoo; Black-eared, 56, 79, 132, 142, 150, 152, 214
  Brush, 47, 62, 213
  Channel-billed, 93, 214
  Chestnut-breasted, 95, 99, 101, 213
  Fan-tailed, 62, 214
  Gould's Bronze-214, 256
  Horsfield's Bronze-62, 130, 131, 214
  Little Bronze-104, 118, 119, 214, 256
  Oriental, 213
  Pallid, 62, 119, 131, 213
  Shining Bronze-, 62, 119, 214
Cuckoo-Shrike; Barred, 82, 83, 84, 91, 249
  Black-faced, 249
  Ground, 79, 110, 129, 131, 174, 175, 249
  White-bellied, 249
Curlew; Eastern, 69, 86, 117, 198
  Little, 38, 88, 89, 116, 118, 120, 198
Currawong; Black, 25, 27, 30, 31, 248
  Grey, 155, 166, 167, 174, 248

Pied, 248
Darter; Australian, 121, 187, 256
  The, 256
Diving-Petrel; Common, 41, 179, 186
  South Georgian, 258
Dollarbird, 218
Dotterel; Black-fronted, 131, 202
  Inland, 52, 53, 77, 132, 172, 175, 202
  Red-kneed, 38, 52, 54, 79, 202
Dove; Bar-shouldered, 206,
  Black-backed Fruit-, 256
  Black-banded Fruit-, 121, 124, 207, 256
  Brown Cuckoo-, 71, 74, 205
  Diamond, 131, 134, 206
  Laughing, 259
  Peaceful, 206
  Rose-crowned Fruit-, 71, 74, 82, 86, 101, 117, 118, 207
  Spotted, 259
  Superb Fruit-, 82, 87, 95, 99, 101, 207
  Wompoo Fruit-, 71, 74, 82, 84, 87, 95, 101, 207
Dowitcher; Asiatic, 14, 68, 147, 199
  Long-billed, 258
Drongo; Spangled, 246
Duck; Blue-billed, 38, 78, 79, 154, 163, 188
  Freckled, 38, 39, 52, 78, 79, 163, 165, 188
  Maned, 189
  Musk, 38, 163, 164, 165, 188
  Pacific Black, 38, 189
  Pink-eared, 38, 61, 189
  Plumed Whistling-, 52, 53, 83, 121, 163, 188
  Spotted Whistling-, 258
  Wandering Whistling-, 83, 92, 118, 121, 141, 188
Dunlin, 259
Eagle; Little, 120, 193
  Wedge-tailed, 193
  White-bellied Sea-, 121, 193
Egret; Cattle, 121, 190
  Great, 121, 190
  Intermediate, 121, 190
  Little, 121, 190
Emu, 17, 152, 182
Emuwren; Mallee, 19, 222, 257
  Rufous-crowned, 129, 133, 134, 135, 149, 150, 222, 257
  Southern, 31, 34, 36, 45, 47, 79, 222
Fairywren; Blue-breasted, 154, 156, 166, 167, 221
  Lilac-crowned, 128, 129, 222
  Lovely, 87, 102, 221, 257
  Red-backed, 92, 221
  Red-winged, 155, 156, 221
  Splendid, 131, 221
  Superb, 221
  Variegated, 124, 221, 257
  White-winged, 129, 133, 150, 221
Falcon; Black, 52, 54, 79, 110, 128, 194
  Brown, 193
  Grey, 58, 78, 79, 128, 133, 147, 170, 172, 194
  Peregrine, 133, 194
Fantail; Grey, 244, 257
  Mangrove, 147, 148, 150, 152, 244, 257
  Northern, 244

BIRD NAME INDEX

Rufous, 244
Fernwren, 83, 91, 94, 95, 225
Figbird, 249
Finch; Black-throated, 92, 93, 95, 102, 254
　Blue-faced Parrot-, 94, 95, 254
　Crimson, 83, 110, 118, 141, 253
　Double-barred, 110, 125, 128, 129, 142, 254
　Gouldian, 102, 112, 125, 126, 127, 128, 129, 142, 254
　Long-tailed, 110, 125, 129, 142, 254
　Masked, 102, 123, 129, 142, 254
　Plum-headed, 48, 74, 75, 79, 102, 253
　Star, 129, 141, 142, 148, 253
　Zebra, 135, 142, 253
Firetail; Beautiful, 25, 27, 30, 31, 36, 37, 45, 253
　Diamond, 12, 22, 48, 53, 54, 61, 62, 74, 166, 253
　Painted, 105, 129, 132, 133, 135, 146, 147, 148, 149, 150, 252
　Red-browed, 95, 253
　Red-eared, 155, 156, 253
Flycatcher; Broad-billed, 102, 104, 114, 118, 119, 147, 245
　Brown-tailed, 147, 148, 237, 257
　Leaden, 121, 245
　Lemon-bellied, 84, 102, 102, 118, 119, 121, 127, 237, 257
　Restless, 22, 65, 119, 245
　Satin, 10, 50, 63, 64, 65, 245
　Shining, 88, 114, 115, 119, 121, 245
　Yellow-legged, 99, 102, 237
Friarbird; Helmeted, 233, 257
　Little, 22, 53, 99, 110, 112, 233
　Noisy, 233
　Silver-crowned, 93, 110, 129, 233
Frigatebird; Christmas Island, 258
　Great, 81, 86, 102, 186
　Lesser, 81, 86, 102, 186
Frogmouth; Marbled, 70, 71, 74, 99, 101, 216
　Papuan, 83, 86, 87, 89, 95, 216
　Tawny, 20, 36, 53, 113, 116, 216
Fulmar; Southern, 179, 183
Galah, 212
Gannet; Australian, 186
　Cape, 258
Garganey, 116, 118, 189
Gerygone; Brown, 228
　Dusky, 147, 148, 150, 228
　Fairy, 84, 227
　Green-backed, 117, 144, 145, 227
　Large-billed, 82, 89, 114, 228
　Mangrove, 69, 82, 104, 147, 228
　Western, 62, 131, 228
　White-throated, 62, 121, 227
Godwit; Bar-tailed, 198
　Black-tailed, 86, 117, 198
　Hudsonian, 258
Goldfinch, 260
Goose; Cape Barren, 29, 165, 188
　Magpie, 116, 118, 121, 141, 187
Goshawk; Brown, 120, 129, 193
　Red, 93, 119, 143, 144, 145, 193
　Variable, 36, 74, 95, 193
Grassbird; Little, 54, 252

Tawny, 116, 252
Grasswren; Black, 143, 144, 223
　Carpentarian, 105, 106, 111, 223
　Dusky, 105, 132, 133, 134, 222
　Eyrean, 167, 170, 171, 223
　Grey, 57, 58, 170, 171, 223
　Striated, 19, 20, 136, 223
　Thick-billed, 150, 151, 169, 170, 222
　White-throated, 122, 123, 223
Grebe; Australasian, 61, 65, 121, 182
　Great Crested, 19, 38, 182
　Hoary-headed, 38, 61, 65, 182
Greenfinch, 260
Greenshank, 82, 117, 198
Gull; Black-headed, 259
　Black-tailed, 259
　Franklin's, 259
　Kelp, 179, 203
　Laughing, 259
　Pacific, 11, 27, 179, 203
　Red-billed, 203, 256
　Sabine's, 259
　Silver, 179, 203, 256
Hardhead, 38, 61, 189
Harrier; Papuan, 258
　Spotted, 110, 120, 132, 174, 175, 193
　Swamp, 193
Heron; Great-billed, 89, 114, 119, 121, 124, 190
　Pacific, 121, 131, 190
　Pacific Reef, 190
　Pied, 121, 190
　Rufous Night-, 79, 112, 121, 125, 190
　Striated, 121, 190
　White-faced, 121, 190
Hobby; Australian, 112, 120, 121, 194
Honeyeater; Banded, 99, 110, 112, 123, 127, 128, 141, 229
　Bar-breasted, 121, 125, 127, 128, 234
　Black, 55, 57, 130, 133, 135, 136, 229
　Black-chinned, 21, 22, 48, 52, 232, 257
　Black-headed, 25, 232
　Blue-faced, 110, 235
　Bridled, 83, 91, 94, 95, 230
　Brown, 124, 128, 229
　Brown-backed, 83, 86, 87, 234
　Brown-headed, 62, 232
　Crescent, 27, 36, 61, 233
　Dusky, 124, 229
　Eungella, 82, 230
　Fuscous, 22, 48, 231, 257
　Golden-backed, 105, 106, 110, 133, 146, 232
　Graceful, 87, 88, 230
　Green-backed, 99, 102, 228
　Grey, 131, 152, 234
　Grey-fronted, 55, 129, 146, 147, 174, 175, 231
　Grey-headed, 77, 79, 105, 133, 231
　Lewin's, 230
　Macleay's, 83, 94, 232
　Mangrove, 69, 82, 230, 257
　New Holland, 233
　Painted, 16, 52, 53, 234
　Pied, 56, 105, 130, 131, 133, 135, 136, 149, 150, 151, 229
　Purple-gaped, 16, 162, 166, 167, 231

INDEX

Red-headed, 102, 104, 114, 118, 229
Regent, 21, 22, 48, 234
Rufous-banded, 118, 119, 234
Rufous-throated, 102, 110, 121, 125, 142, 234
Scarlet, 84, 229
Singing, 230
Spiny-cheeked, 55, 235
Striped, 53, 56, 57, 234
Strong-billed, 27, 232
Tawny-breasted, 99, 102, 232
Tawny-crowned, 41, 45, 155, 166, 167, 234
Varied, 88, 89, 230, 257
White-cheeked, 233
White-eared, 231
White-fronted, 16, 19, 55, 130, 131, 174, 233
White-gaped, 110, 112, 124, 128, 231
White-lined, 121, 124, 230
White-naped, 232
White-plumed, 232
White-streaked, 99, 102, 229
White-throated, 112, 124, 232
Yellow, 83, 87, 92, 99, 230
Yellow-faced, 230
Yellow-plumed, 55, 232
Yellow-spotted, 87, 230
Yellow-throated, 25, 231
Yellow-tinted, 102, 110, 112, 231, 257
Yellow-tufted, 22, 48, 74, 231
Hylacola; Chestnut-rumped, 22, 34, 36, 41, 45, 48, 74, 226
   Shy, 16, 17, 19, 20, 55, 166, 226
Ibis; Australian, 121, 191, 256
   Black-headed, 256
   Glossy, 52, 121, 191
   Straw-necked, 118, 121, 191
Jacana; Comb-crested, 83, 118, 121, 198
   Pheasant-tailed, 258
Jacky Winter, 62, 174, 237
Junglefowl; Red, 259
Kestrel; Australian, 194
Kingfisher; Azure, 44, 89, 114, 115, 121, 217
   Collared, 82, 114, 118, 148, 218
   Forest, 115, 122, 123, 217
   Little, 84, 86, 87, 88, 89, 101, 114, 121, 217
   Red-backed, 104, 127, 130, 131, 150, 217
   Sacred, 218
   Yellow-billed, 99, 101, 218
Kite; Australian, 192, 256
   Black, 120, 192
   Black-shouldered, 256
   Brahminy, 82, 120, 150, 193
   Letter-winged, 52, 110, 168, 170, 172, 192
   Square-tailed, 48, 52, 192
   Whistling, 120, 121, 193
Knot; Red, 86, 199
   Great, 86, 117, 150, 199
Koel; Asian, 256
   Australian, 88, 119, 214, 256
Kookaburra; Blue-winged, 93, 99, 102, 110, 112, 115, 123, 128, 129, 217
   Laughing, 217
Lapwing; Banded, 38, 39, 52, 53, 132, 202
   Masked, 39, 203
Logrunner, 74, 241

Lorikeet; Little, 22, 48, 82, 213
   Musk, 22, 213
   Purple-crowned, 10, 12, 19, 156, 167, 213
   Rainbow, 212, 256
   Red-collared, 110, 128, 129, 213, 256
   Scaly-breasted, 72, 82, 213
   Varied, 113, 114, 119, 141, 213
Lyrebird; Albert's, 71, 73, 219
   Superb, 36, 43, 44, 47, 63, 64, 219
Magpie; Australian, 248
Magpie-Lark, 249
Mallard, 259
Malleefowl, 17, 19, 56, 162, 194
Mannikin; Chestnut-breasted, 254
   Nutmeg, 260
   Pictorella, 102, 112, 141, 144, 255
   Yellow-rumped, 141, 254
Manucode; Trumpet, 99, 102, 247
Martin; Fairy, 251
   Tree, 251
Miner; Bell, 71, 235
   Black-eared, 17, 235, 257
   Noisy, 235
   White-rumped see Miner; Yellow-throated
   Yellow-throated, 17, 235, 257
Mistletoebird, 65, 119, 255
Monarch; Black-faced, 44, 244
   Black-winged, 99, 102, 244
   Frilled, 99, 102, 244
   Pied, 84, 87, 92, 94, 95, 245
   Spectacled, 71, 245
   White-eared, 74, 82, 84, 94, 95, 99, 102, 244
Moorhen; Dusky, 197
Myna; Common, 260
Native-Hen; Black-tailed, 19, 54, 57, 79, 131, 197
   Tasmanian, 29, 197
Needletail; White-throated, 217
Nightjar; Large-tailed, 114, 216
   Spotted, 55, 111, 147, 170, 216
   White-throated, 22, 36, 38, 41, 70, 216
Noddy; Black, 80, 81, 86, 204
   Brown, 80, 81, 86, 204
   Lesser, 148, 205
Origma, 36, 37, 44, 47, 48, 224
Oriole; Olive-backed, 127, 249
   Yellow, 115, 119, 121, 127, 249
Osprey, 82, 150, 167, 192
Ostrich, 259
Owl; Barking, 94, 95, 104, 123, 128, 129, 216
   Barn, 84, 175, 215
   Brown Hawk-, 259
   (Australasian) Grass, 79, 84, 94, 215, 256
   Grass, 256
   Lesser Sooty, 83, 84, 91, 94, 95, 214, 256
   Masked, 28, 40, 41, 50, 84, 94, 215, 256
   Powerful, 10, 12, 40, 43, 44, 46, 65, 70, 215
   Rufous, 84, 94, 99, 101, 113, 115, 123, 124, 215
   Sooty, 36, 41, 43, 44, 70, 71, 74, 76, 77, 215, 256
   Tasmanian Masked, 256
Owlet-Nightjar; Australian, 19, 53, 77, 78, 113, 134, 167, 175, 216
Oystercatcher; Pied, 167, 200

BIRD NAME INDEX

Sooty, 167, 200
Paradise-Kingfisher; Buff-breasted, 87, 94, 99, 101, 218
 Common, 259
Pardalote; Forty-spotted, 25, 26, 27, 29, 224
 Red-browed, 133, 134, 146, 150, 167, 224
 Spotted, 26, 223, 257
 Striated, 26, 224
 Yellow-rumped, 224, 257
Parrot; Australian King-208
 Blue-winged, 11, 12, 14, 41, 210
 Bourke's, 78, 79, 131, 147, 152, 210
 Double-eyed Fig-, 84, 86, 87, 99, 101, 207
 Eclectus, 99, 101, 208
 Elegant, 150, 155, 157, 162, 210
 Golden-shouldered, 97, 99, 209
 Ground, 30, 31, 34, 35, 41, 79, 211
 Hooded, 125, 126, 127, 128, 209
 Mulga, 19, 56, 79, 209
 Night, 211
 Orange-bellied, 11, 12, 13, 14, 31, 210
 Paradise, 210
 Princess, 146, 147, 208
 Red-capped, 156, 157, 208
 Red-cheeked, 99, 101, 207
 Red-rumped, 19, 209
 Red-winged, 57, 77, 99, 102, 208
 Regent, 17, 19, 155, 208
 Ringneck, 134, 157, 256 see also Ringneck, Cloncurry; Mallee; and Port Linoln
 Rock, 155, 156, 162, 166, 167, 210
 Scarlet-chested, 174, 175, 210
 Superb, 51, 52, 53, 54, 208
 Swift, 12, 22, 25, 27, 29, 30, 52, 210
 Turquoise, 21, 22, 48, 54, 74, 75, 210
Peacock, 259
Pelican; Australian, 187
Penguin; Adelie, 257
 Chinstrap, 258
 Erect-crested, 258
 Fiordland Crested, 182
 Gentoo, 257
 King, 257
 Little Blue, 11, 27, 178, 183
 Macaroni, 256
 Magellanic, 258
 Rockhopper, 258
 Royal, 256, 258
 Snares Crested, 258
Petrel; Antarctic, 257
 Barau's, 258
 Black, 178, 179, 185
 Black-winged, 184
 Blue, 179, 184
 Bulwer's, 258
 Cape, 179, 180, 183
 Cook's, 179, 180, 258
 Gould's, 178, 179, 180, 184
 Great-winged, 179, 184
 Grey, 179, 258
 Herald, 184
 Juan Fernandez, 258
 Kerguelen, 184
 Kermadec, 184
 Leach's, 258
 Matsudaira's, 258
 Mottled, 179, 180, 258
 Northern Giant, 179, 183
 Snow, 258
 Soft-plumaged, 179, 184
 Solander's, 178, 179, 184
 Southern Giant, 179, 180, 183
 Tahiti, 180, 184
 Westland Black, 258
 White-chinned, 179, 180, 185
 White-headed, 179, 184
 White-necked, 71, 178, 179, 184
Phalarope; Grey, 259
 Red-necked, 200
 Wilson's, 259
Pheasant; Ring-necked, 259
Pigeon; Chestnut-quilled Rock-, 122, 123, 206, 256
 Crested, 206
 Domestic, 259
 Elegant Imperial-, 259
 Partridge, 114, 120, 121, 123, 145, 206
 Pied Imperial-, 256
 Spinifex, 110, 111, 133, 134, 142, 149, 206
 Squatter, 92, 95, 102, 206
 Topknot, 36, 71, 74, 207
 Torresian Imperial-, 86, 119, 207, 256
 White-headed, 71, 74, 84, 205
 White-quilled Rock-, 128, 129, 141, 142, 144, 145, 206, 256
 Wonga, 207
Pilotbird, 36, 48, 63, 64, 65, 224
Pintail; Northern, 258
Pipit; Australasian, 255, 257
 Red-throated, 259
 Richard's, 257
Pitta; Blue-winged, 259
 Noisy, 71, 73, 84, 87, 102, 218
 Rainbow, 114, 115, 117, 118, 124, 218
 Red-bellied, 99, 102, 218
Plains-wanderer, 52, 53, 200
Plover; American Golden, 258
 Pacific Golden, 38, 89, 116, 117, 120, 201
 Caspian, 258
 Double-banded, 12, 27, 38, 201
 Grey, 117, 201
 Hooded, 29, 41, 166, 167, 202
 Kentish, 258
 Little Ringed, 258
 Oriental, 88, 89, 117, 120, 202
 Red-capped, 38, 201
 Ringed, 258
Pratincole; Australian, 53, 77, 89, 103, 110, 116, 120, 141, 170, 201
 Oriental, 88, 89, 201
Prion; Antarctic, 179, 185
 Broad-billed, 258
 Fairy, 179, 180, 185
 Fulmar, 258
 Salvin's, 258
 Thin-billed, 179, 185
Pygmy-Goose; Cotton, 83, 92, 189
 Green, 83, 92, 112, 118, 121, 141, 189
Quail; Blue-breasted, 70, 79, 115, 116, 195

INDEX

Brown, 30, 48, 70, 112, 116, 122, 195
Californian, 259
Stubble, 53, 175, 194
Quail-Thrush; Chestnut, 17, 19, 20, 56, 166, 243
   Chestnut-breasted, 79, 152, 243, 257
   Cinnamon, 136, 167, 168, 169, 170, 172, 243, 257
   Nullarbor, 175, 243, 257
   Spotted, 47, 48, 64, 71, 74, 243
Rail; Buff-banded, 14, 81, 88, 89, 92, 196
   Chestnut, 114, 117, 197
   Lewin's, 11, 12, 14, 45, 47, 61, 196
   Red-necked, 86, 87, 94, 196
Raven; Australian, 246
   Forest, 246, 257
   Little, 246
   Relict, 50, 246, 257
Redshank; Common, 258
   Spotted, 258
Redthroat, 150, 152, 169, 170, 225
Riflebird; Magnificent, 99, 102, 247
   Paradise, 50, 71, 73, 74, 77, 247, 257
   Victoria's, 83, 91, 94, 95, 247, 257
Ringneck; Cloncurry, 105, 106, 208, 256
   Mallee, 19, 56, 57, 208
   Port Lincoln, 155, 174, 208, 256
Robin; Ashy, 239, 257
   Dusky, 25, 26, 27, 29, 30, 31, 238
   Eastern Yellow, 64, 238
   Flame, 62, 64, 65, 237
   Grey-headed, 83, 91, 92, 95, 239, 257
   Hooded, 48, 54, 62, 131, 238
   Mangrove, 87, 88, 89, 104, 148, 238
   Northern Scrub-, 99, 102, 239
   Pale-yellow, 71, 74, 238
   Pink, 27, 29, 30, 31, 238
   Red-capped, 55, 131, 237
   Rose, 50, 64, 65, 77, 237
   Scarlet, 62, 64, 65, 237
   Southern Scrub-, 16, 17, 19, 20, 55, 166, 167, 239
   Western Yellow, 155, 157, 158, 166, 167, 238
   White-breasted, 155, 156, 238
   White-browed, 93, 96, 102, 123, 124, 142, 239
   White-faced, 99, 102, 238
Rosella; Blue-cheeked, 256
   Crimson, 208, 256
   Eastern, 209, 256
   Green, 27, 208
   Northern, 112, 123, 127, 209, 256
   Pale-headed, 72, 99, 102, 209, 256
   Western, 155, 156, 157, 209
   White-cheeked, 256
   Yellow, 19, 208, 256
Ruff, 200
Sanderling, 199
Sandpiper; Baird's, 258
   Broad-billed, 86, 200
   Buff-breasted, 38, 259
   Common, 116, 118, 199
   Curlew, 200
   Marsh, 38, 83, 103, 118, 141, 198
   Pectoral, 38, 199
   Sharp-tailed, 38, 83, 86, 89, 116, 200
   Stilt, 258
   Terek, 82, 86, 150, 199
   Upland, 258
   White-rumped, 259
   Wood, 52, 118, 199
Sandplover; Greater, 69, 86, 202
   Lesser, 69, 86, 150, 201
Scrub-bird; Noisy, 155, 156, 219
   Rufous, 50, 71, 73, 219
Scrubfowl; Orange-footed, 84, 115, 194
Scrubtit, 27, 30, 225
Scrubwren; Atherton, 91, 94, 95, 225
   Brown, 27, 225, 257
   Large-billed, 47, 225
   Tropical, 99, 102, 225
   White-browed, 166, 167, 225, 257
   Yellow-throated, 225
Shearwater; Audubon's, 258
   Buller's, 178, 179, 185
   Flesh-footed, 179, 180, 185
   Fluttering, 81, 178, 179, 185
   Great, 258
   Hutton's, 178, 179, 185
   Little, 185
   Manx, 258
   Pink-footed, 258
   Short-tailed, 27, 179, 185
   Sooty, 179, 185
   Streaked, 71, 179, 180, 185
   Wedge-tailed, 179, 185
Shelduck; Australian, 189
   Radjah, 116, 118, 121, 128, 141, 189
Shoveler; Australian, 38, 189
   Northern, 258
Shrike-Thrush; Bower's, 83, 92, 94, 95, 241
   Grey, 241
   Rufous, 71, 241
   Sandstone, 111, 128, 129, 142, 144, 241
Shrike-Tit; Crested, 22, 48, 53, 54, 62, 154, 155, 239
Silver-eye, 81, 86, 251
Sittella; Varied, 175, 239
Skua; Arctic, 179, 205
   Great, 256
   Long-tailed, 179, 205
   Pomarine, 179, 205
   South Polar, 259
   Southern, 179, 180, 205, 256
Skylark; Eurasian, 259
Snipe; Latham's, 61, 70, 198
   Painted, 52, 54, 198
   Pin-tailed, 258
   Swinhoe's, 116, 198
Songlark; Brown, 131, 252
   Rufous, 22, 48, 62, 130, 131, 134, 252
Sparrow; House, 260
   Tree, 260
Sparrowhawk; Collared, 110, 125, 193
Spinebill; Eastern, 235
   Western, 155, 156, 235
Spinifexbird, 106, 129, 133, 134, 150, 252
Spoonbill; Royal, 121, 191
   Yellow-billed, 191
Starling; Common, 260
   Metallic, 86, 87, 250

BIRD NAME INDEX

Stilt; Banded, 11, 156, 161, 164, 167, 201
　Black-winged, 200
Stint; Little, 259
　Long-toed, 52, 199
　Red-necked, 38, 69, 116, 199
Stork; Black-necked, 83, 116, 121, 191
Storm-Petrel; Black-bellied, 186
　Grey-backed, 179, 185
　White-bellied, 186
　White-faced, 30, 178, 179, 180, 186
　Wilson's, 178, 179, 180, 185, 187, 188, 202
Sunbird; Olive-backed, 88, 255
Swallow; Barn, 251
　Pacific, 259
　Red-rumped, 259
　Welcome, 250
　White-backed, 130, 136, 250
Swamphen; Purple, 197
Swan; Black, 188
　Mute, 259
Swift; House, 259
　Pacific, 217
Swiftlet; Australian, 89, 217, 256
　Uniform, 259
　White-bellied, 259
　White-rumped, 256
Tattler; Grey-tailed, 69, 82, 86, 150, 152, 199
　Wandering, 70, 71, 86, 199
Teal; Chestnut, 38, 61, 189
　Grey, 38, 61, 189
Tern; Antarctic, 259
　Arctic, 204
　Black, 259
　Black-naped, 81, 86, 204
　Bridled, 80, 81, 86, 204
　Caspian, 27, 82, 150, 203
　Common, 150, 204
　Crested, 150, 203
　Fairy, 11, 12, 150, 204
　Gull-billed, 150, 203
　Lesser Crested, 86, 150, 203
　Little, 204
　Roseate, 80, 81, 203
　Sooty, 86, 204
　Whiskered, 52, 83, 118, 121, 150, 203
　White, 71, 259
　White-fronted, 179, 180, 204
　White-winged, 203
Ternlet; Grey, 71, 259
Thick-knee; Beach, 50, 82, 89, 118, 200
　Bush, 53, 82, 83, 95, 96, 113, 114, 123, 155, 200
Thornbill; Brown, 226, 257
　Buff-rumped, 226
　Chestnut-rumped, 131, 133, 227
　Inland, 131, 133, 175, 227, 257
　Mountain, 84, 91, 94, 95, 226
　Slaty-backed, 131, 152, 175, 227
　Slender-billed, 150, 162, 175, 226
　Striated, 227
　Tasmanian, 25, 27, 30, 227
　Western, 156, 157, 226
　Yellow, 65, 227

Yellow-rumped, 227
Thrush; Bassian Ground-, 27, 29, 30, 44, 47, 50, 64, 71, 74, 84, 250, 257
　Russet-tailed Ground-, 70, 71, 74, 250, 257
　Song, 260
　White's, 257
Treecreeper; Black-tailed, 120, 122, 123, 141, 219
　Brown, 17, 22, 62, 219
　Red-browed, 63, 64, 74, 219
　Rufous, 155, 156, 174, 219
　White-browed, 17, 77, 78, 79, 131, 174, 175, 219
　White-throated, 218
Triller; Varied, 74, 88, 115, 117, 119, 250
　White-winged, 62, 110, 130, 250
Tropicbird; Red-tailed, 71, 80, 81, 158, 179, 186
　White-tailed, 71, 179, 186
Turnstone; Ruddy, 199
Wagtail; Black-backed, 259
　Citrine, 259
　Grey, 259
　Pied, 259
　Yellow, 88, 89, 116, 255
Warbler; Arctic, 259
　Australian Reed, 251, 257
　Clamorous Reed, 257
　Oriental Reed, 259
　Speckled, 48, 54, 61, 62, 225
Wattlebird; Brush, 235, 257
　Little, 155, 156, 236, 257
　Red, 236
　Yellow, 25, 236
Wedgebill; Chiming, 136, 137, 150, 152, 242, 257
　Chirruping, 58, 170, 243, 257
Weebill, 124, 227
Whimbrel, 82, 198
Whipbird; Eastern, 242
　Western, 155, 156, 157, 162, 165, 242
Whistler; Brown, 240, 257
　Gilbert's, 19, 52, 53, 54, 56, 175, 240
　Golden, 240
　Grey, 117, 240, 257
　Mangrove Golden, 104, 119, 147, 148, 240
　Olive, 14, 27, 30, 31, 64, 240
　Red-lored, 16, 54, 55, 56, 240
　Rufous, 104, 241
　White-breasted, 103, 104, 117, 147, 148, 150, 241
White-eye; Pale, 86, 251
　Yellow, 104, 117, 147, 148, 150, 152, 251
Whiteface; Banded, 135, 136, 167, 168, 228
　Chestnut-breasted, 169, 228
　Southern, 53, 136, 228
Willie-wagtail, 244
Woodswallow; Black-faced, 133, 247
　Dusky, 247
　Little, 105, 133, 149, 247
　Masked, 130, 137, 149, 247
　White-breasted, 247
　White-browed, 12, 17, 22, 247
Yellowlegs; Lesser, 258

276   INDEX

Locality Index

Abattoir Swamp (6.41) 95
Abrolhos Islands *see* (8B) 203, 204, 205
Adelaide ICI Saltworks (9.1) 161,188, 199, 200, 201, 204, 210, 226, 236
Adelaide River (7.12) 119, 214, 234, 237, 241, 245, 246, 250, 253
Adventure Bay (3.1f) 27, 240
Airlies Inlet *see* (2.9) 14
Alice Springs (7F) 130
Arnhem Highway (7.13) 119, 193
Atherton Tablelands (6E) 89
Australian National Botanic Gardens (5.1) 61, 205, 212, 221, 223, 233, 235, 236
Avalon Swamp (4.18d) 54, 191, 197, 198, 201, 202, 251, 252
Ayers Rock (7.33) 136, 223, 228, 229, 248
Back Yamma State Forest (4.19) 54, 210, 239, 240, 253
Barkly Homestead (7.1) 110, 192, 193, 194, 196, 201, 206, 236, 249
Barred Creek *see* (8.9) 148, 237, 245
Barren Grounds Bird Observatory (4.1) 34, 193, 207, 211, 212, 220, 222, 224, 226, 231, 233, 234, 242, 244, 253
Barrington Tops (4.13) 50, 219, 220, 238, 245, 247
Barwon Heads (VIC) 202, 204
Bellbird Grove *see* (6.5) 71
Big Billy Bore *see* (2.12) 16
Big Desert Wilderness Park (2.12) 16, 226, 231, 234, 236, 237, 239, 240, 247, 248
Big Mitchell Creek (6.39) 93, 193, 239
Big Swamp (9.7) 165, 188
Billiat Conservation Park (SA) 242
Birdsville Track (9.15) 170, 192, 194, 202, 206, 223, 224, 236, 237, 243, 246, 252
Black Mountain *see* (5.1) 226
Bool Lagoon (9.5) 163, 188, 189, 191, 197
Boroloola (7.3) 111, 206, 209, 213, 222, 223, 229, 231, 233, 241, 248, 254, 255
Botany Bay (NSW) 199, 201, 204
Bourke *see* (4.21) and (4.22) 57, 197, 234
Boxwood Hill (WA) 253
Brindabellas (5.7) 65, 212, 216, 230, 236, 237, 240, 246, 250, 255
Brisbane Pelagics (10.5) 180
Brisbane Ranges National Park (2.7) 12, 205, 215, 245
Bromfield Swamp (QLD) 92
Broome Bird Observatory (8.9) 147, 194, 198, 199, 200, 241, 251, 255
Bruny Island (3.1) 25, 185, 187, 200, 201, 202, 203, 211, 224, 225, 227, 237, 238, 245, 248, 253
Buffalo Creek (7.9) 117, 197, 202, 227, 229, 240, 248, 250
Bundaberg Airport *see* (6.16) 82, 213
Bundaberg and the Reef (6.16) 80, 185, 186, 187, 196, 203, 204, 206, 218, 221, 228, 230
Bunya Mountains National Park (6.10) 76, 205, 215, 238, 241, 247
Burnett Heads *see* (6.16) 82

Cabbagetree Island (NSW) 184
Cairns Botanic Gardens (6.26) 86, 194, 196, 197, 198, 205, 214, 217, 227, 229, 230, 233, 234, 239, 248, 249, 250, 255
Cairns Esplanade (6.24) 86, 190, 198, 199, 200, 201, 202, 203, 204, 207, 214, 230, 233, 250
Caloundra *see* (6.3) 70, 199
Cambridge Gulf (WA) 244
Camelback Firetrail (5.4b) 64, 232, 243
Cameron Corner (9.12) 58, 167, 223, 224
Campbell Park (5.3) 61, 212, 213, 214, 218, 219, 226, 227, 228, 232, 233, 235, 237, 238, 239, 243, 245, 247, 249, 250, 252, 253
Canning Stock Route (8.7) 146, 208, 211, 231, 253
Cape Bruny (3.1g) 27
Cape Crawford (7.2) 110, 206, 229, 231, 232, 233, 234, 254
Cape Hillsborough National Park (6.18) 82, 200
Cape Naturaliste *see* (8.24) 158
Cape Queen Elizabeth (3.1c) 27
Cape Range National Park (8.13) 149, 206, 214, 220, 222, 229, 242, 252
Cape Tribulation National Park (QLD) 207, 221, 244
Cape York Peninsula (6F) 96
Caranbirini Springs *see* (7.3) 111
Cariewerloo Homestead (SA) 243
Carnarvon (8.14) 150, 203, 204, 217, 225, 228, 236, 251
Cathedral Fig Tree (6.35) 92, 241, 245
Channel Country (6B) 77
Charleville *see* (6.14) 77
Chestnut-breasted Whiteface Site (9.14) 169, 216, 221, 222, 225, 226, 228, 235, 236, 237, 243
Chiltern State Forest (2C) 21, 195, 210, 213, 226, 231, 232, 235, 237, 247, 249, 252
Chinaman Creek (7.23) 127, 209, 234, 254
Cloncurry (6.48) 104, 211
Clunes State Forest (2.10) 16, 234
Coffin Bay National Park (9.9) 166, 202, 205, 210, 239
Coffs Harbour (4.14) 50, 192, 246
Cook Airfield (9.17) 175, 202
Cooloola National Park (6.15) 79, 195, 205, 211, 215, 233
Corin Dam (5.5) 64, 224, 240
Cradle Mountain (3.7) 30, 225, 226, 248
Crater National Park (6.32) 91, 215, 220, 225, 226, 230, 239, 241, 247, 249
Croajingolong National Park (VIC) 202
Cronulla Swamp (4.8) 45, 191, 196, 251, 252
Cumberland Gap *see* (6.46) 102
Cunninghams Gap (QLD) 235
Daintree River Cruises (6.31) 89, 190, 216, 217, 218, 228, 230, 239
Daly River (7.4) 113, 215
Darwin (7B) 113
Darwin Botanic Gardens (NT) 207
Denham (8.16) 150, 187, 202, 204, 214, 221, 222, 229, 233, 242, 244, 251
Deniliquin (4.18) 52, 188, 191, 192, 194, 195, 196, 200, 202, 203, 208, 212, 229, 234, 236, 252

LOCALITY INDEX

Derby (8.8) 147, 228, 237, 241, 244, 245, 251
Dharug National Park (4.10) 47, 196, 212, 213, 219, 225, 232, 233, 243
Dingo Creek (7.25) 129, 254
Diversion Dam (WA) 254
Dongara see (8.18) 154, 212
Dryandra State Forest (8.19) 154, 192, 205, 208, 209, 210, 219, 221, 225, 226, 232, 233, 235, 239, 249
Dunham River (8.3) 142, 239, 244
East Gippsland National Park (VIC) 238
East Point Recreation Reserve (7.10) 117, 200, 207, 218, 227, 234, 248, 252
Eden (10.4) 180, 186
Edith River (7.21) 125, 195
Edmonton (6.29) 88, 198, 201, 202, 255
Ellery Creek Big Hole Nature Park (7.30) 133, 222, 233, 252
Elliston (9.6) 164
Erldunda (7.32) 135, 228, 236, 242, 243
Eulo Bore (6.14) 79, 209, 210, 212, 214, 220, 242, 243, 248, 249, 253
Eungella National Park (6.17) 82, 218, 220, 230, 249
Eyre Bird Observatory (WA) 209
Eyre Peninsula (9B) 163
Ferguson River (7.20) 125, 191, 209, 234, 253, 254
Ferntree Gully National Park (2.2) 10, 215, 238, 245
Fishing Gap Firetrail (5.4d) 64, 219, 249
Fitzroy Falls (4.2a) 36, 193, 219, 224, 233
Fogg Dam (7.11) 118, 187, 192, 197, 198, 207, 214, 218, 234, 237, 240, 245, 252, 253
Forest Glen Tea Gardens (3.6) 30, 210
Freycinet National Park (3.5) 30, 243
Georgetown (6.46) 102, 206, 231, 234, 253, 254, 255
Gibb River Road (8.5) 143, 192, 198, 206, 209, 254, 255
Girraween National Park (6.8) 74, 210, 253
Glen Davis (4.12) 48, 195, 210, 226, 231, 232, 235, 237, 238, 239, 243, 249, 250, 253, 254
Great Barrier Reef (6.25) 86, 186, 187, 203, 204, 205, 207 see also (6.16)
Great Ocean Road (2.9) 14, 205, 210, 224, 233, 236, 240
Great Victoria Desert (9.16) 172, 209, 210, 219, 231
Green Cape see (4.6) 41
Gulf Country (6G) 102
Gulpa State Forest (4.18b) 53, 208, 228, 233, 239, 240, 252
Gundagai (NSW) 213
Gypsy Point Lodge (VIC) 212
Hall's Gap see (2.11) 16, 212
Halls Creek (8.6) 146, 224, 231, 232, 253
Hasties Swamp (6.33) 92, 188, 196, 197
Hattah-Kulkyne National Park (2.14) 19, 182, 194, 205, 208, 209, 210, 212, 216, 217, 222, 223, 224, 226, 231, 232, 233, 234, 235, 236, 237, 239, 240, 242, 247, 248
Hay Wildlife Refuge (4.18c) 53, 234
Herdsman Lake (WA) 188, 191, 252

Hobart Airfield (TAS) 202
Holmes Jungle Swamp (7.7) 115, 195, 250, 252
Horseshoe Lagoon (6.19) 83, 189, 253
Howard Springs (7.6) 114, 194, 217, 218, 232, 234, 240, 241, 244, 246, 249, 250, 254
Ingham (6.22) 84, 215
Innes National Park (9.4) 162, 194, 205, 231, 242
Innisfail (QLD) 251
Iron Range National Park (6.45) 99, 182, 186, 193, 194, 196, 198, 200, 207, 208, 211, 213, 214, 215, 216, 217, 218, 220, 221, 225, 227, 228, 229, 230, 232, 233, 237, 238, 239, 240, 241, 244, 245, 246, 247, 248, 249, 250, 253
J C Slaughter Falls (6.2) 70, 215, 216
Jenolan Caves (NSW) 48, 225
Jerrabomberra Wetlands (5.2) 61, 194, 196, 197, 198, 202, 251, 252
Jervis Bay (4.4) 39, 183, 215, 224, 233
Jindalee State Forest see (4.16) 52
John Forrest National Park (WA) 211
Julatten (6.40) 94, 192, 193, 194, 196, 200, 213, 214, 215, 216, 217, 218, 220, 225, 226, 232, 237, 240, 241, 244, 245, 246, 249, 250, 254, 255
Kakadu National Park (7C) 119, 187, 188, 189, 192, 198, 206, 209, 211, 213, 217, 221, 233, 234, 236, 245
Kalamunda National Park (WA) 211
Karumba (6.47) 103, 197, 214, 216, 228, 229, 241, 245, 251
Katherine (7D) 124
Katherine Gorge National Park (7.22) 127, 209, 221, 234, 235, 249
Keep River National Park see (8.1) 141, 206, 216
Kiama (NSW) 200
Kingower see (2.10) 16, 234
Kioloa Rest Area (4.5) 40, 215, 244
Knuckey's Lagoon (7.8) 116, 189, 198, 201, 251, 252, 255
Kunoth Well (7.28) 131, 197, 202, 209, 210, 214, 219, 221, 227, 228, 229, 234, 235, 236, 237, 238, 244, 249
Kununurra (8.2) 141, 190, 214, 253, 254, 255
Lady Elliot Island see (6.16) 81
Lady Loretta Project (6.50) 105, 208, 223, 232, 252
Lady Musgrave Island see (6.16) 81
Lake Argyle (8.1) 141, 198, 236, 255
Lake Barrine (6.34) 92, 188, 192, 220
Lake Bathurst (4.3b) 38, 182, 188, 195, 199, 201, 202, 236, 246, 252
Lake Bindegolly (6.13) 78, 188, 190, 197, 202, 236, 249, 252
Lake Conneware see (2.8) 13
Lake Eacham (6.34) 92, 188, 192, 220
Lake George (4.3a) 38, 182, 188, 191, 201
Lake Gilles Conservation Park (9.10) 167
Lake Gore (WA) 202
Lake Samsonvale (6.4) 70, 195, 198, 252
Lake St Clair (3.9) 31, 238, 248
Lakes Entrance (VIC) 202
Lamington National Park (6.7) 71, 193, 194, 195, 205, 207, 208, 209, 212, 214, 215, 216, 218,

INDEX

219, 220, 224, 225, 228, 229, 230, 232, 238, 239, 240, 241, 242, 244, 245, 246, 247, 250
Laverton Saltworks (2.4) 11, 201
Lawn Hill National Park (QLD) 222
Leaning Tree Lagoon (NT) 118
Lee Point (7.9) 117, 197, 202, 227, 229, 240, 248, 250
Leeton Swamp (4.17) 52, 188, 197, 199, 201, 202, 252
Lincoln National Park (9.8) 165, 221, 225, 231, 234, 236, 238, 239, 242, 243, 248, 253
Loch Ard Gorge see (2.9) 14
Louth Bay see (9.7) 188
Lunawanna (3.1f) 27, 240
Lyrebird Trail (5.4c) 64, 219, 220, 224, 238, 250
Macquarie National Park see (4.1) 36
Mairee Pool (8.12) 148
Maitland River (8.12) 148
Mamukala (7.14) 120, 198, 201, 202, 228, 237
Manjimup (8.23) 158, 211, 226, 238
Manly Yacht Club (6.1) 68, 199
Manning Gorge see (8.5) 144, 191, 193, 223
Maria Island National Park (3.4) 29, 182, 188, 202, 205, 211, 216, 224, 238, 245, 248
Melaleuca (3.10) 31, 210
Melbourne Airport (2.1) 10, 213
Merty-Merty Station (9.12) 167, 223, 224
Michaelmas Cay see (6.25) 86
Middle Arm (7.5) 114, 190, 197, 206, 214, 217, 218, 228, 229, 240, 241, 245, 246, 248
Mission Beach (6.23) 84, 182, 215, 218, 246
Mitchell Falls (8.5b) 144, 191, 193, 195, 206, 221, 223, 227, 230, 233, 241, 244, 248, 249
Monger Lake (8.18) 154, 188, 212, 228
Monkey Mia (8.16) 150, see also Denham
Morton National Park (4.2) 36, 216, 224
Mount Carbine Road (6.42) 95, 198, 206, 254
Mount Elizabeth Station (8.5a) 143, 223
Mount Field National Park (TAS) 238
Mount Glorious (6.5) 70, 192, 195, 205, 207, 215, 216, 220, 229, 235, 238, 241, 243, 245, 246, 247, 249, 250
Mount Isa (6.49) 105, 217, 222, 231, 248, 252
Mount Keira (NSW) 196, 241
Mount Lewis (6.40) 94, see also Julatten
Mount Magnet (8.17) 152, 209, 210, 211, 220, 227, 228, 229, 243
Mount Molloy (6.43) 96, 195, 200
Mount Nebo see (6.5) 71
Mount Remarkable National Park (9.3) 162, 210
Mount Spec National Park (6.21) 83, 196, 205, 218, 220, 225, 226, 230, 232, 241, 245, 247, 249, 250
Mount Taylor (ACT) 254
Mount Todd see (7.22) 127, 254
Mount Wellington (3.2) 27, 211, 225, 227, 238, 240, 245, 248, 250
Mount Whitfield Environmental Park (6.27) 87, 182, 194, 218, 221, 249
Mundaring Weir (WA) 228
Mungo National Park (NSW) 242
Musgrave (6.44) 97, 209, 229, 248, 253, 254
Nadgee Nature Reserve (4.6) 41, 183, 202, 205, 211, 226, 234, 236, 244

Namadgi National Park (5.6) 64, 231, 243
Nardellos Lagoon (6.36) 92, 189
Neumgna State Forest (6.9) 75, 195
New Beach (8.15) 150, 226, 228, 236, 244, 251
North Epping (4.9) 46, 215
North Stradbroke Island (6.6) 71, 184, 185, 186, 199
Nourlangie Rock (7.15) 121, 206, 207, 230, 233
Nullarbor Roadhouse (9.18) 175, 226, 243, 252
Nullica State Forest see (4.6) 41, 215
Nyngan (4.21) 57, 220, 229, 242
Old Darwin Road (7.17) 122, 195, 219
Ormiston Gorge National Park (7.31) 133, 206, 220, 222, 229, 231, 248, 252
Palm Grove National Park (QLD) 219
Perup Nature Reserve see (8.18) 154, 212
Phillip Island (2.3) 11, 183
Pickford Road (6.38) 93, 254
Pierces Pass (4.11) 48, 224, 225
Pittwater Road (3.3) 28, 209, 215
Point Addis see (2.9) 14, 238
Point Hut Crossing (ACT) 230
Point Samson (8.11) 148, 228, 239, 240, 241, 244, 251
Porongurup National Park (8.21) 156, 209, 211, 213, 219, 221, 232, 238, 253
Port Augusta (9.11) 167
Port Cartwright see (6.3) 70
Port Gawler (9.2) 162, 204, 210, 226, 236
Port Hedland Salt Works (WA) 199
Port Phillip Bay (VIC) 201, 204, 226
Port Prime (9.2) 162, 204, 210, 226, 236
Portland (10.2) 179, 183, 184, 185, 186, 187, 204
Pyampa Station (4.23) 57, 223, 236, 243
Raine Island (QLD) 184, 251
Red Rock Caravan Park (4.15) 50, 200
Redcliffe (6.3) 70, 199
Rocky Pool see (8.14) 150
Rottnest Island (WA) 201, 202, 210
Round Hill Nature Reserve (4.20) 54, 194, 196, 205, 209, 212, 214, 216, 220, 221, 224, 226, 227, 228, 229, 231, 232, 233, 234, 236, 237, 239, 240, 242, 243, 247
Royal National Park (4.7) 43, 211, 214, 215, 217, 218, 219, 224, 225, 229, 230, 232, 244, 245
Sherbrook picnic area see (2.9) 14
Sherwood Forest Park (QLD) 191, 196, 252
Shoalhaven River (4.2d) 38, 204
Simpson's Gap (7.29) 132, 194, 222, 231, 248, 252
South Australia Border (7.34) 137, 220, 242
Stag Creek (7.19) 124, 207, 218, 227, 230, 239, 244
Stirling Ranges National Park (8.22) 157, 192, 210, 211, 226, 231, 233, 234, 238, 242
Strahan (3.8) 30, 211, 222, 226, 234, 253
Strzelecki Track (9.13) 168, 192, 194, 228, 236, 243, 246
Sturt National Park see (4.24) 58
Sugarloaf Island (8.24) 158, 186, 211, 253
Swan Island (2.8) 13, 187, 201, 210, 214
Sydney (4B) 42
Tableland Highway (7.1) 110, 192, 193, 194, 196, 201, 206, 236, 249

LOCALITY INDEX

Tasmania Pelagics (10.3) 180, 186
Tennant Creek (7.26) 129, 222, 231, 236, 252
The Arch *see* (2.9) 14
Thomsons Road (6.28) 88, 217, 227, 228, 230, 239, 255
Thornside *see* (6.1) 69, 199, 230
Tibooburra (4.24) 57, 58, 194
Tidbinbilla Nature Reserve (5.4) 63, 207, 211, 212, 218, 221, 223, 231, 232, 237, 238, 243, 244, 245
Tinaroo Creek Road (6.37) 92, 191, 206, 230, 233, 250, 254
Toogoolawah (QLD) 213
Townsville Common Environmental Park (6.20) 83, 188, 189, 190, 202, 203, 228, 230, 232, 234, 252
Triabunna Falls (4.2b) 36, 253
Tuppa Creek Station (4.18e) 54
Two Peoples Bay (8.20) 155, 210, 211, 219, 222, 224, 226, 235, 236, 238, 242, 253
Uluru National Park (7.33) 136, *see also* Ayers Rock
Victoria River Roadhouse (7.24) 128, 194, 206, 216, 222, 229, 231, 233, 234, 241, 249, 253, 254
Wallaman Falls National Park *see* (6.22) 84, 182, 215
Waterfall Creek (7.18) 122, 192, 200, 206, 207, 209, 215, 216, 221, 223, 229, 232, 233, 239, 241, 248, 249, 254
Waterview Hill (3.1b) 26
Weddin Mountains National Park (NSW) 210
Werribee Sewage Farm (2.5) 11, 188, 196, 197, 198, 203, 204, 210
Western Highway (2.11) 16, 212
Wilson's Promontory (VIC) 187, 188, 202
Windorah (6.12) 77, 210, 216, 219, 242, 243
Wirrula *see* (9.16) 174, 219, 233
Wollongong (10.1) 178, 183, 184, 185, 186, 200, 203, 204, 205
Woody Island (WA) 187, 188
Wyndham (8.4) 142, 206, 214, 231, 234, 253, 254
Wyperfield National Park (2.13) 17, 182, 194, 208, 209, 212, 219, 226, 231, 232, 234, 235, 236, 237, 239, 240, 243, 247, 248
Yalgoo National Park (WA) 211
Yalgoo *see* (8.17) 152, 225, 234
Yarrabah Turf Farms (6.29) 88, 198, 201, 202, 255
Yass (4.16) 51, 208
Yellow Waters Boat Cruises (7.16) 121, 188, 190, 192, 198, 206, 214, 217, 246
You Yangs Forest Park (2.6) 12, 210, 213, 227, 232, 237, 253
Yule Point (6.30) 89, 200, 240

Additional Sites

Although all the essential sites are included in the main text of this book, readers are reminded that there are literally thousands of places where it is worth birding in Australia. Below are mentioned a few sites that we did not get around to visiting but they are all outstanding areas.

Munghorn Gap, NSW

Situated near Mudgee, to the north-west of Sydney, this area is fairly close to the Glen Davis valley. From Mudgee head north-east to Budgee Budgee then fork right and then take the road to Wollar. Munghorn Gap is a signposted square parking and picnic area about 30 km from Budgee Budgee on the left hand side. Everywhere in this vicinity is good, but look especially for any trees with flowering mistletoe. **Painted** and **Regent Honeyeaters** are both regularly recorded and **White-throated Nightjars** are commonly seen around the picnic area in the spring from mid-October onwards.

Waychinicup, WA

This is the area that the rangers at Two Peoples Bay now recommend that visitors look for **Noisy Scrub-bird**, **Western Whipbird** and **Western Bristlebird**. Check with them for exact directions. Waychinicup is reached by turning off the South Coast Highway near Manypeaks towards the coast. Just before you reach the coast turn right on a rough limestone track which leads after 10 km to a campsite. All three of the above species can be seen around this campground. The Bristlebird is found in the short heath along the road just before the campground. The Scrub-bird is found around the edge of the creek here and the Whipbird is in the taller denser areas of heath. Another site for the Whipbird is further east where the South Coast Highway crosses the Fitzgerald River. They can be heard all around the area. To the south of the Highway, both the Bristlebird and Whipbird are found in the large Fitzgerald River National Park. Try asking at the rangers station for details of where to see them.

Rottnest Island, WA

Reached by ferry from Freemantle, there are several good species to be found. These include **Banded Stilt**, a large flock of which is usually present and can be seen from the causeway between Government House/Pearse Lakes and Lake Herschell. The former area is probably the most reliable place in Australia to find **Red-necked Phalarope**. Up to 3 birds are found regularly here in the summer. Other regular species of note include **Red-necked Avocet**, **White-fronted Chat** and **Rock Parrot**; check the coastal heath around the sewerage works for the latter.

Gluepot Station, SA

The former RAOU (now Birds Australia) recently announced the purchase of Gluepot Station in South Australia. Birds found there include a high percentage of the last surviving **Black-eared Miners** together with a healthy population of **Scarlet-chested Parrots** and **Red-lored Whistlers**. Contact Birds Australia for further information on visiting this exciting new reserve.